Fundamental Uncertainty

Fundamental Uncertainty

Rationality and Plausible Reasoning

Edited by

Silva Marzetti Dall'Aste Brandolini
and
Roberto Scazzieri

First published 2011 by
PALGRAVE MACMILLAN

Palgrave Macmillan in the UK is an imprint of Macmillan Publishers Limited, registered in England, company number 785998, of Houndmills, Basingstoke, Hampshire RG21 6XS.

Palgrave Macmillan in the US is a division of St Martin's Press LLC, 175 Fifth Avenue, New York, NY 10010.

Palgrave Macmillan is the global academic imprint of the above companies and has companies and representatives throughout the world.

Palgrave® and Macmillan® are registered trademarks in the United States, the United Kingdom, Europe and other countries.

ISBN 978–0–230–59427–2   hardback

This book is printed on paper suitable for recycling and made from fully managed and sustained forest sources. Logging, pulping and manufacturing processes are expected to conform to the environmental regulations of the country of origin.

A catalogue record for this book is available from the British Library.

A catalog record for this book is available from the Library of Congress.

10 9 8 7 6 5 4 3 2 1
20 19 18 17 16 15 14 13 12 11

Printed and bound in Great Britain by
CPI Antony Rowe, Chippenham and Eastbourne

Contents

List of Figures

List of Tables

Preface

The aim of this volume is to take stock of contributions that in recent years have addressed uncertainty from the point of view of an extended conception of rationality. In particular, the volume explores the premises and implications of plausible reasoning when probabilities are non-measurable or unknown, and when the space of possible events is only partially identified. The manifold routes to plausible reasoning under the latter set of conditions (fundamental uncertainty) suggest a multidisciplinary perspective guided by attention to four principal fields of investigation: (*a*) philosophical research into rational decision making, (*b*) artificial intelligence, (*c*) decision theory and statistics, and (*d*) economic theory.

The contributions indicate an emerging consensus distinguished by acknowledgement that decision making under fundamental uncertainty is conducive to the application of rational standards, provided the latter are grounded in a suitable recognition and representation of context. This point of view has far-reaching implications (which are discussed in the volume) for what concerns the variety of rationality constraints, the plausibility of optimization criteria based on means and averages (such as the representative agent), and the relationship between parts and wholes when a system of multiple decision makers is considered.

We are grateful to all the institutions and colleagues whose support has made this volume possible. In particular, the University of Bologna (Department and Faculty of Economics, 'Federigo Enriques' Centre for Epistemology and History of Science) and the University of Cambridge (Gonville and Caius College, Clare Hall, Centre for Research in the Arts, Social Sciences and Humanities, King's College Centre for History and Economics) have provided the research facilities and the intellectual environment necessary for interdisciplinary work. But most of all we are grateful to the colleagues who enthusiastically accepted our invitation to take part in this project and whose collaboration made possible the emergence of an invisible college sharing the view that enhanced and extended rational standards are necessary if fundamental uncertainty is to be successfully addressed.

Silva Marzetti Dall'Aste Brandolini and Roberto Scazzieri
Bologna, April 2010

Notes on Contributors

Masanao Aoki is Professor of Economics at the University of California, Los Angeles (UCLA). His publications include, among others, *Optimal Control and System Theory in Dynamic Economic Analysis* (Amsterdam, North-Holland, 1976); *New Approaches to Macroeconomic Modelling*, Cambridge, Cambridge University Press, 1996; *Modeling Aggregate Behavior and Fluctuations in Economics: Stochastic Views of Interactive Agents*, Cambridge, Cambridge University Press, 2002; 'Uncertainty, Policy Ineffectiveness, and Long Stagnation of the Macroeconomy' (with H. Yoshikawa), *Japan and the World Economy*, 2006; *Reconstructing Macroeconomics. A Perspective from Statistical Physics and Combinatorial Stochastic Processes* (with H. Yoshikawa), Cambridge, Cambridge University Press, 2006; 'The Nature of Equilibrium in Macroeconomics: A Critique of Equilibrium Search Theory' (with H. Yoshikawa), *Economics. The Open-Access, Open-Assessment E-Journal*, 2009.

Domenico Costantini is Emeritus Professor of Probability at the University of Bologna. His publications include *Fondamenti del calcolo delle probabilità*, Milan, Feltrinelli, 1970; *Introduzione alla probabilità*, Torino, Bollati Boringhieri, 1977; and *I fondamenti storico-filosofici delle discipline statistico-probabilistiche*, Torino, Bollati Boringhieri, 2004. He also edited *Statistics in Science: The Foundations of Statistical Methods in Biology, Physics and Economics* (in collaboration with R. Cooke), Dordrecht, Kluwer, 1990; *Probability, Dynamics and Causality. Essays in Honour of Richard C. Jeffreys* (in collaboration with M. C. Galavotti), Dordrecht, Kluwer, 1997; *Stochastic Causality* (in collaboration with M. C. Galavotti and P. Suppes), CSLI Publications/Chicago University Press, 2001; 'Herding and Clustering in Economics: The Yule–Zipf–Simon Model' (with S. Donadio, U. Garibaldi and P. Viarengo), *Computational Economics*, 2006.

Vincenzo Fano is Professor of Philosophy of Science at the University of Urbino. His publications include, among others, *Time Dilations in Special Relativity Theory* (Bologna, Department of Philosophy, 1996); *La filosofia dell'evidenza: saggio sull'epistemologia di Franz Brentano*, Bologna, CLUEB, 1993; 'The Categories of Consciousness: Brentano's Epistemology', *Brentano Studien*, 4, 1992/93; 'The Analogy between Symbols and Intuitions in Modern Physics', *Axiomathes*, 8, 1997; 'Non-Materiality of

Non-Locality', *Foundations of Physics*, 2004; and 'A Meinongian Solution of McTaggart's Paradox', *Meinong Studies*, 2009. He also edited (in collaboration with R. Lupacchini), *Understanding Physical Knowledge* (Bologna, Department of Philosophy, 2002).

Ubaldo Garibaldi is Professor of Statistics at the Department of Physics, University of Genoa. His publications include, among others, 'Exchangeability and Invariance: Classical Aspects of Quantum Mechanics' (in collaboration with D. Costantini), in C. Garola and A. Rossi (eds), *The Foundations of Quantum Mechanics: Historical Analysis and Open Questions*, Dordrecht, Kluwer, 1995; 'An Exact Physical Approach to Market Participation Models' (with M. A. Penco and P. Viarengo), in R. Cowan and N. Jonard (eds), *Heterogeneous Agents, Interactions and Economic Performance*, Berlin and New York, Springer, 2003; 'Herding and Clustering in Economics: The Yule–Zipf–Simon Model' (with D. Costantini, S. Donadio and P. Viarengo), *Computational Economics*, 2006; and 'A Dynamic Probabilistic Version of the Aoki-Yoshikawa Sectoral Productivity Model' (with E. Scalas), *The Open-Access, Open-Assessment E-Journal*, 2009.

Izumi Hishiyama is Late Professor Emeritus of Economics, University of Kyoto and former President of the University of Kagoshima. His publications include, among others, '"Homo Oeconomicus" in J. M. Keynes' *Theory of Investment*, *Shiso*, September 1957; 'Law of Increasing Returns in the Neo-Classical Theory', *Kyoto University Economic Review*, 1958; 'The *Tableau Economique* of François Quesnay: Its Analysis, Reconstruction, and Applications', *Kyoto University Economic Review*, 1960, 'J. M. Keynes' Logic of Uncertainty and Money', *Shiso*, April 1968; 'The Logic of Uncertainty According to J. M. Keynes', *Kyoto University Economic Review*, April 1969; 'On the Theories of Capital and Distribution', *Kyoto University Economic Review*, October 1971; *Quesnay kara Sraffa he* [From Quesnay to Sraffa], Nagoya, Nagoya University Press, 1990; and 'Appraising Pasinetti's Structural Dynamics', *Structural Change and Economic Dynamics*, June 1996.

John Allen Kregel is Professor of Economics at the Tallinn University of Technology, Tallinn, and Research Associate at the Levy Economics Institute, Bard College; University of Missouri-Kansas City. Former Chief, Policy Analysis and Development Branch, United Nations Department of Economic and Social Affairs; Former Professor of Economics, Rutgers University, University of Groningen, Johns Hopkins University, University of Bologna. He is the author of *The Reconstruction* *of Political Economy* (with an introduction by Joan Robinson), London, Macmillan, 1973. He is editor of *Barriers to Full Employment* (in collaboration with E. Matzner and A. Roncaglia), London, Macmillan, 1988 and *Full Employment and Price Stability in a Global Economy* (in collaboration with P. Davidson), Cheltenham and Northampton, Edward Elgar, 1999.

Henry Kyburg is Late Research Scientist and Pace Eminent Scholar, Institute for Human and Machine Intelligence, University of Rochester. Former Professor of Philosophy and Professor of Computer Science, University of Rochester. He was Fellow of the American Academy of Arts and Science, and Fellow of the American Association for Artificial Intelligence. His publications include *The Logical Foundations of Statistical Inference* (Synthèse Library), Berlin, Springer, 1974; *Epistemology and Inference*, Minneapolis, University of Minnesota Press, 1983; *Theory of Measurement*, Cambridge, Cambridge University Press, 1988; *Science and Reason*, New York, Oxford University Press, 1990; *Uncertain Inference* (in collaboration with C. Man Teng), Cambridge, Cambridge University Press, 2001. He also edited *Studies in Subjective Probability* (in collaboration with H. E. Smokler), New York, Wiley, 1964, and *Knowledge Representation and Defeasible Reasoning* (in collaboration with R. P. Loui and G. H. Carlson), Dordrecht and Boston, Kluwer Academic Publishers, 1990.

Isaac Levi is Emeritus John Dewey Professor of Philosophy, Columbia University. Former Visiting Fellow, All Souls College, Oxford; The Institute of Advanced Study, University of Jerusalem; and Wolfson College, Cambridge. His publications include *Gambling with Truth: An Essay on Induction and the Aims of Science*, New York, A. A. Knopf; London, Routledge & Kegan Paul, 1967; *The Enterprise of Knowledge: An Essay on Knowledge, Credal Probability, and Chance*, Cambridge, Mass, MIT Press, 1980; *Decisions and Revisions*, Cambridge, Cambridge University Press, 1984; *Hard Choices: Decision Making under Unresolved Conflict*, Cambridge, Cambridge University Press, 1986; *The Fixation of Belief and its Undoing*, Cambridge, Cambridge University Press, 1991; *For the Sake of Argument: Ramsey Test Conditionals, Inductive Inference and Nonmonotonic Reasoning*, Cambridge, Cambridge University Press, 1996; and *The Covenant of Reason*, Cambridge, Cambridge University Press, 1997. He is an editor of *The Journal of Philosophy*.

Silva Marzetti Dall'Aste Brandolini is Professor of Economics, University of Bologna. Her publications include, among others, 'Tasso ottimale di crescita e bilancio pubblico', *Rivista Internazionale di Scienze Economiche e Commerciali*, April–May 1983; 'Il comportamento razionale del policy maker', *Economia Politica*, 1998; 'Economic and Social Demand for Coastal Protection', *Coastal Engineering*, November, 2005 (co-authored); 'Happiness and Sustainability: A Modern Paradox', in L. Bruni and P. L. Porta (eds), *Handbook on the Economics of Happiness*, Cheltenham, UK and Northampton, Mass., Elgar, 2007; 'Recreational Demand Functions for Different Categories of Beach Visitors', *Tourism Economics*, 2009. She has also edited (in collaboration with A. Pasquinelli), *John Maynard Keynes, Trattato sulla probabilità* (Italian translation of J. M. Keynes's *A Treatise on Probability*) and (in collaboration with R. Scazzieri) *La probabilità in Keynes*, Bologna, CLUEB, 1999.

Eric Nasica is Maître de Conférences en Sciences économiques, Université de Nice Sophia Antipolis. His publications include, among others, 'Comportements bancaires et fluctuations économiques: l'apport fondamental d'H. P. Minsky', *Revue d'Economie Politique*, 1997; *Finance, Investment and Economic Fluctuations*, Cheltenham, UK and Northampton, US, Elgar, 2000; 'Profits, Confidence and Public Deficits: Modeling Minsky's Institutional Dynamics' (with A. Raybaut), *Journal of Post Keynesian Economics*, 2005; 'Incertitude, rationalité et confiance dans les choix d'investissement: une analyse de la relation entre marchés financiers et capital-risque' (with D. Dufour), *Revue d'Economie Industrielle*, 2007; 'Schumpeter on Money, Banking and Finance: An Institutionalist Perspective' (with A. Festré), *European Journal of the History of Economic Thought*, 2009.

Roberto Scazzieri is Professor of Economic Analysis, University of Bologna, Former Visiting Fellow, Gonville and Caius College and Clare Hall, Cambridge, Centre for Research in the Arts, Social Sciences and Humanities (CRASSH), University of Cambridge, Centre for History and Economics, King's College, Cambridge. St Vincent Prize for Economics, 1984 and Linceo Prize for Economics, 2004. Author of *A Theory of Production: Tasks, Processes and Technical Practices*, Oxford, Clarendon Press, 1993. Co-editor of *Foundations of Economics: Structures of Inquiry and Economic Theory*, Oxford, Basil Blackwell, 1986; *Economic Theory of Structure and Change*, Cambridge, Cambridge University Press, 1990; *Production and Economic Dynamics*, Cambridge, Cambridge University Press, 1996; *Knowledge, Social Institutions and the Division of Labour*, Cheltenham, UK and Northampton, US, Elgar, 2001; *Reasoning, Rationality and Probability*, Stanford, CSLI Publications, 2008; *The Migration of Ideas*, Sagamore Beach, Science History Publications/USA, 2008; *Markets, Money and Capital: Hicksian Economics for the 21st Century*,

Cambridge, Cambridge University Press, 2008; and *Capital, Time and Transitional Dynamics*, London and New York, Routledge, 2009.

Alessandro Vercelli is Professor of Economics, University of Siena. Former Visiting Fellow of Clare Hall, Cambridge and of St Anthony's College, Oxford. He was awarded the St Vincent Prize for Economics in 1987. His publications include *Methodological Foundations of Macroeconomics: Keynes and Lucas*, Cambridge, Cambridge University Press, 1991, and *Global Sustainability: Social and Environmental Conditions* (in collaboration with S. Borghesi), Basingstoke, Palgrave Macmillan, 2008. He is the editor or co-editor of *Macroeconomics: A Survey of Research Strategies*, Oxford, Oxford University Press, 1992; *The Economics of Transnational Commons*, Oxford, Oxford University Press, 1997; *Sustainability: Dynamics and Uncertainty*, Dordrecht, Kluwer, 1997; *Psychology, Rationality and Economic Behaviour: Challenging Standard Assumptions*, Basingstoke, Palgrave Macmillan, 2005; *Keynes's General Theory After Seventy Years*, Basingstoke, Palgrave Macmillan, 2010.

Lotfi A. Zadeh is Professor of Computer Science, University of Berkeley and Director, Berkeley Initiative in Soft Computing. He is the founder of fuzzy set theory. He was awarded the IEEE Millennium Medal, 2000 and the IEEE Pioneer Award in Fuzzy Systems, 2000. He has published many research papers and *Fuzzy Sets and Applications: Selected Papers by L. A. Zadeh*, edited by R.R. Yager, New York, Wiley, 1987. He is the editor of *Approximate Reasoning in Intelligent Systems, Decisions and Control* (in collaboration with E. Sanchez), Oxford, Pergamon Press, 1987; *Fuzzy Logic for the Management of Uncertainty* (in collaboration with J. Kacprzyk), New York, Wiley, 1992; *An Introduction to Fuzzy Logic Application in Intelligent Systems* (in collaboration with R. R. Yager), Boston, Kluwer, 1993; *Outline of Computational Theory of Perceptions Based on Computing with Words, Self Computing and Intelligent Systems* (in collaboration with N. K. Sinha and M. M. Gupta), New York, Academic Press, 2000; *Semantic Computing* (in collaboration with P. Sheu, H. Yu, C. V. Ramamoorthy, and A. K. Joshi), Wiley-IEEE Press, 2010.

1
Introduction: Fundamental Uncertainty and Plausible Reasoning

Silva Marzetti Dall'Aste Brandolini and Roberto Scazzieri

1.1 Uncertainty, plausible reasoning and the continuum of inductive methods

Uncertainty and rationality are closely related features of human decision making. Many practical decisions are traditionally reconstructed as attempts to frame uncertain outcomes within the domain of rule-constrained reasoning, and much established literature explores the manifold ramifications of rationality when choice among uncertain outcomes has to be made (as with choice criteria associated with maximization of expected utility). However, this overall picture is changing rapidly as a result of recent work in a variety of related disciplines. Research in cognitive science, artificial intelligence, philosophy and economics has called attention to the open-ended structure of rationality. This point of view stresses the *active* role of the human mind in developing conceptual possibilities relevant to problem solving under contingent sets of constraints. Rationality is conceived of as a pragmatic attitude that is nonetheless conducive to rigorous investigation of decision making. In particular, conditions for rational decision are moved back to its cognitive frame (the collection of concepts and predicates that makes any given representation of problem space possible), and the cognitive frame is associated with the context-dependent utilization of cognitive abilities. This view of rationality distances itself from received conceptions of deductive and inductive inference as it is related to a *situational* conception of reasoning. This means that reasoning comes to be considered as a mental state in which a prior (and only partially structured) set of cognitive abilities takes definite shape, as shifts from one context to another activate one particular set of cognitive procedures after another. As a result, rationality appears to be intertwined with utilization of

1

justified procedures. However, the reduction of rational procedure to any single-minded criterion of instrumental rationality (or rational success) is avoided. Any given problem space is considered, at least partly, as a *mental construction*, so that identification of problem setting and selection of justified procedure go hand in hand (see also Galavotti, Scazzieri and Suppes, 2008a, 2008b).

The above view of problem spaces and solution procedures suggests a description of rationality as a specific configuration of capabilities and procedures, rather than as a particular selection of choice strategies and actions. In particular, a rational cognitive agent is considered as an agent capable of effectively reconfiguring itself after a cognitive shock. In other words, rationality is associated not only with effective utilization of a given set of *cognitive rules* but also with the effective use of *cognitive abilities*. As regards cognitive abilities, however, not all abilities are used at the same time, and new abilities may become available as the cognitive process unfolds. If this point of view is adopted, rationality appears to presuppose a cognitive system capable of self-reference and reflective states. In other words, rational cognitive systems should be endowed with the ability to make sense of their own structure and behaviour. At the same time, a rational cognitive system should be open to the possibility of self-correction and structural change (see above). Reflective rationality is inherently dynamic, due to the emphasis upon reconfiguration ability. It may also be conjectured that reconfiguration is associated with feedback processes (primarily of the non-linear type). The above view of rationality suggests a pragmatic approach highlighting the variety of patterns of reasoning by means of which it is possible to identify effective strategies. It also suggests a cognitive and experimental twist in the analysis of decisions. In this connection, the available bundles of concepts and predicates (*frames*) and the active principles calling attention to *particular* sets of concepts and predicates (*focal points*) may be more relevant than standard computational skills in reaching satisfactory (not necessarily optimal) solutions (see Bacharach, 2003, pp. 63–70).

More specifically, research work in cognitive science and artificial intelligence, decision science and economics suggests an understanding of rationality through a reformulation of the relationship between cognitive states and their material (physical) conditions (the classical mind–body problem[1]). In particular, rationality appears to be grounded in the recognition of associative structures to which the human mind is disposed but which cannot be reduced to any deterministic model of its neural structure. This calls attention to the open-ended configuration of justified procedures, in which the standards of classical epistemology and rational choice decision theory are complemented by close attention for interactive outcomes, analogical reasoning and pattern identification. Contingent constraints and situational reasoning are often associated with uncertainty of individual outcomes. The shift from one set of constraints to another (from one space of events to another) could make it difficult to rely upon any fixed set of inferential rules. It also suggests that cognitive (and pragmatic) success may reflect the individual (or collective) ability to make use of a diversity of cognitive frames and to switch from one frame to another as the need arises.

Reasoning under uncertainty is the most important field of human cognition in which the active role of the human mind is clearly in view. This is primarily because assessment of greater or lower likelihood is critically dependent on the way in which alternative conceptual spaces may give rise to alternative configurations of strategies and outcomes. Uncertainty itself may be assessed in terms of the degree to which the cognitive agent is free to 'structure' the situations associated with it. This manipulative view of uncertainty implies that, for any given state of nature, any given situation would be more uncertain (or, respectively, less uncertain) depending on whether agents are more (or, respectively, less) capable of *configuring* (or *reconfiguring*) that situation, its antecedents and its likely successors. Consideration of the specific domain in which the 'active power' of cognitive agents may be exerted is closely associated with a classification of situations ranging from lower to higher uncertainty. A situation in which the cognitive agent has virtually no freedom in giving shape to the configuration of possible events is one of lower uncertainty. Maximum uncertainty is associated with situations in which the cognitive agent is completely unconstrained in terms of which configuration of possible events he might reasonably consider.

The above point of view is consistent with a primary research avenue in cognitive science, which is to assess the formation of categories and its roots in dispositional attitudes concerning the detection of similarity (see Tversky, 1977; Gardenfors, 2000; Scazzieri, 2001; 2008). It is also consistent with research work in artificial intelligence addressing the interplay of ontological and epistemic abilities (see Gardenfors, 1990; Giunchiglia, 1993; Sánchez, Cavero and Marcos, 2009) as well as with a well established tradition in decision theory and economics recognizing the pervasive *and* multidimensional character of situations characterized by lack of certainty (see Hishiyama, Chapter 10, Vercelli, Chapter 7, and Zadeh, Chapter 6, in this volume). Among the latter contributions, we mention the classical distinction between risk and uncertainty (see Kregel and Nasica, Chapter 11, this volume), introduced by John Maynard Keynes in 1907 and in 1921 by pointing out that 'if we are given two distinct arguments, there is no general presumption that their two probabilities and certainty can be placed in an order' (Keynes, 1973 [1921], p. 41); Frank H. Knight's view that 'a *measurable* uncertainty, or "risk" proper, [...] is so far different from an *unmeasurable* one that it is not in effect uncertainty at all' (Knight, 1946 [1921], p. 20; author's emphasis); and John Hicks's belief that 'of two alternatives, on given evidence, either A is more probable than B, or B [is] more probable than A, or they are equally probable, *or* [...] *they are not comparable*' (Hicks, 1979, p. 114; author's emphasis). Following those acknowledgements, it is increasingly recognized that reasoning under lack of certainty is inherently associated with a complex mix of inferential *and* representational abilities, and that plausible judgements under those conditions presuppose first the ability to identify the cognitive context (most) suitable for the situation and problem(s) in view (see, for example, Suppes, 1981; Gilboa and Schmeidler, 2001, pp. 29–61; Drolet and Suppes, 2008; Suppes, 2010).

The aim of this volume is to address lack of certainty on the basis of the most general conditions for *plausible reasoning*, that is, reasoning that is defensible but not 'beyond controversy' (Polya, 1990 [1954], p. v; see also Polya, 1968; Collins and Michalski, 1989). Fundamental uncertainty provides the framework of the cases of plausible reasoning considered in the following chapters. It is associated with probabilistic ignorance (no relevant probability distribution is known, nor can it be assumed) and, in particular, *ex ante* structural ignorance (the space of events is unknown, or only partially known). In particular, lack of certainty is examined from both the ontic and the epistemic viewpoints, reliability of evidence is assigned a central role, and similarity judgements are considered a necessary condition of probability judgements. The above setting lends itself to a theory of uncertainty associated with the analysis of concept formation, likeness and distance more than with the inferential structure of probabilistic reasoning. The latter part of the volume explores the implications of the above point of view in the analysis of economic decisions, and carries out that investigation by examining the weight of rational arguments under uncertainty, the objective conditions of stochastic equilibrium, and the general structure of economic and social laws in a universe of interacting decision makers. Finally, the volume examines the character of plausible reasoning about moral issues in the light of the theory of uncertainty outlined in the previous chapters.

1.2 A refinement of the distinction between risk and uncertainty: fundamental uncertainty

Rationality may be compatible with a variety of uncertainty assessments, which often reflect different ways of structuring the space of events. Acknowledgement that identification and representation of the space of conceivable events is a necessary condition of plausible reasoning under uncertainty suggests a refinement of the distinction between risk and uncertainty (see section 1.1). In particular, as argued by Itzhack Gilboa and David Schmeidler, it may be reasonable to introduce

> a third category of *structural ignorance*: 'risk' refers to situations where probabilities are given; 'uncertainty'—to situations in which states are naturally defined, or can simply be constructed, but probabilities are not. Finally, decision under 'structural ignorance' refers to decision problems for which states are neither (i) naturally given in the problem; nor (ii) can they be naturally constructed by the decision maker.
>
> (Gilboa and Schmeidler, 2001, p. 45)

This conceptual setting is close to that considered by Keynes in his *Treatise on Probability* (*TP*) (Keynes, 1973 [1921]). There Keynes examined conditions for rational choice when probabilities may not be known and/or could be expressed only in a non-numerical way. Keynesian uncertainty is a setting in which rational decisions are possible but depend upon highly *distinctive* bodies of information depending on situation and context (see Marzetti Dall'Aste Brandolini, Chapter 12, this volume; see also Marzetti Dall'Aste Brandolini and Scazzieri, 1999, Introduction and pp. 139–88).[2] In this case 'The principles of probability logic need not mandate numerical degrees of belief that *a* and that *ab* on the evidence *h* but only that agent *X* is required to be more certain that *a* than that *ab*. According to Keynes, probabilities of hypotheses on given information could even be non comparable' (Levi, Chapter 3, section 3.3, this volume; see also Kyburg, Chapter 2, this volume). Keynes's discussion of the weight of argument (and of the associated issue of the weight of evidence) calls attention to the reliability of human judgement under fundamental uncertainty. In particular, it suggests a way to assess the influence of evidence in attaining a plausible (but not uncontroversial) inference ('proximity to proof').[3] It also allows a formal treatment of unexpected events (potential surprise or disbelief).[4] As some contributors to this volume point out (see Levi, Chapter 3; Vercelli, Chapter 7), this point of view opens up a whole set of new issues, since consideration of the weight of evidence 'turns upon a balance, not between the favourable and the unfavourable evidence, but between *absolute* amounts of relevant knowledge and of relevant ignorance respectively' (Keynes, 1973 [1921], p. 77). In particular, assessment of the degree of relevance calls attention to the fact that '[w]here the conclusions of two arguments are different, or where the evidence for the one does not overlap the evidence for the other, it will often be impossible to compare their weights, just as it may be impossible to compare their probabilities' (Keynes, 1973 [1921], p. 78; see also Runde, 1990).

Fundamental uncertainty calls attention to the role of mental frames in assessing evidence and guiding rational decisions. Probability is associated with degree of rational belief, but different probabilities are not always comparable (primarily because their weights may be different). It may be argued that probabilities 'lie on *paths*, each of which runs from 0 to 1' (Kyburg, Chapter 2, section 2.1.3, this volume). Indeed, the same numerical probability could have entirely different implications for rational choice depending on the weight attached to it. To put it in another way, the same information could be associated with different probabilities depending on the weight we attach to available evidence. In particular, 'probabilities are only partially ordered: two probabilities may be incomparable. The first may be neither greater, nor less than, nor yet equal to the third' (Kyburg and Man Teng, 2001, p. 80). The existence of different 'orders of probability' (Keynes) makes *switches* between probability orders conceivable. This in turn makes the relationship between degrees of rational beliefs and available information to be of the non-monotonic type. Further evidence could initially increase our confidence in a given hypothesis and then prompt us to withdraw it, either because we have shifted to a different order of probability or because new background knowledge has drastically reduced the weight of our evidence. There is an important connection between the cognitive demands of fundamental uncertainty and the idea that probability judgements are always relative to a certain state of mind. This property is clearly stated in Chapter 1 of Keynes's *TP*:

> when in ordinary speech we name some opinion as probable without qualification, the phrase is generally elliptical. We mean that it is probable when certain considerations, implicitly or explicitly present to our minds at the moment, are taken into account [...] No proposition is in itself either probable or improbable, just as no place is intrinsically distant; and the probability of the same statement

varies with the evidence presented, which is, as it were, its origin of reference.

(Keynes, 1973 [1921], p. 7)[5]

This point of view is closely related to the formalization of fundamental uncertainty in terms of conditional probability, a possibility explored in a number of contributions to this volume (see Costantini and Garibaldi, Chapter 8; Fano, Chapter 4; Kyburg, Chapter 2). Keynes called attention to the 'coefficient of influence' (Carnap's 'relevance quotient' as introduced in Carnap, 1950), which may be defined as a measure of the relevance of additional evidence for the degree of acceptance of any given hypothesis (see Costantini and Garibaldi, Chapter 8, this volume). In general, additional evidence has more or less impact upon the degree of acceptance of any given hypothesis H depending on whether the weight of argument leading to its acceptance (or rejection) is increased or reduced. For example, we may conjecture that additional evidence would have greater influence upon acceptance/rejection of H if the weight of the corresponding inductive inference is increased. In other words, the coefficient of influence provides a link between the epistemic and the ontic aspects of probabilities. This is because the coefficient of influence is related *at the same time* to the degree of rational belief in hypothesis H for any given evidence e and to the way in which stochastic interdependence influences the structure of observations (that is, the internal configuration of e). Given a certain amount of new evidence e^*, it is reasonable to conjecture an inverse relationship between the degree of stochastic interdependence and the weight of inductive inference. For a high degree of interdependence makes the configuration of e unstable and reduces the likelihood that new evidence e^* will be conclusive with respect to the given hypothesis. On the other hand, a low degree of interdependence makes the configuration of e^* more stable and increases the weight of inductive inference.

1.3   Plausible reasoning under fundamental uncertainty

Emphasis on the cognitive dimension of rationality enhances the domain in which the plausibility of reasoning criteria can be assessed and compared. In other words, moving beyond the circumscribed assumptions of 'standard' rational choice theory does not lend (by itself) to relaxation of general rationality conditions, such as the propensity to deliberately draw conclusions from premises, to follow any given chain of reasoning step by step, and to identify on that basis connections among seemingly disjointed objects or ideas. It is fully consistent with the recognition that problem spaces are to a large extent a product of the *constructive work* of the human mind, and that assessment of that work presupposes careful consideration of situation and context (see also note 1, and Marzetti Dall'Aste Brandolini, Chapter 12, this volume). However, under conditions of fundamental uncertainty, classical rules for inductive inference (such as the Humean multiplication of instances) may be replaced by a strategy in which inductive arguments are associated with the identification of stochastic regularities for relatively *independent* sets of objects or agents. This approach calls attention to the possibility of representing any given set of heterogeneous objects or agents as a universe of *agent types*, in which each type would be associated with a specific collection of attributes (see Costantini and Garibaldi, Chapter 8, this volume).

Under fundamental uncertainty, rational choices are guided by 'the degree of belief that it is rational to entertain in given conditions' (Keynes, 1973 [1921], p. 4). This means that guesswork is fundamental to rational understanding and acting. Keynes carefully argued this point when he wrote: '[g]iven the body of direct knowledge which constitutes our ultimate premises, [...] further rational beliefs, certain or probable, can be derived by valid argument from our direct knowledge' (Keynes, 1973 [1921], p. 4). The close intertwining of subjective perceptions and objective (intersubjective) relations is outlined by Keynes in the passage that immediately follows the previous quotation:

> [t]his involves purely logical relations between the propositions which embody our direct knowledge and the propositions about which we seek indirect knowledge. What particular propositions we select as the premises of our argument naturally depends on subjective factors peculiar to ourselves; but the relations, in which other propositions stand to these, and which entitle us to probable beliefs, are objective and logical.
>
> (Keynes, 1973 [1921], p. 4)

Plausible reasoning under fundamental uncertainty gives prominence to the identification of what 'given conditions' (in Keynes's sense) are, and the identification of those conditions becomes increasingly important as one moves away from known circumstances to largely unknown sets of possibilities. Fundamental uncertainty is likely to be associated with event fluctuations around the mean that are *not* self-averaging, that is, they do not tend to 0 as the model size n tends to infinity (see Aoki,

Chapter 9, section 9.1, this volume). Once fundamental uncertainty is acknowledged, the constraints associated with a cognitive frame become relevant and may be central for the utilization of available and relevant knowledge in choice situations. In short, fundamental uncertainty is bound to 'twist' our attention towards the ontological and epistemic *premises* for rational arguments, but does not make rationality constraints redundant. Indeed, there are grounds for believing that those constraints may become increasingly important when the 'imprecision' of possibility spaces does not allow unambiguous identification of what may be likely (or unlikely). For in this case rationality constraints narrow down the epistemic source of uncertainty and reduce the set of possibilities that it is reasonable to conceive of. The above argument entails that, under conditions of fundamental uncertainty, rationality may have a twofold role to play. On the one hand, the guesswork needed in identifying suitable problem spaces must be grounded in reasons: cognitive agents should be suitably equipped to sort out relevant information and to construct an effective representation of the world.[6] On the other hand, that preliminary guesswork is often conducive to rationality constraints circumscribing the range of options to be considered for any such representation. It may be interesting to note that the twofold role of rationality in cognition has an equivalent in the domain of reasons for acting. For in this case, too, reasons for accepting a certain view of the world are often associated with reasons inducing us to act upon that particular representation of the world. Conditions of fundamental uncertainty strengthen the relationship between knowing and acting because of the greater freedom acquired by the constructive power of the human mind. Again, we owe to Keynes an effective picture of that relationship: '[t]o believe one thing *in preference* of another, as distinct from believing the first true or more probable and the second false or less probable, must have reference to action and must be a loose way of expressing the propriety of acting on one hypothesis rather than another' (1973 [1921], p. 339).

The above argument calls attention to the relationship between situational judgement and rationality standards (see Marzetti Dall'Aste Brandolini, Chapter 12, this volume). When probability distributions are unknown and even the space of possible events is not fully explored, agents are likely to fall back on judgements of likeness in their search for a suitable representation of problem space and an effective set of epistemic criteria. It is primarily the type of rationality called forth in judgements of similarity rather than in processes of inference. Indeed, the connection between judgements of similarity and judgements of probability had been recognized long ago. Joseph Butler noted that it is a distinctive feature of reasoning under uncertainty: 'when we determine a thing to be probably true, suppose that an event has or will come to pass, it is from the mind's remarking in it a likeness to some other event, which we have observed has come to pass' (Butler, 1834 [1736], p. 2). In this connection, however, the objective (or intersubjective) character of rational judgement might be questioned. As noted by Arthur Cecil Pigou, 'it seems paradoxical to speak of its being rational for me to perceive something, which, from the constitution of my mind, it is impossible for me to perceive' (Pigou, 1921, p. 507). Fundamental uncertainty enhances the dependence of similarity recognition on human judgement (see above). At the same time, the active role of judgement in similarity assessment calls attention to criteria and constraints that make judgement reasonable in any given situation.

The language used for describing uncertain situations also deserves attention, since situations may be described in different ways according to the language used. In this connection, Lotfi A. Zadeh (Chapter 6, section 6.1, this volume) highlights the fact that 'more often than not uncertain knowledge is described in a natural language'. This condition introduces a constraint on the range of descriptions that are feasible for any given language and highlights the need to distinguish between possibility and probability, as well as between 'probabilistic uncertainty and possibilistic uncertainty' (Zadeh, ibid.). In particular, it is emphasized that, since standard probability theory is based on the belief that information is statistical in nature, when information is expressed in a 'natural language', considered as propositions or a system of propositions, uncertainty cannot be dealt with by standard theory. This point of view suggests a generalized theory of uncertainty based on non-bivalent (fuzzy) logic and indicates that different patterns of rational behaviour may coexist within the same social universe due to a variety of linguistic constraints.[7]

1.4   The scope of the volume and its contributions

This volume explores fundamental uncertainty in the light of a set of connected research lines that have taken shape in recent years as a result of investigation in a variety of experimental and theoretical fields. Prominent features of the above research scenario are (i) a shift from general to context-specific (or context-specifiable) canons of rationality; (ii) increasing attention to the heterogeneity of cognitive attitudes; (iii) the central role assumed by framing and focusing; and (iv) interest in non-monotonic inferences and discontinuous changes of cognitive state (cognitive jumps). In particular, lack of certainty is examined from both the ontological and the epistemic viewpoints, reliability of evidence is assigned a central role, and similarity judgements are considered a necessary condition of probability judgements. The above setting lends itself to a theory of uncertainty associated with the analysis of concept formation, likeness and distance more than with the inferential structure of probabilistic reasoning.

The essays in this volume address fundamental uncertainty from the points of view of philosophy, information science, decision theory and statistics, and economic analysis. Many themes are recurrent across those disciplines and the chapters of the volume suggest manifold opportunities for cross-fertilization. In particular, the volume highlights fields of interest such as the justification of intersubjective grounding of judgement under uncertainty after Ramsey's criticism of Keynes (see below), the distinction between individual decisions and the properties of the overall system within which those decisions are taken, and the specific features of plausible decisions (that is, defensible but not uncontroversial decisions) in the economic and moral domains under fundamental uncertainty.

In Chapter 2, 'Keynes and Ramsey on Probability', Henry E. Kyburg calls attention to the discussion between Keynes and Frank P. Ramsey on the proper epistemological role of probability. The author argues that neither side understood the other, and even that they failed to understand the issue that separated them. In particular, Kyburg argues that, although Keynes was at times unclear, he was basically right about the methodological issues. His contribution starts from acknowledgment that 'in the philosophical world of the nineteenth century, "intuition" did not carry overtones of arbitrariness or personal whimsy' (section 2.1.1) so that Keynes's appeal to an intuitive conception of probability would be entirely consistent with his view that 'in the sense important to logic, probability is not subjective' (Keynes, 1973 [1921], p. 4; as quoted in Kyburg, 2.1.2). Kyburg builds upon Keynes's analysis of different ordered series of probabilities (Keynes, 1973 [1921], pp. 36–43) a theory of probabilities as forming 'a lattice structure' such that '[u]pper and lower bounds for any probabilities exist [...]—namely 0 and 1' (Kyburg, section 2.1.3). In this connection, the conjecture that probability values could be conceived as *intervals* is seen as providing an answer to Keynes's problem whether 'the meet and join of any two probabilities exist' (section 2.1.3). After detailed presentation of the exchange between

Keynes and Ramsey, Kyburg goes back to Keynes's interest in partial rankings of probabilities and argues that, from that point of view, 'those probabilities to which Ramsey's arguments apply may constitute a small fraction of probabilities' (section 2.3).

In Chapter 3, 'The Weight of Argument', Isaac Levi examines the role of 'balancing reasons' in inductive arguments and discusses what Keynes called the 'somewhat novel question' of the balance between favourable and unfavourable evidence. In particular, Levi takes up Charles Peirce's criticism of the 'conceptualist' approach to decision making under uncertainty (the approach interpreting terms such as 'certain' and 'probable' as describing degrees of rational belief) and stresses that, according to Peirce, the amount of knowledge relevant to decision making 'cannot be accounted for on the conceptualist view but can on the view that insists that belief probabilities be derivable via direct inference from statistical probability' (section 3.2). Peirce's view presupposes that belief probability can be grounded on statistical probability. Keynes was critical of this assumption while acknowledging that belief probability can itself be indeterminate. Differently from Peirce, Levi thinks that 'one needs to be in a position to make moderately determinate judgements of belief probability without grounding in objective or statistical chance' (section 3.4). He also emphasizes the cognitive-value dimension attached to Keynes's discussion of evidential weight, which 'is in this sense independent of the specific goals of the practical decision problem' (section 3.6). The essay concludes with the proposal of stepping beyond Keynes's own analysis by acknowledging the symmetrical roles of belief and disbelief functions and recognizing that the formal properties of belief and disbelief according to G. L. S. Shackle are closely parallel to the properties that any given argument should have in order to be sufficiently close to proof or disproof'.

Chapter 4 by Vincenzo Fano, 'A Critical Evaluation of Comparative Probability', takes up the discussion of probability judgements as judgements concerning relative (comparative) probability, and outlines an assessment of the Keynes–Ramsey debate starting from the idea that 'it is often possible to establish a comparison between probabilities, but not to determine their quantitative value' (section 4.2). For example, as acknowledged by Keynes, even brokers dealing with disaster insurance 'have to establish only that the probability of the disaster happening is *lower* than a certain value' (section 4.2; see also Keynes, 1973 [1921], p. 23). However, recognition of widespread use of comparative (not quantitative) probability judgements exposes the epistemological dilemma between circumscribing the treatment of uncertainty to the special cases in which Ramsey's argument applies (and quantitative probabilities are identifiable), and extending it to cases beyond Ramsey's circumscription, that is, to cases in which probability can be only of the comparative type and in which rules governing the updating of probability in view of augmented evidence cannot be established. At this point of his argument, Fano turns his attention to comparability itself, and introduces the distinction between homogeneous probabilities, which have either the same hypothesis or the same evidence, and inhomogeneous probabilities: the former are always comparable, whereas this is not generally true for the latter. Comparative probability is shown to have epistemological advantages, such as the possibility to assess comparative probabilities from relative frequencies. However, comparative probability, too, is marred by the lack of a probability measure making it possible to update rational belief in view of augmented evidence.

The relationship between the ontological and epistemic features of uncertainty is taken up by Roberto Scazzieri in his contribution 'A Theory of Similarity and Uncertainty' (Chapter 5). This chapter starts from the premise that, under most general assumptions, uncertainty entails at the same time a lack of determinacy and imprecise knowledge. The former is an ontological property of the universe under consideration; the latter is an epistemic property of the agents in that universe. Scazzieri conjectures that there may be a trade-off between ontological and epistemic precision, and that the domain of reasoning under uncertainty coincides with the collection of intermediate situations *between* ontological precision and epistemic precision. The two polar cases point to the existence of intermediate situations in which ontological precision ('circumscription') is sufficiently low to allow identification of partial similarity but similarity itself is not too high, so that occurrences beyond uniformities (that is, novelties) are possible. Following a suggestion in Keynes's *TP*, Scazzieri examines the analogy between similarity and probability and emphasizes that, like standard similarity judgements, likelihood judgements presuppose a plurality of ordered series in terms of which a reasonable judgement may be expressed. In particular, this contribution highlights the role of crossovers between different serial orders, which may be interpreted as corresponding to situations in which different ontologies coincide at a given point of time. This means that the very plurality of uncertainty dimensions that makes it difficult in general to assess any given situation may turn out to be an advantage when one faces the special circumstances in which the same assessment of the situation in view is grounded in a plurality of different orders of likelihood.

In Chapter 6, 'Generalized Theory of Uncertainty: Principal Concepts and Ideas', Lotfi A. Zadeh outlines a theory of uncertainty in which uncertainty is considered an attribute of information, and information itself is seen as subject to a 'generalized constraint' that determines which propositions, commands and questions can be expressed by means of any given language. Reasoning under uncertainty is thus treated as 'generalized constraint propagation', that is, as a process by which constraints upon the uses of language determine which inferences are possible on the basis of available information (section 6.2). This point of view leads Zadeh to delve into the relationship between the ontological and the epistemic sides of uncertainty and in particular to examine the role of prototypical forms (or *protoforms*), which are considered as abstracted summaries needed to identify 'the deep semantic structure' of the corresponding objects to which they apply (section 6.14). Prototypical forms lead to the concept of granular structure, in which attention is focused on 'a clump of values [for any given variable X] drawn together by indistinguishability, similarity, proximity or functionality' (section 6.1).[8] This approach leads Zadeh to introduce the distinction between probability and possibility and to conjecture that there are manifold kinds of uncertainty: probabilistic uncertainty, uncertainty associated with ontological possibility (possibilistic uncertainty), and various combinations of those two kinds. In short, information should be considered a generalized constraint, with statistical uncertainty being a special case; fuzzy logic should be substituted for bivalent logic; information expressed in natural language should be assigned a central role. This strategy is considered to be the most effective tool in dealing with real-world constraints, which are mostly elastic rather than rigid and have a complex structure even when apparently simple.

The relationship between information and the nature of uncertainty is also central to Keynes's proposal that the probability of arguments cannot be fully assessed unless we also introduce a measure of our confidence in those arguments (Keynes's 'weight of arguments'). Chapter 7 by Alessandro Vercelli, 'Weight of Argument and Economic Decisions', sets out to clarify the relationship between the 'weight of argument' in Keynes's *TP* and some crucial passages of *The General Theory of Employment, Interest and Money* (Keynes, 1973 [1936]) (*GT*). In particular, Vercelli points out that Keynes's most innovative contribution should be found in the utilization of this concept in interpreting economic decisions. After discussing alternative definitions of the weight of argument in *TP* and *GT*, Vercelli emphasizes the need to establish a hierarchical relation between probability and weight of argument: probability is considered a first-order uncertainty measure while 'uncertainty' in the strict sense is associated with second-order uncertainty as measured by the weight of argument. It is nowadays increasingly acknowledged that there are no binding objections that preclude the analysis of different modalities of uncertainty. In particular, Keynes's reaction to Ramsey's criticism should now be reassessed, as Keynes was induced to broaden the scope of non-demonstrative inference that could be seen as relative not only to the premises and background knowledge of arguments but also to their pragmatic and semantic context. Keynes's revised view is central to the treatment of uncertainty and the weight of argument in *GT*, and explains his growing attention to social psychology. According to Vercelli, Keynes's view that it is impossible to insure against the (negative) effects of a change in the weight of argument provides strong decision-theoretical foundations for his fundamental message that the market may be unable to regulate itself, so that full employment can be restored and maintained only through a well thought-out economic policy.

Fundamental uncertainty raises the issue of whether we may be justified in accepting the principle of indifference. In Keynes's words, this principle asserts that 'if there is no *known reason* for predicating of our subject one rather than another of several alternatives, then relatively to such knowledge the assertions of each of these alternatives have an *equal* probability' (Keynes, 1973 [1921], p. 45). The principle of indifference entails comparing 'the likelihood of two conclusions on given evidence' (Keynes, 1973 [1921], p. 58) and must be distinguished from a criterion of relevance, according to which we should consider 'what difference a change of evidence makes to the likelihood of a given conclusion' (ibid.). In the former case (likelihood of conclusions versus indifference), we are asking 'whether or not x is to be preferred to y on evidence h' (Keynes, 1973 [1921], p. 58); in the latter case (relevance versus irrelevance), we should evaluate 'whether the addition of h_1 to evidence h is relevant to x' (Keynes, 1973 [1921], p. 59). Likelihood of conclusions and relevance of evidence are symmetrical features of inductive knowledge under the assumption of a fundamental regularity in nature and society. Chapters 8 and 9 examine the structure of induction by discussing, respectively, Keynes's concept of 'coefficient of influence' and the implications of lack of regularity under uncertainty due to very large coefficients of variation. Chapter 8 by Domenico Costantini and Francesco Garibaldi, 'The Relevance Quotient: Keynes and Carnap', discusses the issue of relevance (that is, the influence of conclusion b upon conclusion a on hypothesis h) by comparing Keynes's 'coefficient of influence' with the concept of 'relevance quotient' introduced by Rudolph Carnap. The authors introduce a condition of invariance for the relevance quotient close to Keynes's coefficient of influence; they argue that the above condition rules the stochastic dependence of a new observation upon data, and is an important tool in solving inductive problems. In particular, they maintain that 'the notion of relevance quotient [...] cannot be introduced without having at one's disposal a relative notion of probability' (section 8.7), and suggest that their relevance quotient is especially useful in contexts, like physics, biology and economics, where probability can be regarded as ontological. Examples of probabilistic dynamics are discussed and the fact is highlighted that changes of long-term expectations are 'indissolubly tied to a probability which is changing with evidence' (ibid.). The authors also call attention to the central role of the invariance condition ensuring that mean values are unaffected by changes in individual distribution. Finally, Chapter 8 asks whether the probability studied in Keynes's *Treatise on Probability* is epistemic or ontic, and concludes by calling attention to the fact that Keynes emphasized his 'fundamental sympathy' with the stochastic approach to biology and statistical physics.

Chapter 9 by Masanao Aoki, 'Non-Self-Averaging Phenomena in Macroeconomics: Neglected Sources of Uncertainty and Policy Ineffectiveness', addresses lack of regularity by examining the behaviour of macroeconomic non-self-averaging models, that is, the behaviour of models in which the coefficient of variation of some random variable (the ratio of standard deviation divided by its mean) does not tend to zero as n tends to infinity. This chapter examines policy effectiveness questions in such models, and shows that in general the larger the coefficient of variation, the smaller is the policy multiplier. There are examples in which policy actions become totally ineffective as the value of the coefficients of variation tends to infinity. It is argued that a particularly important feature of non-self-averaging in macroeconomic simulation is that it can give rise to uninformative or misleading policy results. Specifically, the convergence of non-self-averaging models when simulated using Monte Carlo methods is much slower than in self-averaging models. Policy-effect simulations tend to become uninformative or misleading because a very large number of simulation runs may be required for extreme values to appear to upset the sorts of conclusion based on small numbers of simulations in which only most probable simulation results appear. It is argued that conventional simulations or analysis with quadratic cost criteria are all associated with self-averaging results and do not say anything about behaviour of non-self-averaging models, which points to a serious fault in using representative agents. Aoki's contribution is an important warning that microeconomic exercises leading to 'a better understanding of the dynamics of the *mean* or *aggregate* variables' cannot lead to a better understanding of the overall dynamics of the economic system if non-self-averaging fluctuations are considered (section 9.1; see also Aoki, 2002).

Non-regularity in individual behaviour has far-reaching implications for what concerns the analysis of the economic (or social) system as a whole and the method most suitable to that objective. In particular, non-regularity points to the existence of a wedge between the universe of individual decision makers (micro-world) and the system as a whole (macro-world) as traditionally conceived, and calls for innovative theoretical effort to overcome the problem. Thus, in Chapter 10, 'A Critical Reorientation of Keynes's Economic and Philosophical Thoughts', Izumi Hishiyama addresses the above issue by first considering 'the difficult core of Keynesian thought—"the logical justification of inductive methods"' (Keynes, as quoted in section 10.1). The specific route followed by Keynes in order to justify induction leads to the analysis of the epistemic conditions for inductive knowledge, that is, of the assumptions of 'atomic uniformity' and 'limitation of independent variety'. According to Hishiyama, this point of view may be connected with ethical individualism (as suggested by Keynes himself in *TP*) but it is explicitly rejected in *GT* when Keynes deals with the economic system as an organic unit. In particular, the author deals with the methodological assumptions behind *GT* and takes up Luigi Pasinetti's view that the effective demand principle is 'quite independent of any behavioural relations and thus of any particular adaptation mechanism' (Pasinetti, as quoted in section 10.7). On the other hand, fundamental (non-measurable) uncertainty characterizes Keynes's representation of the micro-world. The dual character of Keynes's thinking calls attention to the whole versus parts issue and leads Hishiyama to look for a way of making Keynes's treatment of uncertainty consistent with the organic approach in the analysis of the economic system as a whole. In this connection, Hishiyama calls attention to Pasinetti's proposal that sectorally differentiated demands should be considered, and to Pasinetti's proposal that one should substitute a general macroeconomic condition (expressed in a multi-sectoral framework) for Keynes's original formulation of effective demand theory. In this way, a criterion for moving back and forth between aggregate and disaggregate levels of investigation is introduced, and fundamental uncertainty is made compatible with a certain degree of determinacy at the macro-level.[9]

John Allen Kregel and Eric Nasica, in Chapter 11 'Uncertainty and Rationality: Keynes and Modern Economics', also highlight the fact that 'the crucial point for Keynes, as for Knight, is the inadequacy of statistical quantification in the form of a probability for the analysis of uncertainty', but this aspect of rational decisions in condition of fundamental uncertainty has been neglected by orthodox economists (section 11.2.1). According to these authors, the consideration of crucial decisions such as those leading to irreversible and non-repeated actions is the boundary line between the Keynesian and the traditional neoclassical approach of uncertainty. Nor does the 'new' classical theory in the version of the rational expectation hypothesis admit situations of fundamental uncertainty, since this theory assumes that the economic system moves according to a stationary stochastic process which also has the characteristic of an ergodic process. Therefore, according to the theory of rational expectations, decisions in condition of fundamental uncertainty are 'excluded, or classified as non rational' (see section 11.3.2); while 'post-Keynesian analysis develops a theory of the formation of expectations applicable to situations in which the degree of rational belief is less than certain' (ibid.). In fact, Keynesian economists admit a non-ergodic environment, and believe that the traditional conception of rationality has to be reformulated in order to describe situations of 'expectational instability'.

The concluding chapter by Silva Marzetti Dall'Aste Brandolini, 'Moral Good and Right Conduct: A General Theory of Welfare under Fundamental Uncertainty', deals with competing moral systems (often associated with competing social philosophies), and aims to identify which general characteristics a general theory of welfare (GTW) must have from the point of view of rationality when also admitting conditions of fundamental uncertainty. Welfare economics consists of a certain number of theoretical models that may be distinguished according to the conception of moral value on which they are grounded and the right conduct they suggest. As regards moral values, two fundamental conceptions of moral good exist, which justify the existence of different approaches to welfare economics: the ethics of motive, which makes reference to subjective values, and the ethics of end, which also admits objective values (see sections 12.2 and 12.4). As regards right conduct, Bayesian reductionism and rational dualism are two different ways of considering uncertainty about economic phenomena. Bayesian reductionism assumes that agents are able to identify numerical subjective probabilities, and admits the maximization procedure only; while rational dualism also admits non-measurable probabilities and procedures other than maximization (see sections 12.3 and 12.5). Since a rational choice between competing moral systems cannot be made, this awareness leads the author to think in terms of a GTW; and in section 12.6 it is shown that, from the point of view of moral values, a GTW must admit all the possible values in which a society *can* believe; while from the point of view of instrumental rationality, it must admit not only situations where decision makers have all the information and computing capabilities needed by the maximization procedure, but also situations where they do not have adequate information and behave under conditions of fundamental uncertainty.

1.5 Epilogue

Uncertainty derives from the intertwining of ontological and epistemic conditions. The relationship between those two sets of conditions emerges as a unifying theme of this volume. Taken in their unity, the different contributions acknowledge that the configuration of any given situation (state of the world) determines whether or not the corresponding epistemic grasp is grounded; they also recognize that the epistemic context may be central in determining whether or not a grounded understanding of that situation is feasible. This point of view is common to the different contributions in the volume and suggests a pragmatic attitude towards uncertain real-world situations and epistemic contexts. This means that the handling of uncertainty cannot be left to a single standard criterion for the description (circumscription) of situations, nor can it be achieved by a uniform rule for the revision of inductive knowledge. Rather, uncertainty calls for agents capable of producing both situation-adequate descriptions and sophisticated inferences. This volume emphasizes that such a need becomes greater as we move towards fundamental uncertainty. It is important to emphasize that the above requirement does not make for arbitrariness in the handling of uncertainty. On the contrary, it would be necessary, in each case, to identify a suitable intersection of ontological and epistemic conditions, and this intersection would normally narrow down the number of relevant ontological and epistemic states. In short, constraints on plausible judgement are increasingly binding as uncertainty increases either for ontological or epistemic reasons (or for both). At the same time, the need to meet multiple relevance conditions (both on the ontological and the epistemic side) discloses the manifold opportunities associated with negative heuristics, that is, with a discovery and choice strategy in which descriptions and/or arguments are gradually discarded as one moves from one reasoning step to another. To conclude, fundamental uncertainty points to a requirement of extended rationality and highlights that prudence may be essential in the application of it.

Notes

1. See Descartes (1986 [1637, 1641, 1644]); Davidson (1980).
2. We follow here F. Giunchiglia's distinction between 'situation', as a way to record 'the state of the world as it is, independently of how it is represented in the mind of the reasoner' (Giunchiglia, 1993, p. 146), and 'context' as 'a *theory* of the world which encodes an individual's subjective perspective about it' (Giunchiglia, 1993, p. 145).
3. According to Maria Carla Galavotti, Keynes's attitude may be explained in terms of his adherence to 'a moderate form of logicism, quite different from the strictly formal approach later developed by Carnap. Keynes' logicism is pervaded by a deeply felt need not to lose sight of ordinary speech and practice, and assigns an important role to intuition and individual judgement' (Galavotti, 2005, p. 147).
4. As noted by Anthony W. F. Edwards, 'the quantification of surprise in terms of probability is likely to tell only half the story' (Edwards, 1992, p. 203). Keynes's weight of argument gives a cue into reasons for disbelief and possible causes of transition from belief to disbelief (or vice versa) as context is changed.
5. We are grateful to Domenico Costantini for calling our attention to this passage of the *Treatise on Probability*.
6. This entails identifying which problems can be addressed and the type of tools that may be used to that purpose. In that connection, Isaac Levi points out that 'we cannot be obliged to recognize all the logical consequences of our full beliefs or even enough of the consequences to solve some particular complicated problem' (Levi, 1997, p. 9).
7. The relationship between language, descriptions and permissible events is also considered in Crisma (1988).
8. The concept of 'prototypical form', in its association with the analysis of granular information, had been anticipated in Adam Smith's *Theory of Moral Sentiments* (Smith, 1976 [1759]). See for example, the following passage: '[T]he beauty of each species, though in one sense the rarest of all things, because few individuals hit this middle form exactly, yet in another, is the most common, because all the deviations from it resemble it more than they resemble one another' (Smith, 1976 [1759], pp. 198–9).
9. This point of view is rooted in the distinction between the way in which events (or situations) are described and the way in which knowledge about those events (situations) may be achieved. As Keynes noted, "[I]f different wholes were subject to different laws *qua* wholes and not simply on account of and in proportion to the differences of their parts, knowledge of a part could not lead, it would seem, even to presumptive or probable knowledge as to its association with other parts. Given, on the other hand, a number of [...] atomic units and the laws connecting them, it would be possible to deduce their effects *pro tanto* without an exhaustive knowledge of all the coexisting circumstances' (Keynes, 1973 [1921], pp. 277–8). Alberto Pasquinelli and Silva Marzetti Dall'Aste Brandolini argue that the above methodological standpoint may be at the root of Keynes's apparent switch to an 'organic' point of view in the *General Theory* (Pasquinelli and Marzetti Dall'Aste Brandolini, 1994, p. xviii).

References

Aoki, M. (2002), *Modeling Aggregate Behavior and Fluctuations in Economics*, Cambridge: Cambridge University Press.

Bacharach, M. (2003), 'Framing and Cognition in Economics: the Bad News and the Good', in N. Dimitri, M. Basili and I. Gilboa (eds), *Cognitive Processes and Economic Behaviour*, London and New York: Routledge, pp. 63–74.

Butler, J. (1834 [1736]), *The Analogy of Religion, Natural and Revealed to the Constitution and Course of Nature*, London: Longman and Co.

Carnap, R. (1950), *Logical Foundations of Probability*, Chicago: University of Chicago Press.

Collins, A. and Michalski, R. S. (1989), 'Plausible Reasoning: A Core Theory', *Cognitive Science*, 13, pp. 1–49.

Crisma, L. (1988), 'Dalla certezza all'incertezza: aspetti dinamici in una impostazione soggettiva', in *Atti del convegno su incertezza ed economia*, Trieste (Università degli Studi di Trieste, Facoltà di Economia e Commercio, 29–30 October 1987): LINT, pp. 11–46.

Davidson, D. (1980), *Essays on Actions and Events*, Oxford: Clarendon Press.

Descartes, D. (1986 [1637, 1641, 1644]), *A Discourse on Method [and] Meditations on the First Philosophy [and] Principles of Philosophy*; translated by John Veitch; new introduction by Tom Sorell, London: Dent.

Drolet, A. and Suppes, P. (2008), 'The Good and the Bad, the True and the False', in Galavotti, Scazzieri and Suppes (2008a), pp. 13–35.

Edwards, A. W. F. (1992), *Likelihood* (expanded edn), Baltimore and London: Johns Hopkins University Press.

Galavotti, M. C. (2005), *Philosophical Introduction to Probability*, Stanford: CSLI Publications.

Galavotti, M. C., Scazzieri, R. and Suppes, P. (eds) (2008a), *Reasoning, Rationality and Probability*, Stanford: CSLI Publications.

——— (2008b), 'Introduction', in M. C. Galavotti, R. Scazzieri and P. Suppes (eds), *Reasoning, Rationality and Probability*, Stanford: CSLI Publications, pp. 1–9.

Gardenfors, P. (1990), 'Induction, Conceptual Spaces and AI', *Philosophy of Science*, 57, pp. 78–95.

——— (2000), *Conceptual Spaces: The Geometry of Thought*, Cambridge, MA and London: MIT Press.

Gilboa, I. and Schmeidler, D. (2001), *A Theory of Case-Based Decisions*, Cambridge: Cambridge University Press.

Giunchiglia, F. (1993), 'Contextual Reasoning', *Epistemologia*, 16 (special issue), pp. 145–63.

Hicks, J. R. (1979), *Causality in Economics*, Oxford: Basil Blackwell.

Keynes, J. M. (1907), *The Principles of Probability*, The John Maynard Keynes Papers, TP/A/1-TP/A/2, King's College Library, Cambridge.

——— (1973 [1921]), *A Treatise on Probability*, vol. VIII of *The Collected Writings of John Maynard Keynes*, London: Macmillan.

——— (1973 [1936]), *The General Theory of Employment, Interest and Money*, vol. VII of *The Collected Writings of John Maynard Keynes*, London: Macmillan.

Knight, F. H. (1946 [1921]), *Risk, Uncertainty and Profit*, with an additional introductory essay hitherto unpublished, London: London School of Economics and Political Science.

Kyburg, H. E. and Man Teng, C. (2001), *Uncertain Inference*, Cambridge: Cambridge University Press.

Levi, I. (1997), *The Covenant of Reason. Rationality and the Commitment of Thought*, Cambridge: Cambridge University Press.

Marzetti Dall'Aste Brandolini, S. and Scazzieri, R. (1999), 'Introduzione', in S. Marzetti Dall'Aste Brandolini and R. Scazzieri (eds), *La probabilità in Keynes. Premesse e influenze*, Bologna: Clueb, pp. 11–23.

Pasquinelli, A. and Marzetti Dall'Aste Brandolini, S. (1994), 'Introduzione', in J. M. Keynes, *Trattato sulla probabilità*, edited by A. Pasquinelli and S. Marzetti Dall'Aste Brandolini, Bologna: CLUEB, pp. ix–xxvi. (Italian translation of J. M. Keynes, *A Treatise on Probability*, London: Macmillan, 1921).

Pigou, A. C. (1921), '*A Treatise on Probability*. By J. M. Keynes', *Economic Journal*, 31, pp. 507–12.

Polya, G. (1968), *Patterns of Plausible Inference*, Princeton: Princeton University Press.

———. (1990 [1954)]), *Mathematics and Plausible Reasoning, vol. I: Induction and Analogy in Mathematics*, Princeton: Princeton University Press.

Runde, J. H. (1990), 'Keynesian Uncertainty and the Weight of Arguments', *Economics and Philosophy*, 6(2), pp. 275–92.

Sánchez, D. M., Cavero, J. M. and Marcos, E. (2009), 'The Concepts of Model in Information Systems Engineering: A Proposal for an Ontology of Models', *The Knowledge Engineering Review*, 24 (1), pp. 5–21.

Scazzieri, R. (2001), 'Analogy, Causal Pattterns and Economic Choice', in M. C. Galavotti, P. Suppes and D. Costantini (eds), *Stochastic Causality*, Stanford: CSLI Publications, pp. 123–39.

——— (2008), 'Context, Congruence and Coordination', in M. C. Galavotti, R. Scazzieri and P. Suppes (eds), *Reasoning, Rationality and Probability*, Stanford: CSLI Publications, pp. 187–207.

Smith, A. (1976 [1759]), *The Theory of Moral Sentiments*, D. D. Raphael and A. L. Macfie (eds), Oxford: Clarendon Press.

Suppes, P. (1981), 'The Limits of Rationality', *Grazer Philosophische Studien*, 12/13, pp. 85–101.

Suppes, P. (2010) 'The Nature of Probability', *Philosophical Studies*, 147 (1), pp. 89–102.

Tversky, A. (1977), 'Features of Similarity', *Psychological Review*, 84 (4), pp. 327–52.

2
Logic, Empiricism and Probability Structures

Henry E. Kyburg, Jr.

2.1 Keynes's *Treatise on Probability*

2.1.1 Logic and empiricism

One[1] of the great and influential events of Keynes's youth was the publication of Whitehead and Russell's *Principia Mathematica* (Whitehead and Russell, 1910–1913). Keynes was enormously impressed by this work, and to some extent took it as the inspiration for *A Treatise on Probability* (*TP*) (Keynes, 1973 [1921]). To some extent only, because Keynes clearly rejected the atomism and some of the empiricism associated with Russell's philosophy of science. Nevertheless he never became a subjectivist with regard to probability.

In 1921, and certainly in 1907 when the first draft of the *Treatise* was completed (Carabelli, 1988), it was widely thought that the basic principles of logic had to be accepted on the basis of "intuition." Lewis Carroll/ John Dodgson wrote a cute spoof, "What the Tortoise Said to Achilles," whose point was that the validity of *modus ponens* (the inference by which, if *p* entails *q* and *p* can be stated, then also *q* can be stated) could not be demonstrated by *modus ponens* (Carroll, 1895). Many people thought that the "first principles" of logic had to be accepted on intuitive grounds. There was no semantic tradition that would have allowed us to "show" that standard logic is truth preserving.

It is important to note that in the philosophical world of the nineteenth century "intuition" did not carry overtones of arbitrariness or personal whimsy. It did not embody the sense of subjectivity that later gave rise to the doctrines of Ramsey (1931), de Finetti (1937; 1964) and Savage (1972). "Intuition" was what allowed us to *see* that *modus ponens* was a valid form of inference, as well as what allowed us to *see* that we were in the presence of a crow or a black patch.

"Empiricism" in probability, for Keynes, also had a specialized and narrow meaning. It referred to a doctrine, stated by Leslie Ellis (1844) and developed by John Venn (1866), according to which probability statements were nothing but statements about empirical relative frequencies.

2.1.2   Probability a logical relation

Keynes is unequivocal in his insistence that probability represents a logical relation that is objective.

> [I]n the sense important to logic, probability is not subjective. It is not, that is to say, subject to human caprice. A proposition is not probable because we think it so. When once the facts are given which determine our knowledge, what is probable or improbable in these circumstances has been fixed objectively, and is independent of our opinion. The Theory of Probability is logical, therefore, because it is concerned with the degree of belief which it is *rational* to entertain in given conditions, and not merely with the actual beliefs of particular individuals, which may or may not be rational.
>
> (*TP*, p. 4)

Having thus laid his cards on the table, Keynes at no point backs down.

> When we argue that Darwin gives valid grounds for our accepting his theory of natural selection, we do not simply mean that we are psychologically inclined to agree with him; it is certain that we also intend to convey our belief that we are acting rationally in regarding his theory as probable. We believe that there is some real objective relation between Darwin's evidence and his conclusions.
>
> (*TP*, p. 5)

Keynes distinguishes three senses of the term "probability." In the most basic sense, it refers to "the logical relation between two sets of propositions" (*TP*, p. 11). Derivatively, the word applies to "the degrees of rational belief arising out of knowledge of secondary propositions which assert the existence of probability relations" (*TP*, p. 12). And then one can apply the term "probable" to the proposition that is so believed.

The epistemology discussed in the second chapter of the *Treatise* is a creation of the early twentieth century. It owes much to Russell and Moore, and is only marginally relevant to the discussion of probability. One phrase, however, is relevant to our treatment of Ramsey's criticism. The distinction is drawn between "direct knowledge" and "knowledge by argument." "In the case of every argument, it is only directly that we can know the secondary proposition which makes the argument itself valid and rational" (*TP*, p. 15). Applied to probability, in its fundamental sense, this entails that the probability relation between premises and conclusion of an argument must be perceived directly.

2.1.3 Probability values

Keynes repeatedly mentions "degrees" of rational belief, and acknowledges that degrees of belief are *in some sense* quantitative and "perhaps capable of measurement." However, he ends up by denying, in Chapter 3 of *TP*, that all probabilities are even capable of comparison. In reviewing arguments in favor of the measurability of probabilities, Keynes (interestingly, vis-à-vis Ramsey) mentions the practice of underwriters when they insure against almost any eventuality: "[b]ut this practice shows no more than that many probabilities are greater or less than some numerical measure, not that they themselves are numerically definite" (*TP*, p. 23).

Keynes also maintains that "there are some pairs of probabilities between the members of which *no* comparison of magnitude is possible . . . [nor is it] always possible to say that the degree of our rational belief in one conclusion is either equal to, greater than, or less than our degree of belief in another" (Keynes, 1973 [1921], pp. 36–7). Indeed he indicates that "the closest analogy [to probability] is that of similarity" (*TP*, p. 39).

This argument suggests, as does the illustration in Keynes (*TP*, p. 39), reproduced below, that probabilities form a lattice structure (see Fig. 2.1; see also Kyburg, 2003, pp. 140–1). Upper and lower bounds for any probabilities exist, of course—namely, 0 and 1—but the question is whether the meet and join of any two probabilities exist. A definitive answer is hard to come by for Keynes, since he never seems to have put the question to himself. Nevertheless, the list of properties on page 41 of *TP* suggests that the answer is affirmative. Probabilities lie on *paths*, each of which runs from 0 to 1. Consider all the paths on which the probability p_1 and p_2 lie. If they have no points in common other than 0 and 1, then these are the meet and join of *pi* and *pi*-. Suppose there is no greatest lower bound, that is, that for every lower bound p such that $p \leq p_1$ and $p \leq p_2$, there is a greater lower bound $p \leq p' \leq p_1$ and $p' < p_2$. It is hard to imagine that Keynes should think it possible that there should be an unbounded sequence of ever greater lower bounds to p_1 and p_2, though it is, of course, mathematically possible.

An alternative, and perhaps more up to date, way of looking at probabilities is to think of them as intervals. This is the view of probability adopted in (Kyburg, 1961) and developed most clearly in Kyburg and

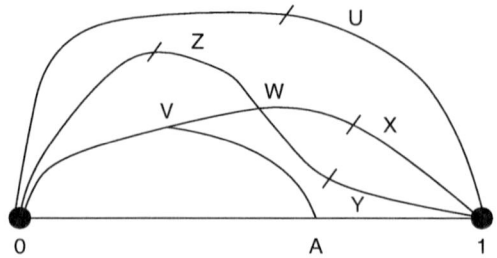

Figure 2.1   Probability structures (from Keynes, *TP*, p. 42)

Teng (2001). The set of sub intervals of (0, 1) does form a lattice under the natural ordering (*p, q*) (*r, s*) if and only if every point in (*p, q*) is less than any point in (*r, s*). The meet of (*p, q*) and (*r, s*) is just the degenerate interval (*min{r, p},min{r, p}*), and similarly for the join. On this interpretation of the *values* of probability we have no difficulty in accommodating Keynes's graph. Furthermore, to the extent that probabilities are based on our knowledge of frequencies—and surely some probabilities are so based—it is natural to suppose that they are often interval valued, since our knowledge of frequencies is inevitably approximate.

In any event, it is clear that we can find a set of objects that has the structure that Keynes assigned to probabilities, and that this structure is consistent and coherent. What is curious is that the mathematician–philosopher, Frank Ramsey, paid no attention to this structure in his review of the *Treatise* (Ramsey, 1922), though he did attack the claims that some probabilities were incomparable and that some were non-numerical.

One writer who did take Keynes's view of seriously was B. O. Koopman (1940a; 1940b; 1941). Koopman showed that if we focus on subsets of probabilities that can be approximated by a numerical net, as can the probabilities generated by well-tuned gambling apparatus, then the standard numerical calculus of probability can be obtained as a limiting approximation.

2.2   Ramsey's criticism

Ramsey's main critique of Keynes's view of probability as set forth in the *Treatise* as it was finally published, as well as the development of his own views, appears in *The Foundations of Mathematics* as the long chapter on "Truth and Probability." Here Ramsey does take note of the fact that

Keynes holds that probabilities are not always expressible by numbers, but "only that there is a one–one correspondence between probability relations and the degrees of belief which they justify" (Ramsey, 1931, pp. 160–1). This renders the manifold of probabilities *similar* (in the technical sense) to the manifold of degrees of belief. This, remarks Ramsey, should have "provided quite as worthy material for his skepticism as did the numerical measurement of probability relations" (Ramsey, 1931, p. 161). This is an odd thing to say, since it is apparently Keynes's intuitions about rational belief that lead him to this view about probability, rather than vice versa. In any event, since the structure of this manifold of probabilities is very different from the structure of the reals between 0 and 1, to which Ramsey wished to reduce all degrees of belief and all probabilities, it is a pity that Ramsey did not provide more motivation for his drastic reduction of Keynes's rich manifold of probabilities to the simple (alleged) structure of degrees of belief.

2.2.1 A logical relation?

A "more fundamental criticism," to which we shall return later, is that "there really do not seem to be any such things as the probability relations he describes" (Ramsey, 1931, p. 161). In support of this Ramsey cites the alleged fact that others are "able to come to so very little agreement as to which of [these probabilities] relates any two given propositions" (Ramsey, 1931, p. 161). Of course, *if* Keynes is right about the structure of probabilities there is another and more natural obstacle to agreement, namely the lack of a vocabulary for naming these relations.

It must be admitted, as Ramsey (1931, p. 163) observes, that Keynes did waffle on the objectivity of the probability relation. Ramsey cites a passage in which Keynes make probability relative to the principles of *human* reason. This is a problem for any normative approach to human activities: our reach must exceed our grasp, or there is no function for the normative theory to perform; but it must not exceed our grasp by too much, or we will be unable to approach the ideal.

At this point Ramsey abandons his criticism of Keynes, and begins to construct his own theory. This theory has had profound and far-reaching effects not only in discussions of probability but in statistics and in the philosophy of science, as well as in other areas of philosophy and in economics.

2.2.2 Dutch Book

The cornerstone of Ramsey's theory is the Dutch Book Argument. This is an argument to the effect that, if an agent has degrees of belief that do not conform to the axioms of the probability calculus, he can have a book made against him, that is, be subjected to a set of bets that entail a certain loss to him. Although not all "Bayesians" accept this argument (Howson and Urbach,1993, do not, for example), many do, and it provides the strongest motivation for many philosophers to become subjectivists.

But let us begin at the beginning.

> The subject of our inquiry is the logic of partial belief, and I do not think we can carry it far unless we have at least an approximate notion of what partial belief is, and how, if at all, it can be measured. . . . It is not enough to measure probability; in order to apportion correctly our belief to the probability we must also be able to measure our belief.
>
> (Ramsey, 1931, p. 166)

Note that here, at the beginning of this section, Ramsey has already committed himself, without visible argument, to the falsity of Keynes's view that "degrees" of belief are no more than partially ordered. Ramsey has now given himself the problem of "measuring" degrees of belief. He sets about solving it in a strictly behavioristic way: my degree of belief in a proposition can be measured by its causal efficacy in making decisions. "[T]his way of measuring beliefs . . . allows validity to betting as a means of measuring beliefs" (Ramsey, 1931, p. 176).

This may provide an "approximate" notion of partial belief, but there is nothing approximate about the corresponding notion of degree. There is exactly one real number, on Ramsey's construction, that corresponds to the odds at which the agent would be willing to accept a bet either on or against a given proposition.

This begs the question against Keynes's claim that the manifold of probabilities is richer than the set of real numbers between 0 and 1. If we leave that issue to one side, there are two objections to the claim that the person whose degrees of belief are not "coherent" (that is, do not satisfy the axioms of probability) will be in a position to have a sure-loss book made against him. First of all, whatever the agent's degrees of belief may be, it requires only prowess in deduction for him to decline to commit himself to a sure loss. I may believe in heads to the degree 2/3 and in tails to the degree 2/3; on Ramsey's behavioristic view this means that I am willing to offer 2:1 odds on tails, and also willing to offer 2:1 odds on heads. But unless I am very confused about the nature of coins, or deductively incompetent, I will decline to make both bets simultaneously.

Second, a more natural, but still behavioristic, way of evaluating degrees of belief is to take the *least odds* at which the agent would accept a bet against a given proposition to be an indication of his degree of belief in it. Thus, that I would accept a bet against heads if offered odds of 2:1 shows that my degree of belief in heads is at least 1/3. If the least odds at which I would accept a bet against tails were also 2:1, then my belief in heads could be characterized by the interval (1/3, 2/3). This idea has been exploited by C. A. B. Smith to develop an interval valued approach to Bayesian probability (Smith, 1961; 1965). Note again that these *intervals* fit precisely the structure that Keynes gives to the manifold of probabilities.

So far, then, Ramsey is not apparently at loggerheads with Keynes; there is a dispute about the structure of the probability manifold; and there is the undisputed fact that if we are to *assess* the rationality of a given "degree" of belief in the manifold, for a given agent, we must have some way of getting into the agent's mind, either by offering alternatives or by a "psychogalvanometer" (Ramsey, 1931, p. 161). In fact, one might think that Ramsey was simply seeking a more thorough foundation for the laws of probability, "which we have proved to be necessarily true of any consistent set of degrees or belief" (Ramsey, 1931, p. 182). This certainly sounds like logic, although the gloss, "If anyone's mental condition violated these laws, . . . [h]e could have a book made against him by a cunning better and would then stand to lose in any event" (Ramsey, 1931, p. 182), is purely pragmatic in tone.

2.2.3 Black and white balls

That there is an out-and-out head-to-head conflict between Keynes and Ramsey—perhaps not fully appreciated by either—becomes clear in the fourth part of Ramsey's essay. He repeats there his claim that he cannot "see what these inconclusive logical relations can be or how they can justify partial beliefs" (Ramsey, 1931, p. 185). Now it is all very well for Ramsey modestly to admit that he sees no logical relation of probability such as the one that Keynes seeks to draw our attention to, but it is clear that Ramsey wants to go further than that. Ramsey wants to claim that there *is* no such relation.

The connection between partial belief and choice behavior, according to Ramsey, is provided by mathematical expectation and the Dutch Book Argument. That we do not find the argument entirely valid does not keep it from being suggestive, and of course there is a connection between mathematical expectation and behavior. Ramsey regards the two interpretations (partial belief and frequency) as "the objective and subjective aspects of the same inner meaning" (Ramsey, 1931, p. 188). Whatever this may mean, it is alleged to relieve us of the need for a principle of indifference—a principle not loved by Keynes, and whose mechanical imposition he inveighs against. It is worth noting, however, that, as Koopman showed, we do not need the full power of the Principle of Indifference to support the mathematics of the probability calculus in those cases in which there is an appropriate approximation.

What is much more to the point is Ramsey's frank avowal of subjectivism: he writes, "we do not regard it as belonging to formal logic to say what should be a man's expectation of drawing a white or a black ball from an urn; his original expectations may within the limits of consistency be any he likes" (Ramsey, 1931, p. 189).

It is true that Ramsey was thinking of the Principle of Indifference here, and emphasizing in his own mind the word "original." It might be thought that Ramsey is saying merely that logic can provide no a priori probability of drawing a white ball. But this is not what he says: what he says is that logic can be of no help, even, one supposes, in the face of a long sequence of draws of black balls. Ramsey does not use the words "prior" or "a priori." It is only *given* his "initial expectations" that he is bound to have certain others. "This is in line with ordinary formal logic, which does not criticize premises but merely declares that certain conclusions are the only ones consistent with them" (Ramsey, 1931, p. 189).

But though this view of uncertain inference is echoed today, for example, by Halpern (Fagin and Halpern, 1988) and Morgan (1998; 2000), it presupposes exactly that complete ordering of the probability manifold that Keynes (and Smith, and many others) was at pains to deny. Perhaps a man's *rational* expectation of drawing a black or a white ball is wholly indeterminate: the whole interval $(0,1)$ or more generally, on Keynes's view, a member of the manifold that is comparable only to 0 and 1. To be sure, this does not solve the problem of induction (but Keynes was very skeptical of any mechanical solution to that problem) for if the initial probability is wholly indeterminate any application of Bayes's theorem will leave the conditional probability wholly indeterminate as well. Furthermore, if a man's initial expectation may be any he likes, he is surely free to adopt that initial expectation that leads to whatever expectation conditioned on the evidence he wants. $P\{h\backslash e\} = P(h \land e)/P(h \land e) + P(\geqslant h \land e)$, so by manipulating the two absolute probabilities in the denominator we can make the conditional probability have any value we want. One can no more admit a little subjectivity into these matters than one can be a little bit pregnant.

The issue that divides Ramsey and Keynes most deeply is the issue of objectivity. Keynes believes that there is an objective logic of non-demonstrative inference; Ramsey takes non-demonstrative inference to be arbitrary and subjective. For Keynes, even though he cannot spell out the conditions of partial validity for this sort of inference, there is a logical fact of the matter that we can often perceive, if only dimly. For Ramsey this is 'metaphysical moonshine' (Levi, 1986, p. 27; see also de Finetti, 1964). It may be conjectured that the plausibility of subjectivism was partly a matter of the popularity of Einstein's theory of relativity at the time. "The degree of a belief is in this respect like the time interval between two events; before Einstein it was supposed that all the ordinary ways of measuring a time interval would lead to the same result if properly performed. Einstein showed that this was not the case" (Ramsey, 1931, p. 167).

Whatever the source of Ramsey's relativism with regard to partial belief, it was clearly far-reaching—in fact more far-reaching than perhaps he understood himself. It is sometimes claimed that Keynes was led to revise his views by Ramsey's essay, but that is not clear. Keynes did write in Ramsey's death notice for *The New Statesman and the Nation*:

> Ramsey argues, as against the view which I had put forward, that probability is concerned not with objective relations between propositions but (in some sense) with degrees of belief, and he succeeds in showing that the calculus of probabilities simply amounts to a set of rules for ensuring that the system of degrees of belief which we hold shall be a *consistent* system, thus the calculus of probabilities belongs to formal logic. But the basis of our degrees of belief . . . is part of our human outfit, ... So far I yield to Ramsey—I think he is right. But in attempting to distinguish "rational" degrees of belief from belief in general he was not yet, I think, quite successful.
>
> (Keynes, 1972 [1933], pp. 338–9)

But this is not throwing in the towel. The issue remains: is there an *objective* difference between "rational" belief and belief in general? It seems to me that Keynes clearly still believes that there is.

Some writers—for example, I. J. Good (1950) and Harold Jeffreys (1954–55)—maintain that it was only briefly that Keynes flirted with objectivity in probability, and that he was primarily a subjectivist. Economists tend to be more balanced; for example, O'Donnell (1989) and Skidelsky (1983), though Carabelli (1988, ch. 3) is uncompromising in taking Keynes to have an objective view. Bateman (1987, p. 107) claims that in 1931 Keynes was willing "to accept a *subjective epistemic* theory." Runde, even in an article subtitled "In Defence of *A Treatise on Probability*," writes, "After all, he [Keynes] does accept Ramsey's demonstration that 'the calculus of probabilities simply amounts to a set of rules for ensuring that the system of degrees of belief which we hold shall be a *consistent* system'" (Runde, 1994, p. 115).[2] This whole issue of subjectivity and objectivity is complicated by the ambiguity of the terms and also by the role that intuition played in Keynes's general epistemology. It is to this philosophical issue, though not to Keynes's treatment of it, that we next turn.

2.3   Assessing the philosophical issues

One of the problems, of course, arises whenever we speak, on the one hand, of the normative, and, on the other, of the subjective. Of course *our* knowledge is subjective, in the sense that it belongs to a subject. On most views it is *individuals* who have knowledge. On the other hand, most of us feel that there is a real if fuzzy distinction between rationality and irrationality, and it was to this feeling that Keynes alluded in his remarks on Ramsey's view of probability. The man who has sampled an urn, in the most scientific manner, and drawn a great many black balls and no white balls, would still be entitled, on Ramsey's view, to be quite sure that the next ball he draws will be white.

These two issues may be usefully distinguished. It seems clear, as Carabelli (1988, ch. 3) emphasizes, that in the *Treatise* Keynes was more attuned to the intuitionism and focus on ordinary discourse of G. E. Moore than to the atomism of Russell and the early Wittgenstein. Moore argued, for example, that the good was an unanalyzable simple property, and therefore subject to direct perception. This did not render the perception of the good "subjective" in the pejorative sense of whimsical or arbitrary or "relative." No more did the fact that the *probability relation* was simple and unanalyzable and therefore indefinable render it arbitrary for Keynes.

Now, accounting for such relations and properties, and especially for our knowledge of them, is another matter, and much of what Ramsey said could be construed as casting doubt on the reality of indefinable relations that cannot be perceived. It is this that led Ramsey to the view that it did not belong to formal logic "to say what a man's expectation of drawing a black ball" should be. This is what divides them: Keynes sees an indefinable logical relation where Ramsey sees nothing.

It is perhaps the current atmosphere of relativism that makes it hard to come to a judgement about this issue. After all, if a man cannot "see" that in itself pleasure is better than pain, what arguments can sway him? If the tortoise cannot "see" that *modus ponens* is truth preserving, to what argument form can Achilles' turn?

We cannot even easily say that the burden of proof should be on the believer: it is as easy to fail to see the moons of Jupiter as it is to succeed in seeing the aura of the saintly. Many writers now, in philosophy and in computer science as well as in economics, agree with Ramsey's position that, once a person's degrees of belief satisfy the probability calculus, there is no more than can be asked of him. The role of probability is analogous to the role of logic: logic embodies our demand that a person's qualitative beliefs be logically consistent; probability embodies our demand that the degrees of a person's beliefs be consistent in the broader sense captured by the probability calculus. (This is to leave aside such issues as finite or countable additivity and the like.)

The one chink in the armor is that these "degrees of belief" do not seem to exist. When I introspect, I can no more find those degrees of belief than Ramsey was able to find the indefinable probability relations to which Keynes referred. We *can* solicit bits of behavior that can be characterized by numbers; some degree of measurement appears to be possible. If I offer you better odds than (say) 6:5 on heads on the toss of a coin, you'll probably take the bet. But a real valued function for a field of alternatives is less plausible. Sometimes it has been suggested that the agent could be "forced" to post odds and make book. Alternatively, it has been suggested that the agent should be forced to choose between finely distinguished alternatives. We have already mentioned that Koopman adopted the idea of throwing a grid over the only partly ordered degrees of probability of Keynes in order to make a connection to ordinary probability theory.

But none of this suggests that people's beliefs come in real values. If intuition suggests anything—the very same intuition that made Ramsey doubt the existence of Keynes's indefinable logical relations—it suggests that there are some relations of probability that are extremely indeterminate. What is the probability that the next species to be discovered will be aquatic as opposed to terrestrial? It might be possible for a biologist to come up with a reasonable constrained interval, but for most of us the answer would be "I haven't the faintest idea," or the whole open interval (0, 1).

Keynes indeed found the vagueness of our assessments of evidence the explanation for our interest in money: "our desire to hold money as a store of wealth is a barometer of the degree of distrust of our own calculations and conventions concerning the future. . . . The possession of actual money lulls our disquietude" (quoted in Carabelli, 1988, p. 169).

But Keynes's real interest was economics and social welfare. He took economics to be a matter of intuitive imagination and practical judgement. He did not devote himself to logic itself other than in the brief foray into probability. It is thus not surprising that Keynes's system of epistemology and logic contained certain unclearnesses and ambiguities.

One of these, which typically remains unremarked on by economists writing on Keynes, is the status of our "probable knowledge." Suppose that e is our total body of knowledge, and that h is some proposition that interests us. If h is "the next toss of this coin will land heads," and e is ordinary knowledge, we would suppose that h/e is close to a half (but not precisely a half!). But Keynes also considers cases in which h corresponds, for example, to "the conclusions of *The Origin of the Species*" (*TP*, p. 118). In these cases the proposition that is rendered probable by the evidence is *accepted*. It is accepted *because*, although the evidence does not entail it—it is not *deducible* from the evidence—the evidence does render it highly probable.

There is an important issue here, one focused on by Carnap (1968). When we say we "accept" the conclusions of Darwin's work, what we mean is ambiguous and loose, but what we are accepting may be one of two quite distinct things: that these conclusions, relative to the evidence we have supporting them, are very highly probable; or we may simply be *accepting* these conclusions. Hempel (1962) noted the distinction between accepting a conclusion because the evidence for it was very great and accepting a *probability* conclusion that assigned a probability to a conclusion. In some cases it may not be clear what is intended. Thus "Between 400 and 500 of the next thousand tosses of this fair coin will land heads" is sometimes what we want to conclude, and sometimes we want to conclude rather "The probability is very high that between 400 and 500 of the next thousand tosses of this fair coin will land heads." Surely we want to say that Darwin's basic conclusions are acceptable, not, except in the context of a discussion of scientific method, that they are "probable." Carnap's view, however, was that we are speaking loosely only when we talk of "acceptance" of general theories.

As a matter of speculation, I suspect that both Ramsey and Keynes supposed that in some sense one could "accept" conclusions that were rendered probable enough by the evidence, in some informal sense of "probable." Although I take this to be a serious epistemological question for philosophy, it is surely not a question that bothers practical people. What separated Ramsey and Keynes very sharply was the issue concerning the nature of probability: was it a psychological property related to actual beliefs? Or was it a logical relation between a proposition and the body of evidence bearing on it to which the actual beliefs of any agent having that evidence should conform?

Although some feel that Keynes gave in on this question in the 1931 notice (Keynes, 1972[1933]), the issue does not seem to be settled. First of all, Keynes never mentioned his thesis that probabilities are only partially ordered, and so those probabilities to which Ramsey's arguments apply may constitute a small fraction of probabilities. Second, of the (possibly) small fraction of probabilities to which Keynes acknowledged that Ramsey's arguments did apply, Keynes felt that there were more *rational* constraints than were captured by mere obedience to the probability calculus.

In a sense, this is an unsatisfying conclusion. That Keynes did not roll over and give in doesn't mean that he was right; and that Ramsey did not succeed in persuading Keynes does not mean that Ramsey was wrong. Nor is this an empty issue—it is an issue of great importance not only in philosophy but in artificial intelligence, in statistical inference, in practical deliberation, and in the social sciences.

It is important in philosophy because, if Ramsey is right, the whole logic of rational belief is captured by the probability calculus; otherwise all is permitted. On the other hand, many people think that the evidence renders certain beliefs irrational.

The issue is important in artificial intelligence for the same reason: are there constraints that degrees of belief should satisfy? Or is one coherent distribution as good as another?

The question of objectivity is very important in statistical inference: if there are no objective constraints, it is hard to know how differences of opinion regarding statistical conclusions can be resolved.

My own conviction is that Keynes was right—that probability is best construed as a *logical* relation. I think of my own efforts to characterize probability along these lines as in Keynes's tradition, though my view of "logic" is rather more conventional than Keynes's. In any event, the large issue, which I commend to your reflection, is suggested by Ramsey: Is it the business of logic to constrain (at all, since we should not dismiss the possibility that probabilities are partially ordered) the belief of a man in drawing black ball from an urn (given any amount of evidence)? Put otherwise: are there degrees of belief that are irrational in themselves given the available evidence, or can degrees of belief be irrational only in relation to other degrees of belief? Allow any admixture of logic in answering these questions—for example, that it is irrational for a man who has conducted a thousand random draws from a bag, obtained only white balls, and is willing to offer ten to one that the next draw will produce a black ball—and you are in conflict with the common and vocal subjectivist interpretation of probability.

If Ramsey is right, then the rational agent has (ideally) a precise real-valued degree of belief in any proposition, though that degree of belief need not be determined on any objective grounds. If that is the case, then perhaps we should not suppose that "high probability" warrants acceptance. If general conclusions are accepted at all, it is for reasons of computational convenience, simplicity, and so on. On the other hand, if Keynes is right, and there is an objective (logical) truth of the matter about probability, it is hard to see how that can fail to involve objective general knowledge—that is, how it can fail to be based on some sort of rational acceptance. For example, what can be the objective basis of assigning a probability of *about* a half to heads on the toss of a coin, if not the empirical and corrigible generalization that in general coins land heads about half the time? Of course, this acceptance would be non-monotonic: further evidence could lead us to withdraw our acceptance of that generalization, since further evidence could lower its probability. We could learn that coins of this specific kind land heads more than three quarters of the time.

This issue of non-monotonic inference or inductive inference raises a whole new collection of problems; and it is true that Keynes did not get very far with these problems, although he devoted many pages of the *Treatise* to them. On the other hand, these are problems that most practical people seem to suppose can be solved somehow or other. They are certainly not problems on which we should turn our backs. To examine them closely, however, is a big job, and a job for another occasion.

Notes

1. This chapter is based upon work supported by the National Science Foundation under Grant IIS 0082928.
2. There are other issues that are equally important from the point of view of economics. For example, the role of observed frequencies, the role, if any, of aleatory probability, the question of the stability of observed frequencies, and the like.

References

Bateman, B. W. (1987), 'Keynes's Changing Conception of Probability,' *Economics and Philosophy*, 3 (1), pp. 97–120.

Carabelli, A. (1988), *On Keynes's Method*, London: Macmillan.

Carnap, R. (1968), 'Inductive Logic and Inductive Intuition,' in I. Lakatos (ed.), *The Problem of Inductive Logic*, Amsterdam: North Holland, pp. 258–67.

Carroll, L. (1895), 'What the Tortoise said to Achilles,' *Mind* (new series), 4 (14), pp. 278–80.

de Finetti, B. (1964), 'Foresight: Its Logical Laws: Its Subjective Sources,' in H. E. Kyburg and H. Smokler (eds), *Studies in Subjective Probability*, New York: Wiley, pp. 93–158.

———— (1937), 'La prévision: ses lois logiques, ses sources subjectives,' *Annales de l'Institute Henri Poincaré*, 7, pp. 1–68.

Ellis, R. L. (1844), 'On the Foundations of the Theory of Probabilities,' *Transactions of the Cambridge Philosophical Society*, 8, pp. 1–6. (Also in R. L. Ellis, *The Mathematical and Other Writings of Robert Leslie Ellis*, Cambridge: Deighton, 1863, pp. 1–11).

Fagin, R. and Halpern, J. Y. (1988), 'Reasoning about Knowledge and Probability,' in M. Y. Vardi (ed.), *Second Conference on Theoretical Aspects of Reasoning about Knowledge*, Los Altos, California: Morgan Kaufmann, pp. 277–93.

Good, I. J. (1950), *Probability and the Weighing of Evidence*, London: C. Griffin.

Hempel, C. G. (1962), 'Deductive-Nomological vs Statistical Explanation,' in H. Feigl (ed.), *Minnesota Studies in the Philosophy of Science III*, Minneapolis: University of Minnesota Press, pp. 98–169.

Howson, C. and Urbach, P. (1993), *Scientific Reasoning: The Bayesian Approach*, LaSalle Ill.: Open Court.

Jeffreys, H. (1954–55), 'The Present Position in Probability Theory,' *British Journal for the Philosophy of Science*, 5 (20), pp. 275–89.

Keynes, J. M. 1972 (1933), 'Ramsey as a Philosopher,' in *Essays in Biography*, vol. X of *The Collected Writings of John Maynard Keynes*, London: Macmillan, pp. 336–9. (Originally published in *The New Statesman and Nation*, 3 October 1931.)

———— (1973 [1921]), *A Treatise on Probability*, vol. VIII of *The Collected Writings of John Maynard Keynes*, London: Macmillan.

Koopman, B. O. (1940a), 'The Axioms and Algebra of Intuitive Probability,' *Annals of Mathematics* (second series), 41 (2), pp. 269–92.

———— (1940b), 'The Bases of Probability,' *Bulletin of the American Mathematical Society*, 46 (10), pp. 763–74.

———— (1941), 'Intuitive Probabilities and Sequences,' *Annals of Mathematics* (second series, 42 (1), pp. 169–87.

Kyburg, H. E., Jr. (1961), *Probability and the Logic of Rational Belief*, Middletown: Wesleyan University Press.

———— (2003), 'Are There Degrees of Belief?,' *Journal of Applied Logic*, 1 (3–4), pp. 139–49.

———— and Man Teng, C. (2001), *Uncertain Inference*, New York: Cambridge University Press.

Levi, I. (1986), 'The Paradoxes of Allais and Ellsberg', *Economics and Philosophy*, 2(1, April), pp. 23–53.

Morgan, C. G. (1998), 'Non-monotonic Logic is Impossible,' *Canadian Artificial Intelligence Magazine*, 42, pp. 18–25.

——— (2000), 'The Nature of Nonmonotonic Reasoning', *Minds and Machines*, 10 (3), pp. 321–60.

O'Donnell, R. (1989), *Keynes: Philosophy, Economics and Politics*, London: Macmillan.

Ramsey, F. P. (1922), 'Mr. Keynes on Probability,' *The Cambridge Magazine*, 11 (1), pp. 3–5.

——— (1931), *The Foundations of Mathematics and Other Essay*, New York: Humanities Press.

Runde, J. (1994), 'Keynes after Ramsey: In Defence of *A Treatise on Probability*,' *Studies in the History and Philosophy of Science*, 25, pp. 97–121.

Savage, L. J. (1972), *The Foundations of Statistics* (2nd edn). New York, Dover Publications.

Skidelsky, R. (1983), *John Maynard Keynes. Vol. I: 'Hopes Betrayed 1883–1920'*, London: Macmillan.

Smith, C. A. B. (1961), 'Consistency in Statistical Inference and Decision,' *Journal of the Royal Statistical Society B*, 23, pp. 1–37.

——— (1965), 'Personal Probability and Statistical Analysis,' *Journal of the Royal Statistical Society A*, 128, pp. 469–99.

Venn, J. (1866), *The Logic of Chance*, Macmillan: London.

Whitehead, A. N. and Russell, B. (1910–1913), *Principia Mathematica*, 3 vols, Cambridge: Cambridge University Press.

3
The Weight of Argument

Isaac Levi

3.1 The somewhat novel question

In Chapter 6 of *A Treatise on Probability* (1973 [1921], hereafter *TP*), John Maynard Keynes raised a question he described as "somewhat novel." This concerned the problem he labeled "The weight of arguments."

Keynes claimed that the magnitude of the probability of an argument depends upon "a balance between what may be termed the favourable and the unfavourable evidence" (*TP*, p. 77). In contrast to this, Keynes introduced a notion of weighing the amount of available evidence.

3.2 Peirce on balancing reasons

Charles Peirce had exploited the metaphors of balancing and weighing evidence in 1878 in his "Probability of Induction." Unlike Keynes, however, he did not contrast "balance" and "weight" but used them more or less interchangeably.

Peirce devoted considerable space in that essay to examining the "conceptualist" view of probability, according to which probability "is the degree of belief that ought to attach to a proposition" (Peirce, 1878, p. 291).

According to conceptualists, degree of belief can be measured by a "thermometer" whose reading is proportional to the "weight of evidence" (Peirce, 1878, p. 294). To explain this, Peirce focused on cases where one is assessing evidence for and against a hypothesis H and where each datum is probabilistically independent of every other relative to information prior to data collection. He derived the probability that two items testify in favor of H conditional on both items agreeing in testifying either for or against H. He then defined the "chance of H" as what is now called the "odds for H given E" or ratio of $P(H/E)/P(\sim H/E)$ where E describes the data. He took the conceptualist practice of invoking insufficient reason to be claiming that the prior odds $P(H)/P(\sim H) = 1$ and with that took the "final odds" (that is, the odds for H given E) to be equal to the "likelihood ratio" $P(E/H)/P(E/\sim H)$. He then argued that the logarithm of this ratio is a suitable "thermometer" for measuring degrees of belief. This logarithm is equal to $\log P(E/H) - \log P(E/\sim H)$. E is a reason for H if this value is positive. E is a reason against H if the value is negative. Peirce also added:

> But there is another consideration that must, if admitted, fix us to this choice for our thermometer. It is that our belief ought to be proportional to the weight of evidence, in this sense, that two arguments which are entirely independent, neither weakening nor strengthening each other, ought, when they concur, to produce a belief equal to the sum of the intensities of belief which either would produce separately (Peirce, 1878, p. 294).

In spite of Irving John Good's allegations to the contrary (Good, 1981), Peirce's characterization of the "independence" of two arguments concurring in their support for or against the hypothesis H is perfectly correct. If $E = E_1 \& E_2$ and independence here means that $P(E/H) = P(E_1/H) P(E_2/H)$ and $P(E/\sim H) = P(E_1/\sim H)P(E_2/\sim H)$, the logarithms of the products become sums. The likelihood ratio becomes a sum of two differences $\log P(E_1/H) - \log P(E_1/\sim H)$ and $\log P(E_2/H) - \log P(E_2/\sim H)$. If the two differences concur—that is, show the same sign—Peirce's contention is that the Fechnerian intensities of belief ought to be the sum. The "weight" of the support has increased. If the two differences are of different signs so that one bit of evidence supports H and the other undermines it, a "balancing of reasons" assesses the overall support (Peirce, 1878, p. 294). Peirce does not say so in so many words but we may call the result an assessment of the "net weight" of the reasons or evidence.

Peirce explicitly associated the balancing of reasons with the conceptualist view of probability that he *opposed*. He took the balancing reasons procedure to be a way of presenting the best case for conceptualism. Peirce pointed out that the approach presupposes a dubious use of the principle of insufficient reason to identify "prior" probabilities for use with Bayes's theorem to obtain posterior probabilities and final odds.

Peirce insisted that the best case is not good enough. Peirce's writings are strewn with diverse arguments attacking the conceptualist view.

Some of the attacks are against the principle of insufficient reason. Some of them are attacks on conceptualism even when it dispenses with insufficient reason and takes a more radically subjectivist turn. Peirce wrote:

> But probability, to have any value at all, must express a fact. It is, therefore, a thing to be inferred from evidence.
>
> (Peirce, 1878, p. 295)

There is some evidence to think that neither Peirce nor John Venn (whom Peirce clearly admired) always interpreted judgements of probability to be judgements of fact—that is, relative frequency or physical probability. Peirce was plainly concerned with issues where a decision maker is faced with a momentous decision in the here and now without the prospect of referring the outcome to a long-run series of outcomes. Judgements of probability used in the evaluation of prospects facing the decision maker are not beliefs about relative frequencies or physical probabilities.

According to Peirce, the probability judgements the inquirer is prepared to make in a given context of choice should be *derived* from the information the inquirer has concerning long-run relative frequencies or physical probabilities in situations of the kind the decision maker takes himself or herself to be addressing. Judgements of numerically determinate belief probability are worthless as a warrant for assessing risks (they have no value at all as Peirce puts his point) unless they "express" a fact. As I understand Peirce, the judgements of numerically determinate belief probability are derived in accordance with principles of "probabilistic syllogism," "statistical syllogism," or, as later authors might put it, "direct inference" from information about objective statistical probabilities of outcomes of an experiment of some kind. That an experiment of type S is also of type T is legitimately ignored if the statistical probabilities of outcomes of trials satisfying both S and T are *known* (or fully believed) to be equal to the statistical probabilities of those outcomes on trials of kind S. (The extra information that the trial is of kind T is *known* to be "statistically irrelevant.") If the inquirer knows the extra information to be statistically relevant or *does not* know it to be irrelevant, it may not be ignored even if this means that no determinate belief probability may be assigned to a hypothesis about the outcome of experiment.

Appealing to insufficient reason to assign probabilities is a way of deriving belief probability judgements that fail to "express" a fact.

For Peirce such derivation would be unacceptable. His opposition to conceptualism was opposition not so much to belief probabilities per se but to the appeal to considerations such as insufficient reason to ground the assessment of belief probabilities.

Peirce offered an illustration of his point of view and in that setting mounted an argument against the "proceeding of balancing reasons."

A bean is taken from a large bag of beans and hidden under a thimble. A probability judgement is formed of the color of the bean by observing the colors of beans sampled from the bag at random with replacement. Peirce considered three cases: (i) two beans are sampled with replacement where one is black and one is white; (ii) ten beans are sampled where four, five, or six are white; and (iii) 1000 are sampled and approximately 500 are black.

The conceptualist (known to us as Laplacian or Bayesian) invokes insufficient reason to assign equal prior probability to each of the $n + 1$ hypotheses as to the number r of white beans in the bag of n beans. Bayes's theorem yields a "posterior distribution" over the $n + 1$ hypotheses. One can then obtain an estimate of the average number r of white beans in the bag of n that is equal to the probability on the data that the bean under the thimble is white. Peirce found this derivation acceptable in those situations where the inquirer could derive the prior probability distribution from knowledge of statistical probabilities. To achieve this in every case, the inquirer would have to assume absurdly that worlds are as plentiful as blackberries.

The alternative favored by Peirce is to consider a rule of inference that specifies the estimate to make of the relative frequency of whites in the bag for each possible outcome of sampling. Indeed, if the rule specifies that the estimate of the relative frequency of whites in the bag falls in an interval within k standard deviations from the observed relative frequency of whites in the sample, it can be known prior to finding out the result of sampling what the statistical probability of obtaining a correct estimate will be. So, in making a judgement about the color of the ball under the thimble, we can no longer take the excess of favorable over unfavorable data as a thermometer measuring degree of belief. Indeed, no single number will do.

In short, to express the proper state of our belief, not *one* number but *two* are requisite, the first depending on the inferred probability, the second on the amount of knowledge on which that probability is based (see Peirce, 1878, p. 295).

In a footnote to this passage Peirce made it clear that "amount of knowledge" is tied to the probable error of the estimate of the "inferred probability." Indeed, Peirce suggested that an infinite series of numbers may be needed. We might need the probable error of the probable error, and so on.

Thus, the "amount of knowledge" or what I am calling the "gross weight of evidence," according to Peirce, cannot be accounted for on the conceptualist view but can be on the view that insists that belief probabilities be derivable via direct inference from statistical probability.

3.3   Keynes as a conceptualist

Peirce would have classified Keynes as a conceptualist. For Keynes "the terms *certain* and *probable* describe the various degrees of rational belief about a proposition which different amounts of knowledge authorize us to entertain" (*TP*, p. 3.) To call the degrees of belief "rational" is to indicate that the "degree of belief" is that degree to which it is rational for X to entertain an hypothesis given the information or evidence available to X.

X is supposed to have a body of "direct" knowledge of logical relations between propositions that includes deductive entailments and judgements concerning the probability relations between data and hypothesis as well general principles characterizing the consistency of probability judgements with each other.

If we strip away the dubious elements of Russellian epistemology that surface in the first two chapters of Keynes's *Treatise on Probability*, the principles of probability logic as Keynes conceived it constitute constraints on the rational coherence of belief. Principles of deductive closure and consistency cover judgements of certainty. Principles of probability logic are constraints of rational coherence imposed on judgements of degree of belief.

Thus, Keynes suggests that if X has a set of exclusive and exhaustive hypotheses given X's background information (or certainties, evidence, or knowledge), and if "[t]here [is] no *relevant* evidence relating to one alternative, unless there is *corresponding* evidence relating to the other," one should assign equal probabilities to each alternative (*TP*, p. 60). Keynes suggested that the judgements of relevance and irrelevance of the evidence required to apply the principle should be based on direct judgement. Such judgements seem to be judgements of a relation of probability between evidence and hypotheses of the sort that Keynes compared to the relation of deductive entailment. Frank Plumpton Ramsey (1990a, pp. 57–9) justly worried about whether one could ground such judgments directly. Nonetheless, Keynes's principle of insufficient reason or "Indifference," as Keynes called it, is a constraint on the coherence or consistency of such judgements of relevance and judgements of equality and inequality in probability judgement. As such it could be considered a "logical principle" in a sense akin to that according to which the requirement that judgements of probability obey the calculus of probability was taken by Ramsey to be a logical principle belonging to a "logic of consistency" for probability judgement.

Keynes's second principle requires the probability of ab given h to be less than the probability of a given h unless the probability of b given ah equals 1. Keynes offered a third principle stating that the probability of a given h is comparable with the probability of a given hh_1 as long as h_1 contains no independent parts relevant to a.

The important point to notice here is that Keynes thought of probability logic as imposing constraints on coherent probability judgement that did not always or, indeed, typically require rational agents to adopt a unique probability distribution over some domain given the evidence. Many systems of quantitative probability judgement might satisfy the constraints given the inquirer's "evidence" or body of certainties. Sometimes numerically determinate probability judgements are mandated. For example, when the principle of insufficient reason is applicable, a rational agent is constrained to adopt degrees of belief on his or her evidence that is representable quantitatively. But probability logic cannot constrain quantitative probability judgement uniquely. According to Keynes, as I understand him, the inquirer is then obliged as a rational agent to adopt a state of probability judgement representable by the set of all the probability functions permissible according to the constraints or, alternatively, by the judgements of comparative probability judgement that are implied by all such logically permissible probability judgements. The principles of probability logic need not mandate numerical degrees of belief that a and that ab on the evidence h but only that X is required to be no less certain that a than that ab. According to Keynes, probabilities of hypotheses on given information could even be non-comparable.[1]

Here then is one point of agreement between Peirce and Keynes: belief probability judgements can be and often are indeterminate. If we ask, however, how the indeterminacy arises in rational probability judgement, Peirce would respond by saying that whenever there is not sufficiently precise information about statistical or physical probabilities on which to base a derivation of belief probabilities via direct inference (and the calculus of probabilities), probability judgement should be indeterminate. Keynes, as I understand him, insisted that his principles, in particular Insufficient Reason or Indifference, could often warrant assigning determinate probabilities on evidence even though indeterminacy can prevail when the requisite conditions are not met.

3.4 Keynes on frequentism

In spite of their differences, Keynes agreed with Peirce that the belief probability judgements one can reach by balancing reasons cannot tell the entire story of how evidence is assessed:

> The magnitude of the probability of an argument . . . depends upon a balance between what may be termed the favourable and the unfavourable evidence; a new piece of evidence which leaves the balance unchanged, also leaves the probability of the argument unchanged. But it seems that there may be another respect in which some kind of quantitative comparison between arguments is possible. This comparison turns upon a balance, not between the favourable and the unfavourable evidence, but between the *absolute* amounts of relevant knowledge and of relevant ignorance respectively.
>
> (*TP*, p. 77)

> As the relevant evidence at our disposal increases, the magnitude of the probability of the argument may either decrease or increase, according as the new knowledge strengthens the unfavorable or the favorable evidence; but *something* seems to have increased in either case—we have a more substantial basis upon which to rest our conclusion. I express this by saying that an accession of new evidence increases the weight of an argument. New evidence will sometimes decrease the probability of an argument, but it will always increase its "weight."
>
> (*TP*, p. 77)

Despite the terminological difference between Peirce who used "weight of evidence" in the sense of net weight or balance of argument, and Keynes who, in the passage cited, was using "weight" in the sense of gross weight, Peirce and Keynes were in agreement that balance of argument or probability alone could not characterize all important aspects of evidential appraisal.

That is where the agreement ended. Peirce insisted that numerically determinate belief probability judgements be grounded or supported by knowledge of statistical or physical probability. Such statistical knowledge itself may be imprecise and subject to some kind of random error. It is that random error that Peirce thought could be used to characterize some of the other aspects of evidential appraisal.

In discussing the frequency interpretation of probability, Keynes complained about the narrowness of Venn's approach, which makes no claims about how to ground belief probabilities in statistical probabilities or long-run frequencies.[2]

Keynes did consider a view of the frequency theory different from Venn's, which he attributed tentatively to Karl Pearson (*TP*, p. 109). On this view, as it is according to Peirce's view, knowledge of statistical probability is used to ground judgements of belief probability. Keynes appreciated, as did Peirce, that, according to this version of the frequency view, the problem of choosing a reference class (or kind of trial) becomes critical.

According to both Peirce and the Keynesian reconstruction of the frequency view, the reference class used in direct inference should contain all relevant information about the specific experiment (see Keynes, *TP*, p. 113).

For Peirce, the judgement of relevance is a judgement of statistical relevance—that is, information about statistical or physical probabilities. This is information X must know. It is, in this sense, grounded in fact.

According to Keynes, the judgement of relevance is not a judgement of fact or grounded in fact but is a direct judgement about belief probabilities. Indeed, Keynes claimed that when belief probability can be "measured" by a known "truth-frequency," the same result can be obtained by a proper use of his Principle of Indifference—that is, insufficient reason. I believe that Keynes had in mind here a thesis suggestive of Bruno de Finetti's use of symmetry conditions on probability judgements to relate belief probabilities of single states to frequencies in reference classes to which they belong. De Finetti thought that he could replace allusion to physical or statistical probability in all contexts where it seemed useful to replace judgements of statistical probability by judgements of subjective or belief probability. It appears that Keynes did also.

In many cases, information available to the inquirer may not be known to be either statistically irrelevant or statistically relevant, so that Peirce's approach offers no clear guidance as to how to draw conclusions about the outcomes of some kind of trial of a certain kind even when the chances of outcomes of that kind on such a trial are known. We may be convinced that a cab from the city is involved in an accident and 85 per cent of the city's cabs are yellow and the remainder blue without being able to judge via direct inference that the belief probability that the cab in the accident is yellow is 0.85. We may not know whether 85 per cent of cabs in the city involved in accidents are yellow. That is to say, we may not know what percentage of cabs in the city involved in accidents are yellow and, hence, we may be ignorant of the stochastic relevance or irrelevance of the information that the cab in question was involved in an accident. In that case, Peirce himself insisted in 1867 that credal probability judgement goes indeterminate. Ignoring the "base rate" information given is no fallacy.

Keynes's criticism of Venn's frequency view carries over to Peirce. The applicability of Peirce's theory is severely limited. However, Keynes should not have made this objection since he himself conceded that credal probability can be indeterminate.

Keynes could have insisted that indeterminacy would be intolerably widespread if one insisted on Peirce's demands. One needs to be in a position to make moderately determinate judgements of belief probability without grounding in objective or statistical chance—at least for the purpose of assessing relevance.

This is not the place to elaborate on the controversy. I shall say only that I am inclined to think that Peirce's position is overly demanding. This point is not sufficient to undermine the importance of frequentist, statistical, or physical probability as Keynes seems to suggest. It does mean that we cannot restrict the use of determinate or relatively determinate belief probabilities to those grounded in knowledge of statistical probabilities.

Return now to the question of the weight of argument. In his 1878 paper and even more emphatically in 1883 Peirce proposed an account of how to make estimates from data about frequencies without appeal to Bayes' theorem that are probabilistically reliable. In this way, Peirce was able to avoid the use of prior belief probabilities while using data as "input" into the procedure without using it as evidence or premises of his "inference" and violating his strictures on direct inference. The method is essentially the method of confidence interval estimation of Neyman–Pearson (see Levi, 1980, ch. 17).

Such a method of estimation can be associated with a measure of its accuracy determined by the standard deviation, as we noted Peirce proposed to do. Keynes recognized the possibility of using measures of dispersion of a probability distribution as measures of weight of argument. In many contexts the variance of posterior distribution of a certain parameter decreases with an increase of information on which the posterior is based. But as Keynes illustrated this need not be so (see *TP*, pp. 80–2). Examples of dispersion increasing with more evidence can be constructed.

3.5   Is more information always a good thing?

Keynes seemed tentatively to be drawn to the conclusion that the (gross) weight of an argument and its probability are two different properties of it (*TP*, pp. 82–3). But this led to a serious worry. In making decisions, Keynes thought, "we ought to take into account the weight as well as the probability of different expectations." Although Keynes reiterated this thought later on in his *Treatise*, he did not propose anything more than a sketch of a positive account of his own of weight of argument or how it bore on decision making or inquiry.

To cut through the metaphors of balancing and weighing, what is the problem to be considered? Here is an illustrative urn model example.

An urn contains 100 black or white balls. If we invoke Insufficient Reason in the manner condoned by Keynes, each possible constitution of black balls and white balls carries equal prior probability. The prior probability of a selection of one ball turning up a black is 0.5, and that should be the betting rate in evaluating a bet on black.

Suppose a sample with replacement of 100 balls is taken at random and 50 per cent are observed to be black. Bayes's theorem gives back a posterior probability of 0.5 for obtaining a black on the next draw. Betting on obtaining a black on the next draw with equal odds for and against is once more the favorite recommendation.

Keynes thought that the decision maker evaluates the balance of arguments in the same way in both cases considered and, hence, this leads to a similar evaluation of the gambles in terms of expectation. Nonetheless, like many decision makers he would prefer to make the decision when the information about the outcome of sampling is available. Keynes saw this preference in a more general setting than the one just described.

> For in deciding on a course of action, it seems plausible to suppose that we ought to take account of the weight as well as the probability of different expectations. But it is difficult to think of any clear example of this, and I do not feel sure that the theory of "evidential weight" has much practical significance.
>
> Bernoulli's second maxim, that we must take into account all the information we have, amounts to an injunction that we should be guided by the probability of that argument, among those of which we know the premises, of which the evidential weight is the greatest.

But should not this be re-enforced by a further maxim, according to which we ought to make the weight of our arguments as great as possible by getting all the information we can? It is difficult to see, however, to what point the strengthening of an argument's weight by increasing the evidence ought to be pushed. We may argue that, when our knowledge is slight but capable of increase, the course of action, which will, relative to such knowledge, probably produce the greatest amount of good, will often consist in the acquisition of more knowledge. But there clearly comes a point when it is no longer worth while to spend trouble before acting, in acquisition of further information, and there is no evident principle by which to determine *how far* we ought to carry our maxim of strengthening the weight of our argument. A little reflection will probably convince the reader that this is a very confusing problem.

(Keynes, *TP*, pp. 83–4)

Sometimes choice is peremptory. Sometimes inquirers have the option to delay making a final decision and collecting more information on which to base a decision where exercising this option is costly. And sometimes the option of postponing choice pending the acquisition of additional information is without cost or nearly so. In the latter case, the question then arises: Would delaying choice and obtaining more information always serve the aims of the decision maker better than making a "terminal" choice without further ado? If not, what considerations determine when we should stop inquiring? This is the question about weight of argument that Keynes found confusing.

Suppose that agent X confronting a decision problem faces a choice at some initial time t between (a) choosing among a set of terminal options and (b) postponing that choice to some later time t' and acquiring additional information in the interim. Keynes's vision seems to have been that the new information would be the result of observation or experimentation of some sort. In that case, the option of postponing choice and acquiring new information via observation or experimentation is contemplated in a setting where X does not know what the new information to be acquired will be.

3.6   Keynes and Ramsey (and Savage and Good)

Ramsey explicitly addressed in an unpublished note (see Ramsey, 1990b)[3] Keynes's question understood as a question about the acquisition of new information about data of observation and experiment. Leonard

Jimmie Savage (1954, s. 6.2) and Irving John Good (1967; reprinted in Good, 1983, ch. 17) offered essentially the same account as Ramsey, apparently independently both of each other and of Ramsey.

Ramsey, Savage, and Good all argued that acquiring the new data and then choosing maximizes expected utility provided certain conditions are satisfied. The collection of data should be cost-free. The inquirer X should be convinced that he will update X's initial probability judgements using Bayes's theorem via conditionalization. The outcome of experimentation makes a difference as to which option maximizes expected utility. If the same option maximizes expected utility regardless of the outcome of experimentation and observation, the expected utility of acquiring the new data and then choosing is the same as the expected utility of choosing without the benefit of the data.

Let us see how this argument works in a simple case. Suppose agent X is told that an urn contains 90 black balls and 10 white balls (H_B), or 10 black balls and 90 white balls (H_W), or 50 black and 50 white balls (H_N). X is also told that whether H_B, H_W, or H_N is true depends on the outcome of random process that assigns equal chance of 1/3 to each alternative. As far as X is concerned the probabilities of the three hypotheses are equal. X is offered three options given in Table 3.1.

X should evaluate the three options equally according to expected utility relative to the initial state of information.

Let X now be offered the opportunity to observe the outcome of a random selection of a single ball before making a choice. The probability $P(\text{black}/H_B) = P(\text{white}/H_W) = 0.9$ and $P(\text{white}/H_B) = P(\text{black}/H_W) = 0.1$. $P(\text{black}/H_N) = P(\text{white}/H_N) = 0.5$. Since $P(H_B) = P(H_W) = P(H_N)$ 0.33, by Bayes's theorem $P(H_B/\text{black}) = P(H_W/\text{white}) = 0.6$. $P(H_N/\text{black}) = P(H_N/\text{white}) = 0.33^+$ and $P(H_B/\text{white}) = P(H_W/\text{black}) = 0.07^-$.

Thus, adding the information that the ball drawn is black to X's body of full beliefs and updating via conditionalization and Bayes's theorem lead to a belief probability of 0.6 for H_B. This equals the expected value of A. The expected value of B is 1/15 and for C is 0.1/3. So the result recommends A as the best option. The addition of the information that

Table 3.1 Random process and evaluation of hypotheses

	H_B	H_N	HW
A	1	0	0
B	0	0	1
C	0	1	0

the ball drawn is white determines B as the best option with the same expected value of 0.6. Thus, on the supposition that X will maximize expected utility on obtaining the new information whatever it may be, X evaluates making the observation and choosing the option that then maximizes expected utility as itself carrying an expected utility of 0.6. This is better than the expected utility 0.33^+ of choosing any one of A, B, or C without the benefit of the observation.

Can X improve X's predicament still further by observing another ball selected from the urn at random? (I shall suppose that the first ball is returned to the urn prior to this second selection.) If the first ball selected is black, the second can be black or white. If black, the posterior for H_B will be boosted even higher (0.76). A will be recommended as before with even higher expectation. If white, the posterior for H_B will be reduced to 0.21. The posterior for H_W will increase to 0.21 and the posterior for H_N will be 0.58. Option C is then optimal. The expected value of obtaining the new information will be 0.75. This is higher than 0.6.

It is demonstrable that collecting new data in this way can never be worse than refusing the new data as long as no extra cost is incurred and we ignore the risk of importing error in acquiring the data.

Appealing to expected utility when deciding whether to obtain more data is not quite the same as appealing to expected utility in choosing between terminal options. Keynes seems quite clear that weight of argument is not relative to any specific decision problem. Moreover, as long as a is not entailed by h, the weight of argument for a can always be increased by strengthening h relevantly. (See the condition "$V\ (a/hh_1) = V\ (a/h)$, unless h_1 is irrelevant, in which case $V\ (a/hh_1) = V\ (a/h)$" in Keynes's *Treatise on Probability*) (*TP*, p. 79).

Nonetheless, Ramsey offered an answer to Keynes's problem. When information is cost free, risk free and relevant to the decision under consideration, it pays to obtain it relative to the aims of the problem at hand.

In spite of its distinguished provenance and the indubitable validity of the argument under the assumptions upon which it is made, the Ramsey argument has severely limited applicability.

Keep in mind that the inquirer X is in a context where X is deciding whether to perform an experiment and then reach a decision or to take the decision without experiment or observation. In that setting, the inquirer does not, as yet, know whether the experiment and observation will be made and, if it is, what it will be. X may be in a position to make determinate probability judgements as to what the outcome of experiment will be conditional on running the experiment or not as the case may be. Ramsey (and Savage and Good) all presupposed that the probabilities would be determinate. If they are not, the import of the argument is quite different.

If we set aside the possibility (which Keynes insisted upon) that probabilities are indeterminate, the calculations upon which the Ramsey–Savage–Good argument is based in our example and in general presuppose that errors of observation are ignored.

Errors of observation would be legitimately ignored if the inquirer X were absolutely certain that no such error could arise. However, to suppose that the inquirer rules out the logical possibility that forming the belief that a black (white) is drawn in response to observation when the ball drawn is white (black) is to suppose that X is more confident of the testimony of the senses than X normally should be. It would not be sound practice to assume in advance of making observations that the observations will be 100 per cent reliable.

Perhaps risk of error should be ignored not because importing false belief is not seriously possible but because it is not important. According to a vulgar form of pragmatism to which Peirce did not subscribe, the inquirer X should not attach any particular value to avoiding false belief unless it impacts on the consequences of X's actions relative to the practical goals X is committed to realizing. X might acknowledge the serious or epistemic possibility of errors of observation and continue to ignore them because they have no impact on X's expectations as to what the practical consequences of X's decisions will be.

Vulgar pragmatists insist that practical considerations always override cognitive goals. So unless risk of error is relevant to promoting or undermining the realization of practical goals, vulgar pragmatists could judge themselves justified in ignoring the possibility of error.

But risk of error can be relevant to the realization of practical goals. Thus, in the case where the issue is to make an observation of the color of one ball drawn from the urn in the case where p (H_B) = 0.33, if the probability of error is greater than 46 per cent the expected value of making an observation will be less than one-third and, hence, will be disadvantageous. In those cases where the Ramsey argument leads to the result that acquiring new information via observation is neither advantageous nor disadvantageous, taking risk of error into account can make no difference. But where the expected value of the new information is positive, taking risk of error into account can undermine the Ramsey argument even when practical considerations alone are considered.

Taking cognitive values including risk of error seriously could deter the making of observations in cases where there is neither practical advantage nor disadvantage otherwise. Thus, if X had already observed a large number of draws from the urn and they were overwhelmingly black, making an additional observation would not make any difference to X's decision to choose option A. But a new observation might incur the risk of a false belief that the ball drawn is black when it is white or white when black. If this risk is slightly greater than the value of the information gained, making the observation would become disadvantageous. Thus, the import of the Ramsey argument is further undermined by insisting on the autonomy of cognitive values.

In the previous section, it was argued that pragmatic justifications for specific inductive inferences should prohibit the overriding of cognitive goals by practical ones. This consideration ought to suffice for the recognition of cognitive values as autonomous dimensions of value and the rejection of vulgar pragmatism and the utilitarianism that so often spawns it.

Ramsey also assumed that the agent X is convinced that, upon obtaining the data, X will update by conditionalizing on the data to form new probability judgements. But even if X is making probability judgements coherently, rationality does not mandate that X update probability judgements in this way any more than it mandates changing probabilities by Jeffrey Conditionalization.[4] Rational agents should change probability judgements on acquiring new data via (temporal credal) conditionalization only if they do not revise their confirmational commitments—that is, their commitments as to what probability judgements should be relative to diverse potential states of full belief or evidence (see Levi, 1974; 1980). So even if we restrict discussion to ideally rational agents, X must predict that X will retain X's current confirmational commitment upon acquiring new information and that such confirmational commitment meets a condition of confirmational conditionalization as a requirement of synchronic rationality. Ideally rational X need not do this.

There is another non-trivial presupposition ingredient in the Ramsey argument. X must assume prior to acquiring new information that, after obtaining the new information, X will choose for the best. At the time t_0 when X is contemplating the acquisition of new information, X may be in a position to decide whether or not to do so. But X is not in control of whether X will maximize in the future once the new information is acquired. X can predict only at the initial stage t_0 whether X will do so or not. And uncertainty may infect this prediction as well.

The reservations registered concerning Ramsey's argument ought not to be taken as a dismissal of its insight. Many of the assumptions tacitly made by advocates of the argument are often reasonably adopted.

The most difficult one, in my judgement, concerns the risk of error. When that risk is sufficiently small, its impact is negligible. A good case can be made for the desirability of acquiring new information when the reservations concerning the assumptions of the Ramsey argument can be overlooked.

Nonetheless, the Ramsey argument does not provide an explication of the notion of weight of argument from evidence h to hypothesis a where the argument is the judgement of probability that a given h. Keynes did suggest that perhaps such an assessment of weight would be useful in determining whether the current total evidence is sufficient for terminating investigation and taking whatever practical decision is at issue. But the threshold level might differ depending upon what the practical decision problem is. Keynes was interested in what sort of measure of weight of argument is suitable for the purpose no matter what the threshold might be. The choice of a threshold might depend on the practical goals of the decision problem. Keynes seemed to have been interested in what the threshold is a threshold of. The assessment of weight of argument is in this sense independent of the specific goals of the practical decision problem. It is clear that the Ramsey argument cannot answer the question raised.

3.7   Inductive warrant and weight of argument

Let E be the information about the relative frequency of blacks and whites obtained in a sample with replacement from the urn confronting X in the toy example. What constitutes an inductive warrant for adding H_B to K^+_E? K is the inquirer's initial state of full belief or background knowledge. K^+_E is the state of full belief obtained by adding E to K together with all the logical consequences. Remember that, relative to K^+_E, X is committed to being certain of the logical consequences of K and E while judging it a serious possibility with positive probability that H_B is false. If there is an inductive warrant for expanding K^+_E by adding H_B, it is a warrant for becoming certain that H_B. After one becomes certain that H_B, there is no point in inquiring further as to the truth or falsity of H_B. As far as that issue is concerned, the weight of argument for or against H_B has reached a maximum.

This line of thinking seems to be consonant with Keynes's own, although his remarks at most gesture in this direction. Keynes explicitly claimed that the weight of argument associated with the probability argument a/h is always equal to the weight of argument associated with $\sim a/h$. For an argument is always as near proving or disproving a proposition as it is to disproving or proving its contradictory (*TP*, p. 84).

Thus, according to Keynes the weight of the argument *a/h*—that is, the weight of the argument *in favor of a* afforded by *h*—is equal to the weight of the argument *~a/h*—that is, the weight of the argument *against a* afforded by *h*. This suggests that lurking behind weight of argument are two dual notions of positive warrant or support b(*a/h*) for *a* by *h* and negative warrant or support d(a/h) for *a* by *h*. Clearly, d(~a/h) = b(*a/h*).

The idea is that given the weight of the argument from *h* to *a*, that weight can support or "prove" to some degree that *a* or it can disprove it or it can do neither. When it supports *a*, it disproves ~a.

Given the pair of values d(*a/h*) and d(~a/h) [i.e., b(~a/h) and b(a/h)], the weight of argument for or against *a* given *h* is the maximum value in the pair.

What happens in cases where the weight of the argument in favor of *a* equals the weight of the argument in favor of ~a? Keynes introduced the idea of "nearness" to proving or to disproving and, hence, of positive and negative warrant. But he did not seem to consider explicitly the case where the negative and the positive warrants for proposition *a* relative to *h* are equal except insofar as it can be teased out of applications of Insufficient Reason to probability judgements. If the probability of *a* given *h* equals the probability of ~a/h, the weight of argument in favor of *a* and in favor of ~a relative to *h* ought to be the same (see *TP*, pp. 79–80).

Let *h* and the background knowledge entail that exactly one of *a*, *b*, and *c* is true and that the conditions for applying the Principle of Indifference obtain. Each of the propositions gets probability 1/3. According to Keynes (*TP*, pp. 78–9) the weights of the arguments from *h* to each of the three alternatives are equal. So are the weights of the arguments for each of the negations.

The circumstances just envisaged are precisely of the sort where the argument inferring *a* from *h* is "as near" proving *a* from *h* as the argument inferring ~a from *h* is near to disproving *a* from *h*.

Consequently, we cannot take a measure of proximity of the inference from *h* to *a* as proof of *a* to be the probability 1/3 of *a* (see Keynes, *TP*, p. 80). The proximity of the inference from *h* to ~a would then be 2/3. But the one inference is supposed to be as close to proof as the other is. We could take the proximity of the inference from *h* to *a* to a proof and the proximity of the inference from *h* to ~a to a proof to be ½ or we could take it to be any non-negative value we like including 0.

The important point is that, whatever value we take, the proximity of *a* given *h* to proof and the proximity of ~a given *h* to proof are both at a minimum. An increase in the proximity of *a* given *h* to proof corresponds to a decrease in the proximity of ~*a* given *h* to proof (that is, to an increase in the proximity of ~*a* given *h* to disproof) and vice versa. Keynes's own appeal to the notion of proximity to proof and disproof as characterizing weight of argument hints at this much.

This suggests that 0 is a convenient value to adopt for the minimum. And, of course, Ramsey's argument is most compelling precisely when the data *h* provide minimum proof for *a* and for ~*h*.

Once more, by Keynes's own principles, the weight of argument for *a* ∨ *b* given *h* ought to be equal to the weight of argument for ~*a* ∨ ~*b* given *h*. The proximity to full proof of the former ought to equal proximity to full disproof of the latter and vice versa.

Here it seems plausible to take a step beyond Keynes's explicit discussion. The proximity of *a* ∨ *b* given *h* to full proof ought to be the minimum of the proximity of *a* given *h* to full proof and of *b* given *h* to full proof. Likewise the proximity of ~*a* ∨ ~*b* given *h* to full proof ought to be equal to the minimum of *a* given *h* to full disproof and of *b* given *h* to full disproof. No argument can come closer to proving *a* ∨ *b* from *h* than the argument from *h* to the conjunct that is least close to full proof.

These observations are based on *very* slender threads of textual evidence in Keynes. The reasoning I have sketched is based, nonetheless, on suggestions that are found in Keynes himself when focusing on the evaluation of the weights of different hypotheses given fixed evidence *h*.

This reasoning points to the idea that the *b*-functions or *d*-functions used to define weight of argument given fixed evidence *h* exhibit the properties of George L. S. Shackle's measures for potential surprise or disbelief and the dual notion of degree of belief (see Shackle, 1952; 1961). The formal properties of Shackle-type belief and disbelief parallel those I have sketched for proximity to proof and disproof. One can use the one measure or the other to represent weight of argument.

Space does not permit illustration of this understanding of weight of argument. Nonetheless, I suggest that the notion of weight of argument that Keynes was seeking might be interpreted by reference to the specificity of conclusions warranted with a Shackle degree of confidence relative to K (see Levi, 1967, 1984, 1996 and 2001 for elaboration).

Notes

1. I am proposing here to reconstruct Keynes's view as recommending that rational agents endorse a rule for adopting states of probability judgement relative to diverse potential states of full belief or certainty, the weakest confirmational commitment in the sense of Levi (1980) allowed by probability logic. Ramsey seemed more inclined to assume that the degrees of belief

or subjective probability would or should be always cardinally measurable, whereas Keynes did not. Like many of his frequentist opponents, Keynes thought that, in the absence of logically compelling determinations, degrees of belief or subjective probability ought to be indeterminate. Ramsey refused to countenance this and deployed some unimpressive and question-begging arguments against Keynes (see Ramsey, 1990a, pp. 56–7.) Ramsey's insight that probability logic could not be both a logic of truth and a logic of consistency registers a more profound objection to Keynes's approach. But that does not touch the reconstruction I am offering.

2. Venn (1888, ch. 9) did make some remarks pertinent to the selection of reference classes and direct inference. But Keynes was essentially correct. Venn thought that the reference class used in direct inference is a practical matter. Keynes complained that Venn was too narrow in restricting probability only to statistical probability. In his review of the 1866 edition of Venn's book, Peirce (1867) complained for the same reason that Venn is too much of a conceptualist because belief probabilities derived from information about frequencies according to Venn are based on appeals to reference classes without objective grounding. Peirce complained especially about Chapter 17 of Venn's book on extraordinary stories.

3. Ramsey did not explicitly mention Keynes's discussion of weight of argument; but there seems little doubt that the note was written in response to Keynes's discussion.

4. B. Skyrms (1990) discusses the Ramsey note (Ramsey, 1990b). Skyrms is anxious to suggest that Ramsey is a forerunner of "Jeffrey updating" or "probability kinematics" and cites this note as an intimation of it along with some notes taken on a paper of Donkin's from the 1850s. I myself can detect no such intimation and suspect that Ramsey may not have even entertained the idea.

References

Good, I. J. (1981), 'An Error by Peirce Concerning Weight of Evidence,' *Journal of Statistical Computation and Simulation*, 13, pp. 155–7.

——— (1983), *Good Thinking: The Foundations of Probability and Its Applications*, Minneapolis: Minnesota, University of Minnesota Press.

Keynes, J.M. (1973 [1921]), *A Treatise on Probability*, vol. VIII of *The Collected Writings of John Maynard Keynes*, London: Macmillan.

Levi, I. (1967), *Gambling with Truth*, New York: Knopf, Cambridge, Mass.: MIT Press. Paperback edn 1973.

——— (1974), 'On Indeterminate Probabilities', *Journal of Philosophy*, 71 (July), pp. 391–418.

——— (1980), *The Enterprise of Knowledge*, Cambridge, Mass.: MIT Press. Paperback edn. 1983.

——— (1984), *Decisions and Revisions*, Cambridge: Cambridge University Press.

——— (1996), *For the Sake of the Argument*, Cambridge: Cambridge University Press.

——— (2001), 'Inductive Expansion and Nonmonotonic Reasoning,' in M. A. Williams and H. Rott (eds), *Frontiers in Belief Revision*, Dordrecht: Kluwer, pp. 7–56.

Peirce, C. S. (1867), 'Review of 1866 Edition of *The Logic of Chance* by J. Venn,' in E. C. Moore (ed.), *Writings of Charles S. Peirce*, 2 Bloomington, Ind., Indiana University Press (1984), pp. 98–102.

———— (1878), 'Probability of Induction,' in C. J. W. Kloessel, (ed.), *Writings of Charles S. Peirce*, 3, Bloomington, Ind.: Indiana University Press (1986), pp. 290–305.

———— (1883), 'A Theory of Probable Inference', in C. J. W. Kloessel, (ed.), *Writings of Charles S. Peirce*, 4, Bloomington, Ind.: Indiana University Press (1986), 408–50.

Ramsey, F. P. (1990a), *Philosophical Papers*, Cambridge: Cambridge University Press.

———— (1990b), 'Weight or Value of Knowledge,' *British Journal for the Philosophy of Science* 41, pp. 1–4, with a preamble by N.-E. Sahlin.

Savage, L. J. (1954), *The Foundations of Statistics*, New York: Wiley; 2nd revised edn 1972, New York: Dover.

Shackle, G. L. S. (1952), *Expectation in Economics*, 2nd edn (1st edn 1949), Cambridge: Cambridge University Press.

———— (1961), *Decision, Order and Time*, Cambridge: Cambridge University Press.

Skyrms, B. (1990), *The Dynamics of Rational Deliberation*, Cambridge. Mass.: Harvard University Press.

Venn, J. (1888), *The Logic of Chance*, 4th edition.

4
A Critical Evaluation of Comparative Probability

Vincenzo Fano

4.1 Introduction

In recent times a partially *logical* perspective on probability has come back into fashion.[1] The deepest modern formulation of the concept of probability is certainly that of John Maynard Keynes's *A Treatise on Probability* (Keynes, 1973 [1921], hereafter *TP*). Elsewhere (Fano, 1999) I have shown that Carnap's logical approach (1950), which attempts to avoid Keynes's reference to the concept of intuition, is obliged to move towards a weakening of his logistic perspective, from both a formal and an epistemological point of view, which results in a more complex position, closer to that of the Keynes's *TP* (Carnap, 1968). Here I would like to retrieve a Keynesian perspective on two aspects: first, proceeding from the datum that most probabilistic evaluations are comparative, not quantitative;[2] second, naturalizing the procedures of ascription of initial probabilities, reaching back beyond Keynes to von Kries (1886), as has been recently presented by Heidelberger (2001).[3]

4.2 Probability as the degree of rational belief

We would all agree that Newton's law of gravitation[4] is more confirmed than the stars as an influence on our character and behaviour. In spite of this it is not easy to *quantify* such a difference as a degree of confirmation. Similarly, given the relative frequencies of fatal car and train accidents, it seems rational to believe that one is more likely to die in a car accident than a train accident. Nevertheless, the difference in probability is difficult to establish with exactitude.

Ever since the pioneering work of Keynes (*TP*), scholars have attempted to find a logic of rational beliefs; these are in most cases neither certainly true nor certainly false. Beliefs are to be expressed by means of sentences, so our first problem is to establish what it means to say that a certain sentence has a certain probability of being true. After Kolmogorov, we know that a probability measure on a set E is a function p, which ascribes a real number belonging to $[0,1]$ to every subset e of E, in such a way that $p(E) = 1$, $p(\phi) = 0$ and if a,b belong to E and their intersection is empty, then $p(a \cup b) = p(a) + p(b)$. If E is a set of sentences, then, if e is a logical truth, $p(e) = 1$, if it is a contradiction, $p(e) = 0$, if a and b are incompatible, $p(a \vee b) = p(a) + p(b)$. But, as we saw in the preceding examples, it is quite difficult to assign a quantitative probability to our rational beliefs when they concern the truth of both scientific and common sentences. In the following we will come back to this point.

A second problem is that rational beliefs are always referred to as a set of already available knowledge. This knowledge is of two kinds: 'foreground evidence' and 'background knowledge'. We are usually interested in finding out the probability of a certain belief with respect to the truth of one or more evidences, keeping the background knowledge unmodified. For instance, if we want to know the probability of experiencing an aircraft accident, given the statistics about the accidents of last year, we implicitly assume that the general situation of the flight we are going to take has undergone no essential changes with respect to last year. Thereafter we can define the conditioned probability of a belief h with respect to one or more evidences e in the following way:

$$p(h/e) = \frac{p(h \wedge e)}{p(e)}. \tag{1}$$

It is possible to prove that, if $p(h)$ is a probability measure, then $p(h/e)$ is a probability measure as well.

If we consider probability as a measure of the degree of rational belief, it seems more sensible to maintain that the conditioned probability is epistemologically primary with respect to absolute probability, because our beliefs are always based on one or more pieces of background knowledge that we are making use of for our cognitive evaluation. However, from the logical point of view, if we move from conditioned probability it is easy to define the absolute probability of a sentence as the conditioned probability with respect to a logical truth. We will return to this point as well in the following.

At this point we emphasize that degrees of rational belief are intended as probabilities that the sentence being considered is true, not as situations of objective indeterminacy. The probabilities we are investigating are, as it were, *de dicto*, not *de re*.

A further problem concerning probabilities as degrees of belief is that of updating them on the basis of new evidences. Indeed, it often happens that the set of relevant evidences for a certain hypothesis is modified, that is, that we acquire new evidences. We usually make use of Bayes's theorem, which is easily derivable from Kolmogorov's third axiom and the definition of conditioned probability:

$$p(h/e) = \frac{p(e/h)p(h)}{p(e)}. \tag{2}$$

In this equation *e* is a new evidence and *h* is the hypothesis we are investigating. In this context $p(h)$ is already a conditioned probability with respect to the old evidence.

On the other hand, the application of Bayes's theorem presupposes that the initial probabilities are already known, that is, first of all the probability of *h* given the old evidences must be known. Thus we return to the problem we posed at the beginning, namely, that of establishing a probability given certain evidences.

From the examples we have proposed it seems that it is often possible to establish a comparison between probabilities but not to determine their quantitative value. Indeed, there are few cases where the probability can be evaluated quantitatively: gambles, some very simple empirical situations and little else. In general, as regards the confirmation of scientific hypotheses, it seems unreasonable to ascribe a probability measure to it, whereas it is often possible to establish that a hypothesis is more probable than another. The same holds for evaluations concerning the common world. In the second chapter of his *TP*, Keynes provides a series of arguments favouring the qualitative character of probability evaluations. He observes that, even for brokers, who determine insurance premiums quantitatively on the basis of statistics, it is enough for the premium to *exceed* the probability of the accident occurring multiplied by the amount to be paid by the insurance company (*TP*, p. 23). Therefore, they have to establish only that the probability of the disaster happening is *lower* than a certain value. Furthermore, he continues, although it is true that a favourable evidence increases the probability of a certain hypothesis, it is difficult to determine *by how much* it increases (*TP*, pp. 30–1).

In order to portray the relation between probabilities, Keynes presents an interesting picture (*TP*, p. 42) in which the impossibility (probability = 0) and certitude (probability = 1) are two points on the plane connected by different lines, of which one is straight and represents a probability measure, whereas the others are curves, which sometimes intersect one another. A quantitative probability (straight line) can be ascribed only in a few cases. In general probabilities are only comparative, that is, curved lines. Furthermore, a comparison is possible only between probabilities that lie on the same curved line. Therefore, in general, probabilities are neither measurable nor comparable. They are measurable in only a very few cases and in only slightly more cases are they comparable.

According to Keynes (*TP*, p. 70), it is certainly possible to compare probability only in the following cases:

$$\text{I. } p(a/c) \text{ and } p(a \wedge b/c)$$

$$\text{II. } p(a/b) \text{ and } p(a/b \wedge c).$$

That is: I. when the two probabilities have the same evidence but the hypothesis is enlarged; II. when the two probabilities have the same hypothesis and the evidence is augmented. This limitation seems excessive because, although it is not possible to compare probabilities from completely different realms, it is possible to compare probabilities that cannot be traced back to the aforementioned patterns. For instance, given the relative frequencies of car and aircraft accidents, we can reasonably maintain that we are more likely to die in the former than in the latter. This comparison is of neither the first nor the second kind, nor can it be traced back to them. We will return to this problem as well.

4.3   The epistemological dilemma between quantitative and qualitative probability

We now investigate how the probabilities in cases I. and II. are modified. Many axiomatizations of comparative probability are available,[5] that is, axiomatizations of a probability relation that is a total order (viz., reflexive, antisymmetric, transitive and linear). However, they are not applicable in this context because here linearity is not satisfied, since from an epistemological point of view not all probabilities are comparable. Nevertheless, we assume we have found a set of sentences Z for which all probabilities are comparable. Then we can ask what happens to the probabilities whenever the hypothesis or the evidence augments. The first case is very simple, because a proposition of this kind may always be derived from the axioms of comparative probability.

If, between two probabilities $p(a/b)$ and $p(c/d)$, the hypothesis a of the first is deducible from the hypothesis c of the second, then $p(a/b) \geq p(c/d)$. Therefore in case I it holds that:

$$p(a/c) \geq p(a \wedge b/c). \tag{3}$$

Keynes analyses the second case in the following way. In case II. comparison is possible if c contains only one further piece of information that is relevant for the hypothesis a. According to the following definition, the evidence c is *mono-relevant*[6] for a in the language Z, iff in Z two sentences b and d such that $c \equiv b \wedge d$, $p(a/b) \neq p(a/\neg b)$ and $p(a/d) \neq p(a/\neg d)$ do not exist.

Thus we assume that c is mono-relevant for a. Then if c is favourable to a – that is, $p(a/c) \geq p(a/\neg c)$ – it follows that:

$$p(a/b \wedge c) \geq p(a/b). \tag{4}$$

If c is unfavourable to a – that is, $p(a/\neg c) \geq p(a/c)$ – then:

$$p(a/b) \geq p(a/b \wedge c). \tag{5}$$

Finally, if $p(a/c) = p(a/\neg c)$, then:

$$p(a/b) = p(a/b \wedge c). \tag{6}$$

All this seems very sensible, but it is not deducible from the current axioms of comparative probability. Indeed it is possible to find counter-examples to such rules. Let us consider as a universe of discourse the inhabitants of Great Britain, who are partitioned into two categories: English and Scottish.[7] Let us assume that all English males wear trousers whereas English females wear skirts, and that all Scottish males wear skirts whereas Scottish females wear trousers. Furthermore, males and females are equi-numerous in both populations. Let us suppose also that there are more English than Scots. We indicate:

with $a \to x$ wears a skirt;
with $c \to x$ is female;
with $b \to x$ is Scottish.

Hence the first case is satisfied, that is, if x is female she is more likely to wear a skirt than trousers, since there are more English than Scots.

However, if we add to the evidence 'x is Scottish' that she is female, the probability that she wears a skirt does not increase but becomes 0, contrary to what Keynes hypothesized.[8]

In other words, even if an evidence b is mono-relevant for and favourable to a certain hypothesis a, it is not certain that b increases the probability of a together with other evidences. In fact, axioms of comparative probability do not support principles suitable for determining an updating of probabilities when the evidence is augmented.

As far as we know, it is possible to establish a principle – Bayes's theorem – which allows the updating of probability if the evidence is augmented *only* when there is a probability measure. Therefore we are faced with a painful *dilemma*:

> Though it is epistemologically more reasonable to deal with most probabilities in comparative terms, we have not yet been able to define a qualitative updating of probability. On the contrary, an updating of probability is possible only if the latter is quantitative. Nonetheless, it is reasonable to maintain that only cases that are very simple from the cognitive point of view allow a reasonable application of a probability measure.

It seems that, if this dilemma is not resolved, the value of the concept of probability, intended as an evaluation of degree of rational belief, loses part of its epistemological relevance: According to the subjectivist solution of the dilemma, Suppes (1994), it is sufficient to find the necessary and sufficient condition for a comparative probability to support a probability measure. But in such a way one renounces completely any logical character of the relation between a priory probabilities and background knowledge.

4.4   Sufficient condition of comparability

We now return briefly to the problem of the relation between conditioned probability and absolute probability. We saw that if p is a probability measure then there is complete symmetry between the two concepts, since it is easy to define a conditioned probability measure in terms of an absolute probability measure and vice versa. In contrast, it is possible to define a comparative absolute probability by moving from a comparative conditioned probability, but the converse is impossible. For this reason it has been maintained (Fine, 1973, pp. 30–1) that the former is an epistemologically primary concept with respect to the latter. Here in our opinion there is confusion between the logical and the epistemological levels. The fact that absolute comparative probability is logically simpler does not mean that it is also epistemo-logically simpler. It seems to me that in general absolute probability is none other than an elliptic probability. As far as we know, among the scholars of comparative probability only Koopman (1940) considers conditioned probabilities as primary, in accordance with the general perspective of Keynes (*TP*, ch. 1, s. 3).

We now look again at the problem of comparability. As mentioned above, all standard axiomatizations of comparative probability presuppose comparability between all sentences of the language considered.[9] Moreover most of these approaches concern the problem of compatibility between qualitative axioms and the introduction of additivity.[10] We mentioned above that the comparability criteria proposed by Keynes are too strict since, when relative frequencies with a certain weight are available, a comparison between them can be affirmed. For this reason it is impossible to establish a priori a necessary and sufficient principle of comparability. But if we leave aside relative frequencies, comparability could be defined in the following way:

Sufficient principle of comparability: at least one between $p(a/c) \geq p(b/c)$ and $p(b/c) \geq p(a/c)$; and one between $p(a/b) \geq p(a/c)$ and $p(a/c) \geq p(a/b)$.

That is, given certain evidence c, it is a always possible to compare the probabilities of two different hypotheses a and b; and, given a certain hypothesis a, it is always possible to compare the probabilities ascribed to it by two different evidences b and c. But, if the evidence and/or the hypothesis are not the same, it is not certain that a comparative evaluation of the probabilities can be provided. Note that this is a sufficient principle of comparability – that is, all probabilities of this kind must be comparable – but it does not exclude the possibility that there are other probabilities which are comparable.

Let us call 'homogeneous' two probabilities which have either the same hypothesis or the same evidence; otherwise they are 'inhomogeneous'. Then we can paraphrase the sufficient principle of comparability by saying that homogeneous probabilities are always comparable; but the same does not generally hold for inhomogeneous probabilities. For instance, the probability that Caesar conquered Gaul given the content of *De bello gallico* is greater than the probability that Caesar conquered Gaul given the content of *De bello civili* (provided that *De bello gallico* is unknown); moreover, the probability that Caesar conquered Gaul given the content of *De bello gallico* is greater than the probability that Brutus plotted against Caesar given the content of *De bello gallico* (provided that Suetonius's *Life of Caesar* is unknown).

The proposed principle seems to be too strong, since it imposes the comparability between dishomogeneous probabilities as well. Indeed, it might be that:

$$P(a/c) \geq p(b/c) \text{ and } p(b/c) \geq p(b/d). \tag{7}$$

For the transitivity of the probability relation, it follows that $p(a/c) \geq p(b/d)$. It is clear that the two inhomogeneous probabilities $p(a/c)$ and $p(b/d)$ have a sort of middle term, that is, $p(b/c)$; but it is easy to imagine a long chain of such intermediations, which would imply comparability of the majority of pairs of probabilities.

In the formal systems of comparative probability the following proposition holds:

$$\text{if } p(a/b) > p(a/\neg b) \text{ then } p(a/b) > 0,$$

where with '0' we mean the probability of any contradiction, whereas with '1' we mean the probability of any logical truth.

Indeed, if the hypothesis holds, the thesis follows from $p(a/\neg b) \geq 0$. In other words, if b favours a, then b is relevant for a. The converse does not hold, as shown by the following counter-example. If the probability of arriving at school on time when leaving home at 8 a.m. is greater than 0, it is not always true that the probability of arriving at school on time when leaving home at 8 a.m. is greater than that of arriving on time without leaving at 8 a.m. Indeed it is better to leave at 7.50 a.m.

Neither does it hold that:

$$\text{if } p(a/b) = p(a/\neg b) \text{ then } p(a/b) = 0.$$

In other words, if b is indifferent for a, then it is also irrelevant for a. For instance, we can arrive at a road junction such that the probability of falling down a slope is positive and equal in both routes. Neither, a fortiori, does the converse of this proposition hold.

In sum, six epistemologically different degrees of cognition can be identified:

$p(a/b) = 0$ impossibility (not only logical impossibility),
$p(a/b) < p(a/\neg b)$ unfavourable evidence,
$p(a/b) > 0$ relevant evidence,
$p(a/b) > p(a/\neg b)$ favourable evidence,
$p(a/b) > p(\neg a/b)$ probable hypothesis,
$p(a/b) = 1$ certitude (not only logical truth).

Note that if b is relevant for a this does not mean that it might not be an unfavourable evidence for a. Moreover, if b is an unfavourable evidence for a, the latter might be impossible. Finally, if a is a probable hypothesis with respect to the evidence b, it is not certain that b is favourable to a.

4.5 Comparative indifference principle

Although the aforementioned principle of sufficient comparability is too strong, it is assumed in order to investigate the problem of initial probabilities. Hence there are two kinds of initial comparative judgements: those with the same evidence and those with the same hypothesis. Following Keynes (*TP*, ch. 4, s. 14), let us call the former 'preference judgements' and the latter 'relevance judgements'. When a relevance judgement is an equality, let us call it an 'irrelevance judgement'. And when a preference judgement is an equality, let us call it an 'indifference judgement':

$$p(a/c) = p(b/c). \tag{8}$$

The latter kind of judgement is very important for determining initial probabilities and so we shall investigate it further. Let us assume that c is constituted by the sentences $c_1...c_N$. To establish whether (8) is true or false, it is sufficient to analyse a series of more elementary irrelevance judgements of the form:

$$p(a/c_i) = p(a/\neg c_i)$$
$$p(b/c_i) = p(b/\neg c_i)$$
$$\text{with } 1 \leq i \leq N.$$

However, in general not all sentences of c are irrelevant for the hypotheses a and b. Let us order the sentences of c so that the first M ($M \leq N$) are relevant for a. That is:

$$p(a/c_i) \neq p(a/\neg c_i) \text{ with } 1 \leq i \leq M.$$

Thereafter, let us order c according to the relevance for the hypothesis b. Let us assume that there are also M elements of c relevant for b – not necessarily the same as in the case of a. If these conditions hold then in order for the indifference judgement (8) to hold it is *sufficient* that for each c_i ($1 \leq i \leq M$) relevant for a there is an element c_j ($1 \leq j \leq M$) belonging to c – not necessarily different – which is equally relevant for b. The correspondence between c_i and c_j must be injective.

In other terms, for (8) to be true, it is sufficient that for each c_i such that $p(a/c_i) \neq p(a/\neg c_i)$ there is a c_j (different for each different c_i) such that:

$$p(a/c_i) = p(b/c_j). \tag{9}$$

To sum up, we have taken indifference judgements of type (8) back to more elementary judgements of type (9).

Moreover, hypotheses a and b must be *indivisible*.[11] We say that hypothesis h is indivisible in the language Z when there are not two sentences k and m belonging to Z, such that $h \equiv k \vee m$, and for both there is at least one relevant sentence in Z. That is, if $h \equiv k \vee m$ for each x must be:

$$p(k/x) = p(k/\neg x) \text{ and/or } p(m/x) = p(m/\neg x). \tag{10}$$

Therefore, it is possible to trace the notion of divisibility back to the evaluation of elementary judgements of irrelevance. It should be emphasized that this notion of indivisibility is efficacious only if the language Z is sufficiently rich. Indeed, if we artificially limit the language Z so that there are no sentences k and m such that $h \equiv k \vee m$ and (10) is violated but conceptually this division is possible, then the notion of indivisibility becomes useless.

Hence, it is possible to evaluate indifference judgements of the form (8) if it is possible to evaluate elementary judgements of type (9) and irrelevance judgements of type (10).

Judgements of form (8) are very important because they are the core of the celebrated 'principle of indifference', which in a context of comparative probability assumes the following form:

> *Comparative indifference principle:* if there are reasons not to prefer any indivisible hypothesis a_i of a set $a_1...a_n$, with respect to the available evidence b, then we can reasonably hold that $p(a_1/b) = p(a_2/b) =...= p(a_n/b)$.

If a and b are indivisible, we avoid the well-known paradoxes arising from the unequal division of the possibilities space. In Chapter 4 of his *TP*, Keynes discusses this problem extensively. Of course, the language in which the sentences whose probability concerns us are to be expressed must be large enough to admit indivisible sentences that are actually equi-possible. Indeed, it is easy to introduce limitations in the expressive capacity of the language, so that it is not reasonable for indivisible hypotheses to be equiprobable.

As mentioned above, evaluations of type (8) are based on judgements of types (9) and (10). How are such evaluations possible? Keynes (*TP*, ch. 5, s. 5) presupposes an intrinsic capacity of human understanding to evaluate a priori elementary judgements of forms (9) and (10). In the next paragraph we follow a different track.

Following Strevens (1998), who unconsciously rediscovers some ideas[12] expressed by von Kries (1886), and going against Keynes (*TP*, ch. 7, s. 8), who blames von Kries for 'physical bias', we state that elementary judgements of forms (9) and (10) could find their justification in the *symmetrical* character of the physical system being considered. As maintained by Franklin (2001), the fact that there are reasons for choosing initial probabilities does not mean that these reasons must be of a logical character, as believed by Keynes (*TP*), and above all by Carnap (1950). As shown by Festa (1993), it is possible to determine initial probabilities on the basis of the cognitive context in which we are operating. As mentioned above, and according to Verbraak (1990) and Castell (1998), the indifference judgements that appear in the principle of indifference do not have the following negative form: there are *no* reasons for choosing one hypothesis rather than another.

Instead, they have the following positive form: there are reasons for *not* choosing one hypothesis rather than another.

These reasons are based on the symmetry of the context of investigation. From this perspective, it is possible to talk about a true *naturalization* of the indifference principle. Paraphrasing a perceptive remark of Bartha and Johns (2001, p. 110), we can say that the principle of indifference is to the probability calculus as the red light district to our big cities; they have always been there and they will always be there, but they will never be altogether respectable.

4.6 Conclusion: epistemological advantages of comparative probability

We now show that in the context of comparative probability it is not possible to formulate certain celebrated paradoxes due to re-parametrization, which fatally affect the quantitative indifference principle.

Let $p(l \in \,]0,0.5]/a)$ be the probability that the length l of the segment S is between 0 (excluded) and 0.5 (included) cm given the evidence a. Then we can say that:

$$p(l \in \,]0,0.5]/a) = p(l \in \,]0.5,1]/a). \qquad (11)$$

If we take the square on both sides, it seems reasonable to accept:

$$p(l^2 \in \,]0,0.25]/a) = p(l^2 \in \,]0.25,1]/a), \qquad (12)$$

which is clearly false.

But (11) is not a suitable indifference judgement, because it is not indivisible. Therefore we have to reformulate it in the following way:

$$p(l = x/a) = p(l = y/a),   \tag{11'}$$

where x belongs to the interval $]0,0.5]$ and y to the interval $]0.5,1]$. Now, in order to obtain the paradoxical equation (12), we have to integrate on the possible lengths of the segment S for x and y. That is

$$\int_{x=0}^{x=0.5} p(l = x/a)dx = \int_{y=0.5}^{y=1} p(l = y/a)dy.$$

Then, if we take the square on both sides:

$$\int_{x=0}^{x=0.5} p(l^2 = x^2/a)dx = \int_{y=0.5}^{y=1} p(l^2 = y^2/a)dy,   \tag{12'}$$

where $x^2 \in]0,0.25]$ and $y^2 \in]0.25,1]$. (12') would obviously be false but, since the probability is not additive, it is not possible to integrate it, that is, (12') is not deducible within the formalism of comparative probability.

We now return to the problem of initial probabilities. So far we have seen that in situations of physical symmetry it is possible to evaluate indifference judgements of the form:

$$p(a/c) = p(b/c),$$

provided that a and b are indivisible.

Nevertheless the comparative principle of indifference is not enough to satisfy the aforementioned principle of comparability, according to which all homogeneous relations of probability can be evaluated. We already know that this principle is too strong. Nonetheless, we can enlarge the extension of the comparable probability relations on the basis of the following statement:

comparative principal principle: if the relative frequency of event e given event f is greater than that of event e given event g; and if a,b,c are descriptions of $e,f,$ and g respectively, then the following is reasonable:

$$p(a/b) > p(a/c).$$

Moreover, if the relative frequency of event *e* given event *f* is greater than that of event *g* given event *f*; and if *a,b,c* are descriptions of *e,f,* and *g* respectively, then the following is reasonable:

$$p(a/b) > p(c/b).$$

This principle enables us to evaluate many comparative probabilities from relative frequencies (provided that the frequencies have enough weight), so that many other probability relations – different from indifference judgements based on physical symmetry – become evaluable. Note that the comparative principal principle seems epistemologically more reasonable than the standard one, which assumes an *identity* between the relative frequency and the rational degree of belief.

Again we meet the aforementioned dilemma: an evaluation of initial probabilities – intended as the evaluation of degrees of rational beliefs – by means of the comparative indifference principle and the comparative principal principle is often more reasonable than a quantitative evaluation. However, without a probability measure we are not able to establish a procedure for updating degrees of rational belief.

Notes

An earlier version of this paper was improved by Margherita Benzi's comments.

1. See Franklin, 2001.
2. Runde (1994) favours this perspective.
3. Strevens (1998) moves in the same research direction.
4. At least when the gravitational field is not too intensive; otherwise general relativity is necessary.
5. See Fine, 1973 and Koopman, 1940.
6. This is a formalization of the concept introduced by Keynes (*TP*, ch. 5, s. 2).
7. With apologies to the Welsh!
8. This counter-example was suggested to me by Angelo Vistoli, who read an earlier version of this chapter and made pertinent observations.
9. de Finetti (1931), Koopman (1940), Fine (1973), Fishburn (1986).
10. See also the recent papers by Coletti and Scozzafava (2001) and Hardy (2002). An important exception is Walley and Fine (1979).
11. The notion of the 'indivisible' appears in Keynes (*TP*, ch. 4, s. 21) as well, but there it is defined in an unsatisfactory way.
12. His point of view was recently reformulated by Heidelberger (2001).

References

Bartha, P. and Johns, P. (2001), 'Probability and Symmetry', *Philosophy of Science*, 68, S109–S122.

72   *Comparative Probability*

Carnap, R. (1950), *Logical Foundations of Probability*, Chicago: University of Chicago Press.

——— (1968), 'Inductive Logic and Inductive Intuition', in I. Lakatos (ed.), *The Problem of Inductive Logic*, vol. II, Amsterdam: North Holland, pp. 258–67.

Castell, P. (1998), 'A Consistent Restriction of the Principle of Indifference', *British Journal for Philosophy of Science*, 49, pp. 387–95.

Coletti, G. and Scozzafava, R. (2001), 'Locally Additive Comparative Probabilities', in *2nd International Symposium on Imprecise Probabilities and their Applications*, Ithaca, New York: Shaker, pp. 77–82.

de Finetti, B. (1931), 'Sul significato soggettivo della probabilità', *Fundamenta Mathematicae*, 17, pp. 298–329.

Fano, V. (1999), 'Keynes, Carnap e l'induzione intuitiva', in S. Marzetti Dall'Aste Brandolini and R. Scazzieri (eds), *La probabilità in Keynes: premesse e influenze*, Bologna: CLUEB, pp. 73–90.

Festa, R. (1993), *Optimum Inductive Methods*, Dordrecht: Kluwer.

Fine, T. L. (1973), *Theories of Probability*, New York: Academic Press.

Fishburn, P. C. (1986), 'The Axioms of Subjective Probability', *Statistical Science*, 1, pp. 335–58.

Franklin, J. (2001), 'Resurrecting Logical Probability', *Erkenntnis*, 55, pp. 277–305.

Hardy, M. (2002), 'Scaled Boolean Algebras', www.arXiv:math.PR/0203249v1, last accessed 14 August 2010.

Heidelberger, M. (2001), 'Origins of the Logical Theory of Probability: von Kries, Wittgenstein, Waismann', *International Studies in the Philosophy of Science*, 15, pp. 177–88.

Keynes, J. M. (1973 [1921]), *A Treatise on Probability*, vol. VIII of *The Collected Writings of John Maynard Keynes*, London: Macmillan.

Koopman, B. O. (1940), 'The Bases of Probability', *Bulletin of the American Mathematical Society*, 46, pp. 763–74.

Runde, J. (1994), 'Keynes after Ramsey: In Defense of *A Treatise on Probability*', *Studies in History and Philosophy of Science*, 25, pp. 97–121.

Strevens, M. (1998), 'Inferring Probabilities from Symmetries', *Nous*, 32, pp. 231–46.

Suppes, P. (1994), 'Qualitative Theory of Subjective Probability', in G. Wright and P. Ayton, eds., *Subjective Probability*, Chichester, Wiley, pp. 18–37.

Verbraak, H. L. F. (1990), *The Logic of Objective Bayesianism: A Theory of Dynamic Probability or Against Orthodox Statistics*, Amsterdam: Insist Pub. Co.

von Kries, J. (1886), *Die Principien der Wahrscheinlichkeitsrechnung*, Freiburg I. B.: Mohr.

Walley, P. and Fine, T. L. (1979), 'Varieties of Modal (Classificatory) and Comparative Probability', *Synthèse*, 41, pp. 321–74.

5
A Theory of Similarity and Uncertainty

Roberto Scazzieri

5.1 Two sides of uncertainty

Uncertainty may entail at the same time lack of determinacy and imprecise knowledge. Lack of determinacy is an ontological property of the universe we are considering. Imprecise knowledge is an epistemic property of the agents in that universe. A desirable feature of a theory of uncertainty is that both properties should be taken into account and integrated within a unifying framework. A possible route to identifying such a framework is suggested by Henry Kyburg's conception of objective (ontological) probability (see Kyburg, Chapter 2, this volume) and Isaac Levi's view concerning the relative autonomy of cognitive objectives (see Levi, Chapter 3, this volume). Kyburg maintains that 'many people think that the evidence renders certain beliefs irrational' (s. 2.3). He also maintains that 'the issue is important in artificial intelligence for the same reason: are there constraints that degrees of beliefs should satisfy? Or is one coherent distribution as good as another?' (s. 2.3). Finally, Kyburg calls attention to the issue of objectivity in statistical inference: 'if there are no objective constraints, it is hard to know how differences of opinion regarding statistical conclusions can be resolved' (s. 2.3). From the point of view of cognitive commitment, Kyburg's claim about the effectiveness of objectivity constraints is close to Isaac Levi's view concerning the autonomy of cognitive values. According to Levi, the specific features of ampliative inference are a clear instance of cognitive autonomy. Ampliative inference allows new information to be obtained from available evidence by making use of an inferential procedure, that is, through a 'legitimate' reasoning procedure that may require calculations but does not presuppose any increase in direct evidence. This cognitive procedure is 'ampliative' in the sense that the new

73

state of full belief 'is "stronger" than the initial one, so that an agent in the new state believes more than an agent in the initial one' (Levi, 1991, p. 10). It is possible to further explore the characteristics of ampliative inference by a comparison with observation and experiment. For the latter are open cognitive procedures whereby the inquirers do not know in advance the type of new information that will eventually be available. In particular, they will not know whether the new information will be reliable or not. The case of ampliative inference is different, since this type of inference is closely associated with what Levi calls 'doxastic commitment', that is, with the type of commitment whereby 'X is committed to recognize fully the truth of the deductive consequences of what he fully believes' (Levi, 1991, p. 9). There is a sense in which this procedure is not open ended, in so far as inquirers are pre-committing themselves to accept the results of the inferences they have accepted to make.

Kyburg's interest in objective constraints and Levi's emphasis on rational commitment call attention to the domain of intermingled ontological and epistemic conditions from which uncertainty arises. And both Kyburg and Levi acknowledge the need to address uncertainty by explicitly accepting the constraining function of a certain commitment (respectively of the ontological and the epistemic types). As a matter of fact, both lack of determinacy (an ontological condition) and imprecise knowledge (an epistemic condition) reflect the organization of similarity in the relevant domain. This is because individual events appear to be determinate or not depending on whether those events are identified in a more (or less) circumscribed way. The more circumscribed the description of any given event is, the more likely it is that that event will be fully accounted for within its own reference domain. For example, any specific historical occurrence will be subject to indeterminacy if it is considered as a particular instance of some larger class of events (say, an economic disturbance generated within the domain of economic crises). On the other hand, the same historical happening will be increasingly determinate if it is considered as a 'singleton', that is, as a unique occurrence with distinctive features making if different from other occurrences of the same type (say, an economic disturbance taking place at a definite time under given conditions). In this case, identification of causation presupposes ability to reconstruct relevant *contexts* rather than ability to identify relevant causal laws.[2] In short, the identification of deterministic versus non-deterministic events is not independent of the way in which events are described. The degree of precision of any given description is inversely related to the degree to which we may be able to identify general principles explaining specific occurrences. On the other hand, more precise descriptions make theoretical explanations more difficult but are conducive to less imprecise narratives of what generates specific outcomes. In short, there seems to be a trade-off between ontological precision and epistemic precision. The *more circumscribed* our view of the world is (ontological precision), the less likely we are to explain specific occurrences in terms of general laws; on the other hand, the *less circumscribed* our view of the world is (ontological imprecision), the more likely we are to make use of law-like explanations.[3] As noted by Lotfi A. Zadeh, successful reasoning under uncertainty presupposes a sophisticated interplay of two distinct cognitive capacities: one is the ability to identify 'granular values', that is, intervals in which a certain variable 'is known to lie' (Zadeh, Chapter 6, this volume, s. 6.13); the other is the ability to recognize, for any given object, its corresponding prototype, or 'protoform', that is, an 'abstracted summary' whose 'primary function [...] is to place in evidence the deep semantic structure' of that object (s. 6.14). Any given circumscription presupposes a protoform which in turn is compatible with a greater or smaller interval of possible values depending on its semantic structure. We may conjecture that epistemic precision (the ability to draw conclusions from premises by deliberately following given rules of inference) is more strongly required in the presence of ontological imprecision, as the latter is associated with less clearly marked dividing lines between different objects (or different qualities). At the same time, it is the existence of partial similarities across different objects that makes law-like statements possible. The domain of reasoning under uncertainty coincides with the collection of intermediate situations *between* ontological precision and epistemic precision.[4] Ontological precision makes inferential reasoning increasingly difficult and ultimately impossible, as an increasingly detailed circumscription of objects reduces the scope of similarity and ultimately makes law-like statements impossible. On the other hand, increasing epistemic precision presupposes increasing approximation to Humean regularity and thus also increasing similarity of situations across different contexts.[5] This makes identification of distinct objects increasingly difficult and ultimately impossible.[6] Uncertainty may be defined as the intersection between a state of the universe and a state of knowledge such that *both* circumscription and similarity are not complete. This means that objects (or situations) are not singletons, so that categorization is possible. On the other hand, objects (or situations) are only partially similar to one another within the relevant similarity classes. This means that categories may be identified but their membership is subject to a degree of arbitrariness depending on context, agents' epistemic propensities, and so on. The above definition entails that uncertainty may be associated with some degree of imprecision both in the representation (description) of the relevant state of the universe and in the 'rational' understanding of it. It is a hybrid condition in which both circumscription and similarity are 'held back': objects are not unique and irretrievable but similarities among objects are only partial.[7] This condition allows human projectibility, which would be impossible were objects unique and/or similarities undetectable. At the same time, projectibility is constrained by limited uniformity, which makes surprises possible.

5.2   Variety and types

5.2.1   Imprecise circumscriptions and limited uniformity

The above discussion highlights the fact that any given state of uncertainty has both an ontological dimension and an epistemic dimension. Both dimensions are associated with the cognitive abilities of human beings. Yet they are clearly distinct from one another.[8] As we have seen, the ontological dimension of uncertainty has to do with the individuation of objects and situations within the domain of experience.[9] Most importantly, ontologies allow us to locate ourselves and others within a shared social domain. On the other hand, the epistemic dimension of uncertainty concerns the drawing of conclusions from premises starting with any given state of knowledge. Clearly uncertainty may be associated with imprecise circumscriptions of objects and situations; it may also be associated with limited uniformity and surprise. The argument of the previous section suggests a taxonomy of uncertain states of the universe, depending on the specific combination of ontological imprecision and epistemic imprecision (see Table 5.1).

5.2.2   Polar and intermediate cases

Table 5.1 calls attention to the two-sided nature of uncertainty. In particular, the circumscription–similarity trade-off calls attention to the

Table 5.1   The circumscription–similarity trade-off and the nature of uncertainty

	High similarity	Low similarity
High circumscription		Ontological uncertainty
Low circumscription	Epistemic uncertainty	

two following polar cases: (i) low circumscription and high similarity and (ii) high circumscription and low similarity. In the former case, uncertainty is generated by defective information and imperfect discriminating abilities (epistemic uncertainty). In the latter case, uncertainty is associated with inadequate similarities and clear distinctions between objects or situations. The two polar cases point to the existence of *intermediate cases* in which circumscription is sufficiently low to allow identification of partial similarity but similarity itself is not too high, so that occurrences beyond uniformities (that is, novelties) are possible. Uncertainty in the intermediate situations is inherently two-sided, as it is associated both with a circumscription gap and with a similarity gap. This means that intermediate cases are associated with variable combinations of epistemic uncertainty and ontological uncertainty. The circumscription–similarity trade-off suggests a relationship between the two types of uncertainty. Polar case (i) is such that, due to low circumscription of objects, uncertainty is primarily of the epistemic type: when uniformity is the rule uncertainty stems more from defective cognitive abilities than from the emergence of novelty. Polar case (ii) is such that, due to high circumscription of objects, uncertainty is primarily of the ontological type: when uniformity is virtually excluded, uncertainty stems more from emergence of novelties (new objects or situations) than from defective cognitive skills. We may conjecture that, as we move from polar case (i) to polar case (ii), there will be a decrease of epistemic uncertainty and an increase of ontological uncertainty. This is because, with higher circumscription, there is more scope for the emergence of novelty and less scope for the exploration of uniformities. Let ω denote ontological uncertainty and ε epistemic uncertainty. We assume $\omega \in [\omega_{max}, \omega_{min}]$, and $\varepsilon \in [\varepsilon_{max}, \varepsilon_{min}]$, where ω_{max} is inversely related with ε_{max}, and ω_{min} is inversely related with ε_{min}. It is reasonable to conjecture that there will be a linear inverse relationship between maximum epistemic uncertainty and maximum ontological uncertainty (this follows from the inverse role of similarity in the two cases). Figure 5.1 shows the ω-ε uncertainty line (uncertainty trade off) for two different contexts.

Figure 5.1 deals with the case in which $\omega \in [0, \omega_{max}]$, and $\varepsilon \in [0, \varepsilon_{max}]$ and represents the relation between the *maximum* values of epistemic uncertainty and ontological uncertainty.

The situation is different if we consider *actual* uncertainty as a combination of epistemic and ontological uncertainty. In this case, linearity can no longer be taken for granted and multiple cross-over points between uncertainty curves are possible (see Figure 5.2).

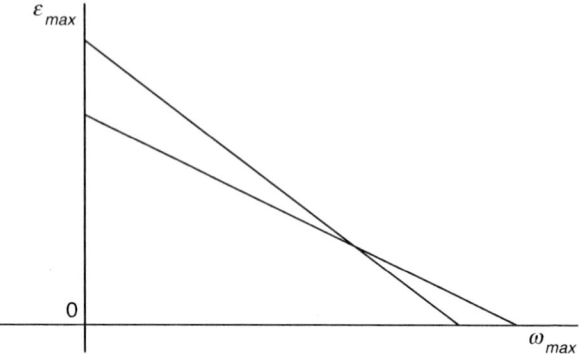

Figure 5.1   Monotonic linear relations between ontological uncertainty (ω) and epistemic uncertainty (ε)

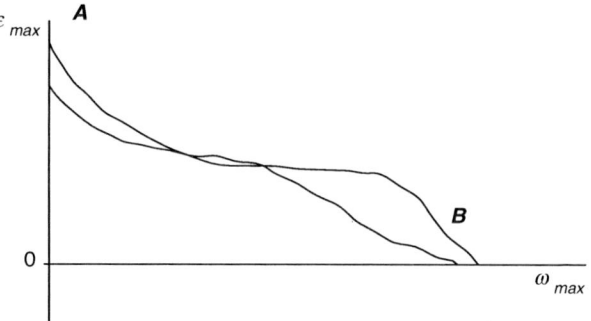

Figure 5.2   Non-linear uncertainty curves and multiple crossover points

Figure 5.2 describes a possible configuration of uncertainty curves ω and ε as we move from 0 towards the corresponding upper bounds ω *max* and ε *max*. The important feature to notice is that the relationship between ε and ω is no longer of the linear type. This is because there is no reason to think that actual epistemic uncertainty and ontological uncertainty, even if constrained within their respective bounds and inversely related to one another, will vary by following a simple rule of proportional change. In most cases an increase of actual epistemic uncertainty will be associated with a more than proportional, or a less than proportional, decrease of actual ontological uncertainty (and vice versa). This entails the possibility of one or more cross-over points between uncertainty curves as one moves across the spectrum of similarity. This could happen for a variety of reasons. For example, a 'fine' description of the universe might give way to a more 'synthetic' description, such that specific events become associated with more comprehensive categories. In this case, the range of *possible* ontological uncertainty will most certainly shrink, as more synthetic descriptions may encompass a greater assortment of individual variations. However, this reduction of ontological uncertainty does not necessarily mean that there will also be a reduction of actual uncertainty. For more synthetic descriptions might be so imprecise that assignment of events to ontological categories might still be in doubt. A similar argument holds for cases in which a 'synthetic' description of the universe gives way to a 'fine' description of the same universe. Here the range of possible ontological uncertainty will most certainly expand, as more analytic descriptions may encompass a smaller assortment of individual variations. However, this increase of ontological uncertainty does not always mean that there will be an increase of actual uncertainty. The reason is that analytic descriptions may be so fine as to be impractical in a variety of situations. (For instance they may presuppose measurement instruments that are not always at hand.) If that is the case, actual uncertainty might *not* increase in spite of what we might expect as a result of the greater precision of individual descriptions. In short, variations in uncertainty ranges should not be confused with variations in actual uncertainty values as far as the human attitude to describing is concerned.

As we have seen, changes in the range of ontological uncertainty are associated with changes in the range of epistemic uncertainty. In particular, more synthetic descriptions allow for greater *possible* epistemic uncertainty even if *actual* uncertainty is not necessarily increased. This is because synthetic descriptions are often too imprecise to be of immediate relevance. (It may be difficult to assess information when categories are at the same time too general and too vague.) In this case, the nature of events may still be to a large extent uncertain, and epistemic considerations may play a relatively minor role in the organization of knowledge.

We are now in a position to discuss the relationship *between* the uncertainty curves of Figure 5.2. Any such curve describes realized combinations of epistemic uncertainty and ontological uncertainty, and both describe non-linear variations that are not necessarily of the monotonic type. When comparing different uncertainty curves (our ω-ε curves), we compare different ways of combining epistemic uncertainty and ontological uncertainty under alternative scenarios. Both curves A and B call attention to the fact that the two types of uncertainty must each fall within a circumscribed range, and that the 'weight' of each component (epistemic and ontological) shows ups and downs as one moves along the two curves. In practice, each curve highlights a different trade-off between the weights of epistemic uncertainty and ontological uncertainty respectively. The specific character of each curve involves the possibility of one of more intersections at which the weighting criterion for the two types of uncertainty is the same. However, what follows from weighting changes along the two curves besides the intersection points is subject to great variety. This highlights the importance of context in the assessment of uncertainty. Indeed we may consider each context to be associated with a particular way of combining ontological uncertainty with epistemic uncertainty, and to vary their relative weights as one moves from one structure of similarity to another in the domain of events.

5.3   Patterns of similarity

5.3.1   Ontological criteria and epistemic criteria

The above argument suggests that similarity is central to the discussion of uncertainty, and that it is grounded in the interplay of structural and epistemic conditions. Any given context, say CT, may be defined, for the purpose of the present analysis, as a coupling (Ω, E), such that Ω is the set of events that can be identified under any given rule of circumscription (or *circumscription set*) and E is the set of the ampliative states that are feasible under any given rule of inference (or *epistemic set*). In general, similarity is specific to any given pair (Ω, E). This means that similarity patterns identified in context $CT = (\Omega, E)$ would normally be different from similarity patterns in contexts (Ω', E), (Ω, E'), and (Ω', E'). In other words, similarity would normally reflect both a rule of circumscription and a rule of ampliative inference, and its character would change depending on which combination of rules we are considering. A particular way of *circumscribing* events (that is, a particular ontology) cannot generate a deliberate pattern of similarity unless it is associated with a particular way of *bringing together* events (that is, a particular set of epistemic criteria).[10] As we have seen, moving from higher to lower circumscription involves the introduction of synthetic descriptions and the possibility of identifying features of similarity that would not otherwise be detected. In short, moving from a world of singletons to a world of categories is a necessary condition for similarity patterns to be identified. However, not all similarity patterns compatible with a given circumscription are in fact 'active' under that circumscription. Actual similarity between objects or situations presupposes epistemic states capable of turning a potential category into an active principle of apprehension. This epistemic criterion allows the very first step of induction, that is, the step by which a collection of attributes are brought together under a common description. However, this latter stage presupposes a definite circumscription of events. In general, it would be hopeless to strive for identification of similarities when events themselves are so described as to make similarities impossible to detect. There is thus a kind of mutual negative implication at work here: circumscription is unproductive if we lack adequate categories, but categorization is infeasible in the absence of adequate circumscription.

Different (Ω, E) pairs are generally associated with different patterns of similarity (see above). An insight into those principles is provided by consideration of which similarity patterns are relevant under given circumscription and epistemic sets. The previous discussion suggests that high circumscription is associated with weak similarities: the more precise and focused our view of the world is, the less likely we are to detect similarities across a wide range of events. Indeed, those similarities that may be detected may be arbitrary as they rely upon relatively 'minor' features quite distant from the central distinctive attributes that are being compared for different objects. For example, medieval and early modern scientists used to assign principal identity to singletons (such as particular species or even individuals within any given species), so that identification of similarities would often derive from secondary features (such as colour, preferred habitat, or even most frequent conceptual associations in creative writings). The situation is different if we consider the case of low circumscription. Here, strong similarities are more likely: a view of the world less centred upon the individual features of objects may allow for identification of similarities closer to the 'internal structure' of a whole *collection* of objects, quite independently of what distinguishes one object from another within any given collection. For example, modern biology is more interested in the determination of identical structures across different individuals or species than in the description of what makes any given individual different from all others. In short, patterns of similarity may be strikingly different depending upon which circumscription we choose to follow. There may, however, be a tension between the similarity patterns allowed under a given circumscription of objects and the similarity patterns allowed by existing epistemic conditions. A circumscription compatible

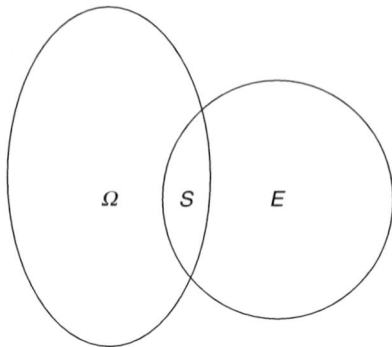

Figure 5.3 Circumscription, epistemic states and similarity

with the 'structural decomposition' of objects and their rearrangement into abstract categories may in fact not be feasible because of epistemic states in which those abstract categories are not allowed.

Figure 5.3 describes the relationship between circumscribed states and epistemic states, and its relevance to the identification of similarity.

Figure 5.3 shows the relationship between the ontology of objects (as shown by the Ω set, which contains all objects conceivable under a given rule of circumscription) and the set of feasible epistemic states, as shown by the E set. Any given Ω set contains all objects conceivable under a given circumscription; any given E set contains all categories available under a given epistemic rule. The intersection S includes the objects (events) for which a similarity relation can be introduced and which are compatible with existing circumscription and epistemic rules.

5.3.2 Similarity relations and measures of distance

More formally, provided that set S is non-empty ($S \neq \varnothing$), a *similarity relation* can be defined as a relation from set S onto itself:

$$R_s\ (s \rightarrow s)$$

such that   (1)
for every object $o_i, o_j \in S$, we have $o_i R_s O_j$.

The above definition does not yet provide a complete picture of the internal structure of the similarity relation. This can be obtained as follows.[11] Let o_i and o_j be vectors belonging to circumscription set Ω. In general, similarity between any two objects presupposes that a minimum number σ^* of features is common between the objects under consideration.[12] This condition may be expressed by assuming that for every pair $o_i, o_j \in R_s$, we have a number of common features σ such that:

$$\sigma \geq \sigma^*. \tag{2}$$

The above definition entails that R_s is a binary relation in set S. However, the way in which the internal structure of R_s is generated makes clear that the domain and range of R_s depends on existing onto-logical (structural) and epistemic conditions. No similarity function and statistics, can be introduced if there are no common elements between sets Ω and E. Indeed, the domain in which similarity functions can be defined is subject to change depending on changes in either the onto-logy or the epistemic rules of the universe under consideration. For example, the switch from a more circumscribed to a less circumscribed ontology (that is, to an ontology less wedded to the principle of individ-uation) may entail a lower threshold σ^*, and thus assignment to binary set R_s of objects that might not have been sufficiently close under the previous similarity threshold. Alternatively, the switch from a less to a more circumscribed ontology (that is, an ontology paying more atten-tion to individuation principles) may entail a higher threshold σ^*, and thus withdrawal from binary set R_s of objects included under the previ-ous threshold. The internal structure of the similarity relation may also change as a result of epistemic variation. For instance, the introduction of a larger set of categories (that is, the expansion of the E set in Figure 5.3) would increase the intersection area with circumscription set Ω, and thus allow the expansion of binary set R_s. Alternatively, contraction in the number of categories available to describe phenomena (that is, contraction of set E) would decrease the intersection area with set Ω, and thus induce contraction of binary set R_s. It is worth noting that both latter processes take place on the assumption of a given ontology (a given Ω set).

The above argument rests on the following assumptions: (i) any given similarity relation is associated with a measure of distance between objects or situations; (ii) distance may change due to a change in the way we identify those objects or situations, and (iii) adequate categories must be available in order to make full use of the opportunities inherent to any given ontology.[13] In general, a reduced circumscription may be associated with a relatively larger R_s set as long as the intersection $\Omega \cap E$ is sufficiently expanded. This means that adequate epistemic enrich-ment is a necessary condition of higher-cardinality R_s sets. Alternatively, enhanced circumscriptions are associated with relatively smaller R_s sets unless the epistemic set E is also sufficiently expanded to *compensate* for the introduction of a richer ontology. In short, epistemic enrichment may induce higher cardinality of the binary R_s set *both* with an expansion and a contraction of the underlying ontology. But the conditions for that enrichment are very different in the two cases: (i) expansion of the Ω set makes ontology more sensitive to individual objects and must be compensated by epistemic expansion (categorization) enabling recognition of increasingly 'fine' similarity structures; (ii) contraction of the Ω set makes ontology less sensitive to individual objects and must be associated with epistemic expansion (categorization) enabling recognition of increasingly 'abstract' similarity structures. To sum up, a change of epistemic conditions may induce a change of similarity relations, but that change would be different depending on the structure and dynamics of the Ω set (see above).

5.4 Uncertainty under similarity structures

5.4.1 Orders of similarity and similarity judgements

John Maynard Keynes argues in *A Treatise on Probability* (1973 [1921], p. 39; hereafter *TP*) that '[w]e say that one argument is more probable than another (i.e. nearer to certainty) in the same kind of way as we can describe one object as more like than another to a standard object of comparison'.[14] In the similarity case, according to Keynes, '[w]hen we say of three objects *A*, *B*, and *C* that *B* is more like *A* than *C*, we mean, not that there is any respect in which *B* is in itself quantitatively greater than *C*, but that, if the three objects are placed in an order of similarity, *B* is nearer to *A* than *C* is' (*TP*, p. 39). In the uncertainty case 'certainty, impossibility, and a probability, which has an intermediate value, for example, constitute an ordered series in which the probability lies *between* certainty and impossibility' (*TP*, p. 37; emphasis in original). The above passages show that, in Keynes's view, the analogy between similarity and probability derives from the serial nature of both types of judgement *and* from the need to adopt in both cases a specific benchmark on which to base judgement (the standard object of comparison in the similarity case, certainty in the probability case). In both cases we place the relevant elements (be they objects or events) along an ordered series identified by a particular precedence relation. Objects are more or less similar depending on the position they hold along the serial order between identity and unlikeness; events are more or less probable depending on the position they hold along the serial order between certainty and impossibility.[15] Keynes's argument suggests a formal analogy between judgements of similarity (in the case of objects) and judgements of likelihood (in the case of events) that is worth further exploration. In practice, according to Keynes, a judgement of likelihood is a special judgement of similarity in which certainty is the standard object of comparison. This point of view has far-reaching implications in view of the argument developed in the previous sections. For a similarity relation as defined above (definition 1) is not immediately conducive to an *order of similarity*. Given a binary relation R_s in set S, we can only say that for every pair of objects (or situations) $o_i, o_j \in S$, we have $o_i R_s o_j$. However, we cannot say 'how similar' o_i and o_j are in each case, nor can we unambiguously identify what the 'standard object of comparison' is as we move from one pair (o_i, o_j) to another. In practice, the definition of similarity as a binary relation is *not sufficient* to ground similarity in the domain of serial comparisons (these are comparisons leading to the arrangement of objects along an ordered series).

The above discussion of the internal structure of similarity (see section 5.3) and Keynes's concept of 'standard object of comparison' provide a clue to what may be done in order to shift from pairwise similarity to similarity of the serial type. This can be seen as follows. First, one should identify the specific similarity domain relevant to the comparison in view. This may not be an easy task. For any two objects (or situations) o_i, o_j may belong to a given similarity relation R_s on the condition that they have a number of common features σ such that: $\sigma \geq \sigma^*$. This means one has to identify a certain number of dimensions relevant to the comparison and a certain threshold (σ^*) below which no similarity can be identified. Indeed, similarity for any given dimension presupposes the possibility of assessing commonality of features across different objects. A practical way to go about that may be to introduce equivalence intervals within which the value taken by any given feature is considered to be the same. For example, if we compare objects (or situations) o_i and o_j along the dimensions of height, length and colour, it may be useful to consider the following equivalence intervals for height, length and colour respectively: $h = [h_l, h_u]$, $w = [w_l, w_u]$, $c = [c_l, c_u]$. Any value for h, w and c falling within the corresponding equivalence interval will be considered the same for the purpose of similarity comparison. We are now in the position to outline a stepwise procedure that allows assignment of objects to similarity relations. First, one has to identify a list of similarity dimensions (the dimensions for which similarity is assessed). Second, one should determine the equivalence intervals for any given, dimension of similarity. Third, it would be necessary to identify for which dimensions the objects under consideration are actually similar. Finally, one would be in the position to assess whether objects o_i and o_j actually meet condition $\sigma \geq \sigma^*$.

The above argument entails consideration of the internal structure of similarity. In particular, it entails the view that any given judgement of overall similarity derives from a composition of *partial* similarity judgements associated with particular dimensions of the objects or situations to be considered. To sum up, objects or situations o_i and o_j may be compared along manifold similarity dimensions (in our example, height, length and colour), and any such dimension gives rise to a particular order of similarity (in our example, the orders of height, length and colour similarity, respectively). It is important to emphasize that, in principle, partial similarity on one dimension (say, weight) is independent of partial similarity on other dimensions (say, length and colour).[16] In other terms, objects or situations o_i and o_j may be close to one another when similarity is assessed in terms of height but not when similarity is assessed in terms of length or colour.[17] As a result, o_i and o_j may be associated with different degrees of similarity depending on which similarity order is considered. On the other hand, the same degree of similarity may be associated with more than one order of similarity (for example, objects o_i and o_j may be 'equally similar' if their height, length and colour fall at exactly the same distance from the two polar situations of perfect likeness and unlikeness). Figure 5.4 shows the relationship between different orders of similarity for any two objects.

Let point 0 be associated with (complete) unlikeness and point 1 with perfect likeness. Any given order of similarity allows the placing of objects

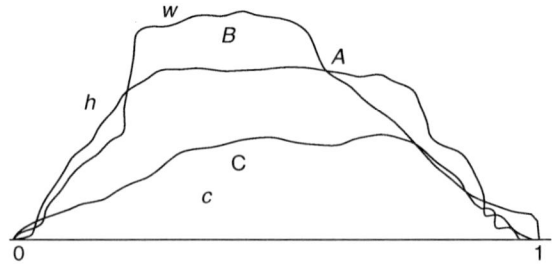

Figure 5.4 Orders of similarity and similarity overlaps

(or situations) on the [0, 1] scale, and the same object (situation) is likely to be located at different points on that scale depending on which particular order of similarity is considered. For example, object o_i would be associated with point A on similarity order h, B on similarity order w, and C on similarity order c relatively to object o_j, which we may take as our standard object of comparison. Only under exceptional circumstances would o_i be located at the same point on different orders of similarity (this would require the special case of qualities such as h, w and c gradually fading into one another, like a colour of different shades). The opposite case would be the one in which a given position on the similarity *scale* [0, 1] were occupied by a certain object by virtue of a perfect alignment of the corresponding qualities. Here, different values for qualities h, w, and c would be associated with the same position on the similarity scale. The most common situation would be the one in which different values for qualities h, w, and c would be associated with *different positions* on the similarity scale. In the latter case, each similarity order provides a different similarity assessment for the same object and (at least in principle) it is impossible to associate the object under consideration with a single position on the [0, 1] scale.

As we let features h, w, and c to vary, we can explore the associated changes in the similarity position of object or situation o_i relatively to the same object of comparison o_j. In this case, similarity of features is matter of degree within the [0, 1] continuum. This means that, for any given feature k (that is, for any given order of similarity), we may take a conventional similarity value, say σ_k^*, and consider σ_k^* as the specific *similarity threshold* for the feature under consideration. In other words, any particular order of similarity is associated with a condition $\sigma_k \geq \sigma_k^*$. Here, overall similarity would depend on whether the number of features for which the latter condition holds is greater than or equal to σ^* (see condition 2, section 5.3.2 above). It is interesting to note that, by the above argument, partial similarity would vary within range [0, 1], while *overall* similarity could be defined as the *number* of relevant similarity features across different similarity domains. This allows the assessment of overall similarity independently of a comparison of features across different orders of similarity.

The above discussion highlights the fact that the internal structure of similarity may have an important influence upon the nature of similarity and ultimately upon whether a similarity relation can be identified. For the distinction between different orders of similarity suggests that, in general, any given object or situation o_i may be 'similar' to another object (the 'standard object of comparison') only if we consider some of its features (that is, some of the associated orders of similarity) but *not* if we consider some other features (that is, some other orders of similarity). In short, consideration of the internal structure of similarity makes partial similarities more likely but, at the same time, makes overall similarity highly conventional and often extremely difficult to achieve.

5.4.2 Similarity, likelihood and uncertainty

The theory of similarity highlights important features of plausible judgement under uncertainty. This is because judgement under uncertainty is essentially judgement about the likelihood that some future event will be 'similar' to some past event (of which it is considered to be a repetition). A first important feature common to similarity and likelihood is the inherent ranking structure of the corresponding judgements. This characteristic was clearly pointed out by John Maynard Keynes, when he wrote:

> [T]he so-called magnitudes or degrees of knowledge or probability, in virtue of, which one is greater and the other less, really arise out of an *order* in which it is possible to place them [...] When, therefore, we say that one probability is greater than another, this precisely means that the degree of our rational belief in the first case lies *between* certainty and the degree of our rational belief in the second case.
>
> (*TP*, p. 37)

Indeed '[p]robability is, so far as measurement is concerned, closely analogous to similarity' (*TP*, p. 30). With both probability and similarity we can say that greater proximity of features increases the likelihood that any given event or object will belong to a certain category (see Keynes, *TP*, p. 30.). However,

> we cannot in these cases *measure* the increase; we can say that the presence of certain peculiar marks in a picture increases the probability that the artist of whom those marks are known to be characteristic painted it, but we cannot say that the presence of these marks makes it two or three or any other number of times more probable than it would have been without them. We can say that one thing is more like a second object that it is like a third; but there will very seldom be any meaning in saying that it is twice as like.
>
> (*TP*, p. 30)

As we have seen, similarity judgements presuppose a fine decomposition of characteristics in order to highlight the different orders of similarity relevant for the case in view, and a more 'synthetic' ability aimed at assessing overall similarity on the strength of the various assessments of partial similarity. In the case of likelihood, its reasonable assessment presupposes a fine decomposition of characteristics so as to highlight the different 'orders of likelihood' relevant for the case in view, that is, the different scenarios relevant to the analysis of whether a certain event is likely to be repeated over time. As with similarity, there is no immediate connection between partial likelihood and overall likelihood. The former is bound to a particular order of likelihood (that is, to a particular set of conditions making a certain event more *or* less likely); the latter presupposes the ability to move beyond likelihood on each specific dimension so as to assess the similarity of future to past events from a more general point of view. In short, evaluation of likelihood is a special similarity judgement made with reference to future outcomes.

5.4.3 Short-term and long-term orders of likelihood

As with standard similarity judgements, with likelihood it is essential to bear in mind the plurality of 'orders' in which a reasonable judgement may be expressed. In short, what is likely under certain conditions (that is, under a given order of likelihood) may turn out to be utterly unlikely if different conditions are considered. For example, we may distinguish between the orders of likelihood associated with different time horizons, and assess the likelihood of any given situation (that is, its greater or smaller closeness to certainty) for different time scales.[18] Figure 5.5 shows the implications of different orders of likelihood for what concerns our ability to assess the overall likelihood of any given situation.

Figure 5.5 shows two different orders of likelihood for the short term (*A*) and the long term (*B*) respectively, and calls attention to the fact that the same situation may be associated with different likelihoods depending on which order is considered. Clearly, likelihood can be the same only under exceptional circumstances, such as those associated with crossover points *A* and *B*. In this case, a crossover point may be interpreted as corresponding to a situation in which two different ontologies coincide at a given point of time. If there are two separate orders of likelihood for the short term and the long term respectively, a crossover point would be a situation at which the circumscription set appropriate for the short term coincides with the circumscription set suitable for long-term analysis: for example, a set of events that can be envisaged only if we take a long-term point of view (say, a slow-moving geological process)

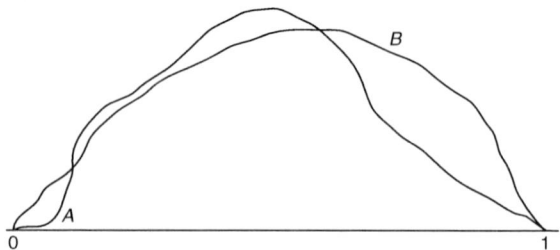

Figure 5.5   Short-term and long-term orders of likelihood

may also be of short-term relevance if it brings about sudden disruption within a narrow time interval.

The previous discussion of similarity orders is relevant for this case too. For we can *directly* compare any two situations if those situations have at least some common value for some of their features or if those situations are associated with the same value on different orders of similarity. In particular, short-term and long-term likelihoods may be directly compared if one or the other of the two following conditions is met: (i) at least one feature is common to the short-term and the long-term orders of likelihood; (ii) a situation has the same similarity value on the short-term and the long-term orders of likelihood. The two above conditions are clearly different. In case (i), different time horizons would give rise to the same set of features; in case (ii), a given situation would take the same likelihood value on different time horizons. The two cases are in fact opposed to one another. For (i) entails that different processes (long-term and short-term) bring about the same situation, whereas (ii) entails that the same situation is equally likely independently of which time horizon is considered. The former statement concerns ontology (that is, the processes by which events are generated from one another); the latter statement concerns the epistemic domain (that is, the criteria by which similarity conditions are assessed across different situations). In general, conditions (i) and (ii) will not be satisfied, and uncertainty cannot be assessed across different orders of likelihood. However, the previous argument suggests a set of practical criteria that may be useful in evaluating more common situations, which are in a sense intermediate with respect to the two polar cases.

Any given situation would have to be assessed differently depending on whether we are considering short-term or long-term orders of likelihood, and we may expect likelihood to be different in the two cases. In Figure 5.6, a specific situation s^* must be separately assessed for short-term likelihood (A) and long-term likelihood (B), respectively. Clearly s^* may be associated with low *or* high likelihood on the long-term likelihood order, and we may conjecture that the likelihood change may be associated with a change in the way s^* is described in the two cases. For example, a change in the similarity features that are being considered is likely to change our perception of the likelihood of future events relatively to some (known) event in the past. The same argument applies to the short-term order of likelihood. Here, the expansion (or contraction) in the number of similarity features may significantly influence the overall likelihood judgement for s^*.

More formally, let s^* be associated with similarity features $(r_1, r_2, ..., r_k)$ on the assumption that all (partial) similarity features $\sigma_r (r = 1, ..., k)$ take values above the corresponding significance thresholds σ_r^* (that is, $\sigma_r \geq \sigma_r^*$). We know that overall similarity σ may be assessed by combining partial similarity features according to the following criterion: $\sigma = k$, where k is the number of partial similarity features for which $\sigma_r \geq \sigma_r^*$. The above argument entails that the likelihood of s^* may increase or decrease depending on changes in the number of significant similarity features. This condition draws us back to the discussion in sections 5.1 and 5.2. For a change of k may be associated with a change of either the circumscription set or the epistemic set. In the former case (that is, in the case of switch to a different ontology), it is likely that less circumscribed descriptions would be associated with an increase in the number of similarity features for which $\sigma_r \geq \sigma_r^*$ (and

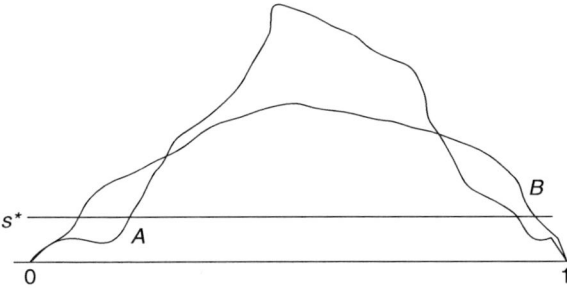

Figure 5.6   Short-term likelihood and long-term likelihood for situation s^*

vice versa if more circumscribed descriptions are considered). In the latter case (that is, in the case of a switch to a different set of categories), it is likely that more comprehensive descriptions would allow identification of partial similarities across a wider range of phenomena than is the case with descriptions of a less comprehensive type (and vice versa). Figure 5.6 highlights the fact that what is apparently the same situation s^* may be associated with different likelihood values, and that this may happen both for any given order of likelihood *and* across different likelihood orders. We may conjecture that likelihood changes for any given order of likelihood may be associated either with ontology change or with epistemic change (or both). On the other hand, changes of likelihood *across* different likelihood orders would be primarily associated with a switch from one particular ontology to another. This latter condition makes cross-order comparisons especially difficult, given that we would have to assess the likelihood of what are in fact two *different* situations, one grounded in the short term and the other in the long term. It is in view of this difficulty that crossover points may be of special interest. For it is precisely at those points that the long-term and the short-term perspectives come to coincide. Crossover points highlight intersections between different ontologies and draw attention to ways in which we can move from one ontology to another. In particular, any given crossover point highlights circumscriptions relevant to both a short-term ontology and a long-term ontology. The fact that only at those points may likelihood be the same on different likelihood orders suggests that, apart from those exceptional cases, uncertainty assessment should be *separately* carried out for different orders of likelihood. However, awareness that crossover points are possible recommends prudence in likelihood assessment. In particular, we may be justified in having more confidence in a statement that is equally likely on different orders of likelihood. For crossover points strengthen the weight of our assessment and make it especially relevant to decision both when a given situation is to be avoided and when it is to be actively promoted.[19]

5.5 Reasoning with uncertainty

5.5.1 Cognitive tension under fundamental uncertainty

The twofold nature of uncertainty (ontological and epistemic) calls attention to the twofold cognitive structure that may be needed in order to cope with its demands. Ontological uncertainty arises from the nature of the world but cannot be expressed except by means of adequate categories. Epistemic uncertainty arises from the cognitive boundaries of human understanding, but is often intermingled with difficulty arising from structural change in the world of objects and situations. Clearly, coping with uncertainty presupposes at the same time representational and inferential abilities, and reasoning with fundamental uncertainty cannot take place unless one is prepared to move back and forth between alternative circumscriptions and alternative ways to single out similarity and likelihood.

The above argument suggests that there is an inherent tension between what may be required for successful handling of ontological uncertainty (that is, how best to circumscribe a changing configuration of objects or situations) and what may be needed for effective handling of epistemic uncertainty (that is, how best to generate the categories needed for that circumscription). A possible way out of this tension is to explicitly acknowledge that fundamental uncertainty is unavoidably associated with the *intermingling* of the ontological and the epistemic components, so that reasoning with fundamental uncertainty would require both the ability to direct attention to changing circumscriptions of objects and situations, and the ability to conceive of the categories that may be needed in order to express precisely those circumscriptions.[20] In particular, reasoning with uncertainty appears to be closely associated with the ability to consider manifold orders of likelihood, so that the likelihood of any given situation would ultimately be assessed after assigning certain 'weights' to the different orders of likelihood relevant for the case in view. For example, the distinction between short-term and long-term likelihood orders suggest a weighting of short-term and long-terms features of similarity (see s. 5.4).

5.5.2 Balancing acts

As we have seen, any given situation (say, s^*) may be associated with different orders of similarity depending on whether we look at its short-term or long-term features. For example, s^* could be similar to other short-term or long-term situations depending on which features we are considering. As the previous argument suggests, different patterns of similarity are normally associated with different orders of likelihood, too. This very possibility points to the need for appropriate 'balancing acts' in the assessment of uncertainty (see above). The open question here is how best to identify alternative sources of uncertainty so as to compare different orders of likelihood and to assess the possibility of crossover points among them. One may tentatively argue that 'hidden similarities' are the most critical ones, and that the recognition of those similarities is made possible by the availability of circumscriptions that are at the same time definite enough to allow effective distinctions among objects or situations and yet permeable enough to allow the discovery of associations among those objects or situations. Clearly, this condition presupposes a specific matching of the ontology and epistemic sets discussed in section 5.3. For structural change within the ontology set (Ω) must be 'within reach' of the available categories included in the epistemic set (E), while a shift to different categories within the epistemic set (E) must be grounded in the existing set of objects and situations (Ω). The above condition may be difficult to achieve, however it is generally possible to identify objective conditions and reasoning criteria by which the intersection $\Omega \cap E$ may be expanded. For example, *structural change* within the Ω set may be identified in terms of change of certain compositional properties (such as hierarchy of constituent processes), which may not all be relevant within the same time horizon. Or, *epistemic change* within the E set may be identified in terms of a change of categories, which may or may not bring about radical innovation depending on the distance between old and new conceptual structures,[21] while at the same time being grounded in the existing cognitive endowments of individuals and societies. For either structural change or epistemic change to be possible, reasoning must allow 'shifts' across different levels of ontology as well as across different levels of cognition. In a way, one must be prepared to drop the existing world of objects and situations so as to glimpse objects and situations that were previously inconceivable. But one must also be prepared to go back to previously conceived (and previously known) objects and situations so as to identify possible bridges between old and new ontologies, or sometimes bridges between old and new ways of looking at things. We may conjecture that this approach would enhance our understanding of the relationship between different orders of likelihood, and would thus allow better identification of critical situations at the juncture of different orders of likelihood, for example of crossover points where short-term and long-term likelihoods happen to coincide.

This framework may be useful in interpreting the distinction between risk and uncertainty. As Frank Knight pointed out in his classical contribution,

Uncertainty must be taken in a sense radically distinct from the familiar notion of Risk, from which it has never been properly separated.

The term 'risk', as loosely used in everyday speech and in economic discussion, really covers two things which, functionally at least, [...] are categorically different [...] The essential fact is that 'risk' means in some cases a quantity susceptible of measurement, while at other times it is something distinctly not of this character.

(Knight, 1940 [1921], pp. 19–20)

We may conjecture that the situations to which the category 'risk' applies must belong to a particular intersection of the circumscription set and of the epistemic set. In other words, assessment of risk pre-supposes both a given ontology and a set of concepts adequate to its understanding. In addition to that, risk assessment presupposes that any given situation belongs to a single order of likelihood, and that such order of likelihood may be grounded in a single order of similarity. A necessary condition of risk measurement is that all relevant situations can be arranged in a single ordered series *and* that such ordered series be associated with a numerical representation of the additive type. In other words, 'arrangement by risk' presupposes a single order of similarity and derives a single order of likelihood from it. The former is provided by the numerical (cardinal) measurement of risk associated with any given situation; the latter is associated with the assumption that the only relevant order of likelihood is the one associated with the above measurement.[22] Knightian uncertainty is related with the collection of all ontological and/or epistemic states for which a single order of similarity and likelihood must be excluded.[23]

5.6 Non-exclusion, uncertainty, and similarity thresholds: concluding remarks

The previous argument calls attention to the ontological and epistemic roots of uncertainty, and emphasizes the plurality of grounds that could make evidence uncertain and induction tentative. In particular, we have seen that the sources of uncertainty are manifold because of the inter-play of circumscription difficulty and epistemic complexity. However, it is precisely this lack of determinacy that allows the handling of uncertainty by means of a *principle of non-exclusion*. This is because the domain of similarity relations coincides with the partial overlap of the ontological and epistemic sets (see above). As a result, we may derive the similarity domain by allowing that ontology separates grounded from ungrounded categories, and that the epistemic endowment separates knowable from unknowable objects and situations. Ontology allows us (at least in principle) to distinguish, within the E set, the categories circumscribing real objects and situations from the categories unfit to that purpose. Similarly, the epistemic endowment allows us (at least in principle) to distinguish, within the Ω set, the objects and situations that may be known from those that lie outside the reach of existing categories. Figure 5.3 suggests a distinction between different types of uncertainty: (i) what belongs to the Ω set but is excluded from its intersection with the E set is clearly unknown and cannot be known in terms of existing categories; (ii) what belongs to the E set but is excluded from its intersection with the Ω set is ungrounded and cannot be grounded in terms of the existing ontology; (iii) what belongs to the intersection of the Ω and E sets may be both known and grounded, and *allows* the introduction of similarity relationships among objects or situations.[24] Of course, degrees of similarity may be different, and the same is true for degrees of likelihood. Indeed, as we have seen, it is generally possible to identify a variety of similarity orders and of likelihood orders. In short, 'pure' ontological uncertainty cannot be handled by means of existing categories, and does not allow the introduction of similarity relationships across objects or situations. On the other hand, 'pure' epistemic uncertainty cannot be associated with existing ontology, and is also incompatible with identifiable similarity relationships. Such relationships are impossible if objects or situations cannot be categorized; they are also impossible if categories do not have a clear association with existing objects and situations. This leaves us with a collection of intermediate states of the world in which objects (and situations) are matched with categories, but multiple orders of similarity are possible (see above). The relationship between similarity and likelihood implies that multiple orders of likelihood are also possible: any given situation may be less or more likely depending on which particular order we are considering. In short, the domain of knowable uncertainty is constrained both on the ontological side and on the epistemic side. Within that domain, uncertainty allows similarity relationships and permits the assessment of likelihood. Multiple orders of likelihood may be associated with different degrees of rational belief as they are not all founded on an equally solid knowledge basis. However, as we have seen, multiple overlaps of likelihood orders may be possible. It is reasonable to conjecture that confidence in the likelihood assessment for any given situation would increase if a variety of different orders of likelihood were to assign the same assessment for that particular situation. For example, situations associated with different orders of likelihood for the short term and the long term may in fact be associated with strongest likelihood confidence in the case of crossover points *A* and *B*, because at those points *both* short-term and long-run considerations are associated with the same assessment of likelihood (see Figure 5.5). In short, uncertainty at its most fundamental level is associated with coexistence of *different* orders of similarity and likelihood. This coexistence makes it very difficult to assess particular situations, as they might look likely or unlikely depending on which features are considered. Clearly this difficulty may arise from the way in which any given situation is circumscribed or from the categories available to make sense of existing circumscriptions. However, different likelihood orders may sometimes intersect one another (see above). This means that the very plurality of uncertainty dimensions that makes it difficult *in general* to assess any given situation may turn out to be an advantage when facing the special circumstances in which the *same* assessment of the situation in view is grounded in a plurality of different orders of likelihood.

Notes

I am grateful to Ivano Cardinale and Silva Marzetti for discussion and comments on this essay and to Vivienne Brown for a stimulating conversation on negative heuristics. The usual caveat applies.

1. In this case, 'the conclusion of an inductive argument broadens the informative content of its premises' (Galavotti, 2005, p. 31).
2. This would be the case if a given set of events (say, the 2007–10 financial crisis) were described not as a particular instance of some general theory but in terms of historical narrative leading from one stage to another along a specific chain of causation.
3. This framework is associated with the view of ontology as a 'system of events' grounded in a specific individuation of agents, objects and situations. Ontology would thus presuppose a way 'of creating a concept of "something" in the world' (Genesereth and Nilsson, 1987 as quoted in Sánchez, Cavero and Marcos, 2009, p. 9). This point of view is consistent with F. Giunchiglia's definition of 'context' as the 'local theory' relevant to the solution of a specific problem (Giunchiglia, 1993). However, not all patterns of individuation need be associated with fully developed categories and conceptual schemes (see below).
4. Lucio Crisma emphasized the relationship between these two dimensions of uncertainty in his criticism of the view that the concept of 'event' could be taken as a primitive in probabilistic reasoning:

   [a] subject, in view of any given problem and considering his own interests, identifies a set *L* of propositions (statements in a natural language), which we shall call language of the problem or simply *language*, which we assume to be closed with respect to finite compositions of its propositions.

> We may then denote by α the *state of information* of the subject, that is, a more or less complex proposition (conjunction of a certain number of elementary propositions) of a known and *true* value ... that describes the *problem data*.
>
> (Crisma, 1988, pp. 16–17)

This approach suggests a twofold development of problem identification, insofar as the concept of event may be extended to include 'increments of language on the one hand and of information on the other hand' (Crisma, 1988, p. 20; see also Koopman, 1940). The interaction between the ontological and the epistemic components of problem setting is also emphasized in Simon (1962), Newell and Simon (1972) and Loasby (1976; 2010).

5. The relationship between individuation of context and pattern of reasoning is discussed in Scazzieri (2001; 2008).

6. A language analogy may be helpful in understanding the distinction. To this end it is important to single out the separate roles of lexicon and grammar. As a matter of fact, any given lexicon is associated with a particular '*construction* of human experience: the same objects, persons and relationships are considered to be worthy of description (to the exclusion of others)' (Rossini Favretti, Sandri and Scazzieri, 1999, p. 3). On the other hand, 'any given grammar entails a standard *communication* of human experience: the objects, persons and relationships considered to be worthy of description, by means of grammar (and its paradigms), enter a meaningful reference space' (Rossini Favretti, Sandri and Scazzieri, 1999, p. 3). Alternative circumscriptions of objects, persons and relationships may be associated with widely different assessments of uncertainty, and thus open up (or alternatively close down) coordination possibilities between individuals or groups (see Scazzieri, 1999; 2006).

7. Siro Lombardini made a reference to this type of situation when he argued that an individual would normally 'divide the class of all possible events (A) into two sub-classes: one is the class of the *n* events that are identified one by one (A_i'), the other is the class of the events that the individual cannot, or deems it convenient not to, consider as independent events (A'')' (Lombardini, 1953, p. 39).

8. Alessandro Vercelli noted a related distinction in his discussion of John Maynard Keynes's *Treatise on Probability* (TP) (Keynes, 1973 [1921]): '[i]n the TP there is an unsolved tension between *causa cognoscendi*, which may be translated as "epistemic cause", and *causa essendi* which could be translated as "ontological cause" according to the philosophical tradition to which the Latin words alluded to' (Vercelli, 2001, p. 145).

9. Analysis of individuation has an established place in philosophy. See also McCarthy (1980) for a treatment of circumscription from the point of view of artificial intelligence.

10. It may be argued that recognition of similarity may take place at different levels of awareness: (i) similarity between elementary features, or 'simple similarity', such that 'we can avoid investigating why and how a subject finds two aspects belonging to different objects similar, because this judgement seems automatic and not based on conscious reasoning' (Cardinale, 2007, p. 51), and

(ii) similarity between objects, or 'complex similarity', which may be associated with 'deliberate comparisons between objects' (Cardinale, 2007, p. 51).

11. The subsequent treatment of the similarity relation follows analytical criteria introduced in Leontief (1947).

12. This view of similarity is discussed in Tversky (1977). It had been anticipated in Keynes (*TP*, pp. 39–41).

13. As argued by Peter Gardenfors, 'concepts group together things that are similar' (Gardenfors, 2000, p. 109; see also Gardenfors, 1990). Indeed, representations may be interpreted as 'representations of similarities' insofar as they 'preserve the similarity relations between the objects they represent' (Gardenfors, 2000, p. 109), However, representations themselves 'need not be similar *to the objects* they represent' (Gardenfors, 2000, p. 109). This argument suggests that the representational aspect of similarity may be due to the mutual 'negative' implication mentioned above: *lack* of adequate circumscription or categorization makes similarity impossible. As a result, similarity itself appears like a mapping from the circumscription set to the epistemic set (or vice versa), and must therefore be grounded both in the structure of reality and in the organization of conceptual spaces.

14. Keynes's emphasis on 'standard objects' is related to his search of an intersubjective foundation for probability judgements. (The epistemic foundations of Keynes's theory of probability are discussed in Galavotti, 2005, pp. 144–53; and Gillies, 2000; 2006.)

15. It is worth noting that orders of similarity are a special case of order of succession insofar as they involve placing objects or situations along a scale associated with a given precedence relation. Adam Smith's discussion of orders of succession in *Essays on Philosophical Subjects* (Smith, 1980 [1795]) is relevant in this connection. In particular, Smith examines the way in which the same sequence of events 'which to one set of men seems quite according to the natural course of things' may look 'altogether incoherent and disjointed' to other observers unless certain 'intermediate events' are supposed (Smith, 1980 [1795], p. 44). This situation is formally close to one in which alternative orders of similarity may be identified depending on which predicate dimensions are considered (see below).

16. For the sake of simplicity, I overlook the case of nested qualities, in which objects must be arranged along similarity orders of primary features first, and only subsequently along similarity orders of secondary features. Keynes had this case in mind when he wrote: 'a book bound in blue morocco is more like a book bound in red morocco than if it were bound in blue calf; and a book bound in red calf is more like the book in red morocco than if it were in blue calf. But there may be no comparison between the degree of similarity which exists between books bound in red morocco and blue morocco, and that which exists between books bound in red morocco and red calf' (*TP*, p. 39).

17. Raimo Tuomela has conjectured that similarity measures are ultimately related to measures of distance: 'as categorical theories speak about the existence and non-existence of the *kinds* of individuals specifiable within L [a given language], the closer their exemplified areas [of common predicates] are to each other and the closer their empty areas are to each other, the closer or more similar must T_1 and T_2 (or what T_1 and T_2 say about their subject matter) be

to each other' (Tuomela, 1978, p. 217). This argument entails that similarity between any two objects may vary depending upon the way in which their respective distance is measured along different predicate dimensions.

18. An early investigation of the relationship between time horizon and order of likelihood is to be found in R. Maggi (1958). There Maggi highlights cases in which, by extending the ontological grounding of decision making, the type of uncertainty (and thus the order of likelihood) are changed: '[o]ne thing ... is to decide by considering a "speculative" type of uncertainty associated with the very short run, something else is to consider a "productive" type of uncertainty associated with a longer maturity' (Maggi, 1958, p. 282).

19. It is worth noting that crossover points, by increasing the reliability of the corresponding likelihood assessments, may turn a continuum of decisions into a sudden break (see also Mandelbrot, 1997).

20. The epistemic–ontological nexus mentioned here calls attention to a cognitive strategy open to epistemic pluralism on the lines suggested by Patrick Suppes (see, for instance, his *Probabilistic Metaphysics*; Suppes, 1984). This set of issues is of special importance in scientific work, in which deep understanding requires 'first, an acute sense of curiosity, and secondly great power of imagination, for the richer the field of imagined possible explanations, the greater the chance of a satisfying one' (Edwards, 1992, p. 203).

21. Paul Thagard discussed the issue of what he calls 'conceptual revolutions' in terms of distance between conceptual structures, where distance is assessed by considering features of similarity across the structures being compared (Thagard, 1992). In particular, he emphasized that 'a conceptual system can be analyzed as a network of nodes, with each node corresponding to a concept, and each line in the network corresponding to a link between concepts' (Thagard, 1992, p. 30). If this view is taken, conceptual change appears to be characterized by change in the network structure of a conceptual system, and primarily by change involving 'the addition, deletion, or reorganization of concepts, or redefinition of the nature of the hierarchy' (Thagard, 1992, p. 36).

22. This condition is independent of particular risk criteria and highlights a requirement common to attempts to arrange situations in a single numerical order of likelihood.

23. Knight pointed out that

[t]he practical difference between the two categories, risk and uncertainty, is that in the former the distribution of the outcome in a group of instances is known (either though calculation *a priori* or from statistics of past experience), while in the case of uncertainty this is not true, the reason being in general that it is impossible to form a group of instances, because the situation dealt with is in a high degree unique.

(Knight, 1940 [1921], p. 233)

Further implications of the principles of exclusion and non-exclusion are discussed in section 5.6.

24. It is important to note that the principle of exclusion works by elimination of what is impossible rather than by determination of what is likely. This feature makes that principle suitable for the assessment of 'unique situations',

that is, of situations whose repetitiveness can be excluded either in principle or in practice. For the nature of those situations is such that assessment of likelihood has more to do with the elimination of negative conditions (conditions making that unique situation impossible) than with the identification of positive conditions (conditions making that particular situation likely). In G. L. S. Shackle's words, in those cases a decision 'may reflect not purely or mainly [the decision maker's] view of the claim of *this* hypothesis to be plausible, but merely his inability to dismiss the like claim of a host of other hypotheses' (Shackle, 1983 [1958], p. 40). In other words, the assessment of uncertainty would be associated with a measure of *disbelief* rather than with one of belief (see Shackle, 1983 [1958], p. 38; see also Carter, Meredith and Shackle, 1957; Shackle, 1979; Loasby, 2003; 2009).

References

Cardinale, I. (2007), Uncertainty, Similarity, and the Logic of Arguments: An Economic Theory of Political Decisions, M.Sc. Dissertation, Faculty of Economics, University of Bologna, academic year 2006–7.

Carter, C. F., Meredith, G. P. and Shackle, G. L. S. (1957), *Uncertainty and Business Decisions*, Liverpool: Liverpool University Press.

Crisma, L. (1988), 'Dalla certezza all'incertezza: aspetti dinamici in una impostazione soggettiva', in *Atti del convegno su incertezza ed economia*, Trieste, 29–30 October 1987, Trieste: LINT, pp. 11–46.

Edwards, A. W. F. (1992), *Likelihood. Expanded Edition*, Baltimore and London: Johns Hopkins University Press.

Galavotti, M. C. (2005), *A Philosophical Introduction to Probability*, Stanford: CSLI Publications.

Gardenfors, P. (1990) 'Induction, Conceptual Spaces and AI', *Philosophy of Science*, 57, pp. 78–95.

——— (2000), *Conceptual Spaces: The Geometry of Thought*, Cambridge, Mass., and London: MIT Press.

Gillies, D. A. (2000), *Philosophical Theories of Probability*, London and New York: Routledge.

——— (2006), 'Keynes and Probability', in R. E. Backhouse and B. W. Bateman (eds), *The Cambridge Companion to Keynes*, Cambridge: Cambridge University Press, pp. 199–216.

Giunchiglia, F. (1993), 'Contextual Reasoning', *Epistemologia*, 16, pp. 345–64.

Keynes, J. M. (1973 [1921]), *A Treatise on Probability*, vol. VIII of *The Collected Writings of John Maynard Keynes*, London, Macmillan.

Knight, F. H. (1940 [1921]), *Risk, Uncertainty and Profit*, with an additional introductory essay hitherto unpublished, London: The London School of Economics and Political Science.

Koopman, B. O. (1940), 'The Axioms and Algebra of Intuitive Probability', *Annals of Mathematics*, 41 (2), pp. 269–92.

Leontief, W. (1947), 'Introduction to a Theory of the Internal Structure of Functional Relationships', *Econometrica*, 15 (4), pp. 361–73.

Levi, I. (1991), *The Fixation of Belief and Its Undoing. Changing Beliefs through Inquiry*, Cambridge, Cambridge University Press.

Loasby, B. (1976), *Choice, Complexity and Ignorance: An Enquiry into Economic Theory and the Practice of Decision-Making*, Cambridge: Cambridge University Press.

——— (2003), *Connecting Principles, New Combinations and Routines*, SCEME Working Paper no. 1, Stirling: University of Stirling Centre for Economic Methodology.

——— (2009), *Imagination, Illusion and Delusion*, SCEME Working Paper no. 27, Stirling: University of Stirling Centre for Economic Methodology.

——— (2010), 'Uncertainty and Imagination, Illusion and Order: Shackleian Connections', The G. L. S. Shackle Biennial Lecture, St. Edmund's College, Cambridge, 4 March.

Lombardini, S. (1953), 'L'incertezza nella teoria economica', in *Studi in memoria di Gino Borgatta*, Bologna: Arti Grafiche, pp. 25–57.

McCarthy, J. (1980), 'Circumscription – A Form of Non-Monotonic Reasoning', *Artificial Intelligence*, 13, pp. 27–39.

Maggi, R. (1958), *Momenti dinamici dell'economia*, Milan: Giuffre.

Mandelbrot, B. (1997), *Fractals and Scaling in Finance: Discontinuity, Concentration, Risk*, with foreword by R. E. Gomory and contributions by P. H. Cootner et al., Berlin and New York: Springer.

Newell, A. and Simon, H. A. (1972), *Human Problem Solving*, Englewood Cliffs, NJ: Prentice Hall.

Rossini Favretti, R., Sandri, G. and Scazzieri, R. (1999), 'Translating Languages: An Introductory Essay', in R. Rossini Favretti, G. Sandri and R. Scazzieri (eds), *Incommensurability and Translation*, Cheltenham, UK and Northampton, Mass.: Edward Elgar, pp. 1–29.

Sánchez, D. M., Cavero, J. M. and Marcos, E. (2009), 'The Concepts of Model in Information Systems Engineering: A Proposal for an Ontology of Models', *Knowledge Engineering Review*, 24 (1 March), pp. 5–21.

Scazzieri, R. (1999), 'Economic Beliefs, Economic Theory and Rational Reconstruction', in R. Rossini Favretti, G. Sandri and R. Scazzieri (eds) (1999), pp. 289–306.

——— (2001), 'Analogy, Causal Patterns and Economic Choice', in M. C. Galavotti, P. Suppes and D. Costantini (eds), *Stochastic Causality*, Stanford: CSLI Publications, pp. 123–39.

——— (2006), 'A Smithian Theory of Choice', *Adam Smith Review*, 2, pp. 21–47.

——— (2008), 'Context, Congruence and Coordination', in M. C. Galavotti, R. Scazzieri and P. Suppes (eds), *Reasoning, Rationality and Probability*, Stanford: CSLI Publications, pp. 187– 207.

Shackle, G. L. S. (1979), *Imagination and the Nature of Choice*, Edinburgh: Edinburgh University Press.

——— (1983 [1958]), *Time in Economics*, Westport, Conn.: Greenwood Press.

Simon, H. A. (1962), 'The Architecture of Complexity', *Proceedings of the American Philosophical Society*, 106 (6), pp. 467–82.

Smith, A. (1980 [1795]), 'The Principles which Lead and Direct Philosophical Inquiries: Illustrated by the History of Astronomy', in W. P. D. Wightman and J. C. Bryce (eds), *Essays on Philosophical Subjects*, Oxford: Clarendon Press.

Suppes, P. (1984), *Probabilistic Metaphysics*, Oxford: Basil Blackwell.

Thagard, P. (1992), *Conceptual Revolutions*, Princeton: Princeton University Press.

Tuomela, R. (1978), 'Theory-Distance and Verisimilitude', *Synthèse*, 38, pp. 213–46.
Tversky, A. (1977), 'Features of Similarity', *Psychological Review*, 84, pp. 327–52.
Vercelli, A. (2001), 'Epistemic Causality and Hard Uncertainty: A Keynesian Approach', in M. C. Galavotti, P. Suppes and D. Costantini (eds), *Stochastic Causality*, Stanford: CSLI Publications, pp. 141–56.

6
Generalized Theory of Uncertainty: Principal Concepts and Ideas[1]

Lotfi A. Zadeh

6.1 Introduction

It is a deep-seated tradition in science to turn to probability theory when one is faced with a problem in which uncertainty plays a significant role. Underlying this tradition is the assumption that there is just one kind of uncertainty—probabilistic uncertainty. The generalized theory of uncertainty (GTU) challenges this assumption. The principal thesis of GTU is that there are many different kinds of uncertainty. Principally, there are two kinds: probabilistic uncertainty and possibilistic uncertainty. In addition, there are various combinations of these uncertainties, principally probabilistic/possibilistic uncertainty and possibilistic/probabilistic uncertainty. In relation to probabilistic/possibilistic uncertainty, a case in point is the Dempster–Shafer theory of evidence. Basically, the Dempster–Shafer theory is a theory of random sets. A random set is a probability distribution of possibility distributions.

The concept of a possibility distribution was introduced and developed in Zadeh (1995). The point of departure in this paper is the thesis that possibility is a matter of degree. There is a basic difference between the concepts of probability and possibility. The concept of probability is rooted in perception of likelihood, while the concept of possibility is rooted in perception of possibility. What is the possibility of squeezing six passengers in a five-passenger car? What is the possibility that Hans may eat four eggs for breakfast?

[1]Sections 6.2–6.18 are a reprint of the paper by Lotfi A. Zadeh 'Generalized Theory of Uncertainty (GTU)-Principal Concepts and Ideas', *Computational Statistics and Data Analysis*, 51, 2006, pp. 15–46. The publishers' permission to reprint the essay is gratefully acknowledged.

Is possibility a disguised form of probability? This issue has been an object of a great deal of discussion and debate, starting with the 1966 paper by Loginov in which it is suggested that a fuzzy set may be defined as a conditional probability distribution. Various links between probability and possibility are discussed in Zadeh (1995). My position has been and continues to be that probability and possibility are distinct concepts, and should be treated as such in theories of uncertainty.

The centerpiece of GTU is the concept of a generalized constraint. In GTU, information is equated to a generalized constraint. The principal generalized constraints are possibilistic, probabilistic, and veristic. As an attribute of information, a particular kind of uncertainty is associated with a particular kind of generalized constraint. In GTU, computation is governed by rules related to propagation and counter-propagation of generalized constraints.

In addition to its capacity to deal with various kinds of uncertainty, GTU has a unique capacity to compute with uncertain information described in a natural language. For this purpose, GTU employs the machinery of Computing with Words (CW)—a system of computation based on fuzzy logic. The importance of this capability derives from the fact that more often than not uncertain knowledge is described in a natural language. Simple example: X is a real-valued random variable. What we know about X is that usually X is much larger than approximately a, and usually X is much smaller than approximately b. What is the probability that X is approximately c? What is the expected value of X?

6.2 Uncertainty and probability theory

There is a long-established custom in science of dealing with uncertainty—whatever its form and nature—through the use of probability theory. Successes of this tradition are undeniable. But as we move further into the age of machine intelligence and automated decision making, a basic limitation of probability theory becomes a serious problem. More specifically, in large measure standard probability theory (PT) cannot deal with information described in natural language; that is, to put it simply, PT does not have NL-capability. Here are a few relatively simple examples:

Trip planning: I am planning to drive from Berkeley to Santa Barbara, with stopover for lunch in Monterey. Usually it takes about two hours to get to Monterey. Usually it takes about one hour to have lunch. It is likely that it will take about five hours to get from Monterey to Santa

Barbara. At what time should I leave Berkeley to get to Santa Barbara, with high probability, before about 6 p.m.?

Balls-in-box: A box contains about 20 balls of various sizes. Most are large. What is the number of small balls? What is the probability that a ball drawn at random is neither small nor large?

Temperature: Usually, the temperature is not very low and not very high. What is the average temperature?

Tall Swedes: Most Swedes are tall. How many are short? What is the average height of Swedes?

Flight delay: Usually, most United Airlines flights from San Francisco leave on time. What is the probability that my flight will be delayed?

Maximization: f is a function from reals to reals described as: If X is small then Y is small; if X is medium then Y is large; if X is large then Y is small. What is the maximum of f?

Expected value: X is a real-valued random variable. Usually, X is much larger than approximately a and much smaller than approximately b, where a and b are real numbers, with $a < b$. What is the expected value of X?

Vera's age: Vera has a son who is in his mid-twenties, and a daughter who is in her mid-thirties. What is Vera's age? This example differs from other examples in that to answer the question what is needed is information drawn from world knowledge. More specifically: (a) child-bearing age ranges from about 16 to about 42; and (b) age of mother is the sum of the age of child and the age of mother when the child was born.

In recent years, important contributions have been made to enhancing the capabilities of PT (Bouchon-Meunier, Yager and Zadeh, 2000; Colubi et al., 2001; Dubois and Prade, 1992; 1994; Nguyen, 1993; Nguyen, Kreinovich and Di Nola, 2003; Puri and Ralescu, 1993; Smets, 1996; Singpurwalla and Booker, 2004; Yager, 2002). Particularly worthy of note are random set-based theories (Orlov, 1980; Wang and Sanchez, 1982; Goodman and Nguyen, 1985), among them the Dempster–Shafer theory (Dempster, 1967; Shafer, 1976); Klir's generalized information theory (Klir, 2004; 2006); and theories of imprecise probabilities (Walley, 1991; de Cooman, 2005). The generalized theory of uncertainty (GTU) differs from other theories in three important respects. First, the thesis that information is statistical in nature is replaced by a much more general thesis that information is a generalized constraint (Zadeh, 1986), with statistical uncertainty being a special, albeit important case. Equating information to a generalized constraint is the fundamental thesis of GTU. In symbolic form, the thesis may be expressed as

$$I(X) = GC(X)$$

where X is a variable taking values in U; $I(X)$ is information about X; and $GC(X)$ is a generalized constraint on X.

Second, bivalence is abandoned throughout GTU, and the foundation of GTU is shifted from bivalent logic to fuzzy logic (Zadeh, 1975a; 1975b; Novak, Perfilieva and Mockor, 1999). As a consequence, in GTU everything is, or is allowed to be, a matter of degree or, equivalently, fuzzy. Concomitantly, all variables are, or are allowed to be, granular, a granule being a clump of values defined by a generalized constraint (Zadeh, 1979a; 1979b; 1997; 1999).

And third, one of the principal objectives of GTU is to achieve NL-capability. Why is NL-capability important capability? Principally because much of human knowledge and real-world information is expressed in natural language. Basically, a natural language is a system for describing perceptions. Perceptions are intrinsically imprecise, reflecting the bounded ability of human sensory organs, and ultimately the brain, to resolve detail and store information. Imprecision of perception is passed on to natural languages. It is this imprecision that severely limits the ability of PT to deal with information described in natural language. NL-capability of GTU is the focus of attention in the present chapter.

A concomitant of GTU's NL-capability is its ability to deal with perception-based information (see Figure 6.1). Much information about subjective probabilities is perception-based. In an earlier paper, a generalization of PT, which leads to a perception-based theory, PTp, of probabilistic reasoning with imprecise probabilities, is described (Zadeh, 2002), PTp is subsumed by GTU.

What follows is a précis of GTU. An exposition of an earlier but more detailed version of GTU may be found in Bouchon-Meunier, Yager and Zadeh (2000), which forms the basis for the present chapter.

The centerpiece of GTU is the concept of a generalized constraint— a concept drawn from fuzzy logic. The principal distinguishing features of fuzzy logic are (a) graduation and (b) granulation. More specifically, in fuzzy logic everything is, or is allowed to be, graduated, that is, to be a matter of degree or, more or less equivalently, fuzzy. Furthermore, in fuzzy logic all variables are allowed to be granulated, a granule being a clump of values drawn together by indistinguishability, similarity, proximity, or functionality (see Figure 6.2). Graduation and granulation underline the

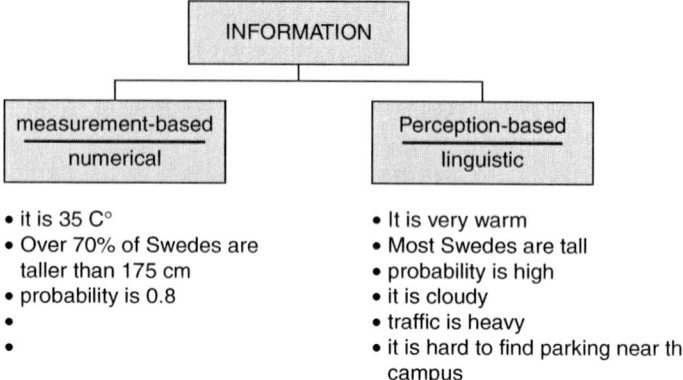

Figure 6.1   Measurement-based vs. perception-based information

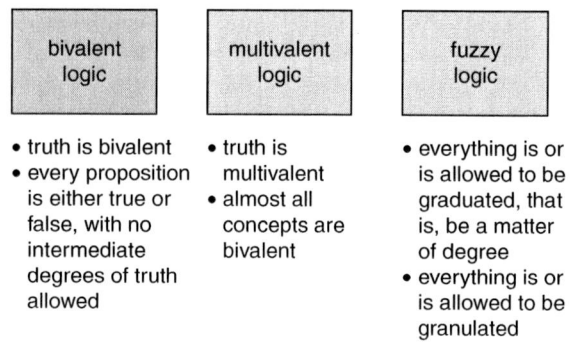

Figure 6.2   Logical systems

concept of a linguistic variable (Zadeh, 1973)—a concept which plays a key role in almost all applications of fuzzy logic (Yen, Langari and Zadeh, 1995). More fundamentally, graduation and granulation have a position of centrality in human cognition. This is one of the basic reasons why fuzzy logic may be viewed in a model of human reasoning.

NL-computation is the core of precisiated natural language (PNL) (Zadeh, 2004a; 2004b). Basically, PNL is a fuzzy logic-based system for computation and deduction with information described in natural language. A forerunner of PNL is PRUF (Zadeh, 1984). We begin with a brief exposition of the basics of NL-computation in the context of GTU.

6.3 The concept of NL-computation

NL-computation has a position of centrality in GTU. The basic structure of NL-computation, viewed as the core of PNL, is shown in Figure 6.3. The point of departure is a given proposition or, more generally, a system of propositions, *p*, which constitutes the initial information set described in a natural language (INL). In addition, what is given is a query, *q*, expressed in a natural language (QNL). The problem is to compute an answer to *q* given *p*, ans(*q*|*p*). In GTU, deduction of ans(*q*|*p*) involves these modules: (a) precisiation module, *P*; (b) protoform module, Pr; and (c) computation/deduction module, *C/D*. Informally, precisiation is an operation which precisiates its operand. The operand and the result of precisiation are referred to as "precisiand" and "precisiand", respectively. The precisiation module operates on the initial information set, *p*, expressed as INL, and results in a precisiand, *p**. The protoform module serves as an interface between the precisiation module and the computation/deduction module. The input to Pr is a precisiand, *p**, and its output is a protoform of *p**, that is, its abstracted summary, *p***. The computation/deduction module is basically a database (catalog) of deduction rules which for the most part are rules that govern generalized constraint propagation and counter-propagation. The principal deduction rule is the Extension Principle (Zadeh, 1965; 1975b). The rules are protoformal, with each rule having a symbolic part and a computational part. Protoformal rules are grouped into modules, with each module comprising rules which are associated with a particular class of generalized constraints, for example, possibilistic constraints, probabilistic constraints,

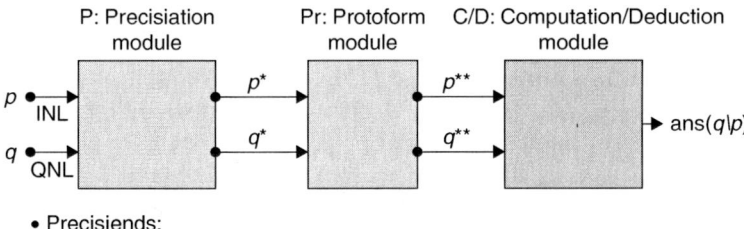

• Precisiends:
    p: proposition or a system of propositions (initial information set, INL)
    q: query
• Precisiands:
    p*, *q**
• Protoforms:
    p**, *q***

Figure 6.3   NL computation—basic structure (pNL)

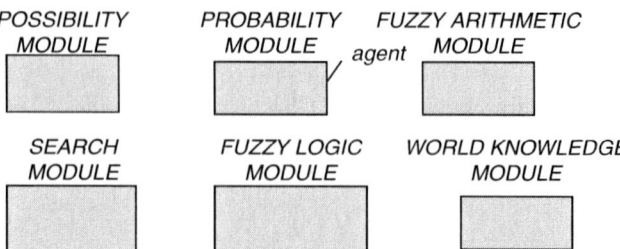

Figure 6.4   Computational/deduction module

veristic constraints, usuality constraints, and so forth (see Figure 6.4). The inputs to the *C/D* module are p^{**} and q^{**}. A module which plays an important role in C/D is the world knowledge module (WK). World knowledge is the knowledge which humans acquire through experience, education, and communication (Zadeh, 2004a; 2004b). Much of the information in WK is perception-based. Organization of knowledge in WK is a complex issue which is not addressed in the present chapter.

6.4   The concept of precisiation

The concept of precisiation has few precursors in the literature of logic, probability theory, and philosophy of languages (Carnap, 1950; Partee, 1976). The reason is that the conceptual structure of bivalent logic, on which the literature is based, is much too limited to allow a full development of the concept of precisiation. In GTU what is used for this purpose is the conceptual structure of fuzzy logic.

Precisiation and precision have many facets. More specifically, it is expedient to consider what may be labeled λ-precisiation, with λ being an indexical variable whose values identify various modalities of precisiation. In particular, it is important to differentiate between precision in value (v-precision) and precision in meaning (m-precision). For example, proposition $X = 5$ is v-precise and m-precise, but proposition $2 \leqslant X \leqslant 6$, is v-imprecise and m-precise. Similarly, proposition "X is a normally distributed random variable with mean 5 and variance 2" is v-imprecise and m-precise.

A further differentiation applies to m-precisiation. Thus, mh-precisiation is human-oriented meaning precisiation, while mm-precisiation is machine-oriented or, equivalently, mathematically based meaning precisiation (see Figure 6.5). A dictionary definition may be viewed as a form

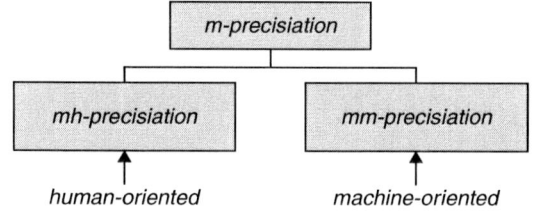

Figure 6.5 *mh*- and *mm*-precisiation

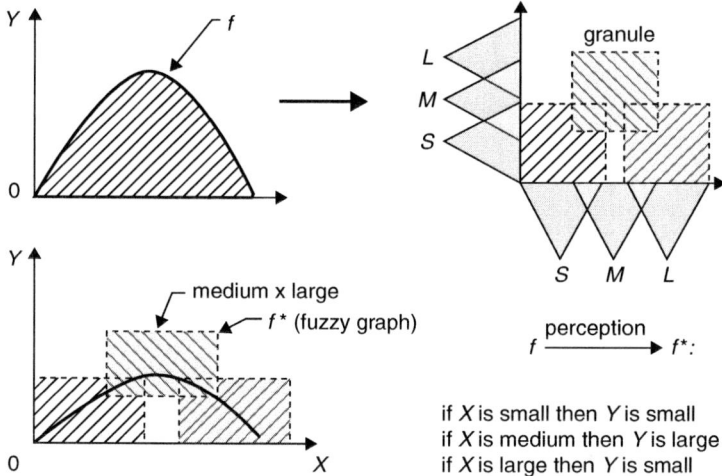

Figure 6.6 Granular definition of a function

of *mh*-precisiation, while a mathematical definition of a concept, such as stability, is *mm*-precisiation whose result is *mm*-precisiand of stability.

A more general illustration relates to representation of a function as a collection of fuzzy if–then rules—a mode of representation which is widely used in practical applications of fuzzy logic (Dubois and Prade, 1996; Yen and Langari, 1998). More specifically, let *f* be a function from reals to reals which is represented as (see Figure 6.6).

f: if X is small then Y is small,
  if X is medium than Y is large,
  if X is large than Y is small,

where small, medium, and large are labels of fuzzy sets. In this representation, the collection in question may be viewed as *mh*-precisiand of *f*.

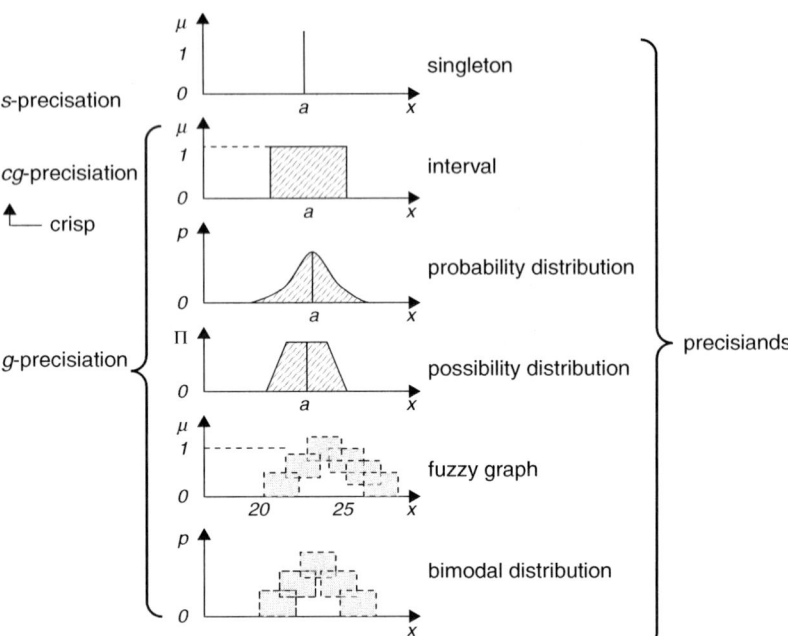

Figure 6.7   Granular precisiation of "approximately *a*." *a

When the collection is interpreted as a fuzzy graph (Zadeh, 1974; 1996) representation of *f* assumes the form.

$$f: \text{small} \times \text{small} + \text{medium} \times \text{large} + \text{large} \times \text{small}$$

which is a disjunction of Cartesian products of small, medium, and large. This representation is *mm*-precisiand of *f*.

In general, a precisiend has many precisiands. As an illustration consider the proposition "*X* is approximately *a*", or "*X* is *a" for short, where *a* is a real number. How can "*X* is *a" be precisiated?

The simplest precisiand of "*X* is *a 'is' *X* = *a*", (see Figure 6.7). This mode of precisiation is referred to as *s*-precisiation, with *s* standing for singular. This is a mode of precisiation that is widely used in science and especially in probability theory. In the latter case, most real-world probabilities are not known exactly but in practice they are frequently computed with as if they are exact numbers. For example, if the probability of an event is stated to be 0.7, then it should be understood that 0.7 is actually *0.7, that is, approximately 0.7. The standard practice is to treat *0.7 as 0.7000, that is, as an exact number.

Next in simplicity is representation of *a is an interval centering on a. This mode of precisiation is referred to as *cg*-precisiation, with *cg* standing for crisp-granular. Next is *fg*-precisiation of *a, with the precisiand being a fuzzy interval centering on a. Next is *p*-precisiation of *a, with the precisiand being a probability distribution centering on a, and so on.

An analogy is helpful in understanding the relationship between a precisiend and its precisiands. More specifically, an *mm*-precisiand, *p**, may be viewed as a model of precisiend, *p*, in the same sense as a differential equation may be viewed as a model of a physical system.

In the context of modeling, an important characteristic of a model is its "goodness of fit." In the context of NL-computation, an analogous concept is that of "cointension." The concept is discussed in the following.

6.5 The concept of cointensive precisiation

Precisiation is a prerequisite to computation with information described in natural language. To be useful, precisiation of a precisiend, *p*, should result in a precisiand, *p**, whose meaning, in some specified sense, should be close to that of *p*. Basically, cointension of *p** and *p* is the degree to which the meaning of *p** fits the meaning of *p*.

In dealing with meaning, it is necessary to differentiate between the intension or, equivalently, the intensional meaning, *i*-meaning, of *p*, and the extension, or, equivalently, the extensional, *e*-meaning of *p*. The concepts of extension and intension are drawn from logic and, more particularly, from modal logic and possible world semantics (Cresswell, 1973; Lambert and van Fraassen, 1970; Belohlavek and Vychodil, 2006). Basically, *e*-meaning is attribute-free and *i*-meaning is attribute-based. As a simple illustration, if *A* is a finite set in a universe of discourse, *U*, then the *e*-meaning of *A*, that is, its extension is the list of elements of *A*, $\{u_1,...,u_n\}$, u_i being the name of *i*th element of *A*, with no attributes associated with u_i. Let $a(u_i)$ be an attribute-vector associated with each u_i. Then the intension of *A* is a recognition algorithm which, given $a(ui)$, recognizes whether u_i is or is not an element of *A*. If *A* is a fuzzy set with membership function μ_A then the *e*-meaning and *i*-meaning of *A* may be expressed compartly as

$$e\text{-meaning of } A : A = A = \{\mu_A(u_i)/u_i\},$$

where $\mu_A(u)/u$ means that $\mu_A(u)$ is the grade of membership of u_i in *A*; and

$$i\text{-meaning of } A : A = \{\mu_A(a(u_i))/u_i\},$$

with the understanding that in the *i*-meaning of *A* the membership function, μ_A is defined on the attribute space. It should be noted that, when *A* is defined through exemplification, it is said to be defined ostensively. Thus, *o*-meaning of *A* consists of exemplars of *A*. An ostensive definition may be viewed as a special case of extensional definition. A neural network may be viewed as a system which derives *i*-meaning from *o*-meaning.

Clearly, *i*-meaning is more informative than *e*-meaning. For this reason, cointension is defined in terms of intensions rather than extensions of precisiend and precisiand. Thus, meaning will be understood to be *i*-meaning, unless stated to the contrary. However, when the precisiend is a concept, which plays the role of definiendum and we know its extension but not its intension, cointension has to involve the extension of the definiendum (precisiend) and the intension of the definiens (precisiand).

As an illustration, let *p* be the concept of bear market. A dictionary definition of *p*—which may be viewed as a *mh*-precisiand of *p*—reads "A prolonged period in which investment prices fall, accompanied by widespread pessimism." A widely accepted quantitative definition of bear market is: We classify a bear market as a 30-per cent decline after 50 days, or a 13-per cent decline after 145 days (Shuster). This definition may be viewed as a *mm*-precisiand of bear market. Clearly, the quantitative definition, *p**, is not a good fit to the perception of the meaning of bear market which is the basis for the dictionary definition. In this sense, the quantitative definition of bear market is not cointensive.

Intensions are more informative than extensions in the sense that more can be inferred from propositions whose meaning is expressed intensionally rather than extensionally. The assertion will be precisiated at a later point. For the present, a simple example will suffice.

Consider the proposition *p*: Most Swedes are tall. Let *U* be a population of *n* Swedes, $U = (u_1,...,u_n)$, u_1 = name of *i*th Swede.

A precisiand of *p* may be represented as

$$\frac{1}{n} \text{ Count (tall.Swedes) is most,}$$

where most is a fuzzy quantifier which is defined as a fuzzy subset of the unit interval (Zadeh, 1983a; Zadeh, 1983b). Let $\mu_{\text{tall}}(u_i)$, $i = (1,...,n)$ be the grade of membership of u_i in the fuzzy set of tall Swedes. Then the *e*-meaning of tall Swedes may be expressed in symbolic form as

$$\text{tall. Swedes} = \mu_{\text{tall}}(u_1)/u_1 + \cdots + \mu_{\text{tall}}(u_n)/u_n.$$

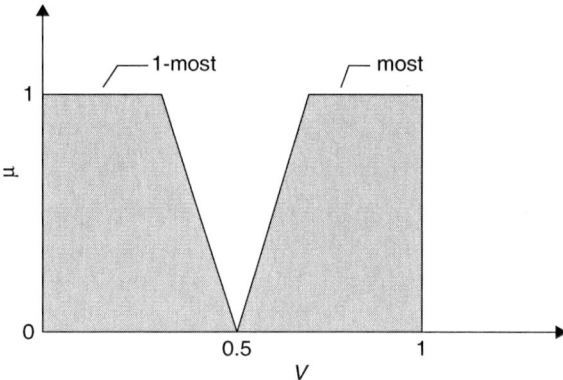

Figure 6.8 "most" and antonym of "most"

Accordingly, the *i*-precisiand of *p* may be expressed as

$$\frac{1}{n} (\mu_{\text{tall}} (u_1) + \cdots + \mu_{\text{tall}} (u_n)) \text{ is most.}$$

Similarly, the *i*-precisiand of *p* may be represented as

$$\frac{1}{n} (\mu_{\text{tall}} (h_1) + \cdots + \mu_{\text{tall}} (h_n)) \text{ is most,}$$

where h_i is the height of u_i.

As will be seen later, given the *e*-precisiend of *p* we can compute the answer to the query: How many Swedes are not tall? The answer is 1-most (see Figure 6.8). However, we cannot compute the answer to the query: How many Swedes are short? The same applies to the query: What is the average height of Swedes? As will be shown later, the answers to these queries can be computed given the *j*-precisiand of *p*.

The concept of cointensive precisiation has important implications for the way in which scientific concepts are defined. The standard practice is to define a concept within the conceptual structure of bivalent logic, leading to a bivalent definition under which the universe of discourse is partitioned into two classes: objects which fit the concept and those which do not, with no shades of gray allowed. This definition is valid when the concept that is defined, the definiendum, is crisp, that is, bivalent. The problem is that in reality most scientific concepts are fuzzy, that is, are a matter of degree. Familiar examples are the concepts of causality, relevance, stability, independence, and bear market. In general,

STABILITY IS A FUZZY CONCEPT

• graduality of progression from stability to instability

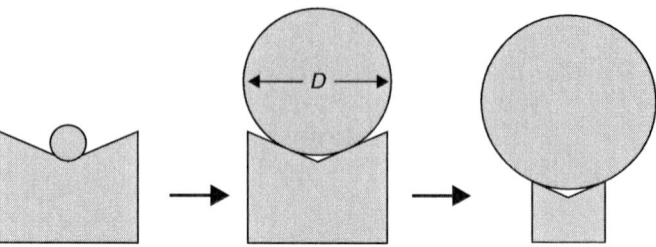

• Lyapounov's definition of stability leads to the
  counterintuitive conclusion that the system is
  stable no matter how large the ball is.
• In reality, stability is a matter of degree.

Figure 6.9   Stability in a fuzzy concept

when the definiendum (precisiend) is a fuzzy concept, the definiens (pre-cisiand) is not cointensive, which is the case with the bivalent definition of bear market. More generally, bivalent definitions of fuzzy concepts are vulnerable to the Sorites (heap) paradox (Sainsbury, 1995).

As an illustration, consider a bottle whose mouth is of diameter d, with a ball of diameter D placed on the bottle (see Figure 6.9). When D is slightly larger than d, based on common sense the system is stable. As D increases, the system becomes less and less stable. But Lyapounov's definition of stability leads to the conclusion that the system is stable for all values of D so long as D is greater than d. Clearly, this conclusion is counterintuitive. The problem is that, under Lyapounov's bivalent definition of stability, a system is either stable or unstable, with no degrees of stability allowed.

What this example points to is the need for redefinition of many basic concepts in scientific theories. To achieve cointension, bivalence must be abandoned.

6.6   A key idea—the meaning postulate

In GTU, a proposition, p, is viewed as an answer to a question, q, of the form "What is the value of X?" Thus, p is a carrier of information about X. From this perspective, the meaning of p, $M(p)$, is the information which p carries about X. An important consequence of the fundamental thesis of GTU is what is referred to as the meaning postulate. In symbolic form, the postulate is expressed as $M(p) = GC(X(p))$, where $GC(X(p))$ is a generalized constraint on the variable which is constrained by *p*. In plain words, the meaning postulate asserts that the meaning of a proposition may be represented as a generalized constraint. It is this postulate that makes the concept of a generalized constraint the centerpiece of GTU.

A point which should be noted is that the question to which *p* is an answer is not uniquely determined by *p*; hence, $X(p)$ is not uniquely defined by *p*. Generally, however, among the possible questions there is one which is most likely. For example, if *p* is "Monika is young," then the most likely question is "How old is Monika?" In this example, *X* is Age(Monika).

6.7   The concept of a generalized constraint

Constraints are ubiquitous. A typical constraint is an expression of the form $X \in C$, where *X* is the constrained variable and *C* is the set of values which *X* is allowed to take. A typical constraint is hard (inelastic) in the sense that if *u* is a value of *X* then *u* satisfies the constraint if and only if $u \in C$.

The problem with hard constraints is that most real-world constraints are not hard, meaning that most real-world constraints have some degree of elasticity. For example, the constraints "check-out time is 1 p.m." and "speed limit is 100 km/hr" are, in reality, not hard. How can such constraints be defined? The concept of a generalized constraint is motivated by questions of this kind.

Real-world constraints may assume a variety of forms. They may be simple in appearance and yet have a complex structure. Reflecting this reality, a generalized constraint, $GC(X)$, is defined as an expression of the form.

$$GC(X) : X \text{ isr } R,$$

where *X* is the constrained variable; *R* is a constraining relation which, in general, is non-bivalent; and *r* is an indexing variable which identifies the modality of the constraint, that is, its semantics. The constrained variable, *X*, may assume a variety of forms. In particular,

- *X* is an *n*-ary variable, $X = (X_1,...,X_n)$,
- *X* is a proposition, for example, $X =$ Leslie is tall,
- *X* is a function,
- *X* is a function of another variable, $X = f(Y)$,
- *X* is conditioned on another variable, X/Y,
- *X* has a structure, for example, $X =$ Location(Residence(Carol)),

- X is a group variable. In this case, there is a group, $G[A]$; with each member of the group, Name$_i$, $i = 1,...,n$, associated with an attribute-value, A_i. A_i may be vector valued. Symbolically,

$$G[A]: \text{Name}_1/A_1 + \cdots + \text{Name}_n/A_n.$$

  Basically, $G[A]$ is a relation.
- X is a generalized constraint, $X = Y$ isr R.

A generalized constraint is associated with a test-score function, $ts(u)$ (Zadeh, 1981a; 1981b) which associates with each object, u, to which the constraint is applicable the degree to which u satisfies the constraint. Usually, $ts(u)$ is a point in the unit interval. However, if necessary, the test-score may be a vector, an element of a semiring (Rossi and Codognet, 2003), an element of a lattice (Goguen, 1969) or, more generally, an element of a partially ordered set, or a bimodal distribution—a constraint which will be described later. The test-score function defines the semantics of the constraint with which it is associated.

The constraining relation, R, is, or is allowed to be, non-bivalent (fuzzy). The principal modalities of generalized constraints are summarized in the following.

6.8   Principal modalities of generalized constraints

(a) *Possibilistic* ($r =$ blank)

$$X \text{ is } R$$

with R playing the role of the possibility distribution of X. For example,

$$X \text{ is } [a, b]$$

means that $[a, b]$ is the set of possible values of X. Another example is

$$X \text{ is small.}$$

In this case, the fuzzy set labeled small is the possibility distribution of X (Zadeh, 1978; Dubois and Prade, 1988). If μ_{small} is the membership function of small, then the semantics of "X is small" is defined by

$$\text{Poss}\{X = u\} = \mu_{\text{small}}(u),$$

where u is a generic value of X.

(b) *Probabilistic* ($r = p$)

$$X \text{ isp } R,$$

with R playing the role of the probability distribution of X. For example,

$$X \text{ isp } N(m, \sigma^2)$$

means that X is a normally distributed random variable with mean m and variance σ^2. If X is a random variable which takes values in a finite set $\{u_1,...,u_n\}$ with respective probabilities $p_1,...,p_n$, then X may be expressed symbolically as

$$X \text{ isp } (p_1 \backslash u_1 + \cdots + p_n \backslash u_n),$$

with the semantics

$$\text{Prob}(X = u_i) = p_i, \quad i = 1,...,n.$$

What is important to note is that in GTU a probabilistic constraint is viewed as an instance of a generalized constraint. When X is a generalized constraint, the expression

$$X \text{ isp } R$$

is interpreted as a probability qualification of X, with R being the probability of X (Zadeh, 1979a; 1981a; 1981b). For example,

$$(X \text{ is small}) \text{ is } p \text{ likely},$$

where small is a fuzzy subset of the real line, means that probability of the fuzzy event $\{X \text{ is small}\}$ is likely. More specifically, if X takes values in the interval $[a, b]$ and g is the probability density function of X, then the probability of the fuzzy even "X is small" may be expressed as (Zadeh, 1968)

$$\text{Prob}(X \text{ is small}) = \int_a^b \mu_{\text{small}}(u)g(u)du.$$

Hence,

$$\text{ts}(g) = \mu_{\text{likely}} \left(\int_b^a g(u)\mu_{\text{small}}(u)du \right).$$

This expression for test-score function defines the semantics of probability qualification of a possibilistic constraint.

(c) *Veristic* $(r = v)$

$$X \text{ isv } R,$$

where R plays the role of a verity (truth) distribution of X. In particular, if X takes values in a finite set $\{u_i,...,u_n\}$ with respective verity (truth) values $t_1,...,t_n$, then X may be expressed as

$$X \text{ isv } (t_1|u_1 + \cdots + t_n| u_n),$$

meaning that Ver $(X = u_i) = t_i$, $i = 1,...,n$.

For example, if Robert is half-German, quarter-French and quarter-Italian, then

Ethnicity(Robert) isv 0.5|German + 0.25|French + 0.25|Italian.

When X is a generalized constraint, the expression

$$X \text{ isv } R$$

is interpreted as verity (truth) qualification of X. For example,

$$(X \text{ is small}) \text{ is very true},$$

should be interpreted as "It is very true that X is small." The semantics of truth qualification is defined by (Zadeh, 1979b)

$$\text{Ver}(X \text{ is } R) \longrightarrow X \text{ is } \mu_R^{-1}(t)$$

where μ_R^{-1} is inverse of the membership function of R, and t is a fuzzy truth value which is a subset of $[0, 1]$, see Figure 6.10.

Note: There are two classes of fuzzy sets: (a) possibilistic, and (b) veristic. In the case of a possibilistic fuzzy set, the grade of membership is the degree of possibility. In the case of a veristic fuzzy set,

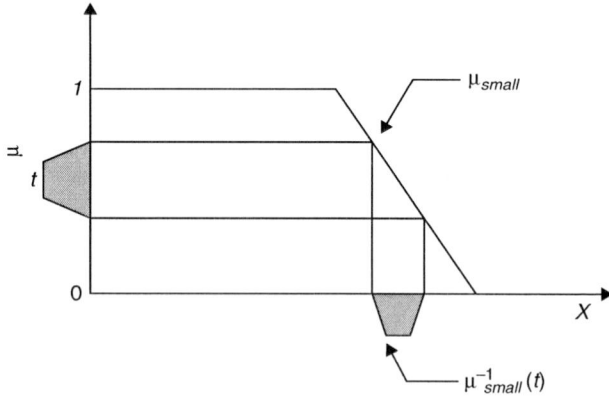

Figure 6.10　Truth qualification: (X is small) is t

the grade of membership is the degree of verity (truth). Unless stated to the contrary, a fuzzy set is assumed to be possibilistic.

(d) *Usuality* $(r = u)$

$$X \text{ isu } R.$$

The usuality constraint presupposes that X is a random variable, and that probability of the event $\{X \text{ isu } R\}$ is usually, where usually plays the role of a fuzzy probability which is a fuzzy number (Kaufmann and Gupta, 1985). For example,

$$X \text{ isu small}$$

means that "usually X is small" or, equivalently,

$$\text{Prob}\{X \text{ is small}\} \text{ is usually.}$$

In this expression, small may be interpreted as the usual value of X. The concept of a usual value has the potential of playing a significant role in decision analysis, since it is more informative than the concept of an expected value.

(e) *Random set* $(r = vs)$
In

$$X \text{ isrs } R$$

X is a fuzzy-set-valued random variable and R is a fuzzy random set.

(f) *Fuzzy graph* $(r = fq)$
In

$$X \text{ isfg } R$$

X is a function, f, and R is a fuzzy graph (Zadeh, 1974; 1996) which constrains f (Figure 6.11). A fuzzy graph is a disjunction of Cartesian granules expressed as

$$R = A_1 \times B_1 + \cdots + A_n \times B_n,$$

where the A_i and B_i, $i = 1, ..., n$, are fuzzy subsets of the real line, and $\times$ is the Cartesian product. A fuzzy graph is frequently described as a collection of fuzzy if-then rules (Zadeh, 1973; 1996; Pedrycz and Gomide, 1998; Bardossy and Duckstein, 1995).

$$R : \text{if } X \text{ is } A_i \text{ then } Y \text{ is } B_i, \ i = 1, ..., n.$$

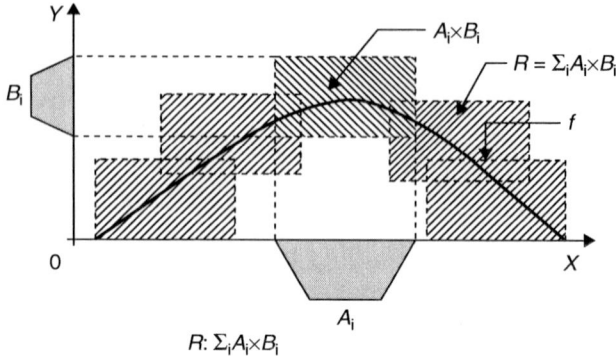

Figure 6.11 Fuzzy graph

The concept of a fuzzy-graph constraint plays an important role in applications of fuzzy logic (Bardossy and Duckstein, 1995; Di Nola et al., 1989; Filev and Yager, 1994; Jamshidi et al., 1997; Ross, 2004; Yen, Langari and Zadeh, 1995).

6.9   The concept of bimodal constraint/distribution

In the bimodal constraint,

$$X \text{ isbm } R,$$

R is a bimodal distribution of the form

$$R : \Sigma_i P_i \backslash A_i, \qquad i = 1,...,n.$$

with the understanding that Prob (X is A_i) is P_i. (Zadeh, 2002), that is, P_i is a granular value of Prob (X is A_i), $i = 1,...,n$. (See next section for the definition of granular value.)

To clarify the meaning of a bimodal distribution it is expedient to start with an example. I am considering buying Ford stock. I ask my stockbroker, "What is your perception of the near-term prospects for Ford stock?" He tells me, "A moderate decline is very likely; a steep decline is unlikely; and a moderate gain is not likely." My question is: What is the probability of a large gain?

Information provided by my stockbroker may be represented as a collection of ordered pairs:

• Price: ((unlikely, steep decline), (very likely, moderate decline), (not likely, moderate gain)).

In this collection, the second element of an ordered pair is a fuzzy event or, generally, a possibility distribution, and the first element is a fuzzy probability. The expression for Price is an example of a bimodal distribution.

The importance of the concept of a bimodal distribution derives from the fact that in the context of human-centric systems most probability distributions are bimodal. Bimodal distributions can assume a variety of forms. The principal types are Type 1, Type 2 and Type 3 (Zadeh, 1979a; 1979b; 1981a). Type 1, 2 and 3 bimodal distributions have a common framework but differ in important detail (see Figure 6.12). A bimodal distribution may be viewed as an important generalization of standard probability distribution. For this reason, bimodal distributions of Type 1, 2, 3 are discussed in greater detail in the following.

- Type 1 (default): X is a random variable taking values in U

  $A_1,...,A_n, A$ are events (fuzzy sets),
  $p_i = \text{Prob}(X \text{ is } A_i), \quad i = 1,...,n,$
  $\sum_i p_i$ is unconstrained,
  P_i = granular value of P_i.

  BD: bimodal distribution: $((P_1, A_1),...,(P_n, A_n))$ or, equivalently,

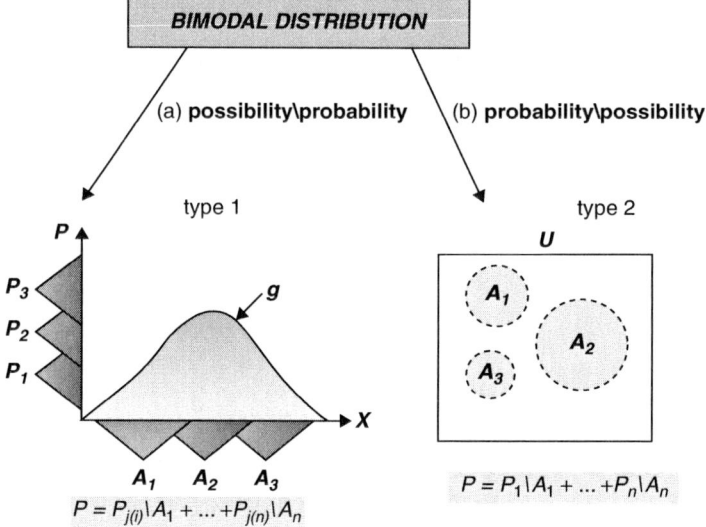

Figure 6.12 Type 1 and Type 2 bimodal distributions

$$X \text{ isbm } (P_1 \backslash A_1 + \cdots + P_n \backslash A_n).$$

Problem: What is the granular probability, P, of A? In general, this probability is fuzzy-set-valued.

A special case of bimodal distribution of Type 1 is the basic bimodal distribution (BBD). In BBD, X is a real-valued random variable, and X and P are granular (see Figure 6.13).

- Type 2 (fuzzy random set): X is a fuzzy-set-valued random variable with values

  $A_1,...,A_n$ (fuzzy sets),
  $p_i = \text{Prob}(X = A_i), \qquad i = 1,...,n,$
  P_i : granular value of p_i.

  BD: X isrs $(P_1 \backslash A_1 + \cdots + P_n \backslash A_n),$
  $\Sigma_i p_i = 1.$

  Problem: What is the granular probability, P, of A? P is not definable. What are definable are (a) the expected value of the conditional possibility of A given BD, and (b) the expected value of the conditional necessity of A given BD.

- Type 3 (Dempster–Shafer) (Dempster, 1967; Shafer, 1976; Schum, 1994): X is a random variable taking values $X_1,...,X_n$ with probabilities $p_1,...,p_n$

  X_i is a random variable taking values in A_i, $i = 1,...,n$.
  Probability distribution of X_i in A_i, $i = 1,...,n$, is not specified,
  X isp $(p_1 \backslash X_1 + \cdots + p_n \backslash X_n).$

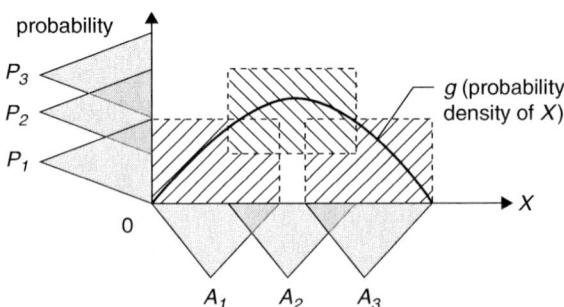

Figure 6.13   Basic bimodal distribution

Problem: What is the probability, p, that X is in A? Because probability distributions of the X_i in the A_i are not specified, p is interval valued. What is important to note is that the concepts of upper and lower probabilities break down when the A_i are fuzzy sets (Zadeh, 1979a).

Note: In applying Dempster–Shafer theory, it is important to check on whether the data fit Type 3 model. In many cases, the correct model is Type 1 rather than Type 3.

The importance of bimodal distributions derives from the fact that in many realistic settings a bimodal distribution is the best approximation to our state of knowledge. An example is assessment of degree of relevance, since relevance is generally not well defined. If I am asked to assess the degree of relevance of a book on knowledge representation to summarization, my state of knowledge about the book may not be sufficient to justify an answer such as 0.7. A better approximation to my state of knowledge may be "likely to be high." Such an answer is an instance of a bimodal distribution.

What is the expected value of a bimodal distribution? This question is considered in the section on protoformal deduction rules.

6.10 The concept of a group constraint

In

$$X \text{ isg } R,$$

X is a group variable, $G[A]$, and R is a group constraint on $G[A]$. More specifically, if X is a group variable of the form

$$G[A]: \text{Name}_1/A_i + \cdots + \text{Name}_n/A_n$$

or

$$G[A]: \Sigma_i \text{ Name}_i/A_i, \text{ for short}, \quad i = 1,\ldots,n,$$

then R is a constraint on the A_i, written in $G[A \text{ is } R]$. To illustrate, if we have a group of n Swedes, with Name; being the name of ith Swede, and A_i being the height of Name_i, then the proposition "most Swedes are tall" is a constraint on the A_i which may be expressed as (Zadeh, 1983a; 2004a)

$$\frac{1}{n} \Sigma \text{ Count (tall Swedes) is most}$$

or, more explicitly,

$$\frac{1}{n} \left(\mu_{\text{tall}} (A_1) + \cdots + \mu_{\text{tall}} (A_n) \right) \text{ is most,}$$

where A_i = Height (Name$_i$), $i = 1,...,n$, and most is a fuzzy quantifier which is interpreted as a fuzzy number (Zadeh, 1983a; 1983b).

6.11   Primary constraints, composite constraints, and standard constraints

Among the principal generalized constraints there are three that play the role of primary generalized constraints. They are:

Possibilistic constraint: X is R,
Probabilistic constraint: X isp R

and

Veristic constraint: X isv R.

A special case of primary constraints is what may be called standard constraints: bivalent possibilistic, probabilistic, and bivalent veristic. Standard constraints form the basis for the conceptual framework of bivalent logic and probability theory.

A generalized constraint is composite if it can be generated from other generalized constraints through conjunction, and/or projection and/or constraint propagation and/or qualification and/or possibly other operations. For example, a random-set constraint may be viewed as a conjunction of a probabilistic constraint and either a possibilistic or a veristic constraint. The Dempster–Shafer theory of evidence is, in effect, a theory of possibilistic random-set constraints. The derivation graph of a composite constraint defines how it can be derived from primary constraints.

The three primary constraints—possibilistic, probabilistic, and veristic—are closely related to a concept which has a position of centrality in human cognition—the concept of partiality. In the sense used here, partial means: a matter of degree or, more or less equivalently, fuzzy. In this sense, almost all human concepts are partial (fuzzy). Familiar examples of fuzzy concepts are: knowledge, understanding, friendship, love, beauty, intelligence, belief, causality, relevance, honesty, mountain, and, most important, truth, likelihood, and possibility. Is a specified concept, C, fuzzy? A simple test is: If C can be hedged, then it is fuzzy. For example, in the case of relevance we can say: very relevant, quite relevant, slightly relevant, and so on. Consequently, relevance is a fuzzy concept.

The three primary constraints may be likened to the three primary colors: red, blue, and green. In terms of this analogy, existing theories of uncertainty may be viewed as theories of different mixtures of primary constraints. For example, the Dempster–Shafer theory of evidence is a theory of a mixture of probabilistic and possibilistic constraints. GTU embraces all possible mixtures. In this sense, the conceptual structure of GTU accommodates most, and perhaps all, of the existing theories of uncertainty.

6.12   The generalized constraint language and standard constraint language

A concept which has a position of centrality in GTU is that of generalized constraint language (GCL). Informally, GCL is the set of all generalized constraints together with the rules governing syntax, semantics, and generation. Simple examples of elements of GCL are:

(X is small) is likely,
((X, Y) isp A) $\wedge$ (X is B),
(X isp A) $\wedge$ ((X, Y) isv B),
Proj_Y((X is A) $\wedge$ (X, Y) isp B),

where $\wedge$ is conjunction. A very simple example of a semantic rule is:

$$(X \text{ is } A) \wedge (Y \text{ is } B) \longrightarrow \text{Poss}(X \text{ is } A) \wedge \text{Poss}(Y \text{ is } B) = \mu_A(u) \wedge \mu_B(v),$$

where u and v are generic values of X, Y; and μ_A and μ_B are the membership functions of A and B, respectively.

In principle, GCL is an infinite set. However, in most applications only a small subset of GCL is likely to be needed.

A key idea which underlies NL-computation is embodied in the meaning postulate—a postulate which asserts that the meaning of a proposition, p, drawn from a natural language is representable as a generalized constraint. In the context of GCL, the meaning postulate asserts that p may be precisiated through translation into GCL. Transparency of translation may be enhanced through annotation. Simple example of annotation,

Monika is young $\longrightarrow$ X/Age (Monika) is R/young.

In GTU, the set of all standard constraints together with the rules governing syntax, semantics, and generation constitute the standard constraint language (SCL). SCL is a subset of GCL.

6.13 The concept of granular value

The concept of a generalized constraint provides a basis for an important concept—the concept of a granular value. Let X be a variable taking values in a universe of discourse U, $U = \{u\}$. If a is an element of U, and it is known that the value of X is a, then a is referred to as a singular value of X. If there is some uncertainty about the value of X, the available information induces a restriction on the possible values of X which may be represented as a generalized constraint $GC(X)$, X isr R. Thus a generalized constraint defines a granule which is referred to as a granular value of X, $Gr(X)$ (see Figure 6.14). For example, if X is known to lie in the interval $[a, h]$, then $[a, h]$ is a granular value of X. Similarly, if X isp $N(m, \sigma^2)$, then $N(m, \sigma^2)$ is a granular value of X. What is important to note is that defining a granular value in terms of a generalized constraint makes a granular value *mm*-precise. It is this characteristic of granular values that underlies the concept of a linguistic variable

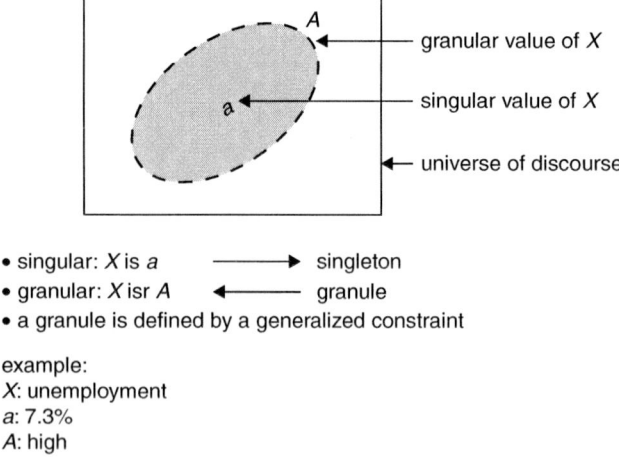

• singular: X is a ⟶ singleton
• granular: X isr A ⟵ granule
• a granule is defined by a generalized constraint

example:
X: unemployment
a: 7.3%
A: high

Figure 6.14 A granule defined as a generalized constraint

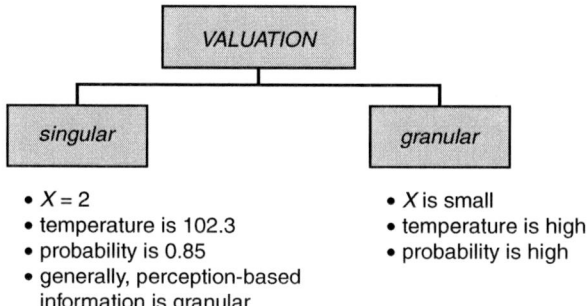

Figure 6.15 Singular and granular values

(Zadeh, 1973). Symbolically, representing a granular value as a generalized constraint may be expressed as $Gr(X) = GC(X)$. It should be noted that, in general, perception-based information is granular (see Figure 6.15).

The importance of the concept of a granular value derives from the fact that it plays a central role in computation with information described in natural language. More specifically, when a proposition expressed in a natural language is represented as a system of generalized constraints, it is, in effect, a system of granular values. Thus, computation with information described in natural language ultimately reduces to computation with granular values. Such computation is the province of Granular Computing. (Zadeh, 1979a; 1979b; 1997; 1998; Lin, 1998; Bargiela and Pedrycz, 2002; Lawry, 2001; Lawry, Shanahan and Ralescu, 2003; Mares, 1994; Yager, 2006).

6.14   The concept of protoform

The term "protoform" is an abbreviation of "prototypical form." Informally, a protoform, A, of an object, B, written as $A = PF(B)$, is an abstracted summary of B (see Figure 6.6). Usually, B is a proposition, a system of propositions, question, command, scenario, decision problem, and so on. More generally, B may be a relation, system, case, geometrical form, or an object of arbitrary complexity. Usually, A is a symbolic expression, but, like B, it may be a complex object. The primary function of $PF(B)$ is to place in evidence the deep semantic structure of B (see Figure 6.16).

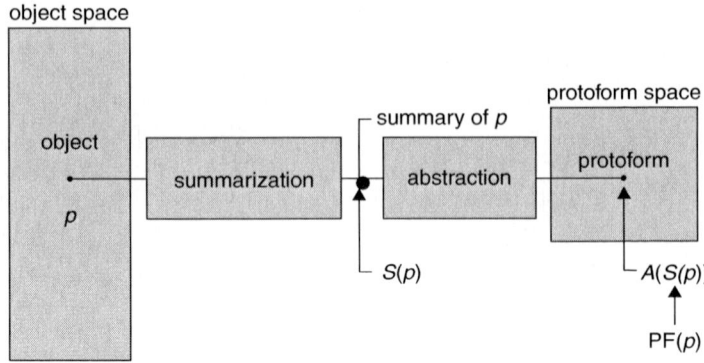

S(p): summary of p
PF(p): abstracted summary of p
     deep structure of p

Figure 6.16   Definition of protoform of p

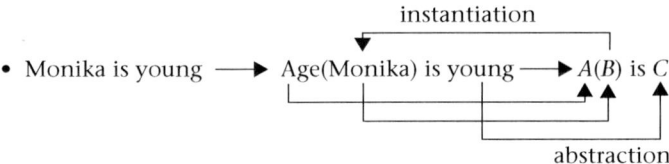

- Monika is young ⟶ Age(Monika) is young ⟶ A(B) is C

- Monika is much younger than Robert ⟶

  Age(Monika), Age(Robert) is much. younger ⟶ D(A(B), A(C)) is E

- What is Monika's age ⟶ Age(Monika) is ?X ⟶

          A(B) is ?X

- Distance between New York and Boston is about 200 mi ⟶ A(B, C) is R

- Usually Robert returns from work at about 6pm ⟶

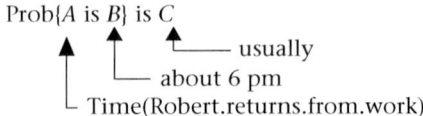

- Carol lives in a small city near San Francisco ⟶ Residence(Carol) is ((city.near.SF) and small.city))

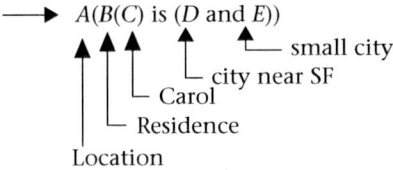

$A(B(C)$ is $(D$ and $E))$

⎿⎯ small city

⎿ city near SF
⎿ Carol
⎿ Residence
Location

- Most Swedes are tall ⟶ $1/n \sum \mathrm{Count}(G[A$ is $R])$ is Q

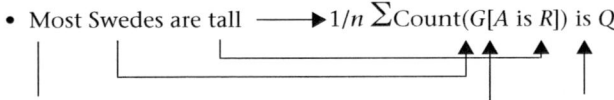

- Alan has severe back pain. He goes to see a doctor. The doctor tells him that there are two options: (1) do nothing; and (2) do surgery. In the case of surgery, there are two possibilities: (a) surgery is successful, in which case Alan will be pain free; and (b) surgery is not successful, in which case Alan will be paralyzed from the neck down. Question: Should Alan elect surgery?

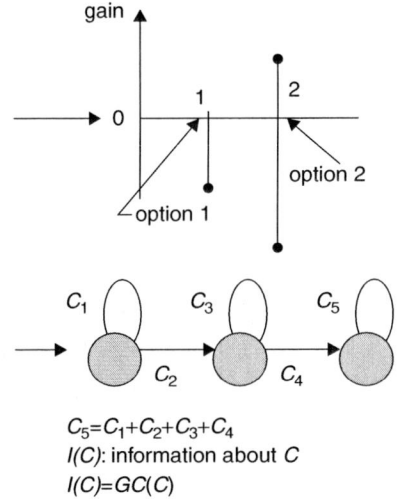

$C_5 = C_1 + C_2 + C_3 + C_4$
$I(C)$: information about C
$I(C) = GC(C)$

- I am planning to drive from Berkeley to Santa Barbara, with stopover for lunch in Monterey. Usually, it takes about two hours to get to Monterey. Usually, it takes about one hour to have lunch. It is likely that it will take about five hours to get from Monterey to Santa Barbara. At what time should I leave Berkeley to get to Santa Barbara, with high probability, before about 6 p.m.?

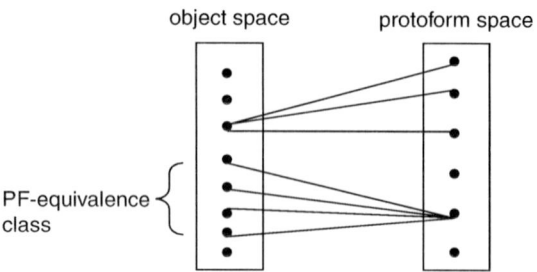

object space   protoform space

PF-equivalence {
class

• at a given level of abstraction and summarization,
objects *p* and *q* are PF-equivalent if PF(*p*) = PF(*q*)

Figure 6.17 Protoforms and PF-equivalence

Abstraction has levels, just as summarization does, including no summarization and/or no abstraction. For this reason, an object may have a multiplicity of protoforms (see Figure 6.17). Conversely, many objects may have the same protoform.

Such objects are said to be protoform-equivalent, or PF-equivalent, for short. For example, *p*: Most Swedes are tall, and *q*: Few professors are rich, are PF-equivalent.

A protoform may be extensional (*e*-protoform) or intensional (*i*-protoform). For example,

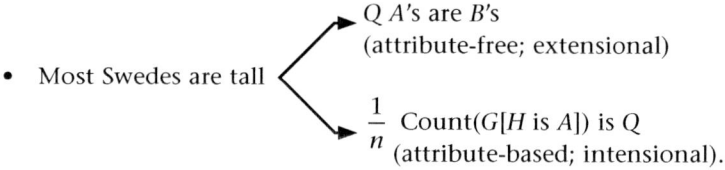

• Most Swedes are tall

Q *A*'s are *B*'s
(attribute-free; extensional)

$\frac{1}{n}$ Count($G[H$ is $A]$) is Q
(attribute-based; intensional).

As in the case of meaning, an *e*-protoform is less informative than an *i*-protoform.

The concept of a protoform serves two important functions. First, it provides a basis for organization of knowledge, with PF-equivalent propositions placed in the same class. And second, in NL-computation the concept of a protoform plays a pivotal role in computation/deduction.

6.15 The concept of generalized constraint-based computation

In GTU, computation/deduction is treated as an instance of question answering. With reference to Figure 6.3, the point of departure is a proposition or a system of propositions, *p*, described in a natural language *p* is referred to as the initial information set, INL. The query, *q*, is likewise expressed in a natural language. As was stated earlier, the first step in NL-computation involves precisiation of *p* and *q*, resulting in precisiands *p** and *q**, respectively. The second step involves construction of protoforms of *p** and *q**, *p*** and *q***, respectively. In the third and last step, *p*** and *q*** are applied to the computation/deduction module, *C/D*. An additional internal source of information is world knowledge, wk. The output of *C/D* is an answer, ans(*q*|*p*).

Examples

> *p:* Monika is young   *p*:* Age(Monika) is young,
> 　　　　　　　　　　 *p**:* A(B) is C,
> *p:* Most Swedes are tall *p*:* Count(tall.Swedes/Swedes) is most,
> 　　　　　　　　　　 *p**:* Count ($G[X$ is $A]/G[X]$) is Q.

The key idea in NL-computation—the meaning postulate—plays a pivotal role in computation/deduction in GTU. More specifically, *p** may be viewed as a system of generalized constraints which induces a generalized constraint on *ans(q|p)*. In this sense, computation/deduction in GTU may be equated to generalized constraint propagation. More concretely, generalized constraint propagation is governed by what is referred to as the deduction principle. Informally, the basic idea behind this principle is the following.

Deduction principle
Assume that the answer to *q* can be completed if we know the values of variables $u_i, ..., u_n$. Thus,

$$\text{ans}(q|p) = f(u_i, ..., u_n).$$

Generally, what we know are not the values of the u_i but a system of generalized constraints which represent the precisiand of *p*, *p**. Express the precisiand, *p**, as a generalized constraint on the u_i.

$$p^*: GC(u_i, ..., U_n).$$

At this point, what we have is $GC(u_i, ..., u_n)$ but what we need is the generalized constraint on ans(*q*|*p*), ans(*q*|*p*) = $f(u_i, ..., u_n)$. To solve this basic problem—a problem which involves constraint propagation—what is needed is the extension principle of fuzzy logic (Zadeh, 1965; 1975b). This principle will be discussed at a later point. At this juncture, a simple example will suffice.

Assume that

$$p: \text{Most Swedes are tall}$$

and

$$q: \text{What is the average height of Swedes?}$$

Assume that we have a population of Swedes, $G = (u_i,...,u_n)$, with h_i, $i = 1,...,n$, being the height of ith Swede. Precisiends of p and q may be expressed as

$$p^{\star}: \frac{1}{n} (\mu_{\text{tall}} (h_1) + \cdots + \mu_{\text{tall}} (h_n)) \text{ is most,}$$

$$q^{\star}: \text{ans}(q|p) = \frac{1}{n} (h_1 + \cdots + h_n).$$

In this instance, what we are dealing with is propagation of the constraint on $p^{\star}$ to a constraint on ans($q|p$). Symbolically, the problem may be expressed as

$$\frac{\dfrac{1}{n}(\mu_{\text{tall}}(h_1)+\cdots+\mu_{\text{tall}}(h_n)) \text{ is most}}{\dfrac{1}{n}(h_1+\cdots+h_n)}$$

with the understanding that the premise and the consequent are fuzzy constraints. Let $\mu_{\text{ave}}(v)$ be the membership function of the average height. Application of this extension principle reduces computation of the membership function of ans($q|p$) to the solution of the variational problem

$$\mu_{\text{ave}}(v) = \sup_{h} \left(\mu_{\text{most}} \left(\frac{1}{n} \left(\mu_{\text{tall}} (h_1) + \cdots + \mu_{\text{tall}} (h_n) \right) \right) \right)$$

subject to

$$v = \frac{1}{n}(h_1 + \cdots + h_n), \qquad h = (h_1,...,h_n).$$

In this simple example, computation of the answer to the query requires the use of just one rule of deduction—the extension principle. More generally, computation of the answer to a query involves application of a sequence of deduction rules drawn from the Computation/Deduction module. The Computation/Deduction module comprises a collection of agent-controlled modules and submodules, each of which contains protoformal deduction rules drawn from various fields and various modalities of generalized constraints (see Figure. 6.4). A proto-formal deduction rule has a symbolic part which is expressed in terms of protoforms, and a computational part which defines the computation that has to be carried out to arrive at a conclusion. The principal proto-formal deduction rules are described in the following.

6.16 Protoformal deduction rules

There are many ways in which generalized constraints may be combined and propagated. The principal protoformal deduction rules are the following:

(a) *Conjunction (possibilistic)*

$$
\begin{array}{ll}
\text{Symbolic} & \text{Computational} \\
X \text{ is } R & T = R \times S, \\
\underline{Y \text{ is } S} & \\
(X, Y) \text{ is } T &
\end{array}
$$

where $\times$ is the Cartesian product.

(b) *Projection (possibilistic)*

$$
\begin{array}{ll}
\text{Symbolic} & \text{Computationial} \\
\dfrac{(X, Y) \text{ is } R}{X \text{ is } S}, & \mu_S(u) = \mu_{\text{Proj}_X R}(u) = \max_{v} \mu_R(u, v),
\end{array}
$$

where μ_R and μ_S are the membership functions of R and S, respectively.

(c) *Projection (probabilistic)*

$$
\begin{array}{ll}
\text{Symbolic} & \text{Computational} \\
\dfrac{(X, Y) \text{ isp } R}{X \text{ isp } S}, & p_S(u) = \int p_R(u,v)dv,
\end{array}
$$

where X and Y are real-valued random variables, and R and S are probability densities of (X, Y) and X, respectively.

(a) *Computational rule of inference* (Zadeh, 1965)

$$
\begin{array}{ll}
\text{Symbolic} & \text{Computational} \\
X \text{ is } A & \\
\dfrac{(X, Y) \text{ is } B}{Y \text{ is } C} & \mu_C(v) = \max_{u}(\mu_A(u) \wedge \mu_B(u,v)).
\end{array}
$$

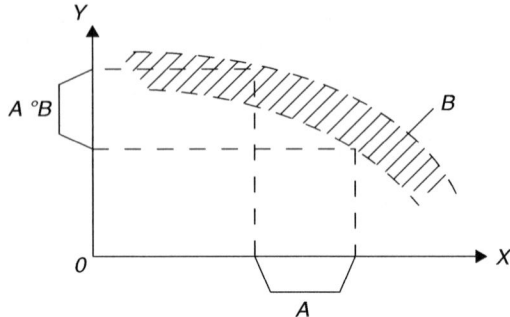

Figure 6.18   Compositional rule of inference

A, *B*, and C are fuzzy sets with respective membership functions μ_A, μ_B, μ_C; $\wedge$ is min or *t*-norm (see Figure 6.18).

(b) *Intersection/product syllogism* (Zadeh, 1983a; 1983b)

Symbolic	Computational
$Q_1 A$'s are B's	
$\dfrac{Q_2(A\&B)\text{'s are } C\text{'s}}{Q_3 A\text{'s are } (B\&C)\text{'s}}$	$Q_3 = Q_1 * Q_2$

Q_1 and Q_2 are fuzzy quantifiers; *A*, *B*, C are fuzzy sets; * is product in fuzzy arithmetic (Kaufmann and Gupta, 1985).

(c) *Basic extension principle* (Zadeh, 1965)

Symbolic	Computational
$\dfrac{X \text{ is } A}{g(X) \text{ is } B}$	$\mu_B(v) = \sup_u (\mu_A(u))$
	subject to
	$v = g(u)$

g is a given function or functional; *A* and *B* are fuzzy sets (see Figure 6.19).

(d) *Extension principle* (Zadeh, 1975b)

This is the principal deduction rule governing possibilistic constraint propagation (see Figure 6.20)

Symbolic	Computational
$\dfrac{f(X) \text{ is } A}{g(X) \text{ is } B}$	$\mu_B(v) = \sup_u (\mu_B(f(u)))$
	subject to
	$v = g(u)$

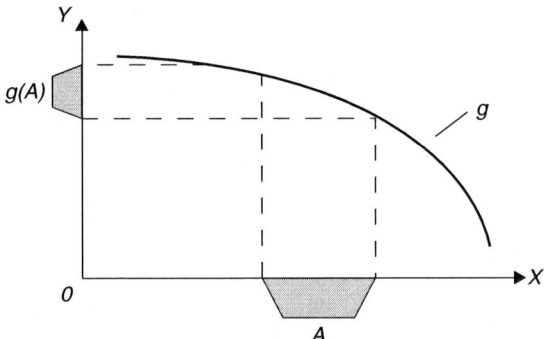

Figure 6.19 Basic extension of principle

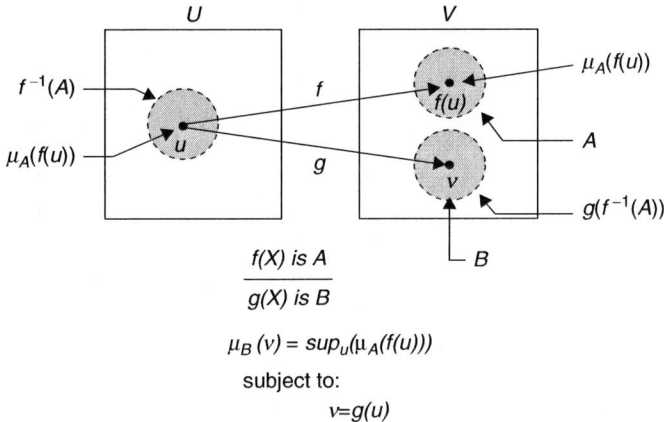

Figure 6.20 Extension principle

The extension principle is an instance of the generalized extension principle

$$Y = f(X)$$
$$Gr(Y) \text{ isr } Gr(X).$$

The generalized extension principle may be viewed as an answer to the following question: If f is a function from $U = \{X\}$ to $V = \{Y\}$ and I can compute the singular value of Y given a singular value of X, what is the granular value of Y given a granular value of X?

Note: The extension principle is a primary deduction rule in the sense that many other deduction rules are derivable from the extension principle. An example is the following rule:

(e) *Probability rule*

Symbolic   Computational

$$\frac{\text{Prob}(X \text{ is } A) \text{ is } B}{\text{Prob}(X \text{ is } C) \text{ is } D} \qquad \mu_D(v) = \sup_r \left(\mu_B \left(\int_U \mu_A(u) r(u) du \right) \right)$$

subject to

$$v = \int_U \mu_C(u) r(u) du$$

$$\int_U r(u) du = 1,$$

where X is a real-valued random variable; A, B, C, and D are fuzzy sets: r is the probability density of X; and $U = \{u\}$. To derive this rule, we note that

$$\text{Prob}(X \text{ is } A) \text{ is } B \longrightarrow \int_U r(u)\mu_A(u)du \text{ is } B$$
$$\text{Prob}(X \text{ is } C) \text{ is } D \longrightarrow \int_U r(u)\mu_C(u)du \text{ is } D$$

which are generalized constraints of the form

$$f(r) \text{ is } B$$
$$g(r) \text{ is } D.$$

Applying the extension principle to these expressions, we obtain the expression for D which appears in the basic probability rule.

(f) *Fuzzy-graph interpolation rule*
This rule is the most widely used rule in applications of fuzzy logic (Zadeh, 1975a; 1976). We have a function, $Y = f(X)$, which is represented as a fuzzy graph (see Figure 6.21). The question is: What is the value of Y when X is A? The A_i, B_i and A are fuzzy sets.
Symbolic part

$$\frac{\begin{array}{l} X \text{ is } A, \\ Y = f(X), \\ f(X) \text{ isfg } \sum_i A_i \times B_i \end{array}}{Y \text{ is } C}.$$

Computational part

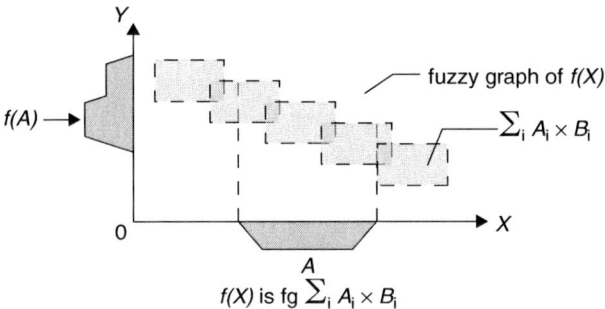

Figure 6.21 Fuzzy-graph interpolation

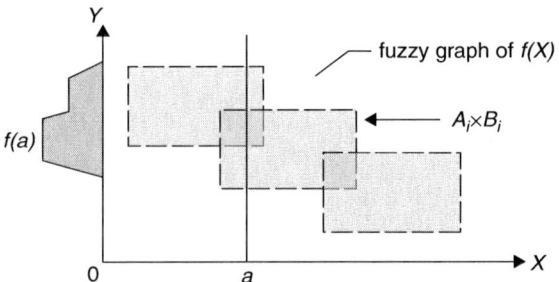

Figure 6.22 Mamdani interpolation

$$C = \sum_i m_i \wedge B_i,$$

where m_i is the degree to which A matches A_i,

$$m_i = \sup_u (\mu_A(u) \wedge \mu_{A_i}(u)), \qquad i = 1, \dots, n.$$

When A is a singleton, this rule reduces to

$$X = a,$$
$$Y = f(X),$$
$$f(X) \text{ isfg } \sum_i A_i \times B_i, \quad i = 1, \dots, n.$$

$$Y = \sum_i \mu_{A_i}(a) \wedge B;$$

In this form, the fuzzy-graph interpolation rule coincides with the Mamdani rule—a rule which is widely used in control and related applications (Mamdani and Assilian, 1975b) (see Figure 6.22).

In addition to basic rules, the computation/deduction module contains a number of specialized modules and submodules. Of particular relevance to GTU are Probability module and Usuality submodule. A basic rule in Probability module is the bimodal distribution interpolation rule which is stated in the following.

(g) *Bimodal distribution interpolation rule*

    With reference to Figure 6.23, the symbolic and computational parts of this rule are:

Symbolic

$$\frac{\text{Prob}(X \text{ is } A_i) \text{ is } P_i}{\text{Prob}(X \text{ is } A) \text{ is } Q}, \quad i = 1,\dots,n.$$

Computational

$$\mu_Q(v) = \sup_{r}\left(\mu_{P_1}\left(\int_U \mu_{A_1}(u)r(u)du\right)\right) \wedge \dots \wedge \mu_{P_n}\left(\int_U \mu_{A_n}(u)r(u)du\right)$$

subject to

$$v = \int_U \mu_A(u)r(u)du$$
$$\int_U r(u)du = 1$$

In this rule, X is a real-valued random variable; r is the probability density of X; and U is the domain of X.

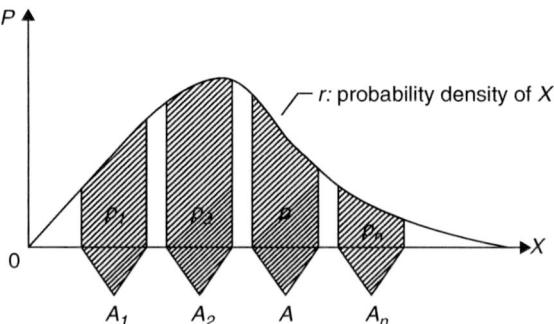

p_i is P_i : granular value of p_i, $i = 1, \dots, n$
(P_i, A_i), $i = 1, \dots, n$ are given
A is given
$(?P, A)$

Figure 6.23   Interpolation of a bimodal distribution

What is the expected value, $E(X)$, of a bimodal distribution? The answer follows through application of the extension principle:

$$\mu_{E(X)}(v) = \sup_{r}\left(\mu_{P_1}\left(\int_U \mu_{A_1}(u)r(u)du\right)\right)\wedge\cdots\wedge\mu_{P_n}\left(\int_U \mu_{A_n}(u)r(u)\,du\right)$$

subject to

$$v = \int_U ur(u)\,du$$
$$\int_U r(u)\,du = 1.$$

Note: $E(X)$ is a fuzzy subset of U.

6.17   Examples of computation/deduction

The following relatively simple examples are intended to illustrate application of deduction rules.

6.17.1 The Robert example

p: Usually, Robert returns from work at about 6:00 p.m. What is the probability that Robert is home at about 6.15 p.m.?

First, we find the protoforms of the information set and the query.
Usually, Robert returns from work at about 6:00 pm. ⟶
⟶ Prob(Time(Return(Robert))) is *6:00 pm.) is usually B/usually, which in annotated form reads
⟶ Prob(X/Time(Return(Robert))) is A/*6:00 pm.) is B/usually, where *a is an abbreviation of about a.
Likewise, for the query, we have
Prob(Time(Return(Robert))) is ⩽ o*6:15 p.m.) is ? D
which in annotated form reads
⟶ Prob(X/Time(Return(Robert))) is C/⩽o *6:15 pm.) is D/usually,

where o is the operation of composition (Pedrycz and Gomide, 1998). Searching the computation/deduction module, we find that the basic probability rule matches the protoforms of the data and the query

$$\frac{\text{Prob } (X \text{ is } A) \text{ is } B}{\text{Prob } (X \text{ is } C) \text{ is } D},$$

where

$$\mu_D(v) = \sup_r \left(\mu_B \left(\int_U \mu_A(u) r(u) du \right) \right)$$

subject to

$$v = \int_U \mu_C(u) r(u) du$$
$$\int_U r(u) du = 1$$

and r is the probability density of X.

Instantiating A, B, C and D, we obtain the answer to the query: Probability that Robert is home at about 6:15 pm. is D, where

$$\mu_D(v) = \sup_r \left(\mu_{\text{usually}} \left(\int_U \mu_{*6:00\,\text{pm}}(u) r(u) du \right) \right)$$

subject to

$$v = \int_U \mu_{\le o^*6:15\,\text{pm}}(u) r(u) du$$

and

$$\int_U r(u) du = 1.$$

6.17.2 The tall Swedes problem

We start with the information set

p: Most Swedes are tall.

Assume that the queries are:

q_1: How many Swedes are not tall
q_2: How many are short
q_3: What is the average height of Swedes.

In our earlier discussion of this example, we found that p translates into a generalized constraint on the count density function, h. Thus,

$$p \longrightarrow \int_a^b h(u) \mu_{\text{all}}(u) du \text{ is most,}$$

where a and b are the lower and upper bounds on the height of Swedes. Precisiands of q_1, q_2 and q_3 may be expressed as

$$q_1: \longrightarrow \int_a^b h(u)\mu_{\text{not.tall}}(u)\,du,$$

$$q_2: \longrightarrow \int_a^b h(u)\mu_{\text{short}}(u)\,du,$$

$$q_3: \longrightarrow \int_a^b uh(u)\,du,$$

Considering q_1, we note that

$$\mu_{\text{not.tall}}(u) = 1 - \mu_{\text{tall}}(u).$$

Consequently,

$$q_1 \longrightarrow 1 - \int_a^b h(u)\mu_{\text{tall}}(u)\,du$$

which may be rewritten as

$$\text{ans}(q_1) \longrightarrow 1\text{-most,}$$

where 1-most plays the role of the antonym of most (Fig. 8).
    Considering q_2, we have to compute

$$A: \int_a^b h(u)\mu_{\text{short}}(u)\,du$$

given that $\int_a^b h(u)\mu_{\text{tall}}(u)\,du$ is most.

    Applying the extension principle, we arrive at the desired answer to the query:

$$\mu_A(v) = \sup_h \left(\mu_{\text{most}} \left(\int_a^b h(u)\mu_{\text{tall}}(u)du \right) \right)$$

subject to

$$v = \int_a^b h(u)\mu_{\text{short}}(u)\,du$$

and

$$\int_a^b h(u)\,du = 1.$$

Likewise, for q_3 we have as the answer

$$\mu_A(v) = \sup_h \left(\mu_{most} \left(\int_a^b h(u)\mu_{tall}(u)du \right) \right)$$

subject to

$$v = \int_a^b uh(u)\,du$$

and

$$\int_a^b h(u)\,du = 1.$$

As an illustration of application of protoformal deduction to an instance of this example, consider

p: Most Swedes are tall
q: How many Swedes are short?

We start with the protoforms of p and q (see earlier example):

Most Swedes are tall $\longrightarrow \dfrac{1}{n}\sum \text{Count}(G[A \text{ is } R])$ is Q,

T Swedes are short $\longrightarrow \dfrac{1}{n}\sum \text{Count}(G[A \text{ is } S])$ is T, where

$$G[A] = \sum_i \text{Name}_i/A_i, \qquad i = 1,...,n.$$

An applicable deduction rule in symbolic form is

$$\frac{\dfrac{1}{n}\sum \text{Count}(G[A \text{ is } R]) \text{ is } Q}{\dfrac{1}{n}\sum \text{Count}(G[A \text{ is } S]) \text{ is } T}.$$

The computational part of this rule is expressed as

$$\frac{\dfrac{1}{n}\sum_i \mu_R(A_i) \text{ is } Q}{\dfrac{1}{n}\sum_i \mu_S(A_i) \text{ is } T},$$

where

$$\mu_T(v) = \sup_{A_1,\ldots,A_n} \mu_Q(\textstyle\sum_i \mu_R(A_i))$$

subject to

$$v = \textstyle\sum_i \mu_S(A_i).$$

What we see is that computation of the answer to the query, *q*, reduces to the solution of a variational problem, as it does in the earlier discussion of this example—a discussion in which protoformal deduction was not employed.

6.17.3 Tall Swedes and tall Italians

p: Most Swedes are much taller than most Italians.
q: What is the difference in the average height of Swedes and the average height of Italians?

Step 1: Precisiation: translation of *p* into GCL.

$S = \{S_1,\ldots,S_n\}$: population of Swedes,
$I = \{I_1,\ldots,I_n\}$: population of Italians,
g_i = height of S_i, $g = (g_1,\ldots,g_m)$,
h_j = height of I_j, $h = (h_1,\ldots,h_n)$,
$\mu_{ij} = \mu_{\text{much.taller}}(g_i,h_j)$ = degree to which S_i is much taller than I_j,
$r_i = \dfrac{1}{n}\sum_j \mu_{ij}$ = Relative ΣCount of Italians in relation to whom S_i is much taller,
$t_i = \mu_{\text{most}}(r_i)$ = degree to which S_i is much taller than most Italians,
$v = \dfrac{1}{m}\sum_i t_i$ = Relative ΣCount of Swedes who are much taller than most Italians, $ts(g, h) = \mu_{\text{most}}(v)$,
$p \longrightarrow$ generalized constraint on S and I,

$$q : d = \frac{1}{m}\textstyle\sum_i g_i - \frac{1}{n}\textstyle\sum_j h_j.$$

Step 2: Deduction via extension principle

$$\mu_q(d) = \sup_{g,\,h} ts(g, h)$$

subject to

$$d = \frac{1}{m}\textstyle\sum_i g_i - \frac{1}{n}\textstyle\sum_j h_j.$$

6.17.4 Simplified trip planning

Probably it will take about two hours to get from San Francisco to Monterey, and it will probably take about five hours to get from Monterey to Los Angeles. What is the probability of getting to Los Angeles in less than about seven hours?

$$BD:(\text{probably},{}^*2) + (\text{probably},{}^*5)$$
$$\uparrow \qquad\qquad \uparrow$$
$$X \qquad\qquad Y$$
$$Z = X + Y$$
$$\uparrow \quad \uparrow \quad \uparrow$$
$$w \quad u \quad v \qquad p_z(w) = \int p_x(u) p_Y(w - u) du$$

query: $\int p_z(w) \mu_{\leq 0^*7}(w) dw$ is ?A

query relevant information:
$$\begin{cases} \pi_{p_X} = \mu_{\text{probably}} \left(\int \mu_{*2}(u) p_X(u) du \right) \\ \pi_{p_Y} = \mu_{\text{probably}} \left(\int \mu_{*5}(v) p_Y(u) dv \right) \end{cases}$$

$$\mu_A(t) = \sup_{p_X, p_Y}(\pi_X \wedge \pi_Y)$$

subject to

$$t = \int p_z(w) \mu_{\leq 0^*7}(w) dw.$$

6.18 Concluding remark

The theory of uncertainty that is outlined in this paper may be viewed as a radical step toward abandonment of bivalence and shifting the foundation of the theory from bivalent logic to fuzzy logic. Though only a step, it is a step that has wide-ranging ramifications. Standing out in importance is achievement of NL-capability. This capability opens the door to extensive enlargement of the role of natural languages in themes of uncertainty, decision analysis, economics, and other fields in which human perceptions play an important role.

Acknowledgments

Research supported in part by ONR Grant N00014-02-1-0294,BT Grant CT1080028046, Omron Grant, Tekes Grant, Chevron Texaco Grant and the BISC Program of UC Berkeley.

References

Bardossy, A. and Duckstein, L. (1995). *Fuzzy Rule-Based Modelling with Application to Geophysical Biological and Engineering Systems*, Boca Raton, FL: CRC Press.

Bargiela, A. and Pedrycz, W. (2002), *Granular Computing*, Dordrecht: Kluwer Academic Publishers.

Belohlavek, R. and Vychodil, V. (2006), 'Attribute Implications in a Fuzzy Setting,' in B. Ganter and L. Kwuida (eds), *ICFCA 2006, Lecture Notes in Artificial Intelligence*, 3874, Heidelberg: Springer, pp. 45–60.

Bouchon-Meunier, B., Yager, R. R. and Zadeh, L. A. (eds) (2000), 'Uncertainty in Intelligent and Information Systems', *Advances in Fuzzy Systems—Applications and Theory*, 20, Singapore: World Scientific.

Carnap, R. (1950), *The Logical Foundations of Probability*. Chicago: University of Chicago Press.

Colubi, A., Santos Dominguez-Menchero, J., Lopez-Diaz, M. and Ralescu, D. A. (2001), 'On the Formalization of Fuzzy Random Variables,' *Information Sciences*, 133 (1–2), pp. 3–6.

Cresswell, M. J. (1973). *Logic and Languages*, London: Methuen.

de Cooman, G. (2005), 'A Behavioural Model for Vague Probability Assessments,' *Fuzzy Sets and Systems* 154 (3), pp. 305–58.

Dempster, A. P. (1967). 'Upper and Lower Probabilities Induced by a Multivalued Mapping.' *Annals of Mathematical Statistics*. 38 (2), pp. 325–9.

Di Nola, A., Sessa, S., Pedrycz, W., and Sanchez, E. (1989), *Fuzzy Relation Equations and Their Applications to Knowledge Engineering*, Dordrecht: Kluwer.

Dubois, D. and Prade, H. (1988). 'Representation and Combination of Uncertainty with Belief Functions and Possibility Measures,' *Computational Intelligence*, 4, pp. 244–64.

—— (1992), 'Gradual Inference Rules in Approximate Reasoning,' *Information Sciences*. 61 (1–2), pp. 103–22.

—— (1994), 'Non-Standard Theories of Uncertainty in Knowledge Representation and Reasoning,' *Conference on Principles of Knowledge Representation and Reasoning (KR)*, pp. 634–45.

—— (eds) (1996), *Fuzzy Information Engineering: A Guided Tour of Applications*, New York: Wiley.

Filev, D. and Yager, R. R. (1994), *Essentials of Fuzzy Modeling and Control*. New York: Wiley-Interscience.

Goguen, J. A. (1969), 'The Logic of Inexact Concepts,' *Synthèse* 19, pp. 325–73.

Goodman, I. R. and Nguyen, H. T. (1985), *Uncertainty Models for Knowledge-Based Systems*, Amsterdam: North-Holland.

Jamshidi, M., Titli, A., Zadeh, L. A., and Boverie, S. (eds) (1997), *Applications of Fuzzy Logic—Towards High Machine Intelligence Quotient Systems*. Environmental and Intelligent Manufacturing Systems Series, vol. 9. Upper Saddle River, NJ: Prentice-Hall.

Kaufmann, A. and Gupta, M. M. (1985), *Introduction to Fuzzy Arithmetic: Theory and Applications*. New York: Von Nostrand.

Klir, G. J. (2004), 'Generalized Information Theory: Aims, Results, and Open Problems,' *Reliability Engineering and System Safety*, 85 (1–3), pp. 21–38.

Lambert, K. and van Fraassen, B. C. (1970), 'Meaning Relations, Possible Objects and Possible Worlds,' in K. Lambert (ed.), *Philosophical Problems in Logic*, Dordrecht: Reidel, pp. 1–19.

Lawry, J. (2001), 'A Methodology for Computing with Words,' *International Journal of Approximate Reasoning*, 28, pp. 51–89.

———, Shanahan, J. G., and Ralescu, A. L. (eds) (2003), *Modelling with Words— Learning, Fusion, and Reasoning within a Formal Linguistic Representation Framework*, Berlin: Springer.

Mamdani, E. H. and Assilian, S. (1975), 'An Experiment in Linguistic Synthesis with a Fuzzy Logic Controller,' *International Journal of Man–Machine Studies*, 7, pp. 1–13.

Mares, M. (1994), *Computation Over Fuzzy Quantities*. Boca Raton, FL: CRC.

Nguyen, H. T. (1993), *On Modeling of Linguistic Information Using Random Sets, Fuzzy Sets for Intelligent Systems*, San Mateo, CA: Morgan Kaufmann Publishers, pp. 242–6.

Nguyen, H. T., Kreinovich, V., and Di Nola, A. (2003), 'Which Truth Values in Fuzzy Logics are Definable?' *International. Journal of Intelligent Systems*, 18 (10), pp. 1057–64.

Novak, V., Perfilieva, I., and Mockor, J. (1999), *Mathematical Principles of Fuzzy Logic*, Boston/Dordrecht: Kluwer.

Orlov, A. I. (1980), *Problems of Optimization and Fuzzy Variables*, Moscow: Znaniye.

Partee, B. (1976), *Montague Grammar*, New York: Academic.

Pedrycz, W. and Gomide, F. (1998), *Introduction to Fuzzy Sets*, Cambridge, MA: MIT Press.

Puri, M. L. and Ralescu, D. A. (1993), *Fuzzy Random Variables, Fuzzy Sets for Intelligent Systems*, San Mateo, CA: Morgan Kaufmann Publishers, pp. 265–71.

Ross, T. J. (2004), *Fuzzy Logic with Engineering Applications* (2nd edn), New York: Wiley.

Rossi, F. and Codognet, P. (2003), 'Soft Constraints,' *Constraints: An International Journal (Special issue on Soft Constraints)*, 8 (1), Dordrecht: Kluwer.

Sainsbury, R. M. (1995), *Paradoxes*, Cambridge: Cambridge University Press.

Schum, D. (1994), *Evidential Foundations of Probabilistic Reasoning*. New York: Wiley.

Shafer, G. (1976), *A Mathematical Theory of Evidence*, Princeton, NJ: Princeton University Press

Singpurwalla, N. D. and Booker, J. M. (2004), 'Membership Functions and Probability Measures of Fuzzy Sets,' *Journal of the American Statistical Association*, 99 (467), pp. 867–89.

Smets, P. (1996), 'Imperfect Information: Imprecision and Uncertainty,' in A. Motro and P. Smets (eds), *Uncertainty in Information Systems*, Boston: Kluwer, pp. 225–54.

Walley, P. (1991), *Statistical Reasoning with Imprecise Probabilities*, London: Chapman & Hall.

Wang, P. Z. and Sanchez, E. (1982), 'Treating a Fuzzy Subset as a Projectable Random Set', in M. M. Gupta, and E. Sanchez (eds), *Fuzzy Information and Decision Processes*, Amsterdam: North-Holland, pp. 213–20.

Yager, R. R. (2002). 'Uncertainty Representation using Fuzzy Measures', *IEEE Transactions on Systems, Man, and Cybernetics, Part B* 32(1), pp. 13–20.

—— (2006), 'Perception-based Granular Probabilities in Risk Modeling and Decision Making', *IEEE Transactions on Fuzzy Systems*, 14, pp. 129–39.

Yen, J. and Langari, R. (1998), *Fuzzy Logic: Intelligence, Control and Information* (1st edn), Englewood Cliffs, NJ: Prentice-Hall.

—— and Zadeh, L. A. (eds) (1995), *Industrial Applications of Fuzzy Logic and Intelligent Systems*, New York: IEEE.

Zadeh, L. A. (1965), 'Fuzzy Sets,' *Information and Control*. 8, pp. 338–53.

——. (1968), 'Probability Measures of Fuzzy Events,' *Journal of Mathematical Analysis and Applications*. 23, pp. 421–7.

—— (1973), 'Outline of a New Approach to the Analysis of Complex Systems and Decision Processes,' *IEEE Transactions on Systems, Man, and Cybernetics*, SMC-3, pp. 28–44.

—— (1974), 'On the Analysis of Large Scale Systems,' in H. Gottinger (ed.), *Systems Approaches and Environment Problems*, Gottingen: Vandenhoeck and Ruprecht, pp. 23–37.

—— (1975a), 'Fuzzy Logic and Approximate Reasoning,' *Synthèse*, 30, pp. 407–28.

—— (1975b), 'The Concept of a Linguistic Variable and its Application to Approximate Reasoning,' *Part I: Information Sciences*, 8, pp. 199–249; *Part II: Information Sciences*, 8, pp. 301–57; *Part III: Information Sciences*, 9, pp. 43–80.

—— (1976), 'A Fuzzy-Algorithmic Approach to the Definition of Complex or Imprecise Concepts,' *International Journal of Man–Machine Studies*, 8, pp. 249–91.

—— (1978), 'Fuzzy Sets as a Basis for a Theory of Possibility,' *Fuzzy Sets and Systems*, 1, pp. 3–28.

—— (1979a), 'Fuzzy Sets and Information Granularity,' In M. Gupta, R. Ragade, and R. Yager (eds), *Advances in Fuzzy Set Theory and Applications*, Amsterdam: North-Holland, pp. 3–18.

—— (1979b), 'A Theory of Approximate Reasoning,' In J. Hayes, D. Michie, and L. I. Mikulich (eds), *Machine Intelligence*, vol. 9, New York: Halstead Press, pp. 149–94.

—— (1981a), 'Possibility Theory and Soft Data Analysis,' in L. Cobb and R. M. Thrall (eds), *Mathematical Frontiers of the Social and Policy Sciences*, Boulder, CO: Westview Press, pp. 69–129.

—— (1981b), 'Test-Score Semantics for Natural Languages and Meaning Representation via PRUF,' in B. Rieger (ed.), *Empirical Semantics*, Bochum: Brockmeyer, pp. 281–349. Also, Technical Memorandum 246, AI Center, Menlo Park, CA: SRI International.

—— (1983a), 'A Computational Approach to Fuzzy Quantifiers in Natural Languages,' *Computers and Mathematics with Applications*, 9, pp. 149–84.

—— (1983b), 'A Fuzzy-Set-Theoretic Approach to the Compositionality of Meaning: Propositions, Dispositions and Canonical Forms,' *Journal of Semantics*, 3, pp. 253–72.

—— (1984), 'Precisiation of Meaning via Translation into PRUF,' In L. Vaina and J. Hintikka (eds), *Cognitive Constraints on Communication*, Dordrecht: Reidel, pp. 373–402.

—— (1986), 'Outline of a Computational Approach to Meaning and Knowledge Representation Based on the Concept of a Generalized Assignment

Statement,' in M. Thoma and A. Wyner (eds), *Proceedings of the International Seminar on Artificial Intelligence and Man-Machine Systems*, Heidelberg: Springer, pp. 198–211.

—— (1996), 'Fuzzy Logic and the Calculi of Fuzzy Rules and Fuzzy Graphs,' *Multiple-Valued Logic*, 1, pp. 1–38.

—— (1997), 'Toward a Theory of Fuzzy Information Granulation and its Centrality in Human Reasoning and Fuzzy Logic,' *Fuzzy Sets and Systems*, 90, pp. 111–27.

—— (1998), 'Some Reflections on Soft Computing Granular Computing and Their Roles in the Conception, Design and Utilization of Information/ Intelligent Systems,' *Soft Computing—A Fusion of Foundations, Methodologies and Applications*, 2 (1), pp. 23–5.

—— (1999), 'From Computing with Numbers to Computing with Words— From Manipulation of Measurements to Manipulation of Perceptions,' *IEEE Transactions on Circuits and Systems*, 45, pp. 105–19.

—— (2002), 'Toward a Perception-Based Theory of Probabilistic Reasoning with Imprecise Probabilities,' *Journal of Statistical Planning and Inference*, 105, pp. 233–64.

—— (2004a), 'A Note on Web Intelligence, World Knowledge and Fuzzy Logic,' *Data and Knowledge* Engineering 50, pp. 291–304.

—— (2004b), 'Precisiated Natural Language (PNL),' *AI Magazine*, 25 (3), 74–91.

—— (2005), 'Toward a Generalized Theory of Uncertainty—An Outline,' *Information Sciences*, 172, pp. 1–40.

7
Weight of Argument and Economic Decisions

Alessandro Vercelli

7.1 Introduction

The *Treatise on Probability* (Keynes, 1973a [1921]; henceforth *TP*), published in 1921, is a crucial reference to understanding in depth the *General Theory* (Keynes, 1973b [1936]; henceforth *GT*) published a few years later (1936). This nexus has been neglected or downplayed for many decades. Only recently has its importance been fully recognized (among the early contributions we mention Carabelli, 1988, and O'Donnell, 1989). However, its importance and scope remain quite controversial.

In this chapter I intend to clarify the controversial concept of 'weight of argument' as introduced in *TP* and explicitly resumed in crucial passages of *GT*, in order to assess its influence on the theoretical framework and methodological approach of *GT*. To this end, I will carry out a preliminary examination of whether, and for what reason, we should expect that the weight of argument has a significant impact on economic decisions. As is well known, Keynes himself admitted being puzzled over the importance to be attributed to this 'somewhat novel' concept (*TP*, p. 77); in particular, he admitted on a few occasions to be uncertain about its 'practical significance' (*TP*, pp. 83, 345, 348), also because 'it is difficult to think of any clear example of this' (*TP*, p. 83) that exemplifies and corroborates its importance. As a matter of fact the concept of weight of argument was not really new when Keynes wrote the *TP*. Keynes himself refers to writers on probability who at the end of the nineteenth century explicitly, although briefly, raised the question, in particular Meinong and Nitsche (*TP*, pp. 84–5). From the theoretical point of view, Keynes's contribution is not much more than a reappraisal of the concept within the framework of his own theory of

151

probability. What is really new is his tentative application of the concept to the explanation of economic decisions in *GT*. In our opinion Keynes's innovative method suggested in *GT* cannot be properly understood without reference to the crucial role played in it by the weight of argument.

As is well known, in *GT* Keynes explicitly refers to the weight of argument in crucial passages of his reasoning showing its significant impact on economic decisions. This provides a crucial example of its practical role, which was missing in *TP*, and shows why the weight of argument should play a crucial role in any satisfactory account of how a monetary economy works. Unfortunately the passages of *GT* referring to the weight of argument have long been neglected by followers and interpreters, for many reasons. One reason is the difficulty of providing an operational definition of the weight of argument and integrating it within analytic or econometric models. Another has been the emergence since the early 1930s of decision theories under uncertainty that are characterized by rigour and operational power (Ramsey, 1931; de Finetti, 1937; von Neumann and Morgenstern, 1944; Savage, 1954); these theories have deeply influenced the foundations of economics, including mainstream Keynesian macroeconomics after the death of Keynes, in such a way to exclude any possible role for the weight of argument. A few recent developments in epistemology and decision theory under uncertainty have reopened the issue, providing at the same time new analytical instruments capable of translating Keynes's intuitions in rigorous and operational instruments.

7.2   Definitions of 'weight of argument'

Given two sets of propositions, the set *h* of premises and the set *x* of conclusions, an argument *x\h* is according to Keynes a logical relation, knowledge of which permits one to infer *x* from *h* with a certain degree of rational belief *p* that defines the probability of *x* given *h*. The epistemic and pragmatic relevance of an argument depends, in his view, not only from its probability but also from its 'weight' (*TP*, pp. 72–85, 345–9; *GT*, pp. 148 and 240). The concept of 'weight of argument' (also called by Keynes 'weight of evidence') has been interpreted in different ways by readers of *TP* and *GT*. We find in *TP* different definitions that at least at first sight do not seem altogether congruent:

1. According to a first definition often repeated in Chapter 6 of *TP*, titled 'The Weight of Argument', 'one argument has more *weight*

than another if it is based upon a greater amount of relevant evidence' (*TP*, p. 84).

2. According to an alternative definition that may be found in the same chapter, the weight of argument 'turns upon a balance ... between the *absolute* amounts of relevant knowledge and of relevant ignorance respectively' (*TP*, p. 77).

3. Finally, in Chapter 26 the weight of argument is defined as 'the degree of completeness of the information upon which a probability is based' (*TP*, p. 345).

Each of these three definitions aims to measure the degree of knowledge relevant for probability; however, the first measure is presented as absolute, the second measure is relative to relevant knowledge, and the third is relative to complete relevant knowledge. In my opinion, contrary to their initial appearance, the three definitions, correctly understood, are fairly consistent and may be represented by the same analytic measure.

Most interpreters picked up the 'absolute' definition, identifying the weight of argument simply with the amount of relevant knowledge K, perhaps because it appears at the very beginning of the Chapter 6 on the weight of argument and it is frequently referred to, explicitly and implicitly, in *TP*. Therefore, most interpreters believe that a satisfactory measure of the weight of argument may be given simply by:

$$V (x/h) = K. \tag{1}$$

In my opinion, however, this measure is inconsistent with Keynes's crucial assertion that additional evidence may increase relevant knowledge without increasing the weight of argument: '[T]he new datum strengthens or weakens the argument, although there is no basis for an estimate how much stronger or weaker the new argument is than the old' (*TP*, p. 34). This reflection clarifies the *rationale* of the second definition. Unfortunately, this important clarification may be found not in Chapter 6, on the weight of argument, but in Chapter 3, on the fundamental ideas of *TP*, before the concept of weight of argument is explicitly introduced, which may explain why Keynes's assertion has been often neglected. We notice that, according to Keynes, new evidence may reduce the weight of argument as it may alert the agent to the fact that the gap between her relevant knowledge and complete relevant knowledge is greater than she previously believed.

Consistently with the preceding considerations and the second definition of weight of argument, Runde (1990) suggests the following measure:

$$V(x/h) = K \setminus I. \tag{2}$$

This simple ratio between relevant knowledge and relevant ignorance takes account of the exigency, emphasized by Keynes in his second definition, of duly taking relevant ignorance into account. This measure implies that, unlike in the first definition, the weight of argument increases only if relevant knowledge increases more (decreases less) than relevant ignorance. However, it is not fully satisfactory because it is meaningless when relevant ignorance tends to zero (complete relevant knowledge) as this measure takes values tending towards infinity.

We may overcome these shortcomings by introducing the following measure, which is derived from the third definition:

$$V(x/h) = K/(K + I). \tag{3}$$

In this case the weight of argument increases only if relevant ignorance diminishes. This measure has the advantage of being clearly defined even in the extreme case of complete relevant knowledge ($V(x/h) = 1$). In addition, its range of values from 0 to 1 is consistent with the usual measures of uncertainty, such as probability, and conforms to the range of values that Keynes seems to have in mind (see *TP*, p. 348).[1] Therefore I conclude that the third definition, as expressed in measure (3), is the most general and satisfactory of the three definitions of weight of argument, as it explicitly takes account of the relation between relevant knowledge and both relevant ignorance and complete knowledge. Therefore, in what follows, I will define the weight of argument as in measure (3).

7.3   Weight of argument and modalities of uncertainty

In *TP* Keynes often illustrates general concepts by examining specific instances considered to be particularly important or emblematic. This method of exposition has the advantage of favouring constant intuitive control of the meaning of arguments, but it may jeopardize the rigorous definition of concepts. In the preceding section we have seen a significant example of this kind of difficulty. In order to clarify the distinction between probability and weight of argument, Keynes insists on the particular case of new evidence that may increase or decrease the probability of an event while increasing at the same time the weight of argument. This happens, we may add, only when the new piece of evidence reduces the relevant ignorance of the decision maker (henceforth DM). This emblematic example illustrates in an intuitive way the semantic difference between probability and weight of argument, but it may mislead the reader if he is induced to believe that an increase in relevant evidence necessarily implies an increase in the weight of argument. This is not necessarily true, because an increase in relevant knowledge may increase the awareness that relevant ignorance is greater than previously believed. As Socrates, Plato and many other eminent philosophers often maintained, 'wisest is he who knows he knows not'.

In order to go deeper into the problem, we have to clarify the concept of uncertainty. We may start from a generic definition that I believe to be consistent with Keynes's epistemic approach: uncertainty is in its essence 'rational awareness of ignorance'. We have to distinguish between ignorance relative to a conclusion x of an argument A (given the premises h) expressed by the probability, and ignorance relative to the argument as expressed by the weight of argument $V(x|h)$. The weight of argument is expressed through a proposition having as its object the argument A. This establishes a hierarchical relation between probability and weight of argument that may be expressed in the following way: the probability of a proposition expressing the conclusion of an argument given the premises is a first-order measure of uncertainty while the weight of argument is a second-order measure having as its object the reliability of the first-order measure.

The concept of weight of argument, as defined and measured here, permits a clear definition of different modalities of (first-order) uncertainty, which may be ordered on the basis of an homogeneous criterion. The range of values of $V(x/h)$, as defined in measure (3), goes from 0 to 1 and allows a distinction between three modalities of (first-order) uncertainty that play a different role in Keynes's analysis in *TP* and then in *GT*. Uncertainty may be defined as 'radical' when the weight of argument is nil. In other words, the DM is aware that he does not know anything relevant about the occurrence of a certain event. For example: '[T]he prospect of a European war is uncertain, or the price of copper and the rate of interest twenty years hence ... about these matters there is no scientific basis on which to form any calculable probability whatever. We simply do not know' (Keynes, 1973c [1937], pp. 113–14). Conversely, uncertainty may be defined as 'soft' (or weak) when the weight of argument is 1. In other words, in this case the DM is uncertain only in the weak sense that he does not know which of a set of possible events will occur but believes that he knows their 'true' probability distribution. This is the typical case in a game of chance, as the emblematic case of roulette well illustrates. If the roulette is fair, the DM knows exactly the complete list of possible events and knows the 'objective' or 'true' probability of each of the possible events. Traditionally only these two extreme cases have been considered. The weight of argument clarifies that between the two extremes – the white of soft uncertainty and the black of complete relevant ignorance – there is a wide grey zone characterized by the DM's awareness that his relevant knowledge is incomplete but not nil. It is thus rational to exploit all relevant knowledge. In other words, the weight of argument allows a measure of the degree of incompleteness of relevant knowledge and provides a guide for its rational exploitation.

The threefold classification of uncertainty that we represent in graphical terms in Figure 7.1 emerges naturally – we believe – from the interpretation of weight of argument suggested here, but it is not universally accepted. Many interpreters of Keynes believe that what Keynes had in mind was a simple dichotomy between weak uncertainty (which may be expressed by probability) and radical uncertainty (or 'uncertainty' in its strict sense): see , for example, Davidson (1988; 1991). There is no doubt that a dichotomy of this kind often appears in Keynes's economic arguments, but in our opinion its role is to emphasize the hierarchy between first-order and second-order uncertainty. In any case, we want to show that the interpretation that focuses on a simple dichotomy raises a series of textual and contextual difficulties.

The first observation refers to radical uncertainty and takes into account a qualification by Keynes. In this case the knowledge relevant for probability is altogether absent, and this prevents the use of probability. Keynes maintains that this is already true for a value of weight of argument inferior to ε. which defines the minimum degree of relevant knowledge that makes probability meaningful. As Keynes emphasizes (*TP*, p. 78):

Figure 7.1 Weight of argument and uncertainty

A proposition cannot be the subject of an argument, unless we at least attach some *meaning* to it, and this meaning, even if it only relates to the form of the proposition, may be relevant in some arguments relating to it. But there may be no other relevant evidence ... in this case the weight of the argument is at its lowest.

According to the dichotomous view of uncertainty modalities, when the weight of argument is maximum (1 in our interpretation) the probability is either 1 or 0. This assertion seems at first sight inescapable as the completeness of relevant knowledge seems to imply the convergence of probability towards one of its extreme values (0 or 1; on this point see in particular O'Donnell, 1989). This thesis, however, is misleading. The knowledge that intervenes in the definition of weight of argument is, according to Keynes, the relevant knowledge that may be acquired by an epistemic subject characterized by bounded rationality. In general, as the weight of argument increases, the probability converges towards a more reliable value, which may be any value between 0 and 1 (extremes included). This conclusion should be obvious as soon as we refer to games of chance. If the DM knows that a dice is fair, the probability of any of the numbers written on its faces is assumed to be equal to $1\backslash6$ and this assertion has the maximum weight (equal to 1). Even if we believe that the outcome of the throw of the dice ultimately depends on deterministic factors, and we agree with Laplace that a demon knowing all the relevant initial conditions would be able to forecast the exact outcome, this is patently beyond human reach. It would be meaningless in a case like this to maintain that an argument based on the probability $1\backslash6$ for each number on the dice has a weight inferior to the maximum, 1. We have thus to conclude that the probability converges towards its extreme values (0 or 1) only in a deterministic argument. In addition, we have to emphasize that the weight of argument has a significant role in decision theory only when uncertainty is hard. As a matter of fact, if uncertainty is radical, probabilities are groundless, while when uncertainty is weak probabilities are seen as fully reliable. Only when uncertainty is hard may a change in the weight of argument affect economic decisions (see ss. 7.4 and 7.5). In *GT* Keynes refers to the weight of argument within a conceptual framework based on the distinction between probability (when the weight of argument is at the maximum) and genuine 'uncertainty' in the other cases. He wants to stress how demanding the hypothesis of soft uncertainty underlying classical economics is and how fragile the approach based on such an extreme assumption is: a small deviation from the assumption that agents have complete relevant knowledge is enough to produce deep modifications in financial and real choices and in the theories that account for them. The prevailing interpretation identifies with radical uncertainty what Keynes calls simply uncertainty in contraposition to probability. This seems justified by a few passages where Keynes refers to uncertainty as complete relevant ignorance (as the famous passage, too well-known to be quoted here, qualifying his reply in 1937 to the early critiques of *GT* (Keynes, 1973c [1937], pp. 113–14). However, this interpretation does not work in different crucial passages of *GT* where Keynes focuses on the effects of changes in one or more crucial variables on the degree of uncertainty perceived by economic agents. The interpretation of these variations as a jump between extreme values of the weight of argument would be misleading. The weight of argument can play an active role in causal analysis only in the hypothesis of hard uncertainty, where a change in the weight may bring about different behaviour.

To avoid confusion we believe that the distinction between probability and uncertainty should be interpreted not as a dichotomy between two extreme modalities of first-order uncertainty, but as a distinction between two levels of a hierarchy: *probability* is a first-order uncertainty measure while 'uncertainty' in its strict sense refers to second-order uncertainty as measured by the weight of argument. We may understand in this way why Keynes relates the weight of argument to uncertainty in the strict sense and why the classical economists, by neglecting altogether this dimension of the analysis, limit themselves to considering probability in the hypothesis of soft uncertainty.

7.4 Practical relevance of the weight of argument: preliminary analysis

Keynes does not make clear why one should take a decision on the basis of an argument having higher weight. As he stresses, Bernoulli's advice that we 'must take into account all the information we have, amounts to an injunction that we should be guided by the probability of that argument, among those of which we know the premises, of which the evidential weight is the greatest' (*TP*, p. 83, 345–6). He then recalls the decision rule suggested by Locke in the following maxim 'he that judges without informing himself to the utmost that he is capable, cannot acquit himself of judging amiss' (quoted in *TP*, p. 84, n. 2; see also p. 6). This second rule links in a crucial way weight of argument and learning: 'when our knowledge is slight but capable of increase, the course of action which will, relative to such knowledge, probably produce the greatest amount of good, will often consist in the acquisition of more knowledge' (*TP*, p. 83). If we take Locke's prescription too literally, we could undermine the practical relevance of the weight of argument by inferring that a rational agent should take a decision only when relevant knowledge is complete. However, Keynes rightly observes that, as soon as we take account of the practical constraints on decisions (the time horizon of the decision and the costs of acquiring new information), it is rational to reduce relevant ignorance and thus to reinforce the weight of argument only up to a threshold that in general is short of its maximum value (*TP*, p. 83). Therefore, the weight of argument cannot be ignored as its value affects the decision strategy of a rational decision maker (*TP*, p. 342).

The reason for taking into account the weight of argument in decision making is not made explicit by Keynes or Bernoulli or Locke in the passages cited. We could speculate that the higher the weight of argument is, the lower is the probability of deviating from the target. However, Keynes maintains that, in principle, the weight of argument is independent of the expected error or 'probable error': 'there is ... no reason whatever for supposing that the probable error must necessarily diminish, as the weight of argument is increased' (*TP*, p. 82). This observation is a source of perplexity for Keynes himself; we believe that this dilemma can be solved by recalling the distinction, routinely made in statistical inference and econometric estimation, between stochastic error and systematic error. We suggest that the weight of argument is altogether independent of stochastic error but is strictly correlated with expected systematic error. A greater weight of argument reduces expected systematic error; and it is exactly this property that confers practical relevance to the weight of argument. Stochastic errors are by definition inevitable as they depend on a host of (by definition) unknowable exogenous factors; however, stochastic errors have a practical relevance for decision making because their properties determine the nature and size of the risk associated with a decision. If we admit the presence only of stochastic errors, the weight of argument is maximum because relevant knowledge cannot be further increased. In contrast, a weight of argument inferior to 1 implies awareness of possible systematic errors that are the more significant the deeper relevant ignorance is. Systematic errors diminish with learning to the extent that learning diminishes relevant ignorance.

Although confidence in the conclusions of a non-demonstrative argument relies upon the expected value of both stochastic and systematic errors, these two determinants should be kept separate as they depend on completely different factors: risk and weight of argument. The practical relevance of risk depends on the attitude towards risk, while the practical relevance of the weight of argument depends on the attitude towards (second-order) uncertainty. The weight of argument, however, is important also for a second fundamental reason that breaks the symmetry with the analysis of risk as it may be interpreted as an index of potential learning. The crucial nexus between the weight of argument and learning is already altogether evident in *TP*, but it is only in *GT* that Keynes formulates the fundamental principle that gives the weight of argument a high degree of practical relevance, in particular in his analysis of liquidity preference: the lower the weight of argument, and thus the higher the potential learning, the higher is the degree of intertemporal flexibility sought by a rational agent (Basili and Vercelli, 1998).

7.5   The weight of argument in the light of theory of decision under uncertainty

To assess in depth the practical relevance of the Keynesian concept of weight of argument, it is sensible to take into account the remarkable advances of decision theory under uncertainty (henceforth DTU) since the publication of *TP* (see Camerer and Weber, 1992).

DTU reaches a stage of maturity with von Neumann and Morgenstern (1944), who succeed in providing sound foundations by axiomatizing it from the point of view of objective probabilities. Its empirical scope, however, is limited to what we have called soft uncertainty. Probabilities are considered by the DM as 'known', that is, as fully reliable. In this case the weight of argument does not have any practical role since by assumption is always equal to 1.

A few years later Savage (1954), building on ideas put forward by Ramsey (1931) and de Finetti (1937), suggests a different axiomatized DTU that pretends to be applicable to any situation characterized by uncertainty. In this subjectivist theory, often called Bayesian, probabilities are conceived of as epistemic weights that assure the consistency of the decisions of a rational agent. De Finetti and Savage believe that the distinction between different modalities of uncertainty, and thus also concepts such as the weight of argument that presuppose it, are inconsistent with rationality. The main argument has been put forward by de Finetti, who has developed in the form of a theorem intuitions put forward by Ramsey. He shows that, if the beliefs of the DM are not represented in the form of a unique distribution of additive probabilities, as in Bayesian theory, he is vulnerable to accept a 'Dutch book', that is, a system of bets whose acceptance is irrational as it does not involve a possible positive pay-off. The assumption that the beliefs are represented by a unique distribution of additive probabilities implies that the DM has complete relevant knowledge, so that his uncertainty is soft. Therefore, in this view only weak uncertainty is consistent with rationality, and this precludes any normative role for the weight of argument. Savage reinforces this conclusion by observing that the introduction of a second-order measure of uncertainty would trigger an infinite regress that in his opinion would be unacceptable from a logical point of view (Savage, 1954).

The state-of-the-art textbook exposition of decision theory under uncertainty makes a basic distinction between 'known' and 'unknown' probabilities to articulate a simplistic division of labour between objectivist and subjectivist theories of decision (Vercelli, 1999). According to this approach, when the probabilities are 'known' (as in the case of a 'roulette game') the use of the objectivist theory introduced by von Neumann and Morgenstern is prescribed, while when the probabilities are 'unknown' (as in the case of a 'horse race') the use of the subjectivist theory introduced by Savage is prescribed. This widespread eclectic view seems to introduce a distinction between two different modalities of uncertainty, providing an opportunity for the use of the weight of argument seen as degree of knowledge of probabilities. However, a deeper analysis shows that the distinction between known and unknown probabilities is confined to their source (stable frequencies in the objective approach and coherent subjective assessment in Bayesian theory), and does not affect the modality of uncertainty that in both cases is represented by a unique distribution of additive probabilities (Vercelli, 1999). As well, the axioms of the two theories are expressed in a different language but are substantially equivalent. In particular, in both cases the axioms preclude the possibility that a rational agent makes systematic mistakes. It is assumed that the probability distribution is not modified by the choices of the agents and that its structural characteristics are perfectly known by them: the DM knows the complete list of possible world states, the complete list of the available options and the consequences of each option or *act* in each possible state of the world. These assumptions presuppose that the world is closed and stationary and that the agent has fully adapted to such a 'world' (Vercelli, 2002; 2005). In this case, the weight of argument is maximum and its explicit introduction would be irrelevant.

This common approach of mainstream DTU explains why, up the mid-1980s, most economists and decision theorists expressed sheer hostility against the concept of weight of argument or any other concept presupposing different modalities of uncertainty. However, since the second half of the 1980s, a series of innovative contributions to DTU has progressively generated a climate of opinion that is more favourable to understanding the Keynesian insights on the weight of argument (Kelsey and Quiggin, 1992). First, the obstructive arguments by de Finetti and Savage proved to be weaker than they were originally believed to be. The Dutch book argument by Ramsey and de Finetti is based upon implicit assumptions that are quite implausible in situations in which the weight of argument has a role, that is, when uncertainty is hard, reflecting an open and non-stationary world. This is true in particular for the assumption that the DM is expected to bet for or against a certain event; this does not take account of the fact that a refusal to bet could be altogether rational when the weight of argument is far from its extreme values. In addition, Savage's argument about the infinite regress is not convincing since the introduction of a second-order measure of uncertainty implies only the possibility of a higher-order measure, not its necessity: whether it is useful to introduce a measure of uncertainty of a higher order is a pragmatic question, not a logical one.

The opinion is now gaining ground that there are in principle no binding objections that preclude the analysis of different modalities of uncertainty. The use of the concept of weight of argument is thus fully legitimate. This shift of attitude is both cause and effect of the emergence of new DTUs, no less rigorous than the aforementioned classical ones that presuppose, or at least are consistent with, hard uncertainty and a weight of argument different from its extreme values. Some of these DTUs assume that the beliefs of DMs are to be expressed through a plurality of probability distributions, none of which is considered fully reliable. This amounts to evaluating the probability of the occurrence of an event or a state of the world through an interval of probability. Other DTUs assume that the beliefs of DMs may be expressed through a unique distribution of non-additive probabilities. This expresses the awareness of the DM that his relevant knowledge is incomplete; in the sub-additive case it reveals that the list of possible states or events is not exhaustive (see Vercelli, 1999). The latter assumption may clarify the theoretical and empirical scope of the Keynesian theory of the weight of argument. It is possible to demonstrate that the measure of uncertainty aversion advanced by Dow and Werlang (1992) within this theory

$$c(P,A) = 1 - P(A) - P(A^c),\qquad(4)$$

where A is an event and A^c is its complement, is strictly related to the weight of argument as here defined. In fact, we may interpret the equation (4) as a measure of relevant ignorance; this is true in general of measures of sub-additivity of the probability distribution. In this case, by utilizing the normalization mentioned in section 7.2, we obtain that the weight of argument is the complement to unity of the measure of uncertainty aversion suggested by Dow and Werlang:

$$c(P,A) = 1 - P(A) - P(A^c) = I/(K + I) = 1 - V(x/h).\qquad(5)$$

We can thus conclude that the recent advances of DTU are rediscovering, in the context of a different language and formalization, the importance of the ideas underlying the Keynesian concept of weight of argument.

7.6 The weight of argument in the *General Theory*

As is well known, the weight of argument is explicitly mentioned by Keynes in *GT* on two occasions (see footnotes on pp. 148 and 240). The importance of these references is confirmed in his correspondence (see, for example, the well-known letter to Townshend of December 1938; Keynes, 1979b [1938], p. 293). Although explicit hints at the weight of argument are scarce, we contend that its role is important as it intervenes in the reasoning in a crucial way, although sometimes only implicitly. Its role looms wherever Keynes refers to uncertainty with a meaning different from that of classical economics and classical decision theory. Actually, as we have seen in section 7.3, uncertainty, as distinct from probability, implies a weight of argument lower than 1 and vice versa. Therefore, the weight of argument is potentially relevant in all the passages in *GT* where uncertainty, confidence and expectations play a crucial role. This is true in particular for the passages where expectations affect economic behaviour. In particular, sudden and discontinuous shifts of the weight of argument induced by variations in the macroeconomic and policy context of agents' decisions determine significant shifts also in the two crucial functions that determine aggregate income: liquidity preference and marginal efficiency of capital.

Before discussing the role of the weight of argument in *GT* we have to dispose of a preliminary objection. According to some interpreters,[2] the references in *GT* to *TP* should not be taken too seriously since Keynes had changed his ideas on probability under the influence of Ramsey (Keynes, 1931). Extrapolating from a famous passage contained in Keynes's review (Keynes, 1931) of Ramsey's posthumous book (Ramsey, 1931), many interpreters claimed that Keynes accepted Ramsey's criticisms of *TP* and adhered from then on to his subjective approach to probability theory. If true, this assertion would destroy the continuity in Keynes's thought not only in the field of probability philosophy but also as between *TP* and *GT*, making meaningless his subsequent references to the weight of argument. O'Donnell rightly maintains that this crucial interpretive issue should be discussed in the light of all the relevant writings of Keynes before and after the alleged conversion around 1931 (O'Donnell, 1990). After an accurate analysis of this kind, he advances seven arguments in favour of the continuity thesis. Further arguments have been put forward by other interpreters (in particular Carabelli, 1988). On this occasion, I do not want to assess these arguments, which on the whole seem to me compelling, but only to complement them with some further considerations from the specific point of view of the weight of argument.

I observe first that both Keynes (1973a [1921]) and Ramsey (1931) believe that the theory of probability is a normative discipline since its rules of inference are based on well-precise rationality requirements. However, according to Ramsey probability theory has to be seen as a branch of formal logic, whereas according to Keynes it has to be treated as an extension of logic to non-demonstrative inference. Before reading Ramsey's own version, Keynes rejected subjective probability theory because of its psychological and arbitrary nature:

> in the sense important to logic, probability is not subjective. It is not, that is to say, subject to human caprice. A proposition is not probable because we think it so. When once the facts are given which determine our knowledge, what is probable or improbable in these circumstances has been fixed objectively, and is independent of our opinion. The theory of probability is logical, therefore, because it is concerned with the degree of belief which is rational to entertain in given conditions.
>
> (*TP*, p. 4)

However, in his review of Ramsey's posthumous book he readily admits that 'Ramsey [...] succeeds in showing that the calculus of probabilities simply amounts to a set of rules for ensuring that the system of degrees of belief which we hold shall be a *consistent* system. Thus, the calculus of probabilities belongs to formal logic' (Keynes, 1972 [1933]), pp. 338–9). According to Keynes, Ramsey's proof that the subjective theory may be conceived of as normative qualifies such a theory as an acceptable theory, but only in the case of demonstrative arguments where the inference may be understood as a logical implication; and the weight of argument is one. This, however, is an extreme case that applies only when probabilities are numerical. On this point Keynes did not change his mind, as explicitly confirmed in his correspondence with Townshend in 1938: 'a main point to which I would call your attention is that, on my theory of probability, the probabilities themselves are non-numerical' (Keynes, 1979a) [1938], p. 289). This argument is sufficient to preclude a conversion of Keynes to subjective probability theory, with the only possible exception of the extreme case of numerical probabilities coupled with a weight of argument equal to 1. In any case, whenever the relevant knowledge is incomplete and the weight of argument is less than 1, the probability inference, to be distinguished from the classical probability calculus to which Ramsey referred, follows different rules from those that Keynes discussed in *TP* and tried to apply to economic decisions in *GT*. This is especially the case with induction, statistical inference (see Carabelli, 1988, chs. 4–7) and causal inference (see Vercelli, 1991; 2001).

The second issue discussed by Keynes in his alleged retreat is the nature of initial, or a priori, probabilities that provide the basis of the inference. Here Keynes declares that he yields to Ramsey, agreeing with him that 'the basis of our degrees of belief – or the *a priori* probabilities, as they used to be called – is part of our human outfit, perhaps given us merely by natural selection' (Keynes, 1931, pp. 338–39). This is not far from his previous point of view as expressed in *TP* (see Carabelli, 1988). It is, however, inconsistent with the assertion, often iterated in *TP*, that probability statements are 'objective' in the sense of logic (see the quotation above). This assertion was a source of countless misunderstandings with his readers since, as became evident with Ramsey's criticisms, many interpreters mainly focused on this specific point. With this assertion Keynes wanted to emphasize the irreconcilable distance between his theory and the pre-Ramsey subjective theory by emphasizing that the degree of probability is not to be taken as psychological or arbitrary belief but as the one 'which it is rational for *us* to entertain' (*TP*, p. 35). The word 'objective' does not aim to have deontological overtones but only to emphasize its non-arbitrary relation with rationality; and the word 'logic' does not refer to formal logic, or to the logic of implication, characterizing demonstrative arguments but the extension of logic to non-demonstrative arguments. The acceptance of Ramsey's assertion that initial probabilities are intersubjective rather than objective does not change Keynes's view of probabilistic inference. The crucial difference with Ramsey, before and after 1931, lies in a radically different view of the relationship between probability theory and rationality: 'in attempting to distinguish "rational" degrees of belief from beliefs in general he was not yet, I think, quite successful' (Keynes, 1972 [1933]), pp. 338–9). In fact, in Ramsey the rationality requirements of probabilistic inference are too strong for a general theory of probability as they apply only to a very limited subset of probabilities when they can be expressed as numerical and the weight of argument is one. In contrast, the initial probabilities may be explained in terms of the logic of discovery, which in Ramsey has no clear-cut rationality requirements. In Keynes, on the other hand, the probabilistic inference continues to be conceived of as 'relative ... to the principles of *human* reason ... does not presume perfect logical insight, and ... is ... relative to human powers' (*TP*, p. 35). Ramsey's approach, as pursued in particular in his sketch of natural logic, induces Keynes to broaden the scope of non-demonstrative inference whose validity is now seen as relative not only to the premises and background knowledge but also to the pragmatic and semantic context. This may explain the growing attention given to social psychology in *GT*, particularly in the passages where Keynes attributes a crucial role to uncertainty, but this does not change the essential outlines of his theory of probability inference.

The new point of view adopted by Keynes blurs the clear demarcation put forward in *TP* between rational and non-rational choice based on 'objective' criteria. This stimulates Keynes to investigate in more depth the grey zone between rational choice in the *TP* sense and non-rational choices[3] based, as in the real world, on the interaction between subjective beliefs and intersubjective beliefs (conventions). As we have seen in section 4, the practical role of the weight of argument refers exactly to this borderline zone of bounded rationality, so that its revival in *GT* is altogether appropriate and must be taken very seriously (Vercelli, 2005).

In *GT* the weight of argument plays a crucial role in the central argument of Keynes. In its absence it would be very difficult to demonstrate the inability of the market to regulate itself. In particular, Keynes does not deny that an excess supply of labour may bring about a reduction in money wages; this would reduce the money supply in real terms and this should reduce the rate of interest, so increasing investment and reabsorbing the involuntary unemployment. The reason why this virtuous interaction between real and monetary markets is unreliable is the increase in perceived uncertainty triggered by deflation, leading to a reduction in the weight of argument that shifts the liquidity preference schedule upwards and the marginal efficiency of capital downwards, offsetting the potentially positive effects of deflation.

If we assume soft uncertainty, as classical economics and DTU do, an increase in the perceived risk of a recession associated with wage deflation does not necessarily shift the two curves in a perverse direction since, at least in principle, the additional risk may be insured through hedging techniques or issuing 'Arrow securities' (see Arrow, 1964). In contrast, in the case of hard uncertainty the effects of a change in the weight of argument cannot be insured, so that uncertainty aversion (or second-order risk aversion) shifts the curves in the wrong direction, jeopardizing the process of market adjustment. From the analytic point of view a way out has been concocted by assuming that the liquidity preference curve becomes horizontal at a level of the rate of interest higher than the one that would assure full employment equilibrium (Modigliani, 1944). This way of giving foundations to Keynesian analysis and policy, promoted by the neoclassical synthesis, should be discarded as ad hoc from the point of view of theory and empirical evidence. In contrast, the approach based on the weight of argument provides the proper foundations for the central message of Keynes, namely, that the market may be unable to regulate itself so that full employment equilibrium can be restored and maintained only through judicious policies of intervention in the economy by the state.

7.7 Concluding remarks

The concept of weight of argument has been neglected for a long time even by interpreters sympathetic to the basic message of *GT* who believed that this concept was unimportant, outdated or even wrong. In this chapter we have suggested an interpretation of the concept of weight of argument that we believe to be consistent with the spirit of Keynes's approach and that permits us to confirm the substantial correctness and analytical potential of that approach in the light of the recent advances of DTU. This interpretation has confirmed the practical relevance of the concept, overcoming the doubts expressed by Keynes himself, as well as its crucial role as a foundation for the crucial theoretical and policy message of Keynes. It is thus possible and opportune to resume the research programme that Keynes suggested, with some timidity, to analyse the role of the weight of argument in economic decisions.

Notes

1. By introducing the usual criterion of normalization of probability measures $K + I = 1$ (a criterion that Keynes himself had utilized in *TP*, for example on page 348), this measure also subsumes the first definition.
2. A list of interpreters emphasizing discontinuity in Keynes's views on probability may be found in O'Donnell (1990, p. 56), while a list of interpreters claiming continuity may be found in Bateman (1990, p. 73).
3. This does not mean that these choices are necessarily irrational in the light of more comprehensive concepts of rationality (see Vercelli, 2005).

References

Arrow, K. (1964), 'The Role of Securities in the Optimal Allocation of Risk-Bearing', *Review of Economic Studies*, 31, pp. 91–6.

Basili, M. and Vercelli, A. (1998), 'Environmental Option Values, Uncertainty Aversion and Learning', in G. Chichilnisky, G. Heal and A. Vercelli (eds), *Sustainability: Dynamics and Uncertainty*, Dordrecht: Kluwer, pp. 223–42.

Bateman, B. W. (1990), 'The Elusive Logical Relation: An Essay on Change and Continuity in Keynes's Thought', in D. E. Moggridge, *Keynes, Macroeconomics and Method*, Elgar: Aldershot, pp. 73–84.

Camerer, C. and Weber, M. (1992), 'Recent Developments in Modelling Preferences: Uncertainty and Ambiguity', *Journal of Risk and Uncertainty*, 5, pp. 325–70.

Carabelli, A. (1988), *On Keynes's Method*, London: Macmillan.

Davidson, P. (1988), 'A Technical Definition of Uncertainty and the Long-run Non-neutrality of Money', *Cambridge Journal of Economics*, 12 (3), pp. 329–37.

—— (1991), 'Is Probability Theory Relevant for Uncertainty? A Post-Keynesian Perspective', *Journal of Economic Perspectives*, 5 (1), pp. 129–43.

de Finetti B. (1937), 'La prévision: ses lois logiques, ses sources subjectives', *Annales de l'Institute Henry Poincaré*, 7, pp. 1–68. Trans.: 'Foresight: Its Logical Laws, Its Subjective Sources', in H. E. Kyburg, Jr. and H. E. Smokler (eds), *Studies in Subjective Probability*, New York (1964): Wiley and Sons, pp. 93–158.

Dow, J. and Werlang, S. R. C. (1992), 'Uncertainty Aversion, Risk Aversion, and the Optimal Choice of Portfolio', *Econometrica*, 60, pp. 197–204.

Kelsey, D. and Quiggin, J. (1992), 'Theories of Choice under Ignorance and Uncertainty', *Journal of Economic Surveys*, 6 (2), pp. 133–53.

Keynes, J. M. (1931), 'Ramsey as a Philosopher', *New Statesman and Nation*, 3 October; in vol. X of *The Collected Writings of John Maynard Keynes*, pp. 336–9.

—— (1972 [1933]), *Essays in Biography*, Vol. X of *The Collected Writings of John Maynard Keynes*, London: Macmillan.

—— (1973a [1921]), *A Treatise on Probability*, Vol. VIII of *The Collected Writings of John Maynard Keynes*, London: Macmillan.

—— (1973b [1936]), *The General Theory of Employment, Interest and Money*, Vol. VII of *The Collected Writings of John Maynard Keynes,*. London: Macmillan.

—— (1973c [1937]), 'From the *Quarterly Journal of Economics*', in *The General Theory and After: 2. Defence and Development*, Vol. XIV of *The Collected Writings of John Maynard Keynes*), London: Macmillan, pp. 109–23.

—— (1979a [1938]), Letter to H. Townshend, 27 July 1938, in *The General Theory and After: A Supplement*, Vol. XXIX of *The Collected Writings of John Maynard Keynes*, London: Macmillan, pp. 288–9.

—— (1979b [1938]), Letter to Hugh Townshend, 7 December 1938, in *The General Theory and After: A Supplement*, Vol. XXIX of *The Collected Writings of John Maynard Keynes*, London: Macmillan, pp. 293–4.

—— (1981), *Activities 1922–1929: The Return to Gold and Industrial Policy*, Vol. XXIX of *The Collected Writings of John Maynard Keynes*, London: Macmillan.

Luini, L. (ed.) (1999), *Uncertain Decisions: Bridging Theory and Experiments*, Dordrecht: Kluwer.

Modigliani, F. (1944), 'Liquidity Preference and the Theory of Interest and Money', *Econometrica*, 17 (1), pp. 45–88.

O'Donnell, R. (1989), *Keynes: Philosophy, Economics and Politics*, London: Macmillan.

—— (1990), 'Continuity in Keynes's Conception of Probability', in D. E. Moggridge, *Keynes, Macroeconomics and Method*, Elgar: Aldershot, pp. 53–72.

Ramsey, F. P. (1931), *The Foundations of Mathematics and Other Logical Essays*, ed. R. Braithwaite, London: Routledge & Kegan Paul.

Runde, J. (1990), 'Keynesian Uncertainty and the Weight of Arguments', *Economics and Philosophy*, 6, pp. 275–92.

Savage, L. J. (1954), *The Foundations of Statistics*, New York: John Wiley and Sons. Revised and enlarged edition, New York: Dover, 1972.

Vercelli, A. (1991), *Methodological Foundations of Macroeconomics. Keynes and Lucas*, Cambridge: Cambridge University Press.

—— (1992), 'Causality and Economic Analysis: A Survey', in A. Vercelli and N. Dimitri (eds), *Macroeconomics: A Survey of Research Strategies*, Oxford: Oxford University Press, pp. 393–421.

—— (1999), 'The Recent Advances in Decision Theory under Uncertainty: A Non-Technical Introduction', in L. Luini (ed.), *Uncertain Decisions: Bridging Theory and Experiments*, Dordrecht: Kluwer, pp. 237–60.

—— (2001), 'Epistemic Causality and Hard Uncertainty: A Keynesian Approach', in M. C. Galavotti, P. Suppes and D. Costantini (eds), *Stochastic Causality*, Stanford, CA: CSLI Publications, pp.141–56.

—— (2002), 'Uncertainty, Rationality and Learning: A Keynesian Perspective', in S. C. Dow and J. Hillard (eds), *Keynes, Uncertainty and the Global Economy*, vol. 2, Elgar: Cheltenham, pp. 88–105.

—— (2005), 'Rationality, Learning and Complexity', in B. Agarwal and A. Vercelli (eds), *Psychology, Rationality and Economic Behaviour: Challenging Standard Assumption*, Basingstoke and New York: Palgrave Macmillan (IEA series), pp. 58–83.

von Neumann, J. and Morgenstern O. (1944), *Theory of Games and Economic Behaviour*, Princeton: Princeton University Press.

8
The Relevance Quotient: Keynes and Carnap

Domenico Costantini and Ubaldo Garibaldi

8.1 Introduction

The well-known, but not widely read, book of John Maynard Keynes, *A Treatise on Probability* (hereafter *TP*) (Keynes, 1973a [1921])—essentially written more than ten years before it was published in 1921 by Macmillan & and Co. in London—consists of five parts. Part II, entitled "Fundamental Theorems," comprises Chapters 10–17. In the introductory chapter of this part the author says

> In Part I we have been occupied with the epistemology of our subject, that is to say, with what we know about the characteristics and the justification of probable knowledge. In Part II I pass to its formal logic. I am not certain of how much positive value this Part will prove to the reader. My object in it is to show that [...] we can deduce by rigorous methods out of simple and precise definitions the usually accepted results.
>
> (*TP*, p. 125)

Here the influence of Bertrand Russell is clear, as the author himself acknowledges at the beginning of Chapter 10. After having stated the axioms of probability and recalled some basic theorems of necessary (logical) inference, Keynes in Chapter 14 of *TP*, titled "The Fundamental Theorems of Probable Inference," gives the proofs of what he calls the "most fundamental theorems of Probability" (*TP*, p. 158). He proves the sum and product rules (after having defined the notions of irrelevance and independence), theorems on relevance, Bayes's theorem (which he calls the "inverse principle", and some theorems on the combination of premises. In section 8 (the final one) he introduces the notion of coefficient of influence or coefficient of dependence. We focus on this coefficient in the present chapter. After sketching a brief history of this notion, we consider a condition of invariance defined in term of a coefficient very close to Keynes's. Then we show some consequences of this condition in both inductive logic and statistical mechanics, and we present two economic applications of the condition of invariance. Finally, we make some comments on probability in economics.

8.2   From the coefficient of influence to the relevance quotient

First of all, we would like to discuss briefly the question of the paternity of the notion of coefficient of influence. Rudolf Carnap, who in 1950 (Carnap, 1950, s. 66) gave to the "coefficient of influence" the name of "relevance quotient," wrote: "Keynes gives a definition of the relevance quotient [...] and a series of theorems on this concept, based upon unpublished notes by W. E. Johnson" (Carnap, 1950, p. 357).

This sentence is obscure. In fact, regarding the coefficient of influence it is not clear whether either the definition or the related theorems are of William Ernst Johnson. On this respect, Keynes is rather clearer. In fact, he explicitly says (Keynes, 1973a [1921], p. 150 footnote)

> The substance of the propositions (41) to (49) below [theorems regarding the coefficient of influence] (Johnson, 1924; 1932) is derived in its entirely from his [Johnson's] notes—the exposition only is mine.

Thus Keynes explicitly recognizes the theorems are from Johnson but this does not regard the definition of the quotient. In this respect he says (*TP*, p. 151):

> It is first of all necessary to introduce a new symbol. Let us write

$$[\text{Def.XV.}]\, a/bh = \left\{a^h b\right\} a/h. \tag{1}$$

We may call $\{a^h b\}$ the *coefficient of influence* of b upon a on hypothesis h [...]; we may also call $\{a^h b\}$ the *coefficient of dependence* between a and b on hypothesis h.

The symbolism of Keynes is cumbersome essentially because he did not use any notation for the probability function, as is clearly shown by (1). In the next section, when we set out the definition in modern symbols, we will make the meaning of (1) clear. At present we note, first, that, with regard to his Definition XV, Keynes speaks of a new symbol; second, that, in saying that propositions (41) to (49) are from Johnson, he implicitly denies that the definition was suggested by this author. Hence we are entitled to suppose that the formal statement of the notion of coefficient of influence is his own. We stress that in no way this diminishes the great intellectual debt Keynes owes to Johnson. To underline this debt we recall the dedication that begins Irving John Good's *The Estimation of Probabilities*: "This monograph is dedicated to William Ernst Johnson the teacher of John Maynard Keynes and Harold Jeffrey" (Good, 1965).

To the best of our knowledge nobody used the coefficient of influence until Carnap began his work on inductive logic. This author stressed the importance of the study of the relevance of a sentence i upon an hypothesis h given evidence e. Carnap singled out two ways of expressing the relevance: one is the relevance quotient, $\dfrac{c(h, e \wedge i)}{c(h, e)}$; the other is the relevance difference $c(h, e \wedge i) - c(h, e)$. These notions are introduced by means of the quantitative concept of confirmation $c(h, e)$, to be read: the degree of confirmation of h with respect to e, which is the probability function Carnap used in his studies on the foundation of probability. After having stated a few theorems about the relevance quotient, Carnap built up his theory of relevance in terms of the relevance difference, thus neglecting the coefficient of influence. However, before moving on to the theory of relevance, referring to this coefficient, Carnap wrote

> The concept explained will hardly be used in the remainder of this book. It has been represented in this section in order to call attention to an interesting concept which deserves further investigation.
>
> (Carnap, 1950, p. 360)

But this investigation was not performed in the following 30 years. Once more the coefficient of influence, in the meantime turned into the relevance quotient, was neglected. At the end of the 1970s we have used this notion to introduce a condition capable of solving a problem Carnap left open. We shall deal extensively with this problem after specifying the context in which we work.

8.3 The formal definition of the relevance quotient

We now move to the formalization of the coefficient of influence, first defining the notion of relevance quotient. But in order to provide this definition we must introduce the probability (function) we are using.

8.3.1 Regular probabilities

Let $X_1, X_2, \ldots, X_n, \ldots$ be a sequence of random variables denoting n individuals of a system each bearing an attribute or, as we prefer to say, belonging to a cell of the class $\{1, \ldots, d\}$. $D := X_1 = j_1 \wedge \ldots \wedge X_i = j_i \wedge \ldots \wedge X_n = j_n$, for each i, $j_i \in \{1, \ldots, d\}$, is the conjunction of n (atomic) propositions specifying the cells to which belong the first n individuals of the sequence. Thus D is the description of the (individuals of the) system with respect to the attributes being considered. Carnap called D a state description. We call an individual distribution D or, until section 8.4, the evidence (data). n, that is, the number of individuals considered in D, is the evidence size.

$$P(X_{n+1} = j \mid D), \quad j \in \{1, \ldots, d\} \tag{2}$$

is the final (conditional) probability of $X_{n+1} = j$ given D. Other names used for (2) are "predictive probability" and "prediction rule."

It is worth noting at this point that the probability function defined by (2) is a relative notion, that is, a function of two variables: $X_{n+1} = j$, the hypothesis, and D, the evidence. Moreover, we recall that Keynes called "premiss" (but sometime also "hypothesis" as in the definition of the coefficient of influence) what we call evidence, "conclusion" what we call hypothesis, and "argument" what we call probability function.

It can be useful to have at one's disposal an absolute probability, too. Such probabilities are to be used when the evidence is devoid of factual content, that is, when data are lacking. We shall denote by V evidence devoid of factual content, briefly, a void evidence. If this is the case, the evidence size is 0. An absolute probability is a function of one variable and can be defined as a special case of (2). In fact, if the evidence is void, (2) becomes $P(X_{n+1} = j \mid V)$, briefly $P(X_{n+1} = j)$. This is the initial (absolute) probability of $X_{n+1} = j$.

The axioms governing probability functions are:

A1. (non negativity) $P(X_{n+1} = j \mid D) \geq 0, j \in \{1, \ldots, d\}$;

A2. (addition rule) $\sum_{j=1}^{d} P(X_{n+1} = j \mid D) = 1$;

A3. (multiplication rule)

$$P(X_{n+1} = j \wedge X_{n+2} = g \mid D) = P(X_{n+1} = j \mid D)P(X_{n+2} = g \mid D \wedge X_{n+1} = j),$$
$$j, g \in \{1, \ldots, d\}.$$

Beside the probability axioms we consider some further conditions. The first is:

C1. (regularity) $P(X_{n+1} = j \mid D) > 0, j \in \{1,\ldots,d\}$.

For regular probability functions we define Keynes's relevance quotient (at D) of g against j, corresponding to (1), as

$$K_j^g(D) := \frac{P(X_{n+2} = j \mid D \wedge X_{n+1} = g)}{P(X_{n+2} = j \mid D)}, \quad j \neq g. \tag{3}$$

The condition of regularity ensures that $K_j^g(D)$ is never meaningless. Considering the Keynes's symbology, we see that a/bh is $P(a \mid h \wedge b)$, the probability of a given h and b while a/h is $P(a \mid h)$. Hence, if in (1) we put $X_{n+2} = j$ for a, D for h and $X_{n+1} = g$ for b, we have (3).

Truly the name of $K_j^g(D)$ should be heterorelevance quotient. The reason is that one can define a homorelevance quotient as

$$K_j^j(D) := \frac{P(X_{n+2} = j \mid D \wedge X_{n+1} = j)}{P(X_{n+2} = j \mid D)}. \tag{4}$$

We have called $K_j^g(D)$ relevance quotient because in what follows we do not deal with homorelevance quotients.

In order to grasp the meaning of the relevance quotient, consider an ordered sequence of individuals. With regard to this sequence we are interested in the cell the $(n + 2)$th term of the sequence, X_{n+2}, belongs to. We know D, that is, the cells the individuals which take up the first n places of the sequence belong to. On the basis of these data we consider the probability that X_{n+2} belongs to the cell j. This is $P(X_{n+2} = j \mid D)$. Now suppose that it becomes known to us that the $(n + 1)$th individual of the sequence belong to the cell g other than j, that is, we know that $X_{n+1} = g$ holds true. With this additional datum, the evidence becomes $D \wedge X_{n+1} = g$ and the probability we are interested in is $P(X_{n+2} = j \mid D \wedge X_{n+1} = g)$. (3) is the ratio between these two probabilities. Thus, the relevance quotient measures the strength of the further, so to speak, adverse datum $X_{n+1} = g$ on the probability of $X_{n+2} = j$.

With this scenario clear, we can imagine a more natural relevance quotient. Suppose that the individuals we are considering are experimental trials, such as the repeated observations of the moon's crater Manilius or the computation of the number of persons killed by horse kicks. For the sake of simplicity, we focus on a familiar experiment, namely, drawing from an urn in which there are balls of d different colors. If this is the case, the evidence describes the colors of the first n drawn balls. On the basis of this data we consider the probability that the color of the next drawn ball, X_{n+1}, is j. This is $P(X_{n+1} = j|D)$. Then we perform a further trial, the $(n + 1)$th, and ascertain that g, different from j, is the color of the $(n + 1)$th drawn ball. The evidence now is $D \wedge X_{n+1} = g$, and we are interested in the color of the ball we shall draw in the next trial, that is, the $(n + 2)$th. Hence the probability we are looking for is $P(X_{n+2} = j|D \wedge X_{n+1} = g)$. If we make the quotient of these two, so to speak, subsequent probabilities we have

$$Q_j^g(D) = \frac{P(X_{n+2} = j \mid D \wedge X_{n+1} = g)}{P(X_{n+1} = j \mid D)}, \quad j \neq g. \tag{5}$$

This is what we call Carnap's relevance quotient, which is slightly different from Keynes's. We refer (5) to Carnap also if it has no role in Carnap's derivation, as it is essential in Carnap's tradition (see Costantini, 1979; 1987). In fact, (3) and (5) refer to two different situations. (5) measures the strength the observation of a color different from j has upon the probability that j is the color of the ball that we shall draw in the next trial. This scenario is much more realistic than that considered in (3). (5) refers to the evolution of a sequence of experimental observations comparing probabilities that it is very natural to compare when referring to such observations. Luckily, when echangeability holds true, the two quotients have the same numerical value.

8.3.2 Exchangeable probabilities

We shall work with exchangeable probabilities. As a consequence both quotients (3) and (5) have the same value, as we shall see. But to show this we must define the next condition we consider:

C2. (exchangeability) $P(X_{n+1} = j \wedge X_{n+2} = g|D) = P(X_{n+1} = g \wedge X_{n+2} = j|D)$.

Keynes did not consider exchageability, but Johnson did. This author called C2 the combination-postulate (see Johnson, 1932). Exchangeability was studied by Frank Plumpton Ramsey in unpublished work from the late 1920s (see von Plato, 1994, p. 246n). This condition became famous when Bruno de Finetti draw from it his celebrated representation theorem (de Finetti, 1930). Carnap called C2 symmetry and based on it his theory of symmetrical c-functions. Exchangeability has many consequences.

The most important is de Finetti's theorem, but we shall not take it into account because we work with a finite number of individuals, while the representation theorem accounts for denumerable domains.

The first consequence of **C2** we consider is the equality of (3) and (5). As we shall see in the next subsection, from **C2** follows the equidistribution of random variables, which means that the probability of belonging to a given cell is unaffected by the considered random variable or individual provided it does not belong to the evidence. Thus

$$P(X_{n+2} = j \mid D) = P(X_{n+1} = j \mid D) \tag{6}$$

and from this follows the equality of (3) and (5).

Another consequence of **C2** is that it becomes superfluous to specify in (2) the individuals involved in the hypothesis and in the data. It is enough to consider attributes and statistical distributions. More exactly, we have

$$P(X_{n+1} = j \mid D) = f(j, n_1, \ldots, n_d), \quad j \in \{1, \ldots, d\} \tag{7}$$

where $\Sigma_{j=1}^{d} n_j = n$. Hence $\mathbf{n} := (n_1, \ldots, n_j, \ldots, n_d)$ is the vector of the frequencies that the evidence indicates in the various cells; it is the frequency distribution of D. We call the frequency n_j the occupation number of the cell j, and $\mathbf{n}$ the occupation vector of D. As we have said, Keynes did not consider exchangeability, and so did not consider occupation vectors. In contrast, Carnap considered such vectors, calling them "structure descriptions" or "statistical distributions." (7) asserts that probability (2) is a function of a cell, j, and an occupation vector, $\mathbf{n}$; that is, what matters is the cell considered in the hypothesis and the numbers of individuals in the various cells, not which ones they are. Then we can write for short:

$$P(X_{n+1} = j \mid D) := P(j \mid \mathbf{n}), \quad j \in \{1, \ldots, d\}. \tag{8}$$

(8) reminds us that we are considering an exchangeable probability. Referring to it, we shall speak of the probability j given $\mathbf{n}$.

In the case in which **C2** holds, the relevance quotient (3), beside j and g, depends upon $\mathbf{n}$ and no longer upon D. We shall recall this by writing $K_j^g(\mathbf{n})$ and $Q_j^g(\mathbf{n})$ instead of (3) and (5). Further, if **C2** and then (6) holds, $K_j^g(\mathbf{n}) = Q_j^g(\mathbf{n})$.

In order to write this quotient using the terminology suggested by (8), it is worth introducing a new symbol for the occupation vector after the new observation, which we suppose relates to an individual belonging to the cell g, has been added to the data. If this is the case the evidence size becomes $n + 1$ and the occupation number of the cell g become $n_g + 1$. We denote by $\mathbf{n}^g = (n_1, \ldots, n_g + 1, \ldots, n_d)$ the occupation vector of this new evidence. Thus the relevance quotients, in the case of exchangeability, can now be written as

$$K_j^g(\mathbf{n}) = Q_j^g(\mathbf{n}) = \frac{P(j \mid \mathbf{n}^g)}{P(j \mid \mathbf{n})}, \quad j \neq g.$$

8.3.3 Exchangeability, independence and relevance quotient

A particular case of great importance is the relevance quotient at V, that is to say, the relevance quotient determined with respect to a void evidence. For Keynes's coefficent this is:

$$K_j^g(V) = \frac{P(X_2 = j \mid X_1 = g)}{P(X_2 = j)}, \quad j \neq g, \tag{9}$$

which we shall call the relevance quotient at V. As is shown by the alternative name Keynes used for the relevance quotient, he recognizes that this quotient is a way to deal with stochastic dependence. If we recall that exchangeability is a particular case of stochastic dependence, it is natural to imagine that exchangeability can be defined *via* the relevance quotient. With a proviso, this is actually the case. For the sake of simplicity, we shall consider only two cells, say H (head) and T (tail), and the relevance quotient at V. What we are saying can be immediately extended to the general case. In the case of two individuals, say X_1 and X_2, we consider the probabilities of $X_i = H \equiv H_i$, $X_i = T \equiv T_i$. If this is the case two relevance quotients can be taken into account

$$K_H^T(V) = \frac{P(H_2 \mid T_1)}{P(H_2)} \quad \text{and} \quad K_T^H(V) = \frac{P(T_2 \mid H_1)}{P(T_2)}.$$

Now let us suppose that the relevance quotient is symmetric, that is

$$K_H^T(V) = K_T^H(V) = q. \tag{10}$$

For (9) and (10) we have

$$P(T_1 \wedge H_2) = qP(T_1)P(H_2),$$
$$P(H_1 \wedge T_2) = qP(X_1)P(T_2).$$

When $P(H_1) = x$ and thus $P(T_1) = 1 - x$, and $P(H_2) = y$ and thus $P(T_2) = 1 - y$, it is easy to check that

$$P(T_1 \wedge H_2) = q(1 - x)y$$
$$P(H_1 \wedge T_2) = qx(1 - y). \tag{11}$$

Exchangeability implies $P(T_1 \wedge H_2) = P(H_1 \wedge T_2)$, which holds true only if in (11), besides the condition of symmetry $Q_H^T(V) = Q_T^H(V) = q$, we have $x = y$, that is, equidistribution of X_1 and X_2. Hence the symmetry of $K_H^T(V)$ is not sufficient for exchangeability.

Futher, we consider

$$P(H_1) = P(H_1 \wedge H_2) + P(H_1 \wedge T_2)$$
$$P(H_2) = P(H_1 \wedge H_2) + P(T_1 \wedge H_2)$$

then, by probability calculus,

$$P(H_1 \wedge H_2) = x - qx(1 - y)$$
$$P(H_1 \wedge H_2) = y - q(1 - x)y,$$

that is

$$y - x = (1 - x)yq - x(1 - y)q = (y - x)q. \tag{12}$$

In only two cases does this equality hold: either $q = 1$ or $q \neq 1 \wedge y = x$.
The case $q = 1$, from (11), implies:

$$P(H_1 \wedge T_2) = P(H_1)P(T_2),$$

that is, X_1 and X_2 are stochastically independent. If this is the case, x and y, that is $P(X_1 = H)$ and $P(X_2 = T)$ can be chosen at pleasure. This means that $P(X_1 = T) \neq P(X_2 = T)$ and $P(X_1 = H \wedge X_2 = T) \neq P(X_1 = T \wedge X_2 = H)$. In fact, as is well known, stochastic independence does not implies equidistribution.

In the second case $q \neq 1 \wedge y = x$ (where $P(X_1 = H) = P(X_2 = H)$, that is equidistribution), the symmetry of the K-relevance quotient implies exchangeability, that is, $P(X_1 = T) = P(X_2 = T)$ and $P(X_1 = H \wedge X_2 = T) = P(X_1 = T \wedge X_2 = H)$. Thus the symmetry of the K-relevance quotient, that is, (10) implies exchangeability only if equidistribution is added.

In this case, when the K-relevance quotient is equal to 1, then independence and equidistribution hold.

The relationship between exchangeability and symmetry is simpler and more powerful with regard to $Q_j^g(\cdot)$. In fact, from $Q_j^g(D) = Q_g^j(D)$ it follows immediately that $P(X_{n+2} = j \wedge X_{n+1} = g \wedge D) = P(X_{n+1} = j | D)$ $P(X_{n+1} = g | D) = P(X_{n+2} = g \wedge X_{n+1} = i \wedge D)$, that is, exchangebility holds true. It means that the symmetry of Carnap's $Q_j^g(\cdot)$ implies exchangeability and the symmetry of Keynes's $K_j^g(\cdot)$, the converse not being true. For this reason Carnap's coefficient has relegated Keynes's in the characterization of predictive inferences. In all the following we shall use Carnap's symmetric coefficient $Q_j^g(\cdot)$, but Keynes's followers can appreciate that its value is equal to Keynes's $K_j^g(\cdot)$.

Recall that $Q_j^g(\cdot)$ is an etero-relevance quotient; it is a measure of the variation of the probability of an attribute after a failure. If it is less (greater) than 1 it denotes, from a subjective or logical standpoint, a decrease (increase) in the degree of belief or confirmation after the failure. It follows that the probability of observing an attribute is an increasing (decreasing) function of the observed successes. If it is equal to 1, the observations are independent and equidistributed. Hence the relevance quotient is a companion of the correlation coefficient.

8.3.4 Invariant probabilities

The last condition we consider concerns the relevance quotient. This condition is stated for exchangeable probabilities. Let **n** and **n**' be occupation vectors whose evidence sizes are n, while $j \neq g$ and $k \neq m$ cells, then

C3 (invariance) $Q_j^g(\mathbf{n}) = Q_l^k(\mathbf{n}')$.

We call invariant a probability function for which **C3** holds. Invariance means that, apart from a parameter that we specify below, the relevance quotient is unaffected by both the considered cells and the occupation vector, but it depends only upon the evidence size. For this reason we shall write $Q(n)$ instead of $Q_j^g(\mathbf{n})$.

A first trivial consequence of **C3** concerns the relevance quotient at V. As we have just seen, there is no need to specify the individuals and the cells involved in the relevance quotient. Moreover, in $Q_j^g(V)$ the evidence size is 0. If we take this into account, it becomes natural to use for this notion a symbol η, following Carnap, that is, we write

$$\eta = Q_j^g(V) = \frac{P(X_2 = j | X_1 = g)}{P(X_1 = j)}, \quad j \neq g.$$

Another immediate consequence of **C3** is that the probability (2), which obviously depends upon j, only depends upon the occupation number of the cell j, that is n_j, and the evidence size, n. In fact, for **C3** we have

$$\frac{P(j \mid \mathbf{n}^g)}{P(j \mid \mathbf{n})} = \frac{P(j \mid \mathbf{n}^k)}{P(j \mid \mathbf{n})}, \quad j \neq g, k.$$

Hence $P(j \mid \mathbf{n}^g) = P(j \mid \mathbf{n}^k)$. This means that the probability of the cell j does not vary, changing the occupation number of cells different from j. In other words,

$$P(j \mid \mathbf{n}) = f(j, n_j, n). \tag{13}$$

Carnap called (13) the λ-principle. Thus we have proved that the λ-principle follows from invariance, and we are in a position to say something about the problem Carnap left open. Essentially Carnap's confirmation theory amounts to a search for a well-defined predictive probability, that is to say, to a search for the value of (2). This was done by stating some conditions Carnap regarded as plausible. Thus, besides the probability axioms, he assumed **C1** and **C2**. But these conditions are not enough to determine the value of (2). To arrive at this value he suggested the λ-principle (Carnap, 1980, p. 84), that is, (13). Exchangeability ensures that the probability of j does not depend upon the full evidence but upon its occupation vector. That is, exchangeability cuts down the influence of the evidence to its statistical distribution. The λ-principle further cuts down the influence of the statistical distribution to n_j, the occupation number of the cell, and n, the size of the system. In other words, the λ-principle turns all families of attributes into dicotomies: the cell j and the cell of all individuals not belonging to j.

8.3.5 The main theorem

The λ-principle enabled Carnap to prove that (2) is a linear function of n_j. In other words, Carnap was able to prove the result expressed by (15) below. Yet the λ-principle effectively restricts the dependence of (2) to n_j and n only when one is considering more than two cells. In the case in which we are considering only two cells, say H and T, like in tossing a coin, the occupation vector is (n_H, n_T), and the λ-principle, being automatically satisfied, does not work. For this reason, Carnap was compelled to state a further condition that he called the principle of linearity (Carnap, 1952, p. 98). This principle states that for two cells, that is, when $d = 2$,(2) is a linear function of $n_j, j = 1,2$. This is tantamount to assuming the validity of the result he was not able to prove. At the end of the 1970s (see Costantini, 1979) one of us proved that both the λ-principle and the principle of linearity follow from a single condition, that is, invariance of $Q_j^g(\mathbf{n})$. This proof was very cumbersome. A clue for a new demonstration, simpler and more intuitive (see also Garibaldi and Scalas, 2010), is the following.

8.3.5.1 A new demonstration

Consider the cell a, and call b its complement, given any evidence $p(a|\cdot) + p(b|\cdot) = 1$. By $p(a|m,s)$ we describe the evidence as the number of successes and the number of trials. Hence, on the same evidence $n_a = m$, $n_b = s - m$, the normalization condition can be written as $p(a|m,s) + p(b|s - m,s) = 1$; $p(a) := p(a|0,0)$ is the initial probability, and $p(a) + p(b) = 1$. To calculate $p(a|m,s)$, we consider the pattern $a_1, a_2, \ldots, a_m, b_{m+1}, \ldots, b_s$. Along $a_1, a_2 \ldots a_m$ we have all failures for b, and they are m: then $p(b|m,m) = Q(0) \ldots Q(m-1)p(b)$, and $p(a|m,m) = 1 - p(b|m,m)$ is a function of $Q(0) \ldots Q(m-1)$ and $p(a) = 1 - p(b)$. Along the second part of the path, that is, $b_{m+1}, \ldots, b_s$, we have $s - m$ failures for a, and then $p(a|m,s) = Q_m \ldots Q_{s-1}p(a|m,m)$. Then $p(a|m,s)$ is a function of $Q(0) \ldots Q(s-1)$ and $p(a)$. The same can be done for $p(b|s - m,s)$ by following the pattern $b_1, b_{s-m}, a_{s-m+1}, \ldots, a_s$, from which results a function of $Q(0) \ldots Q(s-1)$ and $p(b)$. The condition $p(a|m,s) + p(b|s - m,s) = 1$ provides a recurrent equation for $Q(i)$ which can be solved in terms of $Q(0)$:

$$\prod_m^{s-1} Q(i) + \prod_{s-m}^{s-1} Q(i) = 1 + \prod_0^{s-1} Q(i),$$

whose solution is, posing $\lambda = \dfrac{Q(0)}{1-Q(0)} = \dfrac{\eta}{1-\eta}$:

$$Q(i) = \frac{\lambda+i}{\lambda+i+1}. \tag{14}$$

If we substitute (14) in the previous formulas, it follows that $P(X_{n+1} = j | D) = \dfrac{\lambda p_j + n_j}{\lambda + n}$. (Q.E.D.).

It is worth noting that Karl Pearson has referred to the problem of reaching the values of (2) as the fundamental problem of practical statistics (Pearson, 1920). With this specification in mind, we shall call main theorem the solution of the problem posed by Pearson. The main theorem was first proved by Johnson (1932), who presumably did not know that a couple of years before Pearson had faced the same problem. However, Johnson's proof was incomplete because it implicitly assumes the equality of all initial probabilities. A satisfactory proof of the main theorem was given by Kemeny (1963). The proof given by Carnap (see Carnap, 1980) is essentially that of Kemeny. All these proofs are based on the λ-principle and, with the exception of Carnap, assume that $d > 2$ and do not worry about dichotomies.

The main theorem states that, if a probability is regular, exchangeable and invariant, then

$$P(X_{n+1} = j \mid D) = \frac{\lambda p_j + n_j}{\lambda + n} \qquad (15)$$

holds, where $p_j = P(X_{n+1} = j)$ is the initial probability of the cell j and

$$\lambda := \frac{\eta}{1 - \eta}. \qquad (16)$$

p_j and λ are free parameters of (15), and $\lambda > 0$ because of regularity. Thus, in order to arrive at specific predictive probabilities, that is, numerical values of (15), we must choose the initial probabilities of each cell and the value of the relevance quotient at V. As a consequence, considering various values of these parameters we arrive at various values of probability. We call λp_j the initial weight of the cell j and $\lambda = \sum_{j=1}^{d} \lambda p_j$ the total weight. As $\lambda + n = \sum_{j=1}^{d} (\lambda p_j + n_j)$, (15) shows that the probability of j is the normalized final weight of j, this being the sum of both its initial weight and its occupation number. If we write (15) as

$$P(X_{n+1} = j \mid D) = \frac{\lambda}{\lambda + n} p_j + \frac{n}{\lambda + n} \frac{n_j}{n}$$

it becomes apparent that the predictive probability is a weighted mean of a prior factor determined before having performed any observation, the initial probability, and an empirical factor, the relative frequency that can be determined only after observations has been performed.

Referring to the definition of λ given in (16), we see that in the case in which $\eta = 1$, λ is meaningless. This means that in (15) λ can grow without limit but cannot be infinite. Thus, stochastic independence appears in (15) as a limiting case. In this limiting case, the final probability is always equal to the initial probability p_j whatever the evidence is. It is easy to realize that positive values of λ introduce a positive correlation while negative values of λ introduce a negative correlation. All proofs of the main theorem given in the line of thought suggested by Johnson consider $0 < \lambda < \infty$. Thus, referring to these studies, we are not entitled to work with negative values of λ. However, the main theorem has been proved for negative values of λ, too (Costantini and Garibaldi, 1991). This extension is not very important for inductive applications, and this is because in the statistical inference only positive values of λ have been considered. In statistical inferences, negative correlation can be deal with assuming only C2 (see Carnap, 1950, p. 207), that is, considering direct inferences. Carnap called "direct" a statistical inference aiming at determining the probabilities of all the possible statistical distributions of a sample drawn from a population whose statistical distribution is known. In other words, when the statistical distribution of the population is known, by using exchangeability and nothing else it is possible to prove that the hypergeometric distribution specifies the probability of all samples that can be drawn from the population. In this case invariance is automatically satisfied.

8.3.6 Inductive applications

We provide two simple inductive applications of the main theorem. The predictive probability (15) may be used to determine the probability of a further observation. In order to show the most simple application of the main theorem, we come back to the example of drawing balls from an urn. Using (15) we can determine the probability that the color of the next drawn ball, X_{n+1}, is $j \in \{1,2,\ldots,d\}$. In order to do this we must fix the values of p_j for all j, that is, the probability of drawing the first ball of color j, and the value of λ. Choosing this value amounts to fixing in what measure the drawing of a ball of a color other that j affects the probability of drawing a ball of color j.

Another more realistic example concerns a clinical trial with dichotomous responses. In this case the objective was to evaluate the effectiveness of a drug (6-mercaptopurine) for the treatment of a deadly disease (acute leukemia). Patients were randomized in pairs to receive either the drug or a placebo. For each pair it was recorded which patient stayed longer in remission, that is, without symptoms of the illness. If it was the drug patient, then the treatment was judged a success, S, otherwise a failure, F. There were pairs of patients in the trial, and the results were as follows:

$$D = S, F, S, S, S, F, S, S, S, S, S, S, S, F, S, S, S, S, S, S, S.$$

Thus, the drug was better than the placebo with 18 of the 21 pairs.

These are the data. A very natural question the investigators may ask themselves is this: having a pair of patients both suffering from that deadly disease, if the first receives the drug and the second a placebo, what is the probability that the former stays longer in remission? A moment's reflection is sufficient to confirm that in the clinical trial we are considering the hypotheses of the main theorem, that is, regularity, exchangeability and invariance, hold. As a consequence we can apply (15). In the case we are considering the cells are two and the occupation vector is (18,3). With these data (15) becomes

$$P(X = S \mid D) = \frac{\lambda p_S + 18}{\lambda + 21} \qquad (17)$$

where X denotes a future pair of patients. In order to have a probability value we must choose the values of the parameters. This can be done along the following lines. First, we suppose we have no evidence about the effectiveness of the drug. For this reason we fix $p_S = p_F = 1/2$. Second, we do not want our initial probabilities to substantially affect the predictive probability. Hence we chose a small value of λ, say 2 or (which is equivalent) we make the relevance quotient at V equal to two thirds. This choice is tantamount to saying that the patient pairs are strongly (positively) correlated: in other words, that the result with one pair affects in a strongly positive way that with a subsequent pair. With these values (17) becomes

$$P(X_{n+1} = S \mid D) = \frac{1+18}{2+21} = 0.83. \qquad (18)$$

It is worth noting that the values of the parameters giving (18) are those that characterize Laplace's celebrated rule of succession. In *TP* Keynes pays a great deal of attention to this rule, concluding that

> it [the rule of succession] is of interest as being one of the most characteristic results of a way of thinking in probability introduced by Laplace, and never thoroughly discarded to this day.
>
> (*TP*, p. 417)

The relevance quotient is an important tool for solving inductive problems but it is useful in other contexts, too, such as with statistical mechanics, population genetics, and macroeconomic modeling. In these applications negative dependence, as given by negative values of λ, may become important. This is actually what happens in statistical mechanics. In the next sections we give some examples of applications in statistical mechanics and macroeconomic modeling: the former because of its importance in the history of science, the latter because we want to show a way of following the route traced by Keynes by using probability in economics.

8.4   Particle statistics

At the end of the previous section we glimpsed the possibility of applying the relevance quotient to contexts other than induction. In dealing with the foundations of probability, Johnson, Keynes, and Carnap all had inductive statistics in mind, especially Keynes, who in Part V of *TP* provides an excellent and profound review of the statistical inferences in the nineteenth century. Like Keynes and Carnap, we, too, have inductive statistics in mind. Aiming at determining predictive probabilities, we have considered sequences of individuals intended to describe the statistical units of a sample drawn from a population. Just as a sample may not have a definite number of units, the evidence must not have a definite size. That is to say, new individuals may always be added to the sequence. All the axioms and conditions we have stated involve a finite number of individuals; but we have not fixed the evidence size once and for all. The reason for this is that, if we leave aside the trivial case in which one examines the whole population, samples drawn from a finite population may always be brought up to date adding one or more new units. This is the case with the evidence too. In a few words, we have considered evidences that could be called open. By forcing this scenario a little, it becomes possible to deal with certain problems of statistical mechanics, for instance particles statistics, as we shall briefly show in a highly abstract way, greatly simplifying the problem in order to account for the basic ideas. Furthermore, in this way we are preparing to undertake our study of equilibrium, especially in economics, in the next section.

In a sense, a quantity of gas is like a population. The molecules of the gas, endlessly in motion, can be seen as the statistical units of the population whose attributes are different velocities consistent with the environment surrounding the gas. The mean velocity of the molecules determines the temperature of the gas. Suppose we are interested in the assumptions justifying the actual temperature of the gas. In order to arrive at the mean values of the velocity of the molecules, we must know the statistical distribution of the molecules with respect to velocities. The reason for our interest in the statistical distribution is that a mean value is unaffected by a change in the individual distribution that does not change the statistical distribution. The mean velocity, too, is unaffected by knowledge of which molecules have which velocity. Even if molecules could be distinguished one from the other—something that nobody has really achieved—the distinction would have no value for the search for the mean velocity. Being ignorant of the statistical distribution of the molecules, we can guess a probability distribution whose domain is the set of all possible individual distributions. In its simplest formulation, this was the problem Boltzmann (see Bach, 1990) pointed out in the second half of the eighteenth century. Having focused on individual distributions, he used the probability of these distributions in order to determine the probabilities of all statistical distributions. More exactly, supposing that all possible individual distributions (of the molecules with respect to velocities) have the same probability, he arrived at explaining the temperature of the gas, in general, the macroscopic behavior of gases of molecules. We want show that, by using the condition we have stated for predictive probability (2), it is possible to justify the equiprobability assumptions of Boltzmann as well as similar assumptions later made for quantum particles.

The analogy between a gas of particles—classical, or quantum—and a population leads us to consider a system of N particles and d single-particle states. The attributes particles may bear are single-particle states that in physics are often called cells (of the μ-space). It is hardly necessary to observe that the name "cell" for attributes we have used comes from statistical mechanics. For simplicity we state that all cells belong to the same energy level and suppose that the system is a void container into which particles are inserted one at the time. This is the simplification and abstraction we have spoken about. X_i, $i = 1, 2, \ldots, N$, the ith particle, denotes the particle that has been inserted into the container when $i-1$ particles are already in it. Each particle goes in a cell and $X_i = j$, $j \in \{1, \ldots, d\}$ is the event that occurs when the ith particle goes in cell j. Once all the particles has been inserted into the container, the individual description is

$$\mathbf{X}^{(N)} := X_1 = j_1 \wedge \ldots \wedge X_n = j_n \wedge \ldots \wedge X_N = j_N, j_i \in \{1, \ldots, j, \ldots, d\}, 1 \le n \le N. \quad (19)$$

It is worth noting that $\mathbf{X}^{(N)}$, formally equal to D, does not refer to data but rather to the individual distribution of the particles in the cells. When j_i varies over all possible values, (19) takes up all possibilities. For instance,

$$X_1 = 1 \wedge \ldots \wedge X_i = 1 \wedge \ldots \wedge X_N = 1 \quad (20)$$

states that all particles are in cell 1. We are interested in the probability of (19) that can be calculated by using the multiplication rule. This rule ensures that

$$P(\mathbf{X}^{(N)}) = P(X_1 = j_1)P(X_2 = j_2 \mid X_1 = j_1)...$$
$$P(X_N = j_N \mid X_1 = j_1 \wedge .... \wedge X_{N-1} = j_{N-1}).$$

Now we assume that the probabilities on the right side of this equality satisfies C2 and C3. It follows that for these probabilities the main theorem holds, and this enables us to calculate the probability of all individual distributions of the system. This distribution is

$$P(\mathbf{X}^{(N)}) = \frac{1}{\lambda^{[N]}p_j} \prod_{i=1}^{d} (\lambda p_j)^{[N_j]} \tag{21}$$

in which the parameters λ and p_j are the same as in (15) while $x^{[n]} = x(x + 1)...(x - n + 1)$ is the Pochhammer symbol. (21) is a probability distribution on the individual distributions of the gas we are considering. It goes without saying that in order to get an actual distribution one must fix the numerical values of the two parameters of (21).

All macroscopic properties of a gas of particles are mean values. Hence in order to determine these values we must have at our disposal a probability distribution on statistical distributions. The sum rule ensures that this probability can be arrived at in a very simple way: summing up the probabilities of all individual distributions consistent with the considered statistical distribution. On the other hand, it is easy to verify that, given an occupation vector (statistical distribution) $\mathbf{N} = (N_1,..., N_j,...,N_d)$, there are

$$\frac{N!}{\prod_{j=1}^{d} N_j!} \tag{22}$$

individual distributions consistent with it. Thanks to exchangeability, all these individual distributions have the same probability. As a consequence, multiplying (21) by (22) we reach the probability of $\mathbf{N}$, that is

$$P_{Po}(\mathbf{N}) = \frac{N!}{\lambda^{[N]}} \prod_{i=1}^{d} \frac{(\lambda p_j)^{[N_j]}}{N_j!}. \tag{23}$$

This is the (generalized) Polya distribution. It is a probability distribution on statistical distributions.

In order to have a definite probability distribution we must fix the numerical values of the parameters of (23). First of all we consider the Bose–Einstein statistics. Putting $p_j = d^{-1}$, for all j, and $\lambda = d$ in (23) we have

$$P_{BE}(\mathbf{N}) = \binom{N+d-1}{N}^{-1}. \tag{24}$$

$\binom{N+d-1}{N}$ is the number of the statistical distributions (occupation vector) of the system. Thus (24) allots the same probability to each occupation vector. Physicists call this uniform probability distribution Bose–Enstein statistics. (24) is the formula governing the behavior of bosons, the particles with integer spin.

The second distribution we take into account is the statistics of Maxwell–Boltzmann. This arises as a limiting case of (23) when $p_j = d^{-1}$, for all j, and $\lambda \to \infty$. If this is the case (23) becomes

$$P_{MB}(\mathbf{N}) = \frac{N!}{\prod N_j!} d^{-N}, \quad j \in \{1,\ldots,d\}. \tag{25}$$

This is again a uniform distribution, not on the occupation vectors but rather on all individual distributions. In fact, that there are d^N individual distributions and (25) allots to all them the same probability, that is, d^{-N}. The uniform probability distribution (25) is known as Maxwell–Boltzmann statistics. (25) is the formula governing the behavior of classical particles.

The last uniform probability distribution we will consider can be reached using a negative value of λ. If we put $p_j = d^{-1}$, for all j, and $\lambda = -d$, (23) becomes

$$P_{FD}(\mathbf{N}) = \binom{d}{N}^{-1}. \tag{26}$$

$\binom{d}{N}$ is the number of the statistical distributions whose occupation numbers are either 0 or 1. Thus (26) allots the same probability to all occupation vectors in which no more that one particle is in a cell. Obviously, in this case $N \leq d$. Physicists call the probability distribution

(26) Fermi–Dirac statistics. This is the formula governing the behavior of fermions, the particles with half-integer spin.

Before going on we shall make a small change in the symbolism we are using, which will greatly assist our exposition. As we have already noted, the symbolism we have so far used for the (predictive) probability looks at an inductive scenario. In this section dealing with particle statistics, we have continued using the same symbolism. It is now clear in what sense we have forced the inductive scenario. The problem we have tackled did not account for the probability of a succeeding observation. Our problem was: what is the probability that a particle of a sequence inserted into the system will be accommodated in a given cell so that a given distribution comes out? Completely explicitly, at the basis of our calculations there is a system whose size is $n = 0,1,...,N - 1$, which, as a consequence of the entry of a new particle, increases its size by 1. Such an entry increases the occupation number of the cell j from n_j to $n_j + 1$. Physicists speak of the "creation" of a particle in the cell j. We have determined the probability of this creation in such a way that, after a sequence of N creations, that is, the entry of N particles, the probability distribution on occupation vectors of the resulting system is (23). Because each creation in a cell j changes the system size from n to $n + 1$, whose occupation vectors are **n** and **n**^{j}, the probability we have used in this section can be denoted by $P(\mathbf{n}^j|\mathbf{n})$. This is the symbol we shall use in what follows.

8.5 Closed dynamical systems

C2 and C3 may be used in contexts that have nothing to do with induction. As we have just seen, this is the case with statistical mechanics; but the same is true for biology and economics. In these applications, exchangeability and invariance are considered in order to build up theories able to explain and foresee natural phenomena. Sometimes, with the clear intention to underestimate these applications, one speaks of probability models. In what follows we want to show how far this use of probability can be pursued. But in order to do this we must specify the scenario we have in mind.

We shall now consider closed dynamical systems. In order to explain what a closed dynamical system is, first of all we point out that, on account of what we have said about macroscopic quantities, when we speak of the state of a system we shall mean its occupation vector or (which is the same) its statistical distributions. A system is closed when its size does not change over time. A dynamical system is a system whose statistical distribution changes over time. Therefore, a closed dynamical system is a system whose size is constant notwithstanding changes in its statistical distribution. This means that, contrary to what we have done so far, we will consider systems that change not because new individuals enter the system but rather because the system's individuals change their attributes. From now on we shift our interest from induction and open evidence to theories and closed dynamical systems.

In considering closed dynamical systems, we focus on economic applications. Hence, to harmonize our terminology with the scenario we have in mind, we shall call agents the individuals and strategies the cells. As an abridgment, we shall say that "an agent is in j", not "an agent follows the strategy j." If the closed dynamical system is built up of N agents and d strategies, we will analyze the simplest transition the system may undergo. We call such a transition a unary move. Such a move occurs when an agent gives up a strategy (the starting one) and begins to follow another strategy (the resulting one). We shall also take more complex moves into account; but most of what we say concerns unary moves. The moves we are considering were first studied by physicists. When a particle undergoes a collision, for instance with the wall of the container, it changes its momentum. As a consequence, a (momentum) cell, say A, loses a particle and a different one, say B, gains a particle. In this sense a particle is destroyed in A and one is created in B. Physicists have adopted this more or less intuitive way of speaking. The terminology we shall use shows traces of this origin in that we shall speak of the "destruction" and "creation" of an agent in a strategy. More exactly, in order to say that an agent gives up the strategy j, we shall say that an agent is destroyed in j; conversely, we shall speak of creation in j if an agent chooses to follow the strategy j. A unary move can be seen as the juxtaposition of two steps: a destruction immediately followed by a creation. We stress that the starting strategy and the resulting strategy may be the same; obviously if this is the case, then no change occurs in the system. This is the way in which, from a probabilistic perspective, we shall analyze unary moves.

8.5.1 Destruction and creation probabilities

While a unary move taken as a whole does not modify the size of the system, a destruction taken from itself decreases by 1 the size of the system while a creation increases it by 1. We first take destructions into account. **N** being the state of the system, if the n-th agent is destroyed in i, the description of the decreased system could be the following: $X_1 = j_1,...,X_{n-1} = j_{n-1}, X_{n+1} = j_{n+1},...,X_N = j_N$. We denote by $\mathbf{N}_i = (N_1,...,$

$N_i - 1, \ldots, N_d)$ the corresponding occupation vector, that is, the state of a system in which any agent whatsoever is destroyed in i. Moreover, we denote by $P(\mathbf{N}_i|\mathbf{N})$ the destruction probability, that is, the probability that the state (occupation vector) of the system changes from $\mathbf{N}$ to $\mathbf{N}_i$. We assume that the destruction probability is exchangeable and invariant, with parameters $\lambda^{(d)} p_i^{(d)} = -N_i$ (d is for destruction). As a consequence we have

$$P(\mathbf{N}_i|\mathbf{N}) = \frac{N_i}{N}. \qquad (27)$$

This probability can be dealt with as a case of direct inference. In fact, (27) is the probability of drawing from a population whose statistical distribution is $\mathbf{N}$ a sample of size 1, that is, an agent, and the drawn agent is in i. But it is clear that to reach the value of a destruction probability one has to pose in (15) a negative value for λ, that is $\lambda^{(d)} = -N$, and $p_i^{(d)} = N_i/N$. Thus we suppose that destruction is "universal", that is, it does not depend on the type of element involved.

$\mathbf{N}_i$ being the state after the destruction, a creation in j restores the size of the system, and $\mathbf{N}_i^j$ is the state (occupation vector) of the resulting system. The probability of such a creation is $P(\mathbf{N}_i^j|\mathbf{N}_i)$. We suppose that creation probabilities are exchangeable and invariant, with parameters $\lambda^{(c)} p_j^{(c)} = \lambda p_j + N_j$, where N_j is the actual occupation number, p_j is the probability of accommodation when the cell is empty and c is for construction. Now λ is free to depend on the type of correlation among elements. It follows that for these probabilities the main theorem holds. Therefore, the probability we are interested in is (15). Considering a creation probability, we do not compel the creation to occur in a strategy other than that in which destruction has occurred. More clearly, destruction and creation may involve the same strategy. As we have said, if this is the case, the state of the system does not change. Hence, in general the creation probability we shall consider is

$$P(\mathbf{N}_i^j|\mathbf{N}_i) = \begin{cases} \dfrac{\lambda p_j + N_j}{\lambda + N - 1} & \text{for } j \neq i \\[2mm] \dfrac{\lambda p_j + N_j - 1}{\lambda + N - 1} & \text{for } j = i \end{cases} \qquad (28)$$

where the sign of λ induces the sign of accommodation correlations. In both formulae the denominator $N-1$ accounts for the size of the system after a destruction in i, and $N_j - 1$ for $j = i$ follows from the fact that, after the destruction in i, the occupation number of this cell is $N_i - 1$.

8.5.2 Unary moves

As time goes by agents change strategies, and this gives rise to the evolution we want study. The assumptions we have made about destruction and creation probabilities are tantamount to supposing that the probabilistic evolution of the system is regular, exchangeable, and invariant. This evolution is described by a sequence of occupation vectors $N(0), N(1), ..., N(t), ...$. As we shall see, this is a homogeneous Markov chain. Moreover, the elements of its stochastic matrix do not depend on time explicitly. A unary move occurs when an agent from i moves on to j. As a consequence of such a move, the state of the system undergoes a transition from to N to N_i^j. The probability of this transition, that is, $P(N_i^j|N)$, can be arrived at by considering two steps: a destruction immediately followed by a creation, as analyzed above. The probabilities of these steps are given by (27) and (28). Hence, the transition probability we are looking for is

$$P(N_i^j|N) = P(N_i|N)P(N_i^j|N_i) = \frac{N_i}{N} \frac{\lambda p_j + N_j}{\lambda + N - 1} \qquad (29)$$

with the correction stressed by (28) for repeated indices.

In (29) either $\lambda > 0$, or $|\lambda p_j|$ is integer and $|\lambda| \leq N$. Hence, starting from a given state of the system, all states of the system can be reached by repeated applications of (29). Further, all these states are persistent, as no absorbing states exist. Hence, the set of all states is ergodic and there is a (unique) invariant probability, say $\pi(N)$, on this ergodic set. Because (29) accounts for the case $i=j$, too, the chain is not periodic and the invariant probability is the equilibrium distribution. By the Chapman–Kolmogorov equation, and by using the detailed balance between any couple of occupation vectors, it can be proved (see Costantini and Garibaldi, 2000) that the equilibrium distribution is the (generalized) Polya (23), that is,

$$\pi(N) = \frac{N!}{\lambda^{[N]}} \prod_{i=1}^{d} \frac{(\lambda p_j)^{[N_j]}}{N_j!} \qquad (30)$$

in which the parameters are the same as in (15). We recall that the mean value and variance of this probability distribution are respectively

$E(N_i) = Np_i$ and $Var(N_i) = Np_i(1 - p_i)\frac{\lambda + N}{\lambda + 1}$.

To conclude the section, we recall that moves of an order greater than 1 are more complicated but can be handled in the same way as unary moves. The sole difference amounts to which approach rate to equilibrium becomes greater (see Costantini and Garibaldi, 2004). In the extreme case in which all agents are involved in an N-ary move, the equilibrium is reached immediately. In the case in which the equilibrium distribution is reached in this way, it amounts to the juxtaposition of $2N$ steps of which the first N are destructions, ruled by an hypergeometric probability, and the second N are creations, ruled by an exchangeable and invariant probability. What we have shown in the previous section devoted to statistical mechanics is a case of an N-ary creation. In all cases we may consider the equilibrium distribution is always (23). This illustrates certain relations existing between statistical mechanics and economics. We are persuaded that this analysis deserves more attention.

8.6 Two economic applications

We are ready to show that the relevance quotient, via the probabilistic evolution described by (29) and the consequent equilibrium distribution (30), can be used in economics. We take two situations into account. The first involves a town with shops and shoppers; the second a stock market trading in a single asset. Other applications of the relevance quotient have been proposed by Masanao Aoki (1996; 2002) in order to model aggregate behavior in economics. What we are doing enables a better understanding of the meaning of the relevance quotient and of invariance.

8.6.1 Customers and shops: Ewens's limit

Consider a system such a town with N inhabitants and d shops. All the inhabitant buy in some shop in the town, so the number of customers is N too. This system is closed: no new inhabitants come into the town and as a consequence the total number of customers is fixed. The strategy of a customer is to buy from one of the d shops. Customers may change strategy, that is, they may decide to cease buying from one shop and to start buying from another one. The state of the system, $\mathbf{N} = (N_1,\ldots,N_j,\ldots,N_d), \Sigma_{j=1}^{d} N_j = N$, specifies the number of customers of the different shops. Hence, $P(\mathbf{N}_i|\mathbf{N})$ is the probability the number of customers of shop i decreases by 1 while $P(\mathbf{N}_i^j|\mathbf{N})$ is the probability that, the number of customers of shop i having decreased by 1, the number of customers of shop j increases by 1.

As we have seen, the destruction probability is ruled by (27). In this respect it is worth stressing that the probability of decreasing by 1 the number of customers of a shop, being equal to the fraction of customers of the shop, depends only upon the number of customers of the shop, irrespective of the particular shop taken into account. In turn, this holds if and only if all customers have the same probability of being chosen for a destruction irrespective of the shop of which they are customers. In other words, all customers are on a par with respect to destructions or (which is the same) the destruction of a customer in a shop always happens at random regardless of the shop in which the destruction takes place.

If exchangeability holds, then the probability that an inhabitant becomes a new customer of a shop does not depend upon the identity of the customers of the various shops but only on the numbers of its customers. The condition of invariance reduces this dependence on the number of customers of the shop and on the total number of inhabitants of the town. The destruction probability is the probability with which a customer ceases to be customer of a shop. Conversely, the creation probability is the probability with which an inhabitant becomes one of the customers of a shop. Considering this interpretation, one may express doubts about the conditions ruling both probabilities (27) and (15). In fact, one can pose questions like these: Do customers always leave shops at random? Does coming to a shop always depend upon the number of its customers? Does the creation probability not depend upon other factors—for example, which people are customers of the shop? With this interpretation, exchangeability and invariance become empirically testable.

In what we have done the distinctive feature of the system, which is that the number of customers and that of shops are given at the beginning, in particular it is supposed that the number of shops is finite, as is the number of customers. However, it may happen that a shop loses all its costumers or, as we shall say, it becomes void. We wish to analyze what happens in the case in which void shops cannot be reopened, and are possibly replaced by new shops. More exactly, we shall consider the case in which the probability that an empty shop will be reopened is equal to zero, and the probability that a new shop opens is positive. This is a way of saying that all shops that have lost all their customer are replaced by some new shops, the actual number of shops being a random variable.

To implement this scenario, besides the conditions we have already considered we suppose that: the number of shops is d, large but finite; all initial probabilities are equal, that is, $p_j = 1/d$; λ is positive and finite. Now we consider the limit $d \to \infty$, that is, Ewens's limit. In a formal way this amounts to supposing that the probabilistic behaviors of customers are ruled by exchangeability and invariance, that all initial probabilities

$p_j \to 0$, hence for all j and the real number λ, which in this context we denote by θ for historical reasons, is finite. We call these assumptions Ewens's limit because they were first considered by Ewens (1972).

If Ewens's limit holds, the number of customers being finite, at a fixed time no more than N shops can be occupied; moreover, the probability that a specific void shop receives a customer is zero, as $p_j \to 0$. As we have said, the probability that a shop which has lost all his customers will be put in action again is equal to zero. Another consequence of Ewens's limit is that it becomes useless to look at the system through the occupation vectors because these almost all have occupation numbers equal to zero. In order to study the evolution of the system we must consider another way of describing it. Given an occupation vector $\mathbf{N}$, we denote by Z_r the number of its occupation numbers equal to r. Thus Z_r is the number of clusters of size (occupation number) r. A cluster size vector $\mathbf{Z} = (Z_0, Z_1, \ldots, Z_n)$, $\Sigma_{r=0}^{N} Z_r = d$, $\Sigma_{r=0}^{N} Z_r = N$, is an $(N+1)$-dimensional vector specifying the number of shops with exactly $r = 0, 1, \ldots, N$ customers. In fact, Z_0, is the number of void shops, Z_1 is that of the shops with a sole customer, Z_r that of shops with r customers and Z_N is the number of shops with N customers. Clearly Z_N may be either 0 or 1. Moreover, if $Z_N = 1$ in the town there is only one active shop.

To study the effect of Ewens's limit, we consider first a large but finite number of shops of which only the first h are active. This means that the first h shops have at least one shopper while the other $d - h$ are void. Obviously $h \le n$ and $h \ll d$. The transition probability (29) becomes

$$P(\mathbf{N}_i^j | \mathbf{N}) = \begin{cases} \dfrac{N_i}{N} \dfrac{\theta/d + N_j}{\theta + N - 1} & \text{for } i \le h \text{ and } j \le h \\[3mm] \dfrac{N_i}{N} \dfrac{\theta - h\theta/d}{\theta + N - 1} & \text{for } i \le h \text{ and } j \text{ is some void shop.} \end{cases} \tag{31}$$

When Ewens's limit holds, (31) becomes

$$P(\mathbf{N}_i^j | \mathbf{N}) = \begin{cases} \dfrac{N_i}{N} \dfrac{N_j}{\theta + N - 1} & \text{for } i \le h \text{ and } j \le h \\[3mm] \dfrac{N_i}{N} \dfrac{\theta}{\theta + N - 1} & \text{for } i \le h \text{ and } j \text{ is some void shop.} \end{cases} \tag{32}$$

This transition probability shows that, as the initial weights of all shops tends to zero, it is almost certain that sooner or later shops become void; the probability that a well-specified void shop will become active is zero, hence after a shop has become void there is no chance that it will reopen; the probability that some void shop receives a costumer is finite; and with probability 1 all existing active shop close, and the closure is for ever.

To account for the dynamical evolution of the system we consider a sequence of cluster size vectors $Z(0), Z(1), ..., Z(t), ...$. Without entering in the details, we note that as before this is a homogeneous Markov chain, focusing on transition probabilities. As in the Ewens's limit $Z_0 \to d \to \infty$, we consider only $Z = (Z_1, ..., Z_n)$, with the sole constraint $\sum_{r=1}^{N} r Z_r = N$, while $\sum_{r=1}^{N} Z_r = k$ is a random variable. Suppose that $Z = (Z_1, ..., Z_N)$ is the cluster size vector of the town with respect to shops and customers. We look for the partition vector after the destruction of a customer in a shop whose occupation number is i and the creation of a customer in a shop whose occupation number is $j-1$. After the first step, the occupation number of the shop concerned becomes $i-1$. This cut has a double effect on the cluster size vector of the town: Z_i becomes $Z_i - 1$ while Z_{i-1} becomes $Z_{i-1} + 1$. On the other hand, as a consequence of the second step, Z_{j-1} becomes $Z_{j-1} - 1$ while becomes $Z_j + 1$. We denote by $z_i^j = (Z_0, Z_1, ..., Z_{i-1} + 1, Z_i - 1, ..., Z_{j-1} - 1, Z_j + 1, ..., Z_N)$ the partition vector resulting from the transition. The related transition probability can be immediately reached by means of (32), noting that the first step is the Z_i disjunction of events whose probabilities are equal to $\frac{i}{N}$, and that the second is the disjunction of Z_{j-1} events whose probabilities are equal to $\frac{j-1}{\theta+N-1}$. Thus we have

$$P(Z_i^j \mid Z) = \begin{cases} \dfrac{iZ_i}{N} \dfrac{(j-1)Z_{j-1}}{\theta+N-1} & \text{for } j > 1 \\[3mm] \dfrac{iZ_i}{N} \dfrac{\theta}{\theta+N-1} & \text{for } j = 1. \end{cases} \tag{33}$$

The transition probability (33) is that of a homogeneous Markov chain, irreducible and aperiodic. The equilibrium distribution is the Ewens Sampling Formula

$$\pi(Z) = \frac{N!}{\theta^{[N]}} \prod_{r=1}^{N} \frac{\theta^{Z_r}}{r^{Z_r} Z_r!}. \tag{34}$$

According to the derivation we have just shown, (34) can be seen as the fraction of time that the town spends in the state described by Z. Aoki has interpreted the parameter θ as a measure of correlatedness of individual agents. Referring to two agents and using [34] he says, "(t)he closer the value of θ to zero, the larger is the probability that two randomly chosen agents are of the same type. The larger that value of θ, the more likely that two randomly chosen agents are not of the same type" (Aoki, 2002, p. 165). The definition we have stipulated for the parameter θ reveals the root of the correlation, which, in turn, depends upon to the value of the relevance quotient.

8.6.2   Stock-price dynamics: thermodynamic limit

Many meaning can be given to the system we have just considered. In contrast, the application we now examine is quite specific. In fact, we look at a stock market with N agents trading in a single asset, whose log price at time t is $x(t)$. The agents buy, sell, or don't trade, and we shall denote by $j_n(t), n = 1,...,N$, the demand for stock at time t. The strategies from which the agents may choose are: to be a bull, +1, to be neutral, 0, to be a bear, -1. The aggregate excess demand for the asset at time t is then $A(t) = \sum_{n=1}^{N} j_n(t)$, and we suppose that the price return is proportional to $A(t)$, that is,

$$\Delta x(t) = x(t+1) - x(t) = \frac{1}{\gamma} A(t),$$

where $A(t) = \sum_{n=1}^{N} j_n(t)$. γ is the excess demand needed to move the percentage return by one unit. For the sake of simplicity we take $\gamma = 1$. We aim at evaluating the distribution of returns. This means that we must determine the joint distribution of $\{j_n(t)\}_{n=1,...,N}$. Finally we suppose that the agents' changes of strategy are governed by a probability which is exchangeable and invariant in such a way that the main theorem holds.

At a given time, which for the sake of simplicity we do not make explicit, let $N = (N_+, N_-, N_0), N_+ + N_- + N_0 = N$, be the state of the system, that is, N_+ is the number of bulls, N_- that of bears, and N_0 that of neutral agents. Hence, $A = N_+ - N_-$ holds. Moreover, we suppose that p_+, p_- and p_0 are the initial probabilities of the three strategies. At each step one (or more) agent(s) may change strategy. For positive λ the probability that an agent chooses a strategy grows with the number of agents following the considered strategy. Considering a negative value of λ, the probability that an agent chooses a strategy diminishes with the number of agents following the considered strategy. For $|\lambda| \to \infty$ the probability of his choice does not depend on the number of agents following one or the other strategy.

We have seen that in general the equilibrium distribution is (30). In the case we are considering this becomes

$$\pi(\mathbf{N}) = \frac{N!}{\lambda^{[N]}} \frac{(\lambda p_+)^{[N_+]}}{N_+!} \frac{(\lambda p_-)^{[N_-]}}{N_-!} \frac{(\chi p_0)^{[N_0]}}{N_0!}. \tag{35}$$

Now we suppose that the thermodynamic this limit holds, that is $\lambda p_0 \to \infty$, $N \to \infty$, $\frac{N}{\lambda} = \chi = const$. The limit we are considering implies that the total number of agents N, and λp_0, both grow without limit, with the proviso that this does not change the mean number of bulls and bears. This can be interpreted by saying that among the infinite number of neutral agents there are always agents that may become active while among bulls and bears there are agents that may become neutral.

If the thermodynamic limit holds, (35) factorizes. This means that $\pi(\mathbf{N})$ tend (in distribution) to $\pi(N_+)\pi(N_-)$ given these distributions negative binomial, that is

$$\pi(N_+) = \frac{(\lambda p_+)^{[N_+]}}{N_+!} \left(\frac{1}{1+\chi}\right)^{\lambda p_+} \left(\frac{\chi}{1+\chi}\right)^{N_+}$$

$$\pi(N_-) = \frac{(\lambda p_-)^{[N_-]}}{N_-!} \left(\frac{1}{1+\chi}\right)^{\lambda p_-} \left(\frac{\chi}{1+\chi}\right)^{N_-}$$

If this is the case, the moments of the equilibrium distribution of excess demand are functions of λ and χ. In fact, considering that

$$E(N_+) = \lambda p_+ \chi$$

$$Var(N_+) = \lambda p_+ \chi(1+\chi)$$

$$Kurt(N_+) = \frac{1}{\lambda p_+}\left(6 + \frac{1}{\chi(\chi+1)}\right),$$

hence

$$E(A) = E(n_+ - n_-) = (\alpha_+ - \alpha_-)\chi.$$

Due to the stochastic independence of N_+ and N_-, we have

$$Var(A) = Var(N_+ - N_-) = (\lambda p_+ + \lambda p_-)\chi(1+\chi)$$

$$\mathit{Kurt}(A) = \frac{\left[Var(\,N_+)\right]^2 \mathit{Kurt}(N_+) + \left[Var(\,N_-)\right]^2 \mathit{Kurt}(N_-)}{\left[Var(\,N_+) + Var(\,N_-)\right]^2}$$

$$= \frac{1}{\lambda p_+ + \lambda p_-}\left(6 + \frac{1}{\chi(\chi + 1)}\right).$$

The last formula shows that the kurtosis of the negative binomial is large for small $(\lambda p_+ + \lambda p_-)$. A lot can be said about this. We limit ourselves to two remarks. First we note that the value of the kurtosis characterizes the "herd behavior" of the agents. Second, we have derived three equations that link the moments of the probability distribution of the excess demand with the three parameters of this model. As a consequence we have the possibility to estimate these parameters using the corresponding observed values. The estimated values may be inductively used, that is to say, they may be used to calculate the probabilities of future trends of the market. We note that this does not contradict the postulate according to which the behavior of the market is unpredictable. The unpredictability of the market does not prevent us from looking for probabilities, just as the unpredictability of how a tossed coin falls does not prevent us from determining the probabilities of heads and tails. As a matter of fact, searching for probabilities of uncertain events is exactly what people have been doing since the emergence of probability in the Renaissance, and what Keynes with his *Treatise on Probability* recommended to us at the beginning of the twentieth century.

8.7   The role of probability in economics

It is beyond doubt that Keynes extensively used probability notions in builing his economic theory. Moreover, the methodological attitude revealed by his economic writings is essentially the one he displays in *TP* (see Carabelli, 1988, p. 8). The results of his investigations into the foundations of probability and statistics has proven to be of fundamental importance in his economic theory. His works on money, prosperity and the general theory of employment cannot be understood without reference to *TP* together with its preparatory studies. To mention only a few examples, taken from many identified by Carabelli (1988; 1992; 1995), the essential relativity of a probability statement that greatly affects the notion of expectation, to which we shall return; the non-comparability of some probability relations, which Keynes transposed in the incommensurability of some economic quantities; the impossibility of a general measurement of probability relations, which Keynes extended to price relations; the inadequacy of addition or multiplication rules to tackle certain probabilities taken as a paradigm for the impossibility of adding or comparing the value of currencies.

However, Keynes did not use the notion of probability in constructing his economics. Only on very few occasions does he mention probabilistic notions. We focus on two cases. In dealing with long-term expectations, Keynes refers to the weight of arguments he had previously considered as the case in which

> we have a more substantial basis upon which to rest our conclusion. I express this by saying that an accession to new evidence increases the *weight* of an argument. New evidence will sometimes decrease the probability of an argument, but it always increase its "weight".
>
> (*TP*, 77)

The second is the discussion of various types of risk (Keynes, 1973b [1936], ch. 11, s. 4) which cannot be fully understood without reference to his definition of "risk"

> If A is the amount of good which may result, p its probability $(p + q = 1)$, and E the value of the "mathematical expectation", so that $E = pA$, then the "risk" is R where $R = p(A-E) = p(1-p)A = pqA = qE$.
>
> (*TP*, p. 348)

However, in many cases in which Keynes did not explicitly mention the notion of probability it is impossible to gain a full insight into his economic writings without having a clear understanding of the relative character of the notion of probability that Keynes first (and in a very perspicuous mode) suggested:

> No proposition is in itself either probable or improbable, just as no place can be intrinsically distant; and the probability of the same statement varies with the evidence presented, which is, as it were, its origin of reference.
>
> (*TP*, p. 7)

This is especially true for the keystone of his economics, that is, expectation. As a notion which can be introduced only after probability is taken into account, expectation, too, is essentially relative. As a consequence, in order to obtain a full insight into the peculiarities of the notion of expectation, one must have a clear understanding of the conditionalization process at the basis of the updating of probabilities. That is to say, just as a probability changes not only if the hypothesis changes but also when the evidence changes, in the same way the expectation of the unknown value of a quantity may change when the evidence changes.

The explicit acknowledgment of the relative character of probability as well as that of all concepts based on it played a revolutionary role in the history of science. Unfortunately, this role is far from fully understood. This has serious consequences. People which refuse to acknowledge the crucial role of the evidence in probability assertions—as all schools of thought that, notwithstanding the various schisms, pursue in founding probabilities on frequencies—are unable to obtain a clear insight into the notion of expectation. For example, the fact that a long-term expectation changes over time is indissolubly tied to a probability that is changing with the evidence. The notion of relevance quotient, too, cannot be introduced without having at one's disposal a relative notion of probability. And the relevance quotient is the powerful intellectual tool that Keynes envisaged to account for stochastic dependence.

On the other hand, it is well known that Keynes expressed sharp criticisms against the manner in which the character and causes of cyclical fluctuations were submitted to statistical test (see Carabelli, 1988, ch. 10). Keynes was against econometric studies as the mathematical way of formalizing economics (which at the time was done by means of the differential calculus). This could superficially appear to be, as it were, in manifest contrast to the attitude we outlined with examples in section 8.6. But this contrast disappears when we endeavor to reflect upon the role Keynes assigned to probability in economics: a reflection that cannot be carried out without clearly distinguishing between epistemic and ontic probabilities.

Considering first epistemic probabilities, we note that, as is well known, probabilities are extensively used to perform statistical (inductive) inferences. In this respect it should be emphasized that epistemological probabilities may be objective as well as subjective. Statistical inferences are essentially of two types: the control of hypotheses and the estimation of unknown values of quantities. To the control of hypotheses belong tests of significance, that is, the attempt to falsify hypotheses. This is done by assuming the validity of a statistical hypothesis to be used in order to determine hypothetical probabilities. If the observed result has a low probability under the assumed hypothesis, then the hypothesis is rejected. From this point of view statistical estimation is distinct from a test of significance. Such an estimation aims at evaluating the unknown value of a quantity by proceeding from experimental observations, which can be carried out in different ways. Frequentists use methods suitable for identifying the value of that quantity; this is, for example, the goal of Fisher's maximum likelihood estimation. But estimation can also be conducted in probability terms, that is, by specifying a probability distribution on the possible values of the quantity; this is what Bayesians, whether classical or modern, do. A variant of the probabilistic approach to estimation is predictive inferences by means of the relevance quotient and the condition of invariance. Thus, the probabilities used in statistical inferences are merely tools by which it is possible to quantify one's ignorance about a world imagined, in the great majority of cases, as being governed by deterministic laws. The work done by econometricians is of this type. The notion of probability used by econometricians is epistemic. Keynes was opposed to this way of using probability notions in economics. We believe that this is the way in which Keynes's criticism of Tinbergen's view should be interpreted (Keynes, 1939).

Nobody can deny that the use of epistemic probabilities is widespread. We maintain that probability has a true ontic aspect besides its old epistemic aspect. This statement is far from being new. With quantum mechanics it has become popular to acknowledge the existence of ontic probabilities. But we deny that the only ontic use of probability is linked to quantum mechanics. Ontic probabilities appear because of the non-causal character of a theory. This was clearly shown by Paul and Tatiana Ehrenfest, interpreteting and clarifying the work of Ludwig Boltzmann, especially his theorem on the probable increase in entropy over time. In genetics the ontic role of probability has been recognized since the time of Mendel. By contrast, this is not the case in economics. In general, economists do not recognize the fundamental lack of causal relations in the external world and the ensuing unpredictability of the future. This was not Keynes's way of thinking. In his economic writings he used neither tests of significance nor methods of estimation, but he referred to probability. We believe that Keynes took the indeterminateness of the economy for granted and that in order to account for it he referred to ontic probabilities. We are well aware that it is not easy to show the ontic aspect of probability in the economic writings of Keynes. This is for various reasons. First, at the beginning of the twentieth century only very few examples of the ontic use of probability were known. The most important one is the vindication of Boltzmann's *H*-theorem accomplished by means of the stochastic process— the dogs and fleas model—envisaged by the Ehrenfests (Ehrenfest P. and

Ehrenfest T., 1907). Stochastic processes play a very important role in the ontic use of probability. In the bibliography of the *Treatise*, Keynes (1973a [1921]) included about ten works of Markov, yet he was not acquainted with the revolutionary research on stochastic processes. As a consequence he could not use those formal results in his economic theory, and was content with an intuitive treatment of stochastic dependence, which he referred to as organicism (we shall return to this issue). Second, Keynes's economics is not a formal theory and neither stochastic processes nor transition probabilities can be dealt with in it. Third, and most important, Keynes based his probability theory upon a propositional calculus, and could not account for individual random variables. Since that time a lot has changed. As we have shown in section 8.6, a stochastic representation of economic processes is available. Referring to these examples, we shall attempt to clarify the way in which ontic probabilities may enter into a "non-causal" economic theory.

The distinctive mark of the examples we have considered consists in abandoning the attempt to follow the causal (deterministic) changes in state that would take place in a particular economic agent—as is done by the mathematical method usually introduced to formalize economics—and in studying from a probabilistic perspective the economic behavior of single economic agents. The transition probabilities (29), (33), and (35) refer to single agents. To obtain a full insight into the meaning of our examples, one must bear clearly in mind that the probability we have worked with accounts for single agents. We have inquired into the change which takes place in the strategy of an agent over time. The change is governed by probability conditions. These conditions produce the statistical behavior of the economic system expressed by a probability distribution, hence its average behavior too. This approach is clearly adopted in the two examples in section 8.6, especially the example concening customers and shops. We proceeded from a detailed probabilistic description of the behavior of agents with respect to strategies, considering the change of strategy as a mechanism leading actual economic systems to change over time. This is worth noting. The question we have answered is: what is the probability of choosing a new strategy when an agent gives up the old one? The macroscopic properties of the economic system result from the statistical behavior of agents, expressed by means of transition probabilities. Much more important, the analysis we have undertaken leads to a probability distribution that, as it were, characterizes the statistical equilibrium.

The stochastic process and its equilibrium probability distribution follow from the laws governing the probabilistic behavior of economic agents. These are: the basic rules of probability, exchangeability, invariance, the values of the initial probabilities and those of the relevance quotient. As a consequence it is quite natural to suppose that these agents obey the probability conditions from which follow the stochastic processes we have described. Because these conditions probabilistically describe properties of economic agents, they are not outside economics but inside it. Being inside the theory, the probability with which these conditions are expressed is ontic in character. This, too, holds true for the probability notions used by Keynes in economics. For Keynes expectations were not merely tools by which ignorance could be overcome but a way to understand and explain the behavior of economic agents. That is to say, the probability notions, directly or indirectly, used by Keynes are ontic because they supply a way of explaining and understanding economic reality.

These considerations lead us to the core of the problem. We have shown that our approach is able to deduce the equilibrium distributions of an economic system. As a consequence, the following question arises in a very natural way: do these distributions reflect the actual behavior of macroeconomic systems? An answer can only be provided by using a statistical inference. This is a typical task of epistemic probabilities. For example, with reference to stock price dynamics, only a statistical inference can reveal whether the behavior of bulls and bears is governed by negative binomial distributions. This means that the ultimate validity of the considered conditions is to be regarded as resting on the correspondence between deduced results and empirical findings. However, if such a control gives a positive answer, then the probabilistic conditions we have considered describe and explain the behavior of the agents trading in a single asset. In other words, this ought to mean that we have worked with probabilities able to understand and explain some aspects of economic reality.

At this point, another question arises: what about the probability of *A Treatise on Probability*? Or, is the probability studied in *TP* epistemic or ontic? Our answer is very clear: neither or both. The reason is simple. In *TP* Keynes dealt with probability in a formal way. In stating the fundamental theorems of probability he clearly asserts that he is dealing with the formal logic of probable knowledge (*TP* p. 125). Following Leibniz, he treat probability calculus as a branch of logic. For Keynes the probability relation is a primitive notion. As such it needs no explicit definition. All Keynes does is to introduce some axioms, like addition and multiplication rules, to be used in transforming probabilities, that is, in calculating probabilities of events given those of other events.

As a notion only implicitly defined through the axioms of an abstract theory, probability can be seen as both epistemic (objective or subjective) and ontic. As a matter of fact, Keynes used probability in both epistemic and ontic modes. In Part V of *TP*, which is devoted to the foundations of statistical inference, probability is clearly epistemic. This is not the case with the notion of probability used in *The General Theory of Employment, Interest and Money* (Keynes, 1973b [1936]). This probability is ontic.

Unfortunately, the introduction of probability in economics took the epistemic route, and this route is far removed from that suggested by Keynes. The notion of probability that in the first half of the twentieth century began to be explicitly used in economics was epistemological in character. Having in mind a frequentistic notion of probability, econometricians narrowed the use of probability in economics to hypothetical probability, that is, to likelihood, the notion, strongly biased by frequentistic philosophy, which Ronald A. Fisher opposed to probability (see Fisher, 1956). As a matter of fact, tests of significance are based on likelihood. This is also the case with estimation, mainly aimed at specify values of deterministic quantities, which is performed in most cases with the method of maximum likelihood. An econometric model, such as a linear equation characterized by a set of parameters previously estimated, has to be tested against empirical observations. The result in the case of a small hypothetical probability (a fixed significance level) is the rejection (falsification) of the model, or else its (provisional) acceptance. In both testing and estimating econometricians aim at discovering the "true" values of the parameters, that is, the "true" description of a deterministic world. For econometricians probability is no more than a tool to be used under circumstances in which the knowledge of the conditions of the system is less than the maximal knowledge which would be theoretically possible: in other words, a tool able to ascertain the validity of a causal model. This attitude is in plain contrast with the Keynesian philosophy of probability.

We are convinced that a probabilistic perspective is at the core of Keynes's economic theory. But how is it possible to reconcile this perspective with the organicist approach to economics that on many occasions Keynes opposed to the atomistic approach? As Carabelli (1995) notes, this attitude is also present in Keynes's approach to the foundations of probability. The answer has to be found in the Laplacean theory of probability, that is, in the theory of probability Keynes was acquainted with. Moreover, one must not forget that the Laplacean theory was formulated with a view to explaining the outcomes of gambling systems which, from a probabilistic point of view, are independent systems. That theory was well suited to dealing with atomic event. Keynes's criticism is directed against the probability theory of the nineteenth century. Criticism of the principle of indifference is correct but completely out of date. The reason is simply that nobody defends that principle any more. Nowadays the theory of probability is very different from the classical theory criticized by Keynes.

We may now consider Keynes's organicistic attitude. According to Carabelli, this attitude is typical of his approach both to economics and probability. As Carabelli writes:

> The final evidence of Keynes's non-atomistic attitude can be found through the analysis of the economic works he wrote between 1908 and 1921 while revising the *Treatise*. An examination of them clearly reveals that Keynes does not radically change his organicist attitude.
>
> (Carabelli, 1995, p. 153)

We agree with this assessment. Keynes envisages a theory of probability that is not well suited to dealing with stochastic dependence. Rightly, Keynes does not limit his attention to atomic events and consistently rejects this possibility when working in economics. In order to understand this, one has to consider the meaning of stochastic dependence. Without a clear idea of the very meaning of this notion, it is impossible to fully understand the organic interdependence that according to Keynes characterizes a monetary economy. The only way to understand this interdependence is to grasp the difference between the initial (absolute) probability of any given hypothesis and its final (conditional) probability.

At the very beginning of the nineteenth century, stochastic dependence was considered by Albert Einstein in order to explain Brownian motion. Keynes was not aware of this revolutionary turning point, which made it possible to obtain an insight into entangled phenomena. Now, by using appropriate stochastic processes, we are able to deal with stochastic dependence in a very effective way. In section 6 we have given two examples of this. Keynes warns against using correlation coefficients in economics. This was and is an important warning insofar as this coefficient is concerned with descriptive or inductive statistics. But, as we have seen, correlation can be used within the theory, and Keynes is not aware of this possibility. Once again the reason is that Keynes takes neither the works of Einstein nor those of Markov into account.

In the spirit of modern approaches to stochastic processes, we have used the notion of relevance quotient. We have shown that this quotient can be widely used in ascertaining the equilibrium distributions of systems ruled by exchangeability and invariance; that the notion of equilibrium is essentially probabilistic; and, what is more important, how it is possible to describe stochastic macroeconomic patterns by referring to the stochastic microeconomic behaviors of individual agents. In this respect, the notion of relevance quotient plays a crucial role. This quotient on the one hand makes it evident that economic behaviors are essentially stochastic and on the other hand measures the degree of stochastic dependence one will introduce in the theory.

The ontic use of Keynes's relevance quotient is crucial in describing and interpreting the stochastic behavior of economic agents. We are convinced that the only feasible route open to those who wish to follow the approach pioneered by Keynes is to introduce this approach into economics. Accepting this point of view has the notable consequence of getting rid of the paradoxical behavior of econometricians, who are used to maintaining, at least theoretically, a deterministic attitude towards both what happened and what happens but are compelled to refer to probabilities in order to foresee what actually will happen.

A probabilistic theory supplies a form of knowledge that leads to the understanding of both the microscopic and the macroscopic sides of our probabilistic world. We are acquainted with the fact that most writers maintain that probabilistic explanations of economic phenomena are not good enough. We have shown that a good explanation of some economic phenomena can be provided in terms of conditional probabilities. In this respect, our example points with great clarity to the role of conditional probabilities in economics. This role is clearly seen by Keynes, the first author who recognized that probability is a relation. Failure to appreciate the ontic status of probabilities is the true reason why probabilistic explanations have not been considered to be good explanations.

Finally, we would like to conclude our comment on probability and economics by recalling the words with which Keynes ends *A Treatise on Probability*:

> The physicists of the nineteenth century have reduced matter to the collisions and arrangements of particles, between which the ultimate qualitative differences are very few; and the Mendelian biologists are deriving the various qualities of men from the collisions and arrangements of chromosomes. In both cases the analogy with a perfect game

of chance is really present; and the validity of some current modes of inferences may depend on the assumption that it is to material of this kind that we are applying them. Here, though I have complained sometimes at their want of logic, I am in fundamental sympathy with the deep underlying conceptions of the statistical theory of the day. If the contemporary doctrines of biology and physics remain tenable, we may have a remarkable, if undeserved, justification of some of the methods of the traditional calculus of probabilities. [...] and it may turn—reversing Quetelet's expression—that "La nature que nous interrogeons c'est une urne."

(*TP*, p. 468)

Biology and statistical physics are still tenable, and much more so than at the beginning of the nineteenth century. The probability conditions we have supposed to hold in our examples have reduced to transition probabilities the study of agents who are in a condition which is changing over time. This probability mechanism is the same one that governs, as Keynes says above, the "collisions and arrangements of particles" (see for example, Costantini and Garibaldi, 2004). From this perspective, what Keynes expresses when concluding his *Treatise* can be interpreted as being "in fundamental sympathy" with the stochastic approach to economics we have outlined. However, a difference must be emphasized. The particles Keynes refers to are molecules, that is, classical particles whose behavior is governed by stochastic independence. The agents we have considered are comparable not to classical particles but to quantum particles. They are not atomistic agents but organicistic agents, that is, agents whose probabilistic behavior is governed by stochastic dependence.

References

Aoki, M. (1996), *New Approaches to Macroeconomic Modeling*, Cambridge: Cambridge University Press.
—— (2002), *Modeling Aggregate Behavior and Fluctuations in Economics*, Cambridge: Cambridge University Press.
Bach, A. (1990), 'Boltzmann's Probability Distribution of 1877', *Archive for History of Exact Sciences*, 41 (1), pp. 1–40.
Carabelli, A. M. (1988), *On Keynes's Method*, London: Macmillan.
—— (1992), 'Organic Interdependence and Keynes's Choice of Units in the General Theory,' in B. Gerrard and J. Hillard (eds), *The Philosophy and Economics of J. M. Keynes*, Aldershot: Elgar, pp. 3–31.

—— (1995), 'Uncertainty and Measurement in Keynes: Probability and Organicness,' in S. Dow and J. Hillard (eds), *Keynes, Knowledge and Uncertainty*, Aldershot: Elgar, pp. 137–76.

Carnap, R. (1950), *Logical Foundations of Probability* (2nd impression of the 2nd edn, 1963), Chicago: University of Chicago Press.

—— (1952), *The Continuum of Inductive Methods*, Chicago: University of Chicago Press.

—— (1980), 'A Basic System of Inductive Logic, Part II,' in H. Jeffrey (ed.), *Studies in Inductive Logic and Probability, Volume II*, Berkeley: University of California Press, pp. 7–155.

Costantini, D. (1979), 'The Relevance Quotient,' *Erkenntnis*, 14, pp. 149–57.

—— (1987), 'Symmetry and the Indistinguishability of Classical Particles,' *Physics Letters A*, 123, pp. 433–6.

—— and Garibaldi, U. (1991), 'Una formulazione probabilistica del principio di esclusione di Pauli nel contesto delle inferenze predittive', *Statistica* 51, pp. 21–34.

—— (2000), 'A Purely Probabilistic Representation of the Dynamics of a Gas of Particles,' *Foundations of Physics*, 30, pp. 81–99.

—— (2004), 'The Ehrenfest Fleas: From Model to Theory,' *Synthèse*, 139 (1), pp. 107–42.

de Finetti, B. (1930), 'Funzione caratteristica di un fenomeno aleatorio,' *Memorie della Regia Accademia Nazionale dei Lincei*, 12, pp. 367–73.

Ehernfest, P. and Ehrenfest, T. (1907), 'Ueber zwei bekannte Einwaende gegen Boltzmanns H-Teorem', *Physikalische Zeitschrift*, 8, pp. 311–16.

Ewens, W. J. (1972), 'The Sampling Theory of Selectively Neutral Alleles,' *Theoretical Population Biology*, 3, pp. 87–112.

Fisher, R. A. (1956), *Statistical Methods and Scientific Inferences*, Edinburgh: Oliver and Boyd.

Garibaldi, U. and Scalas, E. (2010), *Finitary Probabilistic Methods in Econophysics*, Cambridge: Cambridge University Press.

Good, I. J. (1965), *The Estimation of Probabilities*, Cambridge Mass.: MIT Press.

Johnson, W. E. (1924), *Logic, Part III*, London: Constable and Co. p. 172

—— (1932), 'Probability: The Relations of Proposal to Supposal'; 'Probability: Axioms'; 'Probability: The Deductive and the Inductive Problem,' *Mind*, 41, pp. 1–16, 281–96, 409–23.

Kemeny, J. C. (1963), 'Carnap's Theory of Probability and Induction,' in M. Schilpp (ed.), *The Philosophy of Rudolf Carnap*, La Salle, Ill.: Open Court; London: Cambridge University Press, pp. 711–38.

Keynes, J. M. (1939), 'Professor Tinbergen's Method,' *Economic Journal*, 49, pp. 558–68.

Keynes, J. M. (1973a [1921]), *A Treatise on Probability*, Vol. VIII of *The Collected Writings of John Maynard Keynes*, London: Macmillan.

—— (1973b [1936]), *The General Theory of Employment, Interest and Money*, Vol. VII of *The Collected Writings of John Maynard Keynes*, London: Macmillan.

Pearson, K. (1920), 'The Fundamental Problem of Practical Statistics,' *Biometrika* 12, pp. 1–16.

von Plato, J. (1994), *Creating Modern Probability*, Cambridge, Mass.: Cambridge University Press.

9
Non-Self-Averaging Phenomena in Macroeconomics: Neglected Sources of Uncertainty and Policy Ineffectiveness

Masanao Aoki

9.1 Introduction

The main analytical exercise by mainstream macroeconomists such as Romer (1986), Lucas (1988), Grossman and Helpman (1991), and Aghion and Howitt (1992) is to explicitly consider the optimization by representative agents using quadratic criterion functions in such activities as education, on-the-job training, basic scientific research, and process and product innovations. This approach is found not only in the study of economic growth but also in research on business cycles. In this chapter we argue that this research program, which dominates modern macroeconomics, is misguided because it does not recognize the distinction between self-averaging and non-self-averaging aspects of their optimization problems. Whether in growth or business cycle models, the fundamental motivation for often complex optimization exercises is that they are expected to lead us to a better understanding of dynamics of the *mean* or *aggregate* variables. The standard procedure is to begin with an analysis of optimization for the representative agent and then to translate it into an analysis of the economy as a whole. These exercises presume that different microeconomic shocks and differences among agents will cancel out in the means, and the results can be well captured by the analysis of the representative agents.

We show that the phenomenon of non-self-averaging has material consequences for macroeconomic policy development. Specifically, models that exhibit non-self-averaging—that is, those whose standard deviations divided by the means do not decrease as the systems grow—are ubiquitous, and macroeconomic simulations using them can give rise to uninformative or misleading policy results.

More formally, given a macroeconomic model, some random variable X_n of the model, where n is model size, is called self-averaging if its coefficient of variation (CV), that is, the ratio of standard deviation of X_n divided by its mean, tends to zero as n goes to infinity, and non-self-averaging if the limit is non-zero or if the limit tends to infinity.

This phenomenon is related directly to the magnitude of economic fluctuations and is consistent with the size and scaling of fluctuations observed both recently and in the more distant past.

By way of examples, we show how macroeconomic policy can be rendered totally ineffective solely as a result of non-self-averaging. Altogether three types of non-self-averaging models are discussed: two-parameter Poisson–Dirichlet models; urn models; and two blocks of interdependent macroeconomic models (see Aoki, 2008a; 2008b; 2008c). After a brief introduction to non-self-averaging, we present analytical results on policy ineffectiveness by means of two simple introductory examples. These show (a) the importance of coefficients of variation, (b) how coefficients of variation enter into a well-known economics problem, and (c) that if the coefficient of variation becomes large then policy becomes ineffective. A connection with the two-parameter Poisson–Dirichlet model is then established to show how GDP becomes non-self-averaging. The chapter then discusses relations of urn models to macroeconomic models and exhibits examples of urn models in the literature that are non-self-averaging.

9.2 Coefficient of variation and policy ineffectiveness

In this chapter we examine a non-self-averaging performance index, and question the role of the "mean" dynamics when the measure of approximation errors by quadratic expression does not convey useful information, either in policy multiplier context or in conducting or designing large-scale Monte Carlo studies. Models with large values of coefficients of variation have smaller policy multipliers than models with small coefficients of variation.

9.2.1 Binary choice: model 1

As an example, consider a binary choice model (Aoki, 2002, s. 6.3) in which each agent makes a binary choice. Here we give a simple example and leave more detailed analysis to Aoki and Yoshikawa (2007, p. 63).

Agents are faced with two choices. They have some idea of the mean return of each of the two choices and the associated uncertainty expressed by some variance expressions.

Let two choices have values V_1 and V_2, but we observe them with error ε_i as V^*_i, $i = 1,2$

$$V^*_i = V_i + \varepsilon_i, \quad i = 1,2.$$

Define $\varepsilon = \varepsilon_1 - \varepsilon_2$. Assume that ε is distributed as

$$Pr(\varepsilon < x) = (1 + e^{-\beta x})^{-1},$$

for real number x, and where $\beta > 0$ is a parameter of this distribution.

McFadden models agents' discrete choices as the maximization of utilities U_j, $j = 1,...,K$, where U_j is associated with choice j and K is the total number of available choices. Let $U_j = V_j + \epsilon_j, j = 1,2,...,K$. We are really interested in picking the maximum of V's, not of U's.

McFadden's model (1973) may be used to illustrate a binary choice problem where under suitable conditions we obtain

$$\eta(x) := Pr(V_1(x) > V_2(x)) = 0.5[1 + erf(u)],$$

where

$$erf(u) = \frac{2}{\sqrt{\pi}} \int_0^u e^{-y^2} dy,$$

where $g(x)$ is the mean and $\sigma(x)$ is the variance in

$$u(x) = \frac{g(x)}{\sqrt{2}\sigma(x)} = \frac{1}{\sqrt{2}CV(x)},$$

and where

$$CV(x) = \sqrt{\sigma(x)}/g(x),$$

is the coefficient of variation.

As $CV(x)$ tends to infinity, u approaches zero, and $\eta(x)$ approaches 1/2. This means that the choice between the two alternatives become equally likely, that is, $\eta(x) \to 1/2$.

Galambos (1987, p. 11) discusses the following model. Suppose εs are independent and identically distributed (i.i.d.) with the distribution function F. Writing $F = 1-(1-F)$, we have $n \ln F(x) = n[1 - F(a_n + b_n y] := u(y)$ for some constant a_n and b_n. Then from

$$Pr(max_j \varepsilon_j < x) = [F(x)]^n$$

$$lim_K Pr(max_j u_j) < a_K + b_k y) = exp(-u(y)).$$

Choose $F(x) = 1 - e^{-x}$, $a_n = ln(n)$, and $b_n = 1$. Let $P_i = Pr(max_j U_j = U_i)$.

9.2.2   Policy multiplier in binary choice: model 2

More realistically, consider the following model. A total of N agents adopt one of two production technologies. One produces y^* per agent, and the other y per agent per period, where $y < y^*$. The total output per period is

$$Y = ny^* + (N - n)y = N[xy^* + (1 - x)y],$$

where $x = n/N$ is the fraction of agents which chose the more efficient technology. Stochastically one of $(N - n)$ agent changes its choice at the rate

$$r = N(1 - x)\,\eta_1(x),$$

or one of n agents changes its choice at the rate

$$l = Nx\,\eta_2(x),$$

where $\eta_1(x) = exp(\beta g(x))$ and $\eta_2 = 1 - \eta_1$. Here $g(x)$ is the policy multiplier. Policymaker wants to persuade agents to switch to using the high-yielding technique.

In Aoki and Yoshikawa (2007, s. 4.2) it is shown that the parameter β is $\kappa/\phi(x)$, $\kappa > 0$, which is a constant, where $\phi(x)$ is the standard deviation associated with this binary choice situation. Changing to $g(x)$ to $g(x) + h(x)$ by policymaker has the multiplier

$$E = \delta\phi/h(\phi) = \frac{2}{1 - 2g'(\phi^*)} > 0,$$

is shown where the coefficient of variation is $CV(\phi) = \sigma(x)/g(x)$.

As the CV grows, the fraction x tends to 1/2, that is, no policy effects in attempting to increase output.

9.3   Two-parameter Poisson–Dirichlet distribution of innovation arrival processes

Following the literature on endogenous growth, assume that the economy grows by experiencing innovations over time. Suppose that there are two kinds of innovation. An innovation, when it occurs, either raises productivity and hence output of one of the existing clusters (sectors) or creates an entirely new cluster (of initial size 1).

After the arrival of the nth innovation, there will be a total of K_n clusters (sectors) of sizes n_i, $i = 1, \ldots, k$, say, $n = n_1 + n_2 + \cdots + n_k$, that is, the total number of clusters is $K_n = k$.

In this two-parameter Poisson–Dirichlet process, we have either

$$\Pr(K_{n+1} = k+1 \mid K_1, K_2, \ldots, K_n = k) = \sum_{i=1}^{k} p_i,$$

where

$$p_i = \frac{n_i - \alpha}{n + \theta},$$

because an innovation occurs in one of these existing clusters with probability P_i, or

$$\Pr(K_{n+1} = k \mid K_1, K_2, \ldots, K_n = k) = 1 - \sum_i p_i = \frac{n - k\alpha}{n + \theta}.$$

These give a probability rate of the $(n+1)$th innovation attaching to one of the existing clusters or creating a new cluster.

There are two parameters, α and θ. Parameter θ is the same as that used by Ewens (1972) and used Hoppe (1984) to cast the model as an urn model. The parameter α was introduced by Pitman (2002) when he extended the Ewens model. It controls the rate at which new types of so far unobserved innovation arrive.

Yamato and Sibuya (2000) derived the expression for $E(K_n)$

$$E(K_{n+1}) = \frac{\theta}{n + \theta} + \left[1 + \frac{\alpha}{\theta + n} \right] E(K_n).$$

Solving this recursion equation, they have also obtained the closed form expression for $E(K_n)$.

Using Stirling's formula we obtain an approximate expression

$$E(K_n) \approx n^\alpha \frac{\Gamma(\theta + 1)}{\alpha \Gamma(\theta + \alpha)}.$$

Yamato and Sibuya (2000) have also calculated the coefficient of variation of K_n normalized by n^α to be

$$CV(K_n / n^\alpha) = [\Gamma(\theta + 1 + \alpha) - \Gamma(\theta + 1)] / \Gamma(\theta + 1)]^{0.5}.$$

It is also known that

$$\lim_{n \to \infty} \frac{K_n}{n^\alpha} = L, almost\ surely,$$

where L is called the Mittag–Leffler random variable, to which we return later.

Carlton (1999) has proved that an estimate of α based on n pieces of data converges almost surely to it

$$\hat{\alpha}_n := \frac{\ln K_n}{\ln n} \to \alpha,$$

when θ is known but α is not. Also see Hoppe (1984), Pitman (2002), and Yamato and Sibuya (2000).

Note that K_n/n^α is not self-averaging, for $0 < \alpha < 1$, but is self-averaging with $\alpha = 0$.

9.4 GDP is non-self-averaging

Let Y_n denote the output of a model with K_n cluster discussed below.

Suppose that a cluster of size n_i produces y_i, and the total output from K_n clusters is the sum of outputs of all clusters

$$Y_n = \sum_{i}^{K_n} y_i,$$

where we assume that

$$y_i = \eta \gamma^{n_i}, \quad \eta > 0, \quad \gamma > \;$$

We set η to 1 without loss of generality.

Yamato and Sibuya (2000) show that the coefficient of variation of Y_n/n^α is the same as that of the random variable L.

Proposition: GDP normalized by n^α is non-self-avaraging in the two-parameter Poisson–Dirichlet process.

To see this, define $a_j(n)$ as the number of clusters in which j innovations have occurred out of n total innovations. The vector $a(n)$ consisting of $a_j(n)$, $j = 1,2,..., n$ is called the *partition vector*, where

$$n = \sum_{j}^{n} j a_j(n).$$

Then we can express K_n as

$$K_n = \sum_j a_j(n).$$

We approximate y_i by

$$y_i \approx 1 + \ln(\gamma)n_i,$$

and

$$Y_n \approx K_n + \beta sum_j ja_j(n) = \sum_j (1 + \beta j)a_j(n),$$

where $\beta = ln(\gamma) > 0$.
   Yamato and Sibuya (2000) have shown that

$$\frac{a_j(n)}{n^\alpha} \to^d f_j L,$$

where f_j is defined by

$$f_j = \frac{\alpha(1-\alpha)^{[j-1]}}{j!}$$

where the notation $[j]$ denotes an ascending factorial

$$x^{[j]} = x(x+1)\cdots(x+j-1).$$

Next, normalize the output by n^α. Then

$$\frac{Y_n}{n^\alpha} \to^d \sum_j f_j(1 + \beta j).$$

Yamato and Sibuya (2000) and Pitman (2002) have shown that

$$\frac{K_n}{n^\alpha} \to L,$$

where the convergence is in almost surely sense as well as in distribution, and since $\Sigma_j f_j$ and $\Sigma_j {}^{jf}_j$ are both constants, that is, not random variables, we conclude that

$$CV(K_n/n^\alpha) \to CV(L),$$

and

$$CV(Y_n/n^\alpha) \to CV(L).$$

9.5   Mittag–Leffler function

To calculate the moments of the random variable K_n/n^α we need the generalized Mittag–Leffler distribution, $g_{\alpha,\theta}(x)$.

To do this, we first need to define the Mittag–Leffler function,

$$E_\alpha(x) = \sum_0^\infty \frac{x^k}{\Gamma(k\alpha + 1)}$$

and the generalized version is

$$E_{\alpha,\beta}(z) = \sum_0^\infty \frac{z^k}{\Gamma(\alpha k + \theta)}.$$

The first two moments of the random variable L are

$$E(L) = \frac{\Gamma(\theta + 1)}{\alpha\Gamma(\theta + \alpha)},$$

and

$$E(L^2) = \frac{(\theta + \alpha)\Gamma(\theta + 1)}{\alpha^2\Gamma(\theta + 2\alpha)}.$$

From these we obtain the variance of L as

$$var(L) = \gamma_{\alpha,\theta} \frac{\Gamma(\theta + 1)}{\alpha^2},$$

where

$$\gamma_{\alpha,\theta} = \frac{\theta + \alpha}{\Gamma(\theta + 2\alpha)} - \frac{\Gamma(\theta + 1)}{\Gamma(\theta + \alpha)^2}.$$

The Mittag–Leffler function $g_\alpha(x)$ has the property that its pth moment is given by

$$\int_0^\infty x^p g_\alpha(x)dx = \frac{\Gamma(p + 1)}{\Gamma(p\alpha + 1)},$$

for $p > -1$. (See the Appendix.) Then the coefficient of variation of L is seen to become zero for $\alpha = 0$.

Yamato and Sibuya (2000) and Pitman (2002) have shown that K_n/n^α converges to L in distribution, and almost surely, and

$$CV(K_n/n^\alpha) \to CV(L).$$

In discussing limiting expressions in the preceeding sections we encounter a random variable L with the density function called the Mittag–Leffler function. It is given by

$$g_{\alpha,\theta}(x) = [\Gamma(\theta+1)/\Gamma(\theta/\alpha+1)]x^{\theta/\alpha}g_{\alpha}(x).$$

The p-th moment of L is given by

$$\int_0^\infty x^p g_\alpha(x)dx = \frac{\Gamma(p+1)}{\Gamma(p\alpha+1)},$$

where $P > -1$.

Using this formula, we obtain the first two moments of the random variable L

$$E_{\alpha,\theta}(L) = \frac{\Gamma(\theta+1)}{\alpha\Gamma(\theta+\alpha)},$$

and

$$E_{\alpha,\theta}(L^2) = \frac{(\theta+\alpha)\Gamma(\theta+1)}{\alpha^2\Gamma(\theta+2\alpha)}.$$

From these we calculate the variance of L, and its coefficient of variation as

$$CV(L) = \Gamma(\theta+\alpha)\sqrt{\gamma(\alpha,\theta)/\Gamma(\theta+1)},$$

where

$$\gamma(\alpha,\theta) = \frac{\theta+\alpha}{\Gamma(\theta+2\alpha)} - \frac{\Gamma(\theta+1)}{\Gamma(\theta+\alpha)^2}.$$

Note that the expression $\gamma(\alpha,\theta)$ defined above is zero at $\alpha = 0$, otherwise it is positive for $\alpha > 0$. See Appendix for some additional information on the Mittag–Leffler functions and distributions.

9.6 Ineffective policy choices in non-self-averaging models

9.6.1 The non-self-averaging phenomenon in two blocks of economies

Next, we use a purely analytical method of cumulant generating function to show the existence of non-self-averaging in one block of economies, by positing a master equation for dynamic growth of two blocks of economies with size n_i, $i = 1,2$, and then by first converting it into the probability generation function and second into a set of equations for the first two cumulants. See Aoki (2002, s. 7.1) on master equations and cumulant equations, for example.

We solve the set of cumulant equations to obtain analytic expressions for the means and the elements of the covariance matrix. Finally, we calculate the coefficients of variations for the means of n_1 and n_2, and show that one block can be non-self-averaging while the other is self-averaging when a factor of production (labor or capital) n_2 is growing faster than n_1 and is being exported from country 2 to country 1. We then show that economy 1 is self-averaging but that economy 2 is non-self-averaging.

A limited amount of simulations bear out this theoretical analysis (Ono, 2007). The question of convergence has been addressed in a number of papers in the economic literature. Some give affirmative answers while the others give negative or qualified negative answers; see for example Phillips and Sul (2003) and Mathunjwa and Temple (2006).

We also use a purely analytical framework by positing a master equation for dynamic growth of two blocks of economies with size, $n_i, i = 1,2$, and then converting it into a set of equations for the first two cumulants. Then the cumulant equations are solved and we calculate the coefficients of variations for the means of n_1 and n_2. We show that the coefficient of variation for block 2, which is the exporting block, diverges, while the coefficient of variation for the importing block is self-averaging with nearly zero cross-correlation coefficient between the two blocks.

9.6.2   The master equation, probability generating function and cumulant equations

Consider a system composed of two economies of size n_1 and n_2 with probability $p(n_1\,n_2)$. If we take d_i and c_i to be the death rate and birth rate, respectively, of block i, the net growth of this block becomes $g_i = c_i - d_i$. We assume that $g_2 > g_1$, and denote the rate of migration of agents from block 2 to block 1 by $nu > 0$. For this system, the master equation is

$$\frac{dP(n_1,n_2)}{dt} = I(n_1,n_2) - O(n_1,n_2),$$

where I is the inflow and O is the outflow of agents, and their expressions are

$$I(n_1,n_2) = P(n_1+1,n_2)d_1(n_1+1) + P(n_1,n_2)d_2(n_2+1)$$
$$+ P(n_1,n_2)c_1(n_1-1) + P(n_1,n_2-1)c_2(n_2-1)$$
$$+ P(n_1-1,n_2+1)v(n_2+1),$$
$$O(n_1,n_2) = P(n_1,n_2)\{c_1n_1 + c_2n_2 + d_1n_1 + d_2n_2 + vn_2.\}$$

We define the probability generating function by

$$G(z_1, z_2; t) = \sum_{z_1, z_2} P(n_1, n_2) z_1^{n_1} z_2^{n_2},$$

and convert the master equation for $P(n_1, n_2)$ into

$$\frac{\partial G}{\partial t} = d_1(1 - z_1)\frac{\partial G}{\partial z_1} + [d_2(1 - z_2) + v(z_1 - z_2)]\frac{\partial G}{\partial z_2}$$
$$+ c_1 z_1(z_1 - 1) + c_2 z_2(z_2 - 1).$$

In deriving the above expressions we must collect terms with the coefficients of the same powers of z_1 and z_2.

See Aoki (2002, ch. 7) on the probability generating functions and master equations.

We solve the above by converting it into the equations for the cumulants. The first two cumulants, κ_i are the expected values of n_i, $i = 1,2$, and the covariance matrix elements are given by the cumulant $\kappa_{1,1}$, $\kappa_{2,2}$, and $\kappa_{1,2}$, which are the covariance matrix elements. See Cramer (1949, p. 186), Cox and Miller (1965), Aoki (2002), or Aoki and Yoshikawa (2007, p. 37).

9.6.3 The dynamics for the mean and the covariance matrix elements

The dynamic equation for the two means is given by

$$\frac{d\kappa_1}{dt} = g_1 \kappa_1 + v\kappa_2,$$

and

$$\frac{d\kappa_2}{dt} = g_2 \kappa_2 - v\kappa_1,$$

where we assume that $g_2 > g_1$, that is, block 1 receives an inflow of resources from block 2. The three dynamic equations for the elements of the covariance matrix are

$$\frac{dx}{dt} = Dx + Hm,$$

where x is a vector with elements $\kappa_{1,1}$, $\kappa_{2,2}$, and $\kappa_{1,2}$, and m has elements κ_1 and κ_2.

The matrix D is defined by

$$D = \begin{bmatrix} 2g_1 & 0 & 2v \\ 0 & 2\mu & 2v \\ 0 & v & 2\mu - v \end{bmatrix},$$

where $2g_1 = \mu - v$, and the matrix H is defined by

$$H = \begin{bmatrix} g_1 & -v \\ 0 & -v \\ 0 & v \end{bmatrix}.$$

We use the Laplace transforms to solve the dynamic equations.

First, we assume that the two blocks of economies are expected to grow at the same rate,

$$\mu = (g_1 + g_2)/2.$$

Next, we set

$$v = (g_2 - g_1)/2 > 0,$$

where we recall that $g_2 > g_1$ by assumption, in other words, $g_1 = \mu - v$, and $g_2 = \mu + v$.

Solving the elements of the covariance matrix is straightforward. The cross term $\kappa_{1,2}$ goes to zero asymptotically. This indicates that the growth patterns of the two economies asymptotically becomes uncorrelated.

9.6.4   The behaviour of the coefficients of variation

From the dynamic equations for the means, we derive their Laplace transform equations as

$$\kappa_1(s) = \frac{\Delta_1}{[(s - g_2)\kappa_1(0) + v\kappa_2(0)]},$$

and

$$\kappa_2(s) = \frac{\Delta_1}{[(s - g_1)\kappa_2(0) - v\kappa_1(0)]},$$

where $\Delta_1 = (s - g_1)(s - g_2) + v^2 = (s - \mu)^2$.

The matrix Δ has two equal roots $\mu=(g_2-g_1)/2$ by choice.

Collect ($\kappa_{1,1}$, $\kappa_{2,2}$, $\kappa_{1,2}$), as a three-dimensional vector x, and (κ_1, κ_2) as a two-dimensional vector y.

Solving the equation is straightforward. The results are that we have

$$\frac{\sqrt{\kappa_{1,1}}}{\kappa_1} \approx \frac{e^{-\nu t}}{\sqrt{(t)}} \to 0,$$

and

$$\frac{\sqrt{\kappa_{2,2}}}{\kappa_2} \approx \frac{e^{\nu t/2}}{t} \to \infty.$$

In words, block 1, which is an exporting sector of capital goods or labor, is self-averaging, but block 2 is non-self-averaging. This result is interesting since the block of economies that is importing the factor of production such as labor or innovations is self-averaging but the exporting block is not self-averaging.

9.7 Related simulation studies

A related but more complicated model in Aoki (2002, s. 7.1) was examined by Ono (2007), who simulated several two-sector models using both the cumulants and the Monte Carlo method for the case of one technically advanced sector and another less technically advanced sector. The model has many more parameters than the one described in the section above.

The broad conclusion of this analysis is that the technically advanced sector behaves in a non-self-averaging manner and the other sector in a self-averaging manner.

Sector 1, which is initially of size $n_1 = 250$, and technically advanced, behaves in non-self-averaging way, while sector 2, which is larger with initial size $n_2 = 500,000$ than sector 1 but less advanced technically, behaves in a self-averaging manner. The size of the CVs in Ono's simulation a re approximately 0.07 for sector 1 and about 0.014 in sector 2. In other words, the standard deviation of n_1, that is, the square root of κ_{11} is about 7 percent of the mean of n_1 in sector 1, and that in sector 2 is about 1.5 percent. This conclusion holds both with the cumulant analysis and with Monte Carlo simulations. The correlation between the n_1 and n_2 sectors is completely negligible in both the cumulant analysis and the Monte Carlo runs.

Interestingly, self-averaging behavior was not found to be a robust outcome for one of the two sectors. Altering the rate at which firms change their types in Monte Carlo simulations could induce non-self-averaging behavior in *both* sectors: a result of particular importance for economic policy designs, as mentioned above.

The overall conclusion of the cumulant analysis is the realization on the part of policymakers that in real economies with several sectors CVs are likely not to be the same across sectors but to vary from sector to sector.

9.8 Non-self-averaging triangular urn models

In the previous section we considered a simple innovation-driven growth model in which some macroeconomic variables were non-self-averaging. Stochastic events are not confined to innovations, of course. No wonder modern macroeconomics—rational expectations models, real business cycle theory, labor search theory, and endogenous growth theory— explicitly takes into account stochastic "shocks" in representative models. Most models can be interpreted as a variety of stochastic processes

Now, many stochastic processes can be interpreted as urn models. For example, the Ewens process, which is a one-parameter Poisson–Dirichlet model in which only one type of innovation occurs, has been implemented as an urn model by Hoppe (1984). More generally, by drawing balls not uniformly but at random times governed by exponential distribution urn models can be reinterpreted as stochastic processes, as shown by Athreya and Karlin (1968).

An important characteristic of urn models is that such processes are *path dependent*. Feller (1968, p. 119) calls path dependence an "after-effect." he says that "it is conceivable that each accident has an after-effect in that it either increases or decreases the chance of new accidents."

An obvious example would be contagious diseases. In a classic paper by Eggenberger and Polya (1923), an urn model was introduced to describe contagious diseases. In Polya's urn scheme, the drawing of either color increases the probability of the same color at the next drawing, and we are led to such path dependence as seen in contagious diseases. We can easily conceive of path-dependent phenomena in economies. They can be described by urn models. We next show that a class of urn models displays non-self-averaging behavior.

These examples are meant to demonstrate that non-self-averaging is not pathological but generic.

9.8.1   Balanced triangular urn models

Using the scheme of Flajolet, Dumas and Puyhaubert (2005), we describe urns with two types of colored balls, black and white. The balls may be interpreted as sectors or innovations. The colors of balls represent different kinds of sectors or innovations. Actual interpretations are quite flexible.

We show that this urn has a number of black balls, say, that are non-self-averaging.

The urn model is described in terms of replacement matrix M. Specifically, we use a 2×2 triangular matrix M, with elements $m_{1,1} = a > 0$, $m_{1,2} = b - a$, $m_{2,1} = 0$, and $m_{2,2} = b$.

This matrix M specifies that, if a black ball (ball of type 1) is drawn, it is returned to the urn together with a additional black balls, and $(b - a)$ white balls. If a white ball (ball of type 2) is drawn, then it is returned to the urn together with b white balls. No black ball is added in this case. The replacement matrix M is triangular. The urn is called balanced because the two row sums of M are equal (both sums are b). It means that the total number of balls in the urn is the same regardless of the color of the balls drawn.

We show below that the stochastic process described by this urn model is non-self-averaging. This feature is caused by the fact that the generating mechanism, that is, the mix of balls of two types, is path-dependent for the same reason as the Poisson–Dirichlet model in the preceding section. Note that in this model the ratio of black and white balls is path dependent, and varies endogenously. The number of balls of each type being put into the urn clearly depends on the way the two types of ball have been drawn in the past.

Suppose that there are r black balls and s white balls after n draws. This composition of the types of ball is represented by a monomial as $u^r v^s$. Then, there are altogether $a_0 + b_0 + b \times n$ balls in the urn, where a_0 and b_0 are the numbers of initial black and white balls. Recall that the urn is balanced. Now, with r black balls in the urn, there are r ways of picking a black ball, and each such draw results in a additional black balls and $b - a$ additional white balls.

Therefore, after a draw of a black ball, the monomial $u^r v^s$ is transformed into $r u^{r+a} v^{s+b-a}$. Here variables u and v are dummy variables or place markers to carry information on the numbers of black and white balls.

Likewise, a draw of a white ball changes the monomial into $s u^r v^{s+b-a}$. This evolution is represented by the operator Γ:

$$\Gamma = u^{a+1} v^{b-a} \frac{\partial}{\partial u} + v^{b+1} \frac{\partial}{\partial v}.$$

All possible compositions of this urn at time n are represented by a polynomial in u and v, $f_n(u,v)$. Using the operator Γ defined above, we have

$$f_{n+1}(u,v) = \Gamma f_n(u,v).$$

By defining the exponential generating function

$$H(z,u,v) = \sum_n f_n(u,v)z^n/n!,$$

we obtain its first-order partial differential equation

$$u^{a+1}v^{b-a}\frac{\partial H}{\partial u} + v^{b+1}\frac{\partial H}{\partial v} = \frac{\partial H}{\partial z}.$$

This equation can be solved by the method of characteristics (see Aoki, 2002, A.1), for examples). The partial differential equation above is converted into a set of ordinary differential equations

$$du/dt = u^{a+1}v^{b-a}, \ dv/dt = v^{b+1},$$

and

$$dz/dt = -1.$$

Eliminating dt from the above, we obtain

$$\frac{du}{u^{a+1}} = \frac{dv}{v^{a+1}}.$$

The equation for v can be integrated directly. Then the other equation is integrated, yielding two constants of integration. The general solution is a function of these two constants of integration. To be concrete, suppose that $a = 1$ and $b = 2$. We then obtain the first integral as follows:

$$\phi_1(z,u,v) = z - (2v^2)^{-1},$$

and

$$\phi_2(z,u,v) = 1/v - 1/u.$$

Hence

$$H(z,u,v) = h(z - 1/(2v^2), 1/v - 1/u),$$

where

$$H(0,u,v) = un.$$

With this generating function, we can obtain the probability distribution of X_n, the number of black balls at time n. Note that, because the urn is balanced, and the total number of balls at n is not random, once we know the number of black balls we automatically know the number of white balls as well. Puyhaubert (2003) thus establishes the result that X_n is non-self-averaging. It is noted above that Mittag–Leffler function $g_\alpha(x)$ has the property that its pth moment is given by

$$\int_0^\infty x^p g_\alpha(x)dx = \frac{\Gamma(p+1)}{\Gamma(p\alpha+1)},$$

for $p > -1$.

As we have seen in the previous section, we can show that $CV(X_n)$ remains positive even if n approaches infinity, that is, it is non-self-averaging.

Proposition: The number of black balls in the balanced triangular urn model is non-self-averaging.

Janson (2006) examines triangular urns that are not balanced. Specifically, Janson (2006, th. 1.3) derives that, when the replacement matrix consists of $m_{1,1} = a = c+d, m_{12} = c, m_{2,1} = 0,$ and $m_{2,2} = d$ he obtains the convergence in distribution

$$n^{-d/a}X_n \to^d W,$$

where X_n is the number of black balls, n is the number of drawings, and W has a generalized Mittag–Leffler distribution.

By identifying the two parameters θ nd α in the $PD(\alpha, \theta)$ in the following way

$$(a_0 + b_0)/a = \theta + 1,$$

and

$$b_0/d = \theta/\alpha,$$

where we can observe that these two Mittag–Leffler moment expressions are the same as the random variable L in the two-parameter Poisson-Dirichlet model presented above. This fact means that the two distributions are identical beacuse the moments of Mittag–Leffler distributions uniquely determine the distribution (Bingham, Goldie and Teugels (1987, p. 391). Janson (2006, th. 1.3) shows that, depending on parameters of the replacement matrix, namely, a,c and d, X_n, the number of black balls, becomes non-self-averaging. Puyhaubert (2005) has explicit expressions for the first two moments of X_n, from which it is clear that X_n is not self-averaging.

We can summarize this analysis as follows:

Proposition: In non-balanced triangular urn models, depending on the values of parameters, non-self-averaging emerges. Non-self-averaging is generic in the sense that a set of parameters for which non-self-averaging emerges is not of measure zero.

9.9 Concluding remarks

The analysis of this chapter and the related numerical studies cited in this chapter suggest that the phenomena of non-self-averaging abound in economics, and cannot be ignored. In particular, this chapter suggests that economies may contain both self-averaging and non-self-averaging sectors interacting with each other.

Given this realization, we should not persist in using only self-averaging models in our studies of economic phenomena but amend our attitude and examine in our policy analysis the possibilities of sectors of two or more different types of agent mutually interacting and with non-self-averaging behavior (see also Aoki, 1996, 2000a, 2000b).

We have also established that policy becomes less effective as the value of the CVs falls towards zero.

9.10 Appendix: Mittag–Leffler function and its distribution

A short description of Mittag–Leffler distribution is available in Kotz, Read, Balakrishnan, Vidakovic, eds, 2006. See also Erdelyi (1955).

The Mittag–Leffler function was introduced by G. Mittag–Leffler in (1905) as a generalization of the exponential function. For t non-negative, and $0 < \alpha < 1$, it is given by

$$F_\alpha(t) = \sum_0^\infty \frac{(-t)^k}{\Gamma(1+k\alpha)}.$$

This function is generalized to a two-parameter version. H. Pollard (1948), Feller (1970, vol. 2, XIII.1 XIII.8), Blumenfeld and Mandelbrot (1997), and others have contributed to clarifying the properties of this function.

For example, it is shown that $F\alpha$ is the Laplace transform of a probability measure on R_+.

It is also known that the Mittag–Leffler density F_α has the moment-generating function

$$\int_0^\infty e^{xt} f_\alpha(x)dx = F_\alpha(t).$$

Its density function is given by

$$f_\alpha(u) = F'_\alpha(u) = \frac{1}{\pi}\sum_1^\infty \frac{(-1)^k}{k!} sin(\pi(k\alpha))\frac{1+\alpha k}{u^{\alpha k+1}}.$$

See also Blumenfeld and Mandelbrot (1997) and Pollard (1948).

The moment condition

$$\int_0^\infty x^p f_\alpha dx = \frac{\Gamma(p+1)}{\Gamma(p\alpha+1)}$$

uniquely determines the distribution, which is completely monotone. From this condition we see that the integral of f_α from 0 to infinity is 1, as it should be. Moments uniquely determine the distribution that is completely monotone. The moment-generating function recovers the function $F\alpha(t)$.

Note

The author is grateful for many discussions with Professor M. Sibuya, Professor H. Yoshikawa, and Professor R. Hawkins. Comments by Professor G. Rehme were helpful in clarifying some technical points.

References

Aghion, P., and Howitt, P. (1992), 'A Model of Growth through Creative Destruction', *Econometrica* 60, pp. 323–51.

Aoki, M. (1996), *New Approaches to Macroeconomic Modeling: Evolutionary Stochastic Dynamics, Multiple Equilibria, and Externalities as Field Effects*, New York: Cambridge University Press.

—— (2000a), 'Open Models of Share Markets with Two Dominant Types of Participants,' *Journal of Economic Behavior & Organization*, 49, pp. 199–216.

—— (2000b), 'Cluster Size Distributions of Economic Agents of Many Types in a Market,' *Journal of Mathematical Analysis and Applications*, 249, pp. 32–52.

—— (2002), *Modeling Aggregate Behavior and Fluctuations in Economics: Stochastic Views of Interacting Agents*, New York: Cambridge University Press.

———— (2008a), 'Thermodynamic Limits of Macroeconomic or Financial Models: One- and Two-Parameter Poisson-Dirichlet Models,' *Journal of Economic Dynamics and Control*, 32, pp. 66–84.

———— (2008b), 'Dispersion of Growth Paths of Macroeconomic Models in Thermodynamic Limits: Two-Parameter Poisson–Dirichlet Models,' *Journal of Economic Interaction and Coordination*, 3, 3–13.

———— (2008c), 'Growth Patterns of Two Types of Macro-models: Limiting Behavior of One- and Two-Parameter Poisson-Dirichlet Models,' in R. R. A. Farmer (ed.), *Macroeconomics in the Small and the Large: Essays on Microfoundations, Macroeconomic Applications and Economic Theory in Honor of Axel Leijonhufvud*, Northampton, MA: Edward Elgar, pp. 115–23.

———— and Yoshikawa, H. (2007), *Reconstructing Macroeconomics: A Perspective From Statistical Physics and Combinatorial Stochastic Processes*, New York: Cambridge University Press.

Athreya, K. B. and Karlin, S. (1968), 'Embedding of Urn Schemes into Continuous Time Markov Branching Processes and Related Limit Theorems,' *Annals of Mathematical Statistics* 39, pp. 1801–17.

Bingham, N. H., Goldie, C. M., and Teugels, J. L. (1987), *Regular Variations*, Cambridge: Cambridge University Press.

Blumenfeld, R. and Mandelbrot, B. B. (1997), 'Levy Dusts, Mittag–Leffler Statistics, Mass Fractal Lacunarity, and Perceived Dimension,' *Physical Review E*, 56, pp. 112–18.

Carlton, M. A. (1999), Applications of the Two-Parameter Poisson-Dirichlet Distribution. Ph.D. thesis, Department of Mathematics, UCLA.

Cox, D. R. and Miller, H. D. (1965), *The Theory of Stochastic Processes*, London: Chapman and Hall.

Cramer, H. (1949), *Mathematical Methods of Statistics*, Princeton, N. J.: Princeton University Press.

Eggenberger, F. and Polya, G. (1923), 'Uber die Statistik verketteter Vogange,' *Zeitschrift fur angewandte Mathematik und Mechanik*, 3, 279–89.

Erdelyi, A. (ed.) (1995), *Higher Transcendental Function*, vol 3, New York: McGraw-Hill.

Ewens, W. J. (1972), 'The Sampling Theory of Selectively Neutral Alleles,' Theoretical Population Biology, 3, pp. 87–112.

Feller, W. (1970), *An Introduction to Probability Theory and its Applications*, (3rd edn), New York: Wiley.

Flajolet, P., Dumas, P., and Puyhaubert, V. (2006), 'Some Exactly Solvable Models of URn Process Theory,' Fourth Colloquium on Mathematics and Computer Science, DMTCS Proc., 59–118.

Galambos, J. (1978), The *Asymptotic Theory of Extreme Order Statistics*, New York, Chichester, Brisbane, Toronto: Wiley.

Grossman, G. M. and Helpman, E. (1991) *Innovation and Growth in the Global Economy*, Cambridge, MA, MIT Press.

Hoppe, F. M. (1984), 'Polya-Like Urns and the Ewens Sampling Formula,' *Journal of Mathematical Biology*, 20, pp. 91–4.

Janson, S. (2006), 'Limit Theorems for Triangular Urn Schemes,' *Prob. Theory Related Fields*, 134, pp. 417–52.

Kotz, S., Read, B., Balakrishnan, M. and Vidakovic, B. (2006), *Encyclopedia of Statistical Sciences*, Hoboken, N.J.: Wiley-Interscience.

Lucas, R. E. (1988) 'On the Mechanics of Economic Development', *Journal of Monetary Economics*, 22 (1, July), pp. 3–42.

Mathunjwa, J. and Temple, J. R. W. (2006), 'Convergence Behavior in Exogenous Growth Models,' Discussion Paper No. 06/590, Department of Economics. University of Bristol.

Ono, K. (2007), Numerical Simulation of Stochastic Models, MSc. Thesis, Department of Physics, Chuo University, Tokyo, Japan.

Phillips, P. C. B. and Sul, D. (2003), 'The Elusive Empirical Shadow of Growth Convergence,' Wowles Foundation Discussion Paper No. 1398, Yale University, February.

Pitman, J. (2002), *Lecture Notes of the Summer School on Probability*, St.Flour: Springer-Verlag.

Pollard, H. (1948), 'The Completely Monotone Character of the Mittag-Leffler Function,' *Bulletin of the American Mathematical Society Series* 2, 54, pp. 1115–16.

Puyhaubert, V., (2005), 'Analytic Urns of Triangular Form,' *Algorithms Seminar*, 2002–4, F. Chyzak (ed.), INRIA (2005), pp. 61–4.

Romer, P. M. (1986), 'Increasing Returns and Long Run Growth', *Journal of Political Economy*, 94 (5, October), pp. 1002–1037.

Yamato, H., and Sibuya, M. (2000), 'Moments of Some Statistics of Pitman Sampling Formula,' *Bulletin of Information and Cybernetics*, 6, pp. 463–88.

10
A Critical Reorientation of Keynes's Economic and Philosophical Thoughts

Izumi Hishiyama

10.1 Introduction

To Keynes, probability is a property, not of natural and social events, but of an individual's knowledge; an idea that originated, it would appear, from the views of Locke and Hume.[1] That position is clearly distinguished from the character of 'frequency theory'.

Probability in Keynes is not the 'probability of events' but the 'probability of propositions', stated in the same way as in the case of Wittgenstein. Note that Keynes does not mention Wittgenstein in the index of *A Treatise on Probability* (*TP*) (Keynes, 1973a [1921]). Probability is, however, a property inherent not in propositions themselves but in our 'degrees of rational belief'. We entertain these in the conclusive propositions that are arrived at, in virtue of our inferences based on the premise, that is, of 'a *corpus* of knowledge, actual or hypothetical' (*TP*, p. 4).

To this extent, Keynes's probability is subjective, but he considers it as objective and logical by emphasizing the logical relation between propositions. Keynes states:

> What particular propositions we select as the premises of *our* argument naturally depends on subjective factors peculiar to ourselves; but the relations, in which other propositions stand to these, and which entitle us to probable beliefs, are objective and logical.
>
> (*TP*, p. 4)

According to Keynes, this 'objective and logical' concept of probability[2,3] has not been treated as a subject worthy of consideration. He is, nevertheless, sure that such 'probable beliefs' are the basis of arguments in almost all the empirical sciences and serve in the decision-making process of our everyday lives. In other words, in order to consider the principal logical properties of probability through a consistent scheme, we must establish 'une nouvelle espèce de logique qui traitroit des degrés de probabilité', as Leibniz wrote (*TP*, p. 3). And that is precisely Keynes's main theme in *TP*.

This chapter, among other things, breaks through the difficult core of Keynesian thought – the 'logical justification' of inductive methods (*TP*, p. 241). It focuses on the assumption of methodological individualism, or the 'atomic' hypothesis,[4] with regard to the 'whole' versus 'parts' question both in *TP* and in *The General Theory of Employment Interest and Money* (*GT*) (Keynes, 1973b [1936]). Emphasis is then placed upon clarifying whether, and to what extent, inductive methods justify methodological individualism, and what differences and limits with respect to that assumption exist in those works. Moreover, as for the whole–parts question, this chapter examines the viewpoints of eminent scientists and scholars selected from the fields of natural and moral sciences, and compares them with Keynes' s conception. The chapter concludes by proposing a way to critically reorient Keynes's economic theory in order to coordinate and integrate it with Sraffa's theory.

10.2   Induction and the 'atomic' universe

Starting from evidence shown in the similarity (or positive analogy) and dissimilarity (or negative analogy) observed between particular instances, one may arrive at or infer a probability of a general conclusive proposition – what is known as a method of 'inductive generalization'. It is interesting in this connection to note that Keynes explicitly states: 'An inductive argument affirms, not that a certain matter of fact *is* so, but that *relative to certain evidence* there is a probability in its favour' (*TP*, p. 245).

There are two kinds of hypothesis to rationalize the validity of inductive methods: the hypothesis of 'atomic uniformity' and the hypothesis of 'the limitation of independent variety'.[5] The hypothesis of atomic uniformity is, it would seem, reflected in a scientific view of the universe and nature. In this regard, Keynes states

> The system of the material universe must consist, if this kind of assumption [about the *atomic* character of natural law] is warranted, of bodies which we may term (without any implication as to their size being conveyed thereby) *legal atoms*, such that each of them exercises its own separate, independent, and invariable effect, a change of the

total state being compounded of a number of separate changes each of which is solely due to a separate portion of the preceding state. [...] Each atom can, according to this theory, be treated as a separate cause and does not enter into different organic combinations in each of which it is regulated by different laws.

(*TP*, pp. 276–7)

However, what if a natural law holds an organic rather than an atomic character? Keynes would obviously respond to this question as follows:

If every configuration of the universe were subject to a separate and independent law, or if very small differences between bodies – in their shape or size, for instance – led to their obeying quite different laws, *prediction would be impossible and the inductive method useless* ... if different wholes were subject to different laws *qua* wholes and not simply on account of and in proportion to the differences of their parts, knowledge of a part could not lead, it would seem, even to presumptive or probable knowledge as to its association with other parts. *Given,* on the other hand, *a number of legally atomic units and the laws connecting them, it would be possible to deduce their effects pro tanto* without an exhaustive knowledge of all the coexisting circumstances.

(*TP*, pp. 277–8, emphasis added)

In short, if the parts–whole relation concerning the universe has an organic, not an atomic, character and, along with this, natural laws have organic, not atomic, features, it would be impossible to deduce probable knowledge about the system as a whole from knowledge of the parts constituting that system. In a nutshell, inductive inference would be useless. To confirm the validity of inductive methods, the universe must be composed of 'legally' atomic units and the laws connecting them must be atomic, certainly not organic. Keynes's answer is that the method of inductive generalization does not subsist without the assumption of atomic uniformity: 'The system of nature is finite' (*TP*, p. 290). A finite system in this sense renders inductive generalization effective. In Keynes' view, the independent variety of the universe as well should not be infinite for inductive generalization to be possible.

It should be noted that Keynes, on this point, asserts that

[T]he almost innumerable apparent properties of any given object all arise out of a finite number of generator properties, which we may call $\phi_1 \phi_2 \phi_3$ ... Some arise out of ϕ_1 alone, some out of ϕ_1 in conjunction with ϕ_2, and so on. The properties which arise out of ϕ_1 alone form one group [f_1]; those which arise out of ϕ_1 ϕ_2 in conjunction form another group [f_2] and so on. *Since the number of generator properties is finite, the number of groups also is finite.*

(*TP*, p. 282; emphasis and bracketed notation added)

In this context, a categorical statement that 'the number of generator properties is finite' plays, as it were, a definitive role. However, this is, it would appear, an a priori intuition, or rather a kind of axiom; moreover, it is not based on empirical understanding. In any event, if the number of such generator properties ϕ_1, ϕ_2, ... ϕ_k ... is *n*, the number of generated groups [f_1, f_2, f_3...] must be 2^n. Thus, whenever the number of ϕ is finite, the number of *f* is necessarily finite, and therefore one never encounters infinite quantities in this field. It is perhaps in view of this effect that Ramsey in his review article of *TP* (Ramsey, 1999 [1922], p. 255), explicitly states that 'the Hypothesis of Limited Variety is simply equivalent to the contradictory of the Axiom of Infinity'. In such a manner, 'the system of nature is finite', that is to say, 'the hypothesis of limited independent variety' generating a finite system of nature is, in fact, the assumption *sine qua non* for the validity of inductive methods.[6]

Although, as shown above, the method of inductive generalization is based on 'the hypothesis of atomic uniformity' and 'the hypothesis of limited independent variety', these hypotheses, according to Keynes, result basically in the same conception of the system of nature. It is interesting to single out his assertion in this regard:

The *hypothesis of atomic uniformity*, as I have called it, while not formally equivalent to *the hypothesis of the limitation of independent variety, amounts to very much the same thing.* If the fundamental laws of connection changed altogether with variations, for instance, in the shape or size of bodies, or if the laws governing the behaviour of a complex had no relation whatever to the laws governing the behaviour of its parts when belonging to other complexes, there could hardly be a limitation of independent variety in the sense in which this has been defined. And, on the other hand, a limitation of independent variety seems necessarily to carry with it some degree of atomic uniformity. *The underlying conception as to the character of the system of nature is in each case the same.*

(*TP*, p. 290, emphasis added)

In sum, these two inductive hypotheses are based purely upon an atomistic conception of the system of nature and of its natural laws. Part III in *TP* ('Induction and Analogy') forms, it would seem, the hard core – the main theme of which is the fundamental relationship between the validity of inductive methods and Keynesian probability. There Keynes undoubtedly adopts his atomistic views about 'universe', 'nature' and 'natural laws'.

10.3   A model of ethical behaviour and the atomic hypothesis

Keynes's analysis of alternative choices for courses of ethical action amounts to a critique of Moore's model. Moore was concerned with 'the relation of ethics to conduct' in *Principia Ethica* (Moore, 1903, pp. 146–55), which has a sophisticated utilitarian flavour based on the frequency theory of probability.

Moore's ethical model is an original type or prototype of a classical economist's model of economic behaviour which was stubbornly attacked by Keynes, both in *GT* and in subsequent publications. It should, therefore, not be neglected by studies of the evolution of Keynes's philosophical thoughts. The target of Keynes's attack is the doctrine of 'mathematical expectations' assumed in Moore's model.

The doctrine explains the situation in which an individual is facing a choice of alternatives from which he or she must choose. The order of degrees of 'mathematical expectations' attached to each alternative course of action represents an 'échelle d'intervalles', as it were, in one's preference. According to this doctrine, one must assume that an individual can forecast the future with certainty. In addition, one must introduce two further assumptions: (a) the degrees of goodness attached to each course of action must be not only numerically measurable but also arithmetically additive, and (b) their degrees of probability must be numerically measurable. According to Keynes, both assumptions stand on a doubtful and unsteady foundation. In particular, assumption (b) runs directly counter to his conception of probability as put forward in *TP*. In short, the doctrine of 'mathematical expectations' adopted in Moore's ethical model is based on neither firm nor plausible assumptions. Another serious shortcoming is that it overlooks the 'weights' of arguments; this means that it fails to consider the amount of evidence at the basis of each probability and the element of 'risk'.[7]

The following statement by Keynes relates to the choice of correct action. Interestingly, it seems somewhat similar to his later views.

> Thus even if we know the degree of advantage which might be obtained from each of a series of alternative courses of actions and know also

the probability in each case of obtaining the advantage in question, it is not always possible by a mere process of arithmetic to determine which of the alternatives ought to be chosen. *If, therefore, the question of right action is under all circumstances a determinate problem, it must be in virtue of an intuitive judgement directed to the situation as a whole, and not in virtue of an arithmetical deduction derived from a series of separate judgements directed to the individual alternatives each treated in isolation.*

(*TP*, pp. 344–5, emphasis added)

As described above, Moore's version of ethical behaviour depends on the doctrine of 'mathematical expectations', and it is obviously based on an empirical and frequency theory of probability. This is one of the reasons why Keynes tries to reject the frequency theory. Keynes sums up the importance of his own conception of probability thus:

> Probability begins and ends with probability. ... The proposition that a course of action guided by the most probable considerations will generally lead to success, is not certainly true and has nothing to recommend it but its probability.
>
> The importance of probability can only be derived from the judgement that it is *rational* to be guided by it in action; and a practical dependence on it can only be justified by a judgment that in action we *ought* to act to take some account of it. It is for this reason that probability is to us the 'guide of life'.
>
> (TP, p. 356)

What needs to be emphasized here is that, while the 'universe' view forms a sort of scheme in which Keynes considers the model of ethical behaviour, he seems to grasp such a 'universe' in virtue of its dependence upon the atomic hypothesis. Here it should be noticed that Moore expressed the difficulty associated with the decision of alternative courses of action thus: 'the first difficulty in the way of establishing a probability that one course of action will give a better *total* result than another, lies in the fact that we have to take account of the effect of both throughout an infinite future' (Moore, *Principia Ethica*, p. 152; *TP*, p. 341; emphasis added).

It is worth pointing out Keynes's caution against this difficulty suggested by Moore. Keynes states

> The difficulties which exist are not chiefly due, I think, to our ignorance of the remote future. The possibility of our knowing that one

thing rather than another is our duty depends upon the assumption that a greater goodness in any part makes, in the absence of evidence to the contrary, a greater goodness in the whole more probable than would the lesser goodness of the part. *We assume that the goodness of a part is favourably relevant to the goodness of the whole. Without this assumption we have no reason, not even a probable one, for preferring one action to any other on the whole. If we suppose that goodness is always organic,* whether the whole is composed of simultaneous or successive parts, *such an assumption is not easily justified.* The case is parallel to the question, whether physical law is organic or atomic, discussed in chapter 21.

(TP, pp. 342–3, my emphasis)

Whether an increase in the goodness or advantage of any 'part' contributes to the increase in goodness for the 'whole' of society, such a problem requires as a *sine qua non* condition the *atomic* hypothesis in order that a *positive* or favourable parts–whole relation could be established. This does not mean that the goodness of the units ought to be exhaustively atomistic; it may be as well to suppose that 'the units whose goodness we must regard as organic and indivisible are not always larger than those the goodness of which we can perceive and judge directly' (*TP*, p. 343).

10.4   The *Quarterly Journal of Economics* article and the atomic hypothesis

In 'The General Theory of Employment', an article by Keynes published in *The Quarterly Journal of Economics* (Keynes, 1937), the model of ethical behaviour investigated in *TP* seems to metamorphose into the model of economic behaviour adopted by the 'classical economists' such as Arthur Cecil Pigou. Keynes's critique focuses on the methods of classical economic theory based on this model. He describes the characteristics of the model as follows:

> [In the classical economic system] at any given time facts and expectations were assumed to be given in a definite and calculable form; and risks, of which, though admitted, not much notice was taken, were supposed to be capable of an exact actuarial computation. The calculus of probability, though mention of it was kept in the background, was supposed to be capable of reducing uncertainty to the same calculable status as that of certainty itself; just as in the Benthamite calculus of pains and pleasures or of advantage and disadvantage,

by which the Benthamite philosophy assumed men to be influenced in their general ethical behavior.

(Keynes, 1937, pp. 212–13)

One of the most important subjects in economic theory is 'wealth, or the accumulation of wealth'. However, it should not be compatible with 'the world of certainty' underlying the model of classical economists. Keynes is confident enough to assert that:

> The whole object of the accumulation of Wealth is to produce results, or potential results, at a comparatively distant, and sometimes at an indefinitely distant, date. Thus the fact that our knowledge of the future is fluctuating, vague and uncertain, renders Wealth a peculiarly unsuitable subject for the method of the classical economic theory.

(Keynes, 1937, p. 213)

To sum up, the subject of 'wealth, or the accumulation of wealth' inherently concerns a vague and uncertain future; as a result, it is something intractable for classical economic theory, because it would always reduce uncertainty into certainty by means of numerically measurable concepts of probability.

It is worth pointing out that the possibility of appraising 'uncertain' knowledge on Keynesian assumptions concerning economic behaviour is based on a restricted concept. In this regard, Keynes explains that:

> By 'uncertain' knowledge, let me explain, I do not mean merely to distinguish what is known for certain from what is only probable ... About these matters [the prospect of a European war, the price of copper and the rate of interest 20 years hence, and so on] there is no scientific basis on which to form calculable probability whatever. We simply do not know.

(Keynes, 1937, p. 214)

Let me state proposition (a), for example 'the price of copper 20 years hence will be about x Euro or dollars'. And then, suppose Keynes's 'rational, economic men' try to derive their probable beliefs [α] of this proposition from their actual or hypothetical knowledge [h]. In this case, they cannot find a scientific basis on which to form the proposition (premise or evidence) [h] intimately relating to their knowledge. Therefore, it is basically impossible to establish the probability relation $\alpha = \alpha/h$. Indeed, this is what 'uncertain' knowledge means.[8]

It is worth recalling here that Keynes asks an interesting question: 'How do we manage in such circumstances to behave in a manner which saves our faces as rational, economic men?' In order to rationalize their behaviour, Keynes's 'rational, economic men' will adopt certain strategic assumptions. I want to focus exclusively upon the last of those assumptions, as it would seem to be the most important in my subject matter. That is to say:

> Knowing that our own individual judgement is worthless, we endeavour to fall back on the judgement of the rest of the world which is perhaps better informed. That is, we endeavour to conform with the behaviour of the majority or the average. *The psychology of a society of individuals each of whom is endeavouring to copy the others leads to what we may strictly term a conventional judgement.*
>
> (Keynes, 1937, p. 214; emphasis added)

It seems to me that most economic men – individuals obsessed with such a conventional judgement – emerge on the stage of an organized investment market, namely, the stock exchange. In *The General Theory*, Keynes calls them the average private investor or the general public in contrast to professional experts. They have, to be sure, no definite preferred list of various kinds of securities, since there is, for them, no certain basis to foresee rationally the events likely to arise in the future.

Thus their behaviour, based on such conventional judgements, would be easily influenced by mass psychology fluctuating in accordance with day-to-day circumstances in the market. It is interesting to note, here, that Keynes would add

> In particular, being based on so flimsy a foundation, it is subject to sudden and violent changes. The practice of calmness and immobility, of certainty and security, suddenly breaks down. New fears and hopes will, without warning, take charge of human conduct. The forces of disillusion may suddenly impose a new conventional basis of valuation.
>
> (Keynes, 1937, pp. 214–15)

But, what, then, is the behaviour of professional experts or professional investors? Keynes clearly answers this question:

> Most of these persons are, in fact, largely concerned, not with making superior long-term forecasts of the probable yield of an investment

over its whole life, but with foreseeing changes in the conventional basis of valuation a short time ahead of the general public.

(*GT*, p. 154)

Actually, most professionals will exclusively endeavour 'to guess better than the crowd how the crowd will behave' (*GT*, p. 157).

It is, therefore, obvious that all of them – the general public and even the professional experts – emerging on the stage of the stock exchange could never be entitled to be the 'individual' assumed in the atomic hypothesis, because, being influenced by mass psychology, they do not, it would seem, behave as distinct, independent and rational economic men. Moreover, it is worth pointing out that a strictly defined 'conventional judgement', which consists basically of the psychology of a society of individuals, runs directly counter to a rational probable judgement of the 'individual' as defined in *TP*.

To sum up, all this, I think, renders the atomic hypothesis an unsuitable assumption for the analysis of the behaviour of economic subjects in organized investment markets such as explained in *GT*, since we cannot regard them as the legally atomic units based on their own rational and distinct preferences.

10.5 The *General Theory* and the atomic hypothesis

Discerning the role of the atomic hypothesis in *GT* is, I think, not a simple matter but a rather delicate and somewhat intricate one. It seems quite different from the example of economic men's *conventional* behaviour in the stock exchange identified in the *Quarterly Journal of Economics* article.

First of all, here is Keynes's definitive assertion about the main topic that we intend to consider:

I have called my theory a *general* theory. I mean by this that I am chiefly concerned with the behaviour of the economic system as a whole,—with aggregate incomes, aggregate profits, aggregate output, aggregate employment, aggregate investment, aggregate saving.... And I argue that *important mistakes have been made through extending to the system as a whole conclusions which have been correctly arrived at in respect of a part of it taken in isolation.*

(*GT*, p. xxxii, Preface to the French Edition [1939], emphasis added)

Though an individual whose transactions are small in relation to the market can safely neglect the fact that demand is not a one-sided transaction, it makes nonsense to neglect it when we come to aggregate demand. *This is the vital difference between the theory of economic behaviour of the aggregate and the theory of the individual unit, in which we assume that changes in the individual's own demand do not affect his income.*

(GT, p. 85; emphasis added)

A typical example of this 'difference between the theory of economic behaviour of the aggregate and the theory of the individual unit' is (though it might be needless to mention) the fallacy of composition shown by the so-called savings paradox. Any individual is, whatever his own motive of saving, able to increase his wealth by increasing his savings. This is, undoubtedly, a 'correct proposition' to him. But we cannot maintain that his saving behaviour contributes to increasing pro tanto *aggregate* wealth as well through extending to the system as a whole such a correct conclusion. Actually, such reasoning falls within the category of the 'fallacy of composition'. In this respect, a reduction in the individual's consumption associated with his or her saving behaviour affects the incomes of other people as well, so that we may expect changes in the aggregate income through such a series of chain reactions. In short, a manner of reasoning aiming at general proposition valid in the *whole* through the adding up of micro-level conclusions valid in a *part* of it obviously overlooks such complicated chain reactions ultimately affecting aggregate income.

Although 'the amount of saving is an outcome of the collective behaviour of individual consumers' (*GT*, p. 63), the existence of the savings paradox is absolutely not compatible with methodological individualism, the crux of which is to construct general laws or uniformity in the system as a whole through reducing it into the separate distinct and rational behaviours of individual units and then basically relying on normal individual behaviour.

Another typical example of the 'difference between the theory of economic behaviour of the aggregate and the theory of the individual unit' is the demand schedule for labour. Since Keynes's world explicitly accepts the 'first classical fundamental postulate', he is obliged to admit the inverse functional relation of employment to wages in particular industries. Thus, Keynes states that 'no one would wish to deny the proposition that a reduction in money-wages *accompanied by the same aggregate effective demand as before* will be associated with an increase in employment' (*GT*, p. 259; emphasis in original).

It is precisely a fallacy of composition that one endeavours to obtain 'a demand schedule for labour in industry as a whole' through extending by analogy such conclusions in respect of a particular industry and to find therein the inverse functional relation as well.

The reason such an analogy is wrong is that, according to Keynes, it entirely overlooks the effects of chain reactions starting from a particular industry and ultimately changing aggregate effective demand, just as in the savings paradox.

Since we do not mean to admit (though we do not discuss it further) the 'first classical fundamental postulate', that is, that 'the wage is equal to the marginal product of labour', we cannot regard 'the demand schedule for labour in the industry relating the quantity of employment to different levels of wages' (*GT*, p. 259) as a consistent and solid ground for economic theory.[9]

However, when Keynes comes to the cost side his approach suddenly and fundamentally changes. A suitable approach on the cost side must be 'to extend by analogy its conclusions in respect of a particular industry to industry as a whole' (*GT*, p. 260). It is worth recalling that this is precisely the method rejected by Keynes on the demand side. In rough terms, since the behaviour of an individual part and the behaviour of the whole are, on the cost side, not basically distinct from each other (except for the degree of aggregation), one is liable to adopt the method by which one first disaggregates the whole into separate parts and then extends by analogy the conclusions arrived at in respect of a particular component part to the system as a whole. This is, I think, nothing other than methodological individualism, or the atomic hypothesis.

In any case, it is interesting to note what Keynes asserts:

> In a single industry its particular price-level depends partly on the rate of remuneration of the factors of production which enter into its marginal cost, and partly on the scale of output. *There is no reason to modify this conclusion when we pass to industry as a whole.* The general price-level depends partly on the rate of remuneration of the factors of production which enter into marginal cost and partly on the scale of output as a whole, i.e. (taking equipment and technique as given) on the volume of employment.
>
> (*GT*, p. 294; emphasis added)

As seen above, it is obvious that the Marshallian short-run and diminishing returns (that is, increasing costs) industry are the starting point of Keynes's cost analysis. What is rather peculiar to Keynes's approach and makes it somewhat different from Marshall's is that it extends to industry as a whole the positive monotonic relation of marginal cost to output in respect of a single industry without any modification. As a result, Keynes's production economy (viewed from the 'cost' angle) seems to be something like a gigantic industry composed of homogenous and continuous elements.[10] It forms a conspicuous contrast with the analysis of Piero Sraffa, in which the economic system generates the objective technological network among various industries, and the general price-level associated with industry as a whole must be represented explicitly as a set of particular prices. But, according to the assumption of increasing costs, the Keynesian marginal cost of such an economy-wide industry, if it were to be, is assumed to rise as the scale of output as a whole increases.

It is true that, since Keynes maintains that 'when we pass to output as a whole, the costs of production in any industry partly depend on the output of other industries' (*GT*, p. 294), he would seem to take into account the technological network among industries. But, in fact, this remains on the fringe of his attention. This is shown by the fact that, starting from the short-run diminishing returns of a particular industry considered in isolation, Keynes extends by analogy the conclusions attained in respect of a single industry (increasing marginal cost) to the output as a whole. This is, I think, unquestionable.

Thus Keynes, within the above conceptual framework, insists that the importance of his remarkable and revolutionary contribution lies on the demand side of economic theory. And he states:

> It is *on the side of demand that we have to introduce quite new ideas when we are dealing with demand as a whole* and no longer with the demand for a single product taken in isolation, with the demand as a whole assumed to be unchanged.
>
> (*GT*, p. 247; emphasis added)

Be that as it may, it follows from what we saw above, first, that Keynes explicitly grounds the atomic hypothesis on the side of cost and, second, that he conceives as the starting point of his cost analysis the Marshallian short-run supply curve for a single product taken in isolation.[11]

10.6   The 'theory' of effective demand

Nobody could deny by now that the core of *GT* is a theory of the determination of output (or employment) by effective demand. Let us begin by discussing that theory, which is explained in a clear and succinct way in the article in *The Quarterly Journal of Economics* (Keynes, 1937).

It is to be noted, among other things, that the theory supposes a certain mature capitalist market economy like that of the United Kingdom in the 1930s. Keynes's following statement is worth quoting in that connection:

> The theory can be summed up by saying that, given the psychology of the public, the level of output and employment as a whole depends on the amount of investment. I put it in this way, not because this is the only factor on which aggregate output depends, but because it is usual in a complex system to regard as *causa causans* that factor which is most prone to sudden and wide fluctuation.
>
> (Keynes, 1937, p. 221)

In contrast to the relatively stable behaviour of consumption, unstable investment, depending on uncertain and doubtful long-term prospects, plays a strategic role as *causa causans* in determining output as a whole.[12] That proposition has, it should be noted, a crucial importance in the case of schematizing the 'causal nexus' in complex systems such as those considered by Keynes.

In the article in *The Quarterly Journal of Economics*, Keynes explicitly assumes a two-sector model composed of one consumption-goods industry and one investment-goods industry. Then he explains the multiplier formula thus:

> [T]here is always a formula, ... relating the output of consumption goods which it pays to produce to the output of investment goods; and I have given attention to it in my book under the name of Multiplier.
>
> (Keynes, 1937, p. 220)

This formula would, I think, be verified not with reference to an individual unit, but merely with reference to the behaviour of aggregates, namely, aggregate investment, aggregate consumption, aggregate saving, and aggregate output, in such a way that, given a certain marginal propensity to consume, when there is an increment of aggregate investment, aggregate output will necessarily increase by an amount which is k times the increment of investment. As to consumption, it will increase by an amount which is $k - 1$ times the increment of investment.

It is very important to note that the quantitative and deterministic character of the multiplier is decisively significant in Keynes's theory of effective demand, and that its working will proceed *quite independently of any individual's behaviour.*

The *theory* of effective demand, though disclosed in the formula of the investment multiplier process, would essentially be a behavioural mechanism under the institutional set-up of a capitalist market economy. However, that theory is a typical instance which clarifies 'the vital difference between the theory of economic behaviour of the aggregate and the theory of the individual unit' (*GT*, p. 85). Therefore, it is obvious that one could never grasp it in virtue of the atomic hypothesis, even though the amount of investment is an outcome of 'the collective behaviour of individual entrepreneurs' (*GT*, p. 63).

10.7   The 'principle' of effective demand: Pasinetti's view

Luigi Pasinetti points out that, though '"The Principle of Effective Demand" is the title of a crucial chapter – Chapter 3 – of Keynes's *General Theory*, [...] the "principle" of effective demand is not studied' (Pasinetti, 1997, p. 93).

According to Pasinetti, what is worth denoting as the 'principle' should belong to a more fundamental level of investigation which concerns a basic characteristic of a production economy, independently of any behavioural relations, of market structure and even of any institutions.

It is generally recognized that Keynes's theory of effective demand, which focuses on the physical quantity-adjustment mechanism and operates through the multiplier process, is based on aggregate behavioural functions – that is, aggregate demand functions and aggregate supply functions.

In order to specify the basic characteristics of a 'monetary production economy', Pasinetti decides to abandon all those behavioural functions.

Above all, the replacement of a 45° line for the original aggregate supply function $[Z = \Phi(N)]$ is required. Thus, he states:

> It meant abandoning a level of analysis that was aimed at explaining the actual behaviour of entrepreneurs acting in a specific market structure (imperfect or perfect competition) in order to uncover more fundamental relationships. It meant giving up the details of firms' behaviour in order to gain deeper insight into the more basic— institutionally free—characteristics of the economic system.
>
> (Pasinetti, 1997, p. 98)

On the other hand, when considering the demand side, Pasinetti leaves aside Keynes's consumption and investment functions. Thus, one may deprive the usual 45° line diagram of every behavioural content, therefore 'remaining simply with the two axes and the 45° line' (Pasinetti, 1997, p. 99).[13]

What is behind such a modified diagram is that

> at any given point in time a production economy is characterized by a specific and well-differentiated productive capacity and by a corresponding labour force (with specific skills and training) [...] The productive capacity and labour force are whatever they are: in the short run they cannot be changed. But they only represent *potential* production. *Actual* production will thus turn out to be whatever effective demand is expected to be. In this sense, effective demand generates production.
>
> (Pasinetti, 1997, p. 99)

Very interestingly, Pasinetti adds the following:

> This process (of production-generation by effective demand) is a basic characteristic of any production economy. It is quite independent of any behavioural relations and thus of any particular adaptation mechanism. It is independent of market structure, it is even independent of the particular consumption and investment functions introduced by Keynes. Basically, it is independent of institutions, by simply being inherently characteristic of the way in which industrial economy (in contrast with agricultural and artisan economy) have come to be set up.
>
> It is this basic, non-institutional, or if we like pre-institutional, characteristic, lying at the very foundations of industrial societies, that – I should venture to say – represents the 'principle' of effective demand.
>
> (Pasinetti, 1997, p. 100)

Mitsuharu Itô clearly makes the same point but from a different perspective:

> The production price of Sraffa represents the exchange-ratio of commodities to make possible the circular process of the system as a whole, quite independently of any behaviour of economic agents. In this sense, the characteristic of Sraffa's theory is 'objective' and is different from the ordinary price theory based on a specific behaviour of economic agents. Thus, Sraffa's theory may be comparable

with Keynes's macrolaw formalized in the Multiplier mechanism operating entirely independently of the behaviour of individual economic agents.

(Itô, 1987, pp. 154–5)

At any rate I think it is hardly necessary to point out that the *principle* of effective demand explicitly analysed by Pasinetti is not based on the atomic hypothesis. This is because the hypothesis always requires the specific behavioural assumption of the atomic unit, whereas the 'principle' is thoroughly independent of all behavioural relations.

It is not unreasonable to say that even the *theory* of effective demand formalized by Keynes would be totally unsuitable for the atomic hypothesis. For the multiplier mechanism depends on genuine behavioural functions, but the multiplier process as such would proceed on its own whatever line of action the individual units prefer.

10.8   The Keynesian world view: deterministic uniformity in the macro world versus the uncertainty of an individual unit in the micro world

It may be necessary for us to take a roundabout journey in order to shed light on the Keynesian 'parts–whole' question from an interdisciplinary point of view.

Let us begin by looking at Rudolf Carnap's *Philosophical Foundations of Physics* (1966). As for the deterministic view of science in the nineteenth century, he states:

Nineteenth century physicists and many philosophers as well took for granted that, behind all the macrolaws, with their inescapable errors of measurement, are microlaws that are exact and deterministic ... The behavior of molecules must depend on *something*. It cannot be arbitrary and haphazard. The basic laws of physics must be deterministic.

(Carnap, 1966, p. 281)

In fact, certain scholars conceive of nineteenth-century natural science, in particular physics, as a typical model and reconstruct moral science on the basis of it. They would probably share the confidence of nineteenth-century physicists described above. It seems to me that such confidence forms the background to their adopting an atomic hypothesis in the field of moral sciences. I think it is not unreasonable to say that a striking example of that attitude is neoclassical economic theory as it emerged from the 'marginal revolution', particularly the Walrasian scheme of general economic equilibrium in its complete logical consistency.

Compared with the history of natural sciences, Keynes in *TP* might occupy the intermediate place between nineteenth-century classical physics and twentieth-century modern physics. The reason for this is that, from the standpoint of a theory of knowledge, Keynes is interested in the uncertainty involved in the behaviour of individuals – 'the twilight, as I may so say, of Probability' (Locke's words as quoted by Keynes) – and also in the doubtful and inconclusive feature of their judgement. In short, he was exclusively concerned with the rational but indeterministic character of individual consciousness. In broad terms, it may be said that Keynes rooted 'the principle of uncertainty' in the ground of moral science by proposing a new logic of probability.

It may not, however, be unreasonable to think that Keynes himself came to hold doubts about his own standpoint concerning 'science and universe' once the implications of the 'doctrine of relativity' are considered. However, he would not enter a discussion of this issue, and his doubt remains confined to a footnote of *TP*: '[i]s *this interpretation of the principle of the uniformity of nature* affected by the doctrine of relativity?' (TP, p. 276n; emphasis added).

It would seem that what 'this interpretation of the principle of the uniformity of nature' entails, is the proposition that 'it is in respect of such positions in time or space that "nature" is supposed' (*TP*, p. 252). Briefly put, it can be traced back to the view of nature in classical mechanics, according to which, given the position and momentum of a certain elementary body in space at a point of time, we can exactly predict the position (and momentum) of it at any future point of time by relying on some fundamental laws connecting those bodies.

When, following Cambridge philosophers like Bertrand Russell, Ludwig Wittgenstein and George Edward Moore, Keynes endeavours to picture the 'universe', he assumes, I think, the world of Newtonian classical physics. If so, his interpretation of 'the uniformity of nature', or rather of 'the atomic uniformity' must be radically influenced by the emergence of modern physics, as he himself anticipated with uneasy feeling.

However, when Keynes comes to grips with the human world, he is mainly concerned with the uncertainty of human conduct. This kind of uncertainty originates from rational but inconclusive judgement arrived at by virtue of probable inference in decision-making processes. And it is by reference to the properties of probable arguments that Keynes endeavours to secure the foundation of a new type of probability.

To sum up, a conspicuous feature of Keynes's thought is that there exists a unidirectional and deterministic uniformity (or regularity) in the macroeconomic world. This uniformity is explicitly based on the principle of effective demand, the core of which is the multiplier mechanism. By contrast, we meet an ambiguous and uncertain multiplicity within the domain of individuals' activities. Those activities cannot be reduced to the scheme of rational behaviour assumed by neoclassical economists, except within a given narrow field.[14] In short, Keynes's thoughts seem to show an ambivalent, dual characteristic. In so far as Keynes's ideas as a system are concerned, a deep gulf still lies between the 'whole' of the system and its component 'parts'.

Our next step consists in discussing the views of eminent scientists and scholars in order to find a way to critically reorient Keynes's theory so as to highlight his unsettled *problématique*.

10.9 The 'whole–parts' issue: views of scientists and scholars in the natural and moral sciences[15]

10.9.1 Physicists' views of natural laws

First of all, let us examine Nobelist Richard Feynman's interesting book *The Character of Physical Law* (Feynman, 1994 [1965]), in particular Chapter 6: 'Probability and Uncertainty – The Quantum Mechanical view of Nature'. In discussing well-known experiments and observing which hole (between two holes) an electron goes through, Feynman writes:

> I only know that each time I look it [an electron] will be one hole or the other; *there is no way to predict ahead of time which hole it will be. The future, in other words, is unpredictable.* It is impossible to predict in any way, from any information ahead of time through which hole the thing will go, or which hole it will be seen behind. *That means that physics has, in a way, given up, if the original purpose was – and everybody thought it was – to know enough so that given the circumstances we can predict what will happen next.*
>
> (Feynman, 1994, p. 146; emphasis added)

It should be noted that this is entirely opposite to the view of classical physics as mentioned above (section 10.8). It was possible to exactly predict the course of movement of a legal atom in *TP*, whereas, by contrast, it is impossible to predict the course of movement of an electron in Feynman's experiments.

Feynman decisively asserts:

> It must then be impossible to have any information ahead of time, about which hole the electron is going to go through ... It is not our ignorance of the internal gears, of the internal complications [of the instruments used for the experiment], that makes nature appear to have probability in it. It seems to be somehow intrinsic. Someone has said it this way – '*Nature herself does not even know which way the electron is going to go*'.
>
> (Feynman, 1994 [1965], p. 147; emphasis added)

In this respect, he concludes: 'But here what we are proposing ... is *that there is probability all the way back that in the fundamental laws of physics there are odds*' (Feynman, 1965, p. 145; emphasis added).

It would be interesting to compare this categorical assertion with Keynes's words: 'Yet nature might still be uniform, causation sovereign and laws timeless and absolute' (*TP*, p. 277). And it is worth quoting here yet another of Keynes's assertions: '[i]t is in respect of such positions in time or space that "nature" is supposed "uniform"' (*TP*, p. 252). In the subatomic world of modern physics, however, such uniformity in nature, namely, the atomic uniformity that Keynes confidently assumes in *TP*, never exists. If so, it would be difficult, or rather impossible, for us to derive the presumptive or probable knowledge of the 'whole' from actual and/or hypothetical knowledge of the 'parts' of the world. When the hypothesis of atomic uniformity fails, does not the method of inductive generalization fail as well?

In short, modern physics is not likely to accept this claim by Keynes:

> Given, on the other hand, a number of legally atomic units and the laws connecting them, it would be possible to deduce their effects *pro tanto* without an exhaustive knowledge of all the existing circumstances.
>
> (*TP*, p. 278)

In the case of physics, one cannot make the above statement insofar as a determinate course of movement for an elementary particle in the quantum mechanical world does not exist.

Another Nobelist, Shinichiro Tomonaga explicitly answers this point in *Quantum Mechanics and I*:

An elementary particle is *something* that does not simultaneously have both position and momentum.

(Tomonaga, 1997, p. 27)

[As a conclusion resulting from the above property] an elementary particle does not have inherently the feature of taking a determinate course of movement ... Something not having such a feature is not only an elementary particle but also an atom and a nucleus. Since such particles do not in general have a given course of movement, their behaviour cannot be ruled by the usual mechanics. For mechanics is essentially the theory of a particular movement ... As far as a quantum particle is concerned ... we do not know how to determine both its position and momentum simultaneously.

(Tomonaga, 1997, pp. 272–3)

In the experiments [very similar to Feynman's] to observe which hole [of two holes] an electron goes through, we cannot determine whether the electron has passed through hole *A* or through hole *B*. Unless we think that at that point of time the electron goes through both holes simultaneously, it is impossible for us to reasonably explain those phenomena.

(Tomonaga, 1997, p. 274).

To sum up, Takeshi Inoue, one of the disciples of Hideki Yukawa, celebrated for the theory of the mesotron, briefly discusses one important implication of the 'quantum mechanical world':

Since probability plays the basic role in quantum mechanics, it is impossible for us to make a deterministic prediction. It is quite contrary to the case of Newtonian mechanics and Maxwell's electromagnetic model. In short, in a subatomic world governed through quantum mechanics, inconclusive probability comes out in place of deterministic causality. In this sense, the appearance of quantum mechanics represents a truly revolutionary outcome that radically changes the human understanding of nature.

(Inoue, 1964, p. 393)

Let us examine in this connection the following Keynes's statement:

> We do habitually assume, I think, that the size of the atomic unit is for the mental events an *individual consciousness*, and for material events an object small in relation to our perceptions.
>
> (*TP*, p. 278; emphasis added)

It is true that individual consciousness reflects an image of mental events; in the background of mental events lies the human world; and it is individuals who constitute the human world. But, compared with 'legal atoms' in the material world, these individuals meet various intrinsic uncertainties throughout their entire lives because of their (albeit not absolute) free will, incomplete and inconclusive knowledge and, in particular, unforeseen alterations in intractable circumstances. Therefore, it is not easy, or rather it is impossible, to predict how individuals will behave and where they will go in the same manner as seen in the case of an elementary particle in quantum mechanics. In a nutshell, it is basically impossible to predict their future action.

Nevertheless, in each domain of the human world academic inquiry continues at all times to build a complete and logically consistent theory as far as the system as a whole is concerned. According to Feynman, 'science goes on in spite of it – although the same conditions do not always produce the same results' (Feynman, 1994 [1965], p. 147).

10.9.2 The sociological view according to Emile Durkheim

This section examines the analyses of systems by Emile Durkheim, Ferdinand de Saussure and Antoine Meillet, and in particular their views of the relationship between the whole and its component parts.

As for the 'whole–parts' question, Durkheim states briefly:

> C'est qu' un tout n'est pas identique à la somme de ses parties, il est quelque chose d'autre et dont les propriétés diffèrent de celles que présentent les parties dont il est composé. [*A whole is not identical to the sum of its parts, it is something different, whose properties are different from those of the parts of which it is composed*].
>
> (Durkheim, 1999 [1895], p. 102)

It should be noted that this statement by Durkheim is very similar to Moore's definition in his *Principia Ethica* (Moore, 1903, p. 28): '[t]he value of a whole must not be assumed to be the same as the sum of the values of its parts'.

Keynes, too, when referring to Edgeworth's *Mathematical Psychics*, sets forth a similar conception:

> The atomic hypothesis which has worked so splendidly in physics breaks down in psychics. We are faced at every turn with the problems of organic unity, of discreteness, of discontinuity – *[T] he whole is not equal to the sum of the parts ... the assumptions of a uniform and homogeneous continuum are not satisfied.*
>
> (Keynes, 1972 [1933], p. 262; emphasis added)[16]

We can find a *locus classicus* of these discussions in Bertrand Russell's *The Principles of Mathematics* (Russell, 1903). In Chapter 16 of Volume 1 of that work ('Whole and Part') he refers to 'two very different classes of whole', that is, 'unities' and 'aggregates'.[17]

It is interesting to note here Durkheim's own view about the superiority of society to the individual:

> Sans doute, nous faisons de la contrainte la caractéristique de tout fait social ... Elle est simplement due à ce que l'individu se trouve en présence d'une force qui le domine et devant laquelle il s'incline; mais cette force est naturelle. Elle ne dérive pas d'un arrangement conventionnel que la volonté humaine a surajouté de toutes pièces au réel; elle sort des entrailles mêmes de la réalité; elle est le produit nécessaire de causes données.... Comme la supériorité que la société a sur lui [l'individu] n'est pas simplement physique, mais intellectuelle et morale [*Undoubtedly, we make constraint to be the distinguishing feature of any social fact ... This is because the individual finds himself confronted by a force that dominates him and to which he yields; but that force is natural. It is not derived from a conventional arrangement that the human will has added to reality; it comes out of the internal structure of reality itself; it is the necessary product of given causes ... Just as the dominance of society over, the individual is not simply physical but intellectual and moral as well.*]
>
> (Durkheim, 1999 [1895], pp. 121–2)

In his explanatory notes on Durkheim, Takashi Miyajima breaks through the central ideas of Durkheimian sociology. Note the following comment:

> What is a social fact? It is a kind of unique reality acknowledged by the properties of both externality and coercion and distinguished from some individual's mirror image of it. Institutions, laws, customs

and morals etc.—nearly all of them are transmitted from former generations, they govern an individual's life by means of their own logic, and form at times an irresistible coercive force. Without appropriately recognizing the objectivity and reality of these factors as such, the science of society could not be established. *It is utilitarian individualism* reducing exhaustively a social fact to individual and subjective elements *that Durkheim considered as a great enemy obstructing the existence of sociology.*

> (Miyajima, 1978, pp. 289–90; emphasis added)

As the above passage makes clear, Durkheim decisively rejected the view of society reduced to ultimate atoms, namely, logical atomism. Moreover, he always opposed Gabriel Tarde. It cannot be said that Tarde supports simplistic atomism. Rather, he adopts *une psychologie sociale* (a social psychology) or rather *une interpsychologie sociale* (social interpsychology) against Durkheim's 'sociologisme'. However it is, I think, undeniable that Tarde found the ultimate basis of his sociology in '*la croyance*' (belief) and '*le désir*' (desire) of individuals as simply suggested in the sentence: 'Tout ce qui est génial est individuel, même le crime [*Everything that is inspired pertains to the individual, even crime.*]'[18, 19]

10.9.3 Saussure's view of 'système'

It is, I think, unquestionable that the Swiss linguist Ferdinand de Saussure is one of the leading scholars who profoundly influenced the humanities and the social sciences in the twentieth century. Here I shall consider solely his discussion of the parts–whole question. In this regard, it is worth pointing out what Saussure explicitly disclosed about his view of 'système':

> Il ne faut pas commencer par le mot, le terme, pour en déduire le système. Ce serait se figurer que les termes ont d'avance une valeur absolue, qu'il n'y a qu'à les échafauder les uns sur les autres pour avoir le système. Au contraire, c'est <du système>, du tout solidaire qu' il faut partir. [*One should not start with the single word, the term, and deduce from it the system. It would be like assuming that terms have an absolute value from the very start, and that one should simply put one term on top of the other in order to have the system. On the contrary, it is from the system, from the organic whole, that one should start.*]
>
> (Saussure, 1989, p.256)[20]

Keizaburô Maruyama's comments on Saussure's concept of 'système' are worth considering: 'Saussure's conception of the "system" is an explicit denial of atomism underlying a taxonomy. It is always the whole from which one must start. The whole is not equal to the sum of the parts' (Maruyama, 1981, p. 95).

Antoine Meillet, who was at the Collège de France at the same time as Saussure (1881–91), attempted a synthesis of the points of view of Saussure and Durkheim:

> Le langage a pour première condition l'existence des sociétés humaines ... le langage est donc éminemment un fait social. En effet, il entre exactement dans la définition qu'a proposée Durkheim; une langue existe indépendamment de chacun des individus qui la parlent, et, bien qu'elle n'ait aucune réalité en dehors de la somme de ces individus, elle est cependant, de par sa généralité, extérieur à chacun d'eux;...Les caractères d'extériorité à l'individu et coercition par lesquels Durkheim définit le fait social apparaissent donc dans le langage avec la dernière évidence. [*Language has as its first condition the existence of human societies ... language is thus characteristically a social fact. As a matter of fact, language fits exactly the definition of it proposed by Durkheim: a language exists independently of any particular individual who is using it and, although it does not have any real existence outside the sum total of those individuals, it is however, due to its general character, external to any one of them. The two features of external existence relative to the individual and coercion, by which Durkheim defines the social fact, are thus unquestionably apparent in the case of language.*]
>
> (Meillet, 1982 [1905–6], p. 230)

In Meillet's view, a social fact is a kind of unique reality identified by the properties of externality and coercion. It is quite different from an individual's image of it.

10.10　Sraffa's production system: a theory independent of the atomic hypothesis

We now consider Sraffa's system of production, as it is an essential step towards a critical reorientation of Keynes' s theory.

In the field of economic theory, it is precisely Sraffa's system that can be compared to Saussure's 'system', or rather to his '*système synchronique*'. In fact, neither a particular industry nor an individual unit (such as an economic agent) can be the ultimate basis of his system. Such a basis is nothing but 'the "objective" relationship among the various sectors, as determined by the particular technology of production of the system' (Baranzini and Scazzieri, 1986, p. 33), and it is represented by Sraffa's system of equations. This is precisely why Sraffa's starting point is equivalent to Saussure's *'le tout solidaire'*.[21]

Sraffa's 'production economy' is based on the view of a 'circular process' that originates from Quesnay's *Tableau économique* (Quesnay, 1972 [1759]). This standpoint is in contrast to the unidirectional view of neoclassical economists leading from 'factors of production' to 'consumption goods' (its functional representation being the 'production function'). In Sraffa's system, the commodity price is not determined through the interaction of producers and consumers (that is, by the behavioural relations underlying the notion of supply and demand for a particular commodity, as in the case of Marshall's *Principles of Economics* (Marshall, 1961 [1890])). Rather, commodity prices are objectively determined so as to make it possible to repeat the process of production of the whole system. In fact, Sraffa's price mechanism, unlike in the usual manner of thinking, has an external and purely objective character and does not depend upon any behavioural function.

Sraffa's fundamental standpoint is, I think, explicitly disclosed in his 'Production for Subsistence' model, in which 'an extremely simple society which produces just enough to maintain itself' is considered (Sraffa, 1960, p. 3). In such a simple model, the kernel of Sraffa's price mechanism comes to light:

> There is a unique set of exchange–values which if adopted by the market restores the original distribution of the products and makes it possible for the process to be repeated; *such values spring directly from the methods of production.*
>
> (Sraffa, 1960, p. 3; emphasis added)

In Sraffa's system, the commodities that play the most notable role are the means of production, that is, the commodities that enter, directly or indirectly, the whole process of production. Therefore, the 'market' that is being considered in this system is not that for the consumption goods purchased by the housewife with her shopping bag, but the exchange market between industries, the market for basic products. In the end, such an exchange is ultimately governed by the objective technological relationship among the various industries of the system.

Sraffa's assumption of a uniform rate of profits associated with the generation of surplus is quite distant from the usual manner of thinking, as it is not based on the competitive, profit-maximization behaviour of entrepreneurs. The assumption is rather a non-behavioural and logical device introduced in order to overcome an internal contradiction within the system, and to make it determinate.[22] It follows that, if such an assumption could not be introduced, the system itself would become indeterminate and the annual cycle of production as well would not be feasible. In view of this, the following statement of Sraffa has decisive importance:

> The result is that the distribution of the surplus must be determined through the same mechanism and at the same time as are the prices of commodities.
>
> (Sraffa, 1960, p. 6.)

This sentence suggests a solution not only of the above analytical issue but also of the so-called Marxian transformation problem.

In Chapter 2, section 8, of Sraffa's book, the division of the surplus between capitalists and workers is considered and, corresponding to it, the quantity of labour employed in each industry and the wage per unit of labour, along with the rate of profits, are explicitly represented. Up to this point Sraffa's basic system of production is inherently a pre-institutional scheme and should be placed on almost the same logical level as Keynes's 'principle' of effective demand (see section 10.7 above), even if it is expressed in terms of a disaggregate multi-sectoral model. It follows that Sraffa's basic system of production is independent of behavioural relations, of assumptions about the market structure (as usually considered), and even of any institution, precisely in the same way as Keynes's principle of effective demand is. And it is hardly necessary to add that Sraffa's system of production is not based on logical atomism.

10.11   A critical reorientation of Keynes's economic theory

In the system of *GT* we find two sides that are logically inconsistent with each other.

On the demand side, the central aim of Keynes's analysis is, it would appear, to outline a theory of the determination of output (or employment) by effective demand. The core of that theory is a physical quantity-adjustment mechanism for the whole economic system – in a word, the 'multiplier' process. It is generally recognized that this is the central feature of the Keynesian Revolution. As argued especially in sections 10.4–10.7 of this chapter, we cannot say that Keynes consistently adopted the atomic hypothesis, in particular for the demand side of his system. Indeed, when we consider Keynes's philosophical thoughts, attention must be paid to his suggestion that there is deterministic uniformity for the 'whole' system versus the uncertain and varied behaviour of individuals, or its 'parts'. By contrast, the cost side of *GT* explicitly depends on the atomic hypothesis, as shown by Keynes's intention to extend by analogy to a whole industry conclusions arrived at in respect of the cost behaviour of a single industry.

The other important property of *GT* is, as it were, its two-layered logical structure. Its fundamental layer is the 'principle' of effective demand. It is entirely independent of any behavioural relations and even of any particular institutional set-up. As indeed mentioned in section 10.7, though Keynes seems to grasp it intuitively, he can never formulate it explicitly. Nevertheless, the principle of effective demand plays a basic role in what concerns a 'production economy', particularly a technologically advanced and developed economy. In such industrialized economies, effective demand generates production in a simple but fundamental way. The other layer of the logical structure, as formulated explicitly in *GT* and in the article in *The Quarterly Journal of Economics*, is the 'theory' of effective demand. This layer is based on a particular institution, that is, a capitalist market economy, and on specific behavioural relations of economic agents (such as entrepreneurs, workers and consumers, and so on). Its kernel is, of course, the notion of an 'investment multiplier'. In short, Keynes's theory, as composed of this two-layer structure, is undoubtedly a genuine 'aggregate' model in respect of the economic system as a whole.

Compared with Keynes's approach, Sraffa's production system also forms, in a sense, a kind of two-layered structure. Its fundamental layer is the system of production before the emergence of capitalists and workers. It is independent of any behavioural relations and even of a particular institutional set-up. And its primary feature, which is ultimately found in any kind of 'production economy', is the process of value generation by the methods of production, that is, by technological inter-industry relations. Thus, we may say that this layer is situated on nearly the same logical level as Keynes's 'principle' of effective demand. The other layer is the system of production after the emergence of capitalists and workers. It explicitly assumes a particular institutional set-up, that is, a technologically advanced capitalist economy. However, Sraffa's 'distribution variables' – either the unit wage or the rate of profits – are incompatible with the case assumed by neoclassical economists, since one of them is determined from outside the system of production. In other words, they are not determined only by the price mechanism. All this implies that the values of commodities are independent of the behavioural relations of demand and supply, as they are determined 'objectively' by technological inter-industry relations – in a word, by the technology of the system. In this sense, Sraffa's theory of prices is a thoroughly non-behavioural and objective system.

A fundamental line of critical reorientation of Keynes's economic theory can be outlined as follows.

1. At first, the most serious difficulty of Keynes's theory lies in the logical inconsistency between its demand side and its cost side.

    In that connection, we should, above all, leave out the micro foundation provided by the Marshallian increasing (marginal) cost based on the first classical postulate, as that may be considered as the most fragile building block in Keynes's construction. And we should replace it with the more solid foundation proposed by Sraffa, a critical successor of the classical economists (Smith, Ricardo, Marx).

2. In view of the logical consistency and formal elegance of Sraffa's system, which is a disaggregated multi-sector model, it would seem natural to transform Keynes's system, too, into a kind of disaggregate model, although the latter was originally aimed at the formulation of aggregate theory. Or it may be more desirable to generalize the field of application of Keynesian theory by using the original aggregate model for some purposes and the disaggregate model for other purposes. But what should not be overlooked is that there is need for a sort of disaggregation of Keynes's original model in order to integrate both its demand side and its supply side into a consistent theoretical scheme.

3. In order to transform the Keynesian aggregate model into a disaggregate one, the demand for output as a whole (that is, effective demand) must be subdivided into as many components as there are commodities. In this case, as Pasinetti (1993; 1997) suggests, we need to introduce the so-called macroeconomic condition[23] as the overall condition of full employment, instead of the principle of effective demand.

Sraffa's subsystems (Sraffa, 1960, p. 89) represent a type of vertical integration model. This point of view provides a connection between Sraffa's system and that of Keynes (see below):

1. Let us partition Sraffa's original system into as many components as there are commodities. Any such component (that is, any 'subsystem') forms a smaller self-replacing system producing a net product consisting of only one kind of commodity. In order to produce the

net product, each subsystem uses directly or indirectly not only labour but also means of production.

However, in any one subsystem, the amount of means of production existing at the starting point of the annual cycle is fully replaced during the production cycle, so that it would be possible to leave aside such means of production altogether. The primary aim would be, first, to single out merely two quantities, that is, the 'net product' and the 'amount of "labour"' required (directly or indirectly) to produce it, and, second, to relate *directly* the former to the latter.

In his discussion of the model of 'reduction to dated quantities of labour' (Sraffa, 1960, ch. 6), Sraffa states:

> [I]n the sub-systems we see at a glance, as an aggregate, the same quantity of labour that we obtain as the sum of a series of terms when we trace back the successive stages of the production of the commodity.
>
> (Sraffa, 1960, p. 89)

2. If we suppose a general case including 'joint production', it would appear that Sraffa devised the notion of 'subsystems' in order to evaluate unambiguously the extent of validity of the classical labour theory of value, whereas Pasinetti (1990) in his 'multi-sector vertical integration' analysis proves stringently that Sraffa's idea of 'subsystems' serves as a fruitful analytical tool from the point of view of effective demand as well. Thus, the method of singling out the direct relationship between 'net product' or 'final product' and 'the amount of labour' represents, in a sense, a device to get away from the whole set of means of production used up directly or indirectly to produce the net product.

In outline, the attempt to integrate Sraffa's system with that of Keynes elucidates the fact that the theoretical scheme of a 'production economy' must be completely separated into a quantity system <Q> and a price system <P> independent of each other.

Thus, in a certain period of time, given the technology and the productive organization of the economy, the price system is determined by technological relations while the quantity system is determined by sectorally differentiated effective demand, that is to say:

Technology → <P>; Demand → <Q>

This simple but clear analytical scheme is, I think, a fundamental point of departure for disclosing the fundamental features of the structural dynamics of a 'production economy' in which the *primum movens* is, without doubt, continuous technological progress.

Notes

I should like to thank for valuable suggestions and comments on my earlier draft, Yuji Aruka, Eiichi Asano, Mitsuharu Itô, Kunitake Itô, Myoung-Kyu Kang, Atsushige Matsushima, David McMurray and Satoshi Sechiyama.

1. Indeed, Keynes avoided an empirical interpretation of probability, but it is often overlooked that he sidestepped the empiricist philosophy of John Locke and David Hume by following two distinct routes: (a) insofar as the *category of knowledge* is concerned, he distinguished between knowledge and probability, which means between absolute, certain knowledge and doubtful, uncertain, probable knowledge based on experience; and (b) he also distinguished two kinds of uncertainty, that is, uncertainty in the object itself and uncertainty in human judgement. In this respect, see J. Locke (1975 [1690]), Chapter 15 ('Of Probability'), and particularly, D. Hume (1978 [1739]), Part III ('Of Knowledge and Probability'). See also K. Itô's (2001), 'Hume no Kakuritsu-ron' (*Hume's Theory of Probability*) which includes a discussion of the relevance of Hume's theory to Keynes's interpretation of probability.

2. The term 'objective' is polysemic and its meaning depends upon which writer is referring to it. In this regard, one can call attention to a number of well-known treatments: M. Weber, 'Die "Objektivität" sozialwissenschaftlicher und sozialpolitischer Erkenntnis' (1971 [1904]), Emile Durkheim, *Les règles de la méthode sociologique* (1999 [1895]), and V. Pareto, *Trattato di sociologia generale* (1916).

   A certain probability relation (between a premise and a conclusion) is taken to be 'objective' because several other (not just a few) thoughtful and prudent people who qualify as 'rational spectators' consider it to be 'reasonable' and 'objective'. If so, Keynes's view of 'objective' seems to be rather similar to the meaning of *'logique'* in Pareto's expression *'action logique'*, which means an individual's rational action suited (subjectively or objectively) to its purpose (see Pareto, 1917, p. 67, and Busino, 1987, p. 803). In that connection, Keynes wrote: 'the theory of probability is logical, therefore, because it is concerned with the degree of belief in which it is *rational* [emphasis in original] to entertain in given conditions, *and not merely with the actual beliefs of particular individuals, which may or may not be rational*' (TP, p. 4; emphasis added). It may be said that Keynes is concerned not with *'actual* beliefs' but with *'ideal* beliefs'. But this assertion could not elude Ramsey's severe criticism. See his critique beginning with the passage: 'But we are concerned with the relation which *actually* holds between two propositions' (Ramsey, 1999 [1922], p. 253; emphasis added).

3. Rudolf Carnap (1950, p. 43; 1966, p. 29), although he is in a sense a critical successor of Keynes's *TP*, calls Keynesian probability 'a *logical* probability'.

But Carnap's conception is generally recognized as 'a *rationalist* theory' (cf. Hacking, 1987, p. 2). According to Hacking, the label 'subjective theory' should be applied not to Keynes's probability but to the tradition stemming from Frank Ramsey (Ramsey, 1926). This is of course not wrong, but I am mostly interested in the classification of probability concepts proposed by Gilles-Gaston Granger (1988, pp. 282 ff.). According to Granger, the theories of probability may be classified in the following terms: (a) '*l'interprétation objectiviste*' (including Kolmogorof and von Mises) in which 'les fréquences de réalisation des événements' are considered to be 'les probabilités', and (b) '*l'interprétation subjectiviste*', which is further subdivided into two sub-classes: (i) the stream of Wittgenstein–Keynes–Carnap, in which 'la probabilité' is regarded as 'une mesure d'un degré de liaison logique entre deux *propositions*', and (ii) the stream of F. Ramsey, von Neumann and Morgenstern, and Savage, in which 'la probabilité' is 'une mesure du degré de crédibilité d'un *événement*'. Incidentally, it would seem that my own interpretation has much in common with that of Granger (see Hishiyama, 1983 [1969]).

4. According to the atomic hypothesis, or logical atomism, it should be possible to reduce the 'world' to individual units or 'atoms'. According to Bertrand Russell and Wittgenstein, a general proposition must ultimately be reducible to elementary or atomic propositions, the former may be completely construed from the latter. To this effect, Wittgenstein (1971 [1918]) presents his basic standpoint as follows: '[i]f all true elementary propositions are given, the result is a complete description of the world' (Wittgenstein, 1971 [1918], s. 4. 231) and '[t]he world is completely described by giving all elementary propositions, and adding which of them are true and which false' (Wittgenstein, 1971 [1918], s. 4. 232). The most typical example of logical atomism in the social sciences is neoclassical economic theory, especially the Walrasian scheme of general equilibrium theory.

5. In this regard, see Kunitake Itô (1999, p. 150 ff.).

6. It is interesting to note here that Shinichirô Tomonaga was also puzzled by the infinite quantities appearing in his quantum electrodynamics model. This kind of infinity concerned 'the infinities appearing in the field reaction, particularly in the scattering process'. He would break through this difficulty by creating 'the theory of renormalization' or, more precisely, 'the theory of renormalization of mass and charge'. This 'theory' serves, it would seem, as *deus ex machina* for him because it helped him to solve the difficulty of infinity and to make his model determinate. See his Nobel lecture ('Development of Quantum Electrodynamics. Personal Recollections'), 6 May 1966, reprinted in Tomonaga (1997, Appendix, pp. 10–33).

7. Let us denote the concept of 'risk' by R and recall its definition. Let A be the amount of good which may result from some course of ethical behaviour, p its probability (assume $p + q = 1$), and E the value of 'mathematical expectation'. As a result, $E = pA$. Then 'risk' R is defined according to the following equations: $R = p(A - E) = p(A - pA) = p(1 - p)A = pqA = qE$. The value of 'mathematical expectation' E, that is, pA, represents 'the net immediate sacrifice which should be made in the hope of obtaining A' (Keynes, *TP*, p. 348) – in other words, opportunity cost associated with hope. Since q is 'the probability that this sacrifice will be made in vain' (*TP*, p. 348), qE measures 'risk'. Keynes adds: '[t]he ordinary theory supposes that

the ethical value of an expectation is a function of E only and is entirely independent of R' (*TP*, p. 348).

8. There is a need to refer to the two cases mentioned in *TP*, as these are somewhat similar to the one considered here: (a) a court case brought by a breeder of racehorses to recover damages for breach of contract (taken from the *Times Law Reports*), and (b) the case of an offer of a beauty prize (taken from the *Daily Express*). Keynes sums up as follows: '[w]hether or not such a thing is theoretically conceivable, no exercise of practical judgment is possible, by which a numerical value can actually be given to the probability of every argument. So far from our being able to measure them, it is not even clear that we are always able to place them in an order of magnitude. Nor has any theoretical rule for their evaluation ever been suggested' (*TP*, p. 29).

9. This 'first classical fundamental postulate' is not admitted here because, as a result of the controversy in the 1960s over the theory of capital, the general applicability of the neoclassical production function, whether it concerns the industries as a whole or a single industry, was definitively disproved. See Pasinetti (2000, pp. 408–12) for the reconstruction of the process whereby this result was suppressed by influential economic theorists and finally disappeared as if the controversy had never taken place.

10. As for the assumption of Marshallian increasing costs, Sraffa rejects Marshall's device by which 'the whole industry [is considered] as a single firm which employs the "whole of the constant factor" and employs successive doses of the other factors' (Sraffa, 1998 [1925], pp. 341–2; Japanese translation by Hishiyama, 1956, p. 41). Of course 'the whole industry' (*tutta l'industria*) here means a particular industry, so that we should reasonably leave out Keynes's peculiar device of 'an economy-wide huge industry', whose marginal cost increases would correspond to an increase in the scale of output as a whole.

11. One of the main topics of Sraffa's critique of Marshall's cost analysis (Sraffa, 1925), in a sense, is its emphasis upon its logical incompatibility with the so-called partial equilibrium framework. While Keynes must have been aware of the implications in Sraffa's critique, he simply includes in *GT* the Marshallian (increasing-costs) supply curve as a cornerstone of his theoretical scheme. This is somewhat surprising, but also a rather interesting sign of the prevailing intellectual atmosphere among his fellow economists. Eiichi Asano (1987, p. 174 ff.) conjectures that Keynes adopted the Marshallian short-run supply curve probably because Richard Kahn advised him to. But it should also be noted that in his 'Notes on Ohlin's Final Section' (April, 1937), Keynes clearly states: 'I have always regarded decreasing physical returns in the short period as one of the very few incontrovertible propositions of our miserable subject!' (Keynes, J. M. 1973c [1937], p. 190).

12. There is a sense in which, unlike in the physical sciences, in the moral sciences, and particularly for investment decisions in economics, future exert an influence upon the present. The following statements by Keynes are worth recalling: '*The schedule of the marginal efficiency of capital* is of fundamental importance because *it is mainly through this factor* (much more than through the rate of interest) *that the expectation of the future influences the present*' (*GT* p. 145; emphasis added). But the type of entrepreneurial

behaviour behind that schedule is, it would seem, essentially similar to the ethical behaviour of human beings facing choices among alternative courses of action, as considered in *TP*. Of course the 'indefinite future' in the case of an ethical act is transformed into a series of discrete periods $(t_1, t_2, ..., t_n)$ and, correspondingly, the 'goodness or advantage' of the particular chosen course is changed into a series of values for the 'prospective yield' of the chosen investment $(Q_1, Q_2, ..., Q_n)$.

We may conjecture that the values of prospective yields should probably be based on 'probable beliefs' arrived at by virtue of probabilistic inference proceeding from actual or expected knowledge (or information). The kernel of this approach, somewhat differently from the case of *TP*, would be the method of capitalization by which one is able to roughly reduce a 'future' value to a 'present' one. Moreover, while 'the state of confidence' is considered by Keynes to be one of the major factors determining the investment demand schedule (see *GT*, pp. 148–9), this is in a certain sense a reformed formulation of the 'probable beliefs' of *TP*, which is obtained by explicitly taking into account both 'risk' and 'weights' of arguments. In the case of investment, 'risk' means 'the likelihood of our best forecast turning out quite wrong' (*GT*, p. 148). On the other hand, 'weights', that is, the amount of evidence, strengthens, as it were, the *credibility* of probable belief independently of its *degree*. In short, we might say that, though the state of confidence may be a decreasing function of 'risk', the increase in 'weight', that is, the amount of evidence associated with probable arguments, does not always strengthen the state of confidence because the latter may be either weakened or strengthened according to whether the increase of evidence strengthens the unfavourable case or the favourable one. The emphasis upon 'the state of *confidence*' in *GT* might in part reflect F. P. Ramsey's criticism of Keynes's *TP* (Ramsey, 1931, pp. 62–8).

13. Pasinetti's views of the 'principle' of effective demand can be traced to his book *Growth and Income Distribution* (Pasinetti, 1974, pp. 31–3). But the original formulation seems to have been made much earlier. In fact, I learned at Cambridge University in 1969–70 that Pasinetti had displayed the graphic representation of the 'principle' in his lectures there.

14. See on this issue this statement by Keynes:

> We are merely reminding ourselves that human decisions affecting the future, whether personal or political or economic, cannot depend on strict mathematical expectation, since the basis for making such calculations does not exist; and that it is our innate urge to activity which makes the wheels go round, *our rational selves choosing between alternatives as best we are able, calculating where we can*, but often falling back for our motive on whim or sentiment or chance.
>
> (*GT*, pp. 162–3; emphasis added)

15. As far as the interpretation of Keynes's philosophical thought is concerned, I have always assumed the following simple classification of the sciences (excluding metaphysics):

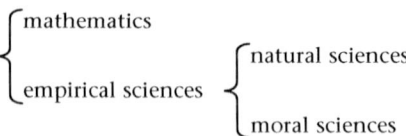

While empirical sciences in general, and especially the reconstruction of their fundamental logic, are the main theme of *TP*, the moral sciences, and particularly the logic of economics as a branch of the moral sciences, are considered in *GT*. Keynes emphasizes 'the point about economics being a moral science', not a natural science, in letters to Roy Harrod after *GT*. This does not, it would appear, require any change in our interpretation of *GT*. (See Keynes' s letters to Harrod, dated 4 and 16 July 1938, in Keynes, 1973d [1939], pp. 295–7, 299–301.) However, I wonder with an uneasy feeling why Harrod does not, in his reply, pay attention to the 'point' mentioned above.

16. It seems clear that when Keynes published this article in 1926 he undoubtedly believed that 'the atomic hypothesis [had] worked so splendidly in physics' (Keynes, 1972 [1933], p. 262). In *TP*, he takes for granted that 'atomic uniformity' is generally applicable in the material universe.

17. As Bertrand Russell writes: 'there are two very different classes of wholes, of which the first will be called *aggregates*, while the second will be called *unities*.... Each class of wholes consists of terms not simply equivalent to all their parts; but in the case of unities, the whole is not even specified by its parts' (Russell, 1903, pp. 140–1). Aggregates are quite different: Russell had also written: '[s]uch a whole [the aggregate] is completely specified when all its simple constituents are specified; its parts have no direct connection *inter se*, but only the indirect connection involved in being parts of one and same whole' (Russell, 1903, p. 140).

In this respect, see R. M. O'Donnell's noteworthy book *Keynes: Philosophy, Economics and Politics* (1989). O'Donnell is interested in the 'parts–wholes' issue, and explicitly mentions the *locus classicus* in Russell's *Principles of Mathematics* (O'Donnell, 1989, pp. 177–8). He writes: 'His [Keynes's] philosophical position on this issue may be described as "pluralist"'. He adds that 'in economics, Keynes' position was, I suggest, similarly pluralist', because 'the principle of atomism or methodological individualism was applicable in some situations, and the principle of organic unity in others' (O'Donnell, 1989, p. 177). Indeed, O'Donnell's general point of view may not be wrong, but there is need, I think, to further investigate the issue so as to arrive at the ultimate ground. In that sense, my point of view might be somewhat different from O'Donnell's.

18. In this respect, see Tarde's article 'La croyance et le désir' in Tarde (1895, pp. 235–308). Tarde summed up his thoughts with regard to the ultimate elements of 'phénoménes internes' into 'trois termes irreductibles, la croyance, le désir, et leur point d'application, le sentir pur' [*Three irreducible terms, belief, desire and their point of application, mere feeling*]. And he adds: 'les deux premiers termes sont les formes ou forces innées et constitutives du sujet, les moules où il reçoit les matériaux bruts de la sensation [*The two former terms are the innate and constitutive forms of the subject, the springs from which*

he receives the rough materials of sensibility]' (Tarde, 1895, p. 240). See also 'Monadologie et sociologie', in Tarde (1895, pp. 371–2).

19. It is worth noting what K. Maruyama (1985) writes about Durkheim:

> Durkheim endeavours to derive the notion of 'society' as an objective fact depending on a rigorous inductive method. According to Durkheim 'society' cannot be reduced to the psychological and physiological characteristics of individuals. The notion of 'society' specified in such a manner is not obtained from adding up individuals' voluntary intentions. On the contrary, it is a system of constraints that moulds those individuals from outside.
>
> (Maruyama, 1985, p. 135)

20. We find a similar statement in Saussure's *Les sources manuscrites du cours de linguistique générale* edited by R. Godel:

> Dès que nous disons: terme au lieu de mot, l'idée de système est évoquée.... Mais de plus, ne pas commencer par le mot ou le terme pour en déduire le système. Ce serait croire que les termes ont d'avance une valeur absolue; au contraire, c'est du système qu'il faut partir, du tout solidaire. Ce dernier se décompose entre certains termes qui ne sont pas si faciles à dégager qu'il peut sembler' [*As soon as we say 'term' instead of 'word', the idea of system is invoked ... Furthermore, never start with the term or the word in order to deduce the system. That would entail thinking that terms have since the very beginning an absolute value. On the contrary, we should start with the system, with the organic whole. This latter must be decomposed into terms that are not so easy to disentangle as it may seem.*]
>
> (Godel, 1969, p. 228).

21. Sraffa's 'system', unlike Durkheim's, consists not of institutions, laws, customs and morals, and so on but of the economic structure based on technological interrelationships among various industries. In Marxian terms, Sraffa identifies the starting point of his theory with the material *base*, not the *superstructure* of society. Nevertheless, it would seem that Sraffa's system of production is a system of constraints similar to Durkheim's system: individuals' economic behaviour ultimately adapts to the operation of an objective system of production. Moreover, there is a sense in which it shares the methodological standpoint of Saussure, which tends to a complete denial of atomism. The following statement is, I think, precisely applicable to Sraffa's view: 'c'est du système, du tout solidaire qu'il faut partir'. Whereas Durkheim makes a direct attack on 'utilitarian individualism', that point of view would also be unacceptable to Sraffa and perhaps also to Keynes.

22. Pierangelo Garegnani explicitly accepts the hypothesis of classical free competition when he writes: '[a]gain, hasn't that assumption [that of the uniform rate of profits for all industries] been generally held as the necessary implication of the hypothesis of free competition?' (Garegnani, 1990, p. 350).

23. For a multi-sector production system, the 'macroeconomic condition' is determined by the production coefficients per unit of output and by the per capita demand coefficients associated with each sector (or commodity) in

the system. It is a *necessary condition* for full employment, or the full expenditure of income. In other words, the condition basically depends upon the configuration of technology and the composition of demand in terms of sectors or commodities (on this point, see Pasinetti, 1993; 1997).

References

Asano, E. (1987), *Keynes' General Theory Keisei-shi* [The Making of Keynes's *General Theory*], Tokyo: Nippon Hyôron Sha.

Baranzini, M. and Scazzieri, R. (1986), 'Knowledge in Economics: A Framework', in M. Baranzini and R. Scazzieri (eds), *Foundations of Economics: Structures of Inquiry and Economic Theory*, Oxford and New York: Basil Blackwell, pp. 1–87.

Busino, G. (1987), 'Pareto Vilfredo (1848–1923)', in P. Newman, J. Eatwell and M. Milgate (eds), *The New Palgrave Dictionary of Economics*, vol. 3, London: Macmillan, pp. 799–804.

Carnap, R. (1950), *Logical Foundations of Probability*, London: Routledge and Kegan Paul.

——— (1966), *Philosophical Foundations of Physics*, ed. M. Gardner, New York and London: Basic Books.

Durkheim, E. (1999 [1895]), *Les règles de la méthode sociologique*, Paris: Quadrige/ Presses Universitaires de France.

Feynman, R. (1994 [1965]), *The Character of Physical Law*, Introduction by J. Gleik, New York: Modern Library.

Garegnani, P. (1990), 'Comment' on A. Asimakopulos, 'Keynes and Sraffa: Visions and Perspectives', in K. Bharadwaj and B. Schefold, eds., *Essays on Piero Sraffa – Critical Perspectives on the Revival of Classical Theory*, London: Unwin Hyman, pp. 345–52.

Godel, R. (1969), *Les sources manuscrites du cours de linguistique générale de F. de Saussure* (2nd impression), Geneva: Librairie Droz.

Granger, G. G. (1988), *Essai d'une philosophie du style* (revised and corrected edition), Paris: Editions Odile Jacob.

Hacking, I. (1987), 'Probability', in P. Newman, J. Eatwell and M. Milgate (eds), *The New Palgrave Dictionary of Economics*, vol. 3, London: Macmillan, pp. 1–13.

Hishiyama, I. (1956), 'Seisanhi to Seisanryô no Kankei nitsuite', A Japanese translation of Sraffa's Italian paper (1925), in I. Hishiyama and Y. Taguchi, *Keizaigaku niokeru Koten to Kindai* [Classic and Modern in Economics], Tokyo: Yuhikaku, pp. 1–88.

——— (1960), 'The Tableau Economique of Quesnay – its Analysis, Reconstruction, and Application', *Kyoto University Economic Review*, 30, pp. 1–46; reprinted in Italian in G. Candela and M. Palazzi (eds), *Dibattito sulla Fisiocrazia*, Florence: La Nuova Italia (1979), pp. 119–60; reprinted also in M. Blaug (ed.) (1991), *François Quesnay (1694–1774)*, vol. 1, Aldershot, UK and Broofield, Vt: Elgar, pp. 115–59.

——— (1966), 'Keizaijin no Ketsui to Fukakujitsusei – Keynes Keizaigaku Kenkyû Josetsu' [Economic Man's Decisions and Uncertainty – Introduction to Inquiry into Keynesian Economics], *Keizai-Ronsô* [Economic Review], 98 (6), Kyoto University Economic Society, pp. 1–21.

—— (1967a), 'Keynes niokeru Fukakujitsusei no Ronri' [Keynes's Logic of Uncertainty], *Shisô*, no. 514, pp. 10–26.

—— (1967b), 'Keynes no Tôshi-Riron niokeru "Keizaijin"' ['Homo Oeconomicus', in J. M. Keynes's Theory of Investment], *Shisô*, no. 519, pp. 47–62.

—— (1968), 'Keynes no Kahei to Fukakujitsusei no Ronri' [J. M. Keynes's Logic of Uncertainty and Money], *Shisô*, no. 526, pp. 41–58.

—— (1977–8), 'Alfred Marshall', originally a series of lectures televised on NHK (Japanese Broadcasting Corporation), reprinted in Chapter 8 of H. Mizuta and Y. Tamanoi (eds), *Keizaishisôshi Tokuhon* [A Reader in the History of Economic Thought], Tokyo: Tôyôkeizai.

—— (1979), *David Ricardo*, Tokyo: Nipponkeizai Shinbun-sha.

—— (1983 [1969]), 'The Logic of Uncertainty According to J. M. Keynes', *Kyoto University Economic Review*, 39, pp. 22–44; reprinted in J. C. Wood (ed.), *John Maynard Keynes: Critical Assessments*, vol. 1, London: Croom Helm.

—— (1993), *Sraffa Keizaigaku no Gendaiteki Hyôka* [Modern Critical Assessment of Sraffian Economics], Kyoto: Kyoto University Press.

—— (2000), 'Keizaishisô Kenkyû to Jakkan-no Kihon-Mondai' [Inquiry into Economic Thought and Some Basic Issues], *Annals of the Society for the History of Economic Thought*, 38, pp. 66–75.

Hume, D. (1978 [1739]), *A Treatise of Human Nature* (2nd edn, with text revised and variant readings by P. H. Nidditch), Oxford: Clarendon Press.

Inoue, T. (1964), 'Ryoshirikigaku-teki Sekai' [Quantum Mechanical World], in *Nippon Hyakka Daijiten* [Grand Encyclopedia Japonica], vol. 13, Tokyo: Shôgakukan.

Itô, K. (1999), *Keynes no Tetsugaku* [Philosophy of J. M. Keynes], Tokyo: Iwanami Shoten.

—— (2001), 'Hume no Kakuritsu-ron' [Hume's Theory of Probability], *Tetsugaku Ronsô* [Philosophical Review], 28, pp. 58–68.

Ito, M. (1987), '1930 nendai no Keizaigaku Saikô' [The Economics of the 1930s Reconsidered], *Keizai-Ronsô* [The Economic Review]: *In commemoration of Prof. I. Hishiyama*, Kyoto: Kyoto University Economic Society.

—— (1998), *Gendai-keizai no Riron* [Contemporary Economic Theory], in *The Collected Writings of Mitsuharu Itô*, vol. 3, Tokyo: Iwanami Shoten

Keynes, J. M. (1937), 'The General Theory of Employment', *Quarterly Journal of Economics*, 51, pp. 209–23.

—— (1972 [1933]), *Essays in Biography*, Vol. X of *The Collected Writings of John Maynard Keynes*, London: Macmillan.

—— (1973a [1921]), *A Treatise on Probability*, Vol. VIII of *The Collected Writings of John Maynard Keynes*, London: Macmillan.

—— (1973b [1936]), *The General Theory of Employment Interest and Money*, Vol. VII of *The Collected Writings of John Maynard Keynes*, London: Macmillan.

—— (1973c [1937]), 'Notes on Ohlin's Final Section', in Vol. XIV of *The Collected Writings of John Maynard Keynes*, London: Macmillan, pp. 188–91.

—— (1973d [1938]), 'Letters to R. F. Harrod, 4 July and 16 July 1938', in Vol. XIV of *The Collected Writings of John Maynard Keynes*, London, Macmillan.

Locke, J. (1975 [1690]), *An Essay Concerning Human Understanding*, edited with a foreword by P. H. Nidditch, Oxford: Clarendon Press.

Marshall, A. (1961 [1890]), *Principles of Economics* (9th (variorum) edn, 2 vols), ed. C. W. Guillebaud, London: Macmillan.

Maruyama, K. (1981), *Saussure no Shisô* [The Thoughts of Ferdinand de Saussure], Tokyo: Iwanami Shoten.

—— (1985), *Saussure shô Jiten* [A Little Encyclopedia of Saussure], Tokyo: Daishûkan Shoten.

Meillet, A. (1982 [1905–06]), *Linguistique historique et linguistique générale*, Geneva and Paris: Slatkine/Champion.

Miyajima, T. (1978), *Kaisetsu (explanatory notes) of Durkheimian sociology*, (Japanese translation of *Les règles de la méthode sociologique*), Tokyo: Iwanami Shoten.

Moore, G. E. (1903), *Principia Ethica*, Cambridge: Cambridge University Press.

O'Donnell, R. M. (1989), *Keynes: Philosophy, Economics and Politics*, Macmillan: London.

Pareto, V. (1916), *Trattato di Sociologia Generale*, 2 vols, Florence: Barbera.

Pareto, V. (1917–19), *Traité de sociologie générale* (French edn, ed. P. Boven), 2 vols, Lausanne: Payot.

Pasinetti, L. L. (1974), *Growth and Income Distribution. Essays in Economic Theory*, Cambridge: Cambridge University Press.

—— (1977), *Lectures on the Theory of Production*, London: Macmillan; New York: Columbia University Press.

—— (ed.) (1980), *Essays on the Theory of Joint Production*, London: Macmillan,

—— (1981), *Structural Change and Economic Growth: A Theoretical Essay on the Dynamics of the Wealth of Nations*, Cambridge: Cambridge University Press.

—— (1990), 'Sraffa's Circular Process and the Concept of Vertical Integration', in K. Bharadwaj and B. Schefold (eds), *Essays on Piero Sraffa: Critical Perspectives on the Revival of Classical Theory*, London: Unwin Hyman, pp. 229–60.

—— (1993), *Structural Economic Dynamics: A Theory of the Economic Consequences of Human Learning*, Cambridge: Cambridge University Press.

—— (1997), 'The Principle of Effective Demand', in G. C. Harcourt and P. A. Riach (eds), *A 'Second Edition' of The General Theory*, vol. 1, London and New York: Routledge, pp. 93–104.

—— (2000), 'Critique of the Neoclassical Theory of Growth and Distribution', *Banca Nazionale del Lavoro Quarterly Review*, no. 215, pp. 383–431.

Quesnay, F. (1972 [1759]), *Quesnay's Tableau Economique*, ed. M. Kuczynski and R. L. Meek, London: Macmillan.

Ramsey, F. P. (1926), 'Truth and Probability', in F. P. Ramsey, *The Foundations of Mathematics and other Logical Essays*, ed. R. B. Braithwaite, London, Kegan Paul, Trench, Trubner and Co.; New York, Harcourt, Brace and Company, chapter VII, pp. 156–98.

Ramsey, F. P. (1999 [1922]), 'A Treatise on Probability of J. M. Keynes', in Silva Marzetti Dall' Aste Brandolini and Roberto Scazzieri (eds), *La Probabilità in Keynes: Premesse e Influenze*, Bologna: CLUEB, pp. 252–6. Originally published in *Cambridge Magazine*, January, 1922.

—— (1931), *Foundations. Essays in Philosophy, Logic, Mathematics and Economics*, ed. D. H. Mellor, London and Henley Routledge & Kegan Paul.

Russell, B. (1903), *The Principles of Mathematics*, vol. 1 (1st edn), Cambridge: Cambridge University Press.

Saussure, F. de (1989) *Cours de linguistique générale*, vol. 1, ed. R. Engler, Wiesbaden: Otto.

Smith, A. (1981 [1776]), *An Inquiry into the Nature and Causes of the Wealth of Nations*, vol. II of *The Glasgow Edition of the Works and Correspondence of Adam*

Smith, ed. R. H. Campbell, A. S. Skinner and W. B. Todd, Indianapolis: Liberty Fund.

Sraffa, P. (1925), 'Sulle relazioni fra costo e quantità prodotta', *Annali di Economia*, 2 (1), pp. 277–328.

—— (1960), *Production of Commodities by Means of Commodities*, Cambridge: Cambridge University Press.

—— (1998 [1925]), 'On the Relations between Cost and Quantity Produced' (An English translation by J. Eatwell and A. Roncaglia), in L. L. Pasinetti (ed.), *Italian Economic Papers*, vol. III, Bologna: il Mulino; Oxford: Oxford University Press, pp. 323–63.

Tarde, G. (1895), *Essais et mélanges sociologiques*, Paris: A. Maloine.

Tomonaga, S. (1997), *Ryoshirikigaku to Watakushi* [Quantum Mechanics and I], Tokyo: Iwanami Shoten.

Weber, M. (1971 [1904]), 'Die 'Objectivität' sozialwissenschaftlicher und sozial-politischer Erkenntnis', *Archiv für Sozialwissenschaft und Sozial Politik*, London, New York: Johnson Reprint corporation, pp. 22–87.

Wittgenstein, L. (1971 [1918]), *Prototractatus, An Early Version of Tractatus Logico-Philosophicus*, ed. B. F. McGuinness, T. Nyberg and G. H. von Wright with a translation by D. F. Pears and B.F. McGuinness, and an historical introduction by G. H. von Wright, New York: Cornell University Press.

11
Uncertainty and Rationality: Keynes and Modern Economics

John Allen Kregel and Eric Nasica

11.1 Changing views about the future in a monetary economy

The intellectual revolution triggered by Keynes's *General Theory of Employment, Interest and Money* (1973c [1936]; hereafter *GT*) is often described as a shift in emphasis from microeconomics to macroeconomics, and as a shift from study of optimal behaviour of the individual consumer or the individual firm to study of broad statistical aggregates, such as income and employment, or consumption and investment. For a long time macroeconomists thought it unnecessary to provide a special explanation of individual behaviour, but eventually traditional microeconomics was introduced into the Keynesian model to provide 'micro foundations' to explain individual decision making. However, Keynes never used the term 'macroeconomics', and it soon became obvious that there was an inherent tension between the traditional approach to optimal individual behaviour and the Keynesian explanation of the movements of income and employment.

Keynes in *GT* drew a distinction between analysis of an economy 'subject to change, but where all things are foreseen from the beginning' and 'the problems of the *real world* in which our previous expectations are liable to disappointment and expectations concerning the future affect what we do to-day' (*GT*, pp. 293–4; emphasis added). In the preface to the book he had already emphasized that his intention was to analyse 'A monetary economy' which he defined as 'one in which changing views about the future are capable of influencing the quantity of employment and not merely its direction'. He went on to add that this would require a 'method of analysing the economic behaviour of the present under the influence of changing ideas about the future'

272

which was more general than the method employed by traditional theory (*GT*, p. vii).

Far from ignoring the problems of explaining the behaviour of economic agents, Keynes calls for a more general explanation of behaviour in more realistic conditions. He thus sought to substitute the assumptions of traditional theory that 'all things are foreseen from the beginning' with a theory of behaviour based on the assumption that 'previous expectations are liable to disappointment and expectations concerning the future affect what we do to-day' (*GT*, p. vii). The traditional view of Keynes's theory as 'macroeconomics' rather than the theory of a 'monetary economy', has thus quite naturally overlooked what it did not expect to be there, but which Keynes considered to be the very heart of his approach, namely, a theory of individual behaviour.

The aim of this chapter is to spell out Keynes's ideas on this subject in more detail, pointing to the crucial influence of his earlier *Treatise on Probability* (1973a [1921]; hereafter *TP*) on the views expressed in the *General Theory*. Although economists who had written before Keynes had not ignored the analysis of the behaviour of economic agents, he felt that they had not adequately analysed the implications of a changing, unknown future. Yet most economists who have written after Keynes have ignored his suggestions for a more general approach. Section 11.2 investigates the essential differences, drawing on the recent contributions of a number of Post-Keynesian economists. Section 11.3 builds on this discussion to show how those extensions of Keynes's approach provide the basis for a criticism of the traditional definition of economic 'rationality', as well as providing the foundation for an alternative approach to the analysis of rational economic behaviour.

11.2 Non-ergodicity, Keynesian uncertainty and probabilistic risk

11.2.1 Knight's and Keynes's distinction between risk and uncertainty

As noted above, Keynes drew a sharp distinction between the analysis of decision making in traditional theory and the conditions faced by decision makers in the 'real world'. But Keynes was not alone in noting the failure of traditional theory.

One of the first economists to call attention to the difficulty of analysing uncertainty was Frank Knight. Knight considered uncertainty to exist when an agent faced what he called a 'unique situation'. Since the agent cannot fall back on past experience to provide a guide, there will be no frequency distribution to provide the basis for the formulation of a probable estimate of the possible outcome (Knight, 1921, p. 233). Any formulation of a numerical probability could be based only on 'pure judgement'. Knight was interested in such cases because he considered them to describe the conditions which entrepreneurs actually face when they take business decisions. It was essential to analyse them in order to be able to understand the evolution of the actual economy.

An example of such a situation would be the formulation of a plan of action based on the proposition 'investing in technology *y* is profitable'. In the absence of any prior quantitative knowledge or experience of the operation of technology *y*, the businessman's evaluation of the returns to be earned from adopting the technology can be based only on personal intuition.

Knight contrasted such cases with what he called 'risk', a situation in which there was 'measurable uncertainty' (see Knight, 1921, pp. 224–5). Here it was possible to formulate 'a priori probabilities' (determined mathematically) or 'statistical probabilities' (determined by empirical observation of frequency of occurrence). By drawing this sharp distinction between risk and uncertainty, Knight sought to highlight the important characteristics of uncertainty that he believed standard theory had neglected. Thus, Knight's concerns are very similar to what we have identified as Keynes's attempt to outline a more 'general' approach to decision making in the face of uncertainty as applying to cases in which the future is not perfectly known so that probabilities can be defined over the set of all possible results.[1]

Keynes makes a distinction between events that are uncertain and events that are only probable in his famous article in the 1937 *Quarterly Journal of Economics*:

> By 'uncertain' knowledge, let me explain, I do not mean merely to distinguish what is known for certain from what is only probable. The game of roulette is not subject, in this sense, to uncertainty .... The sense in which I am using the term is that in which the prospect of a European war is uncertain, or the price of copper and the rate of interest twenty years hence, or the obsolescence of a new invention .... About these matters, there is no scientific basis on which to form any calculable probability whatever. We simply do not know.
>
> (Keynes, 1973e [1937], pp. 113–14)

Keynes even denies the possibility of describing the game of roulette as being uncertain even though it is the most common example of uncertainty cited by traditional theory. The crucial point for Keynes, as for Knight, is the inadequacy of statistical quantification in the form of a probability for the analysis of uncertainty since 'human decisions affecting the future, whether personal or political or economic, cannot depend on strict mathematical expectation, since the basis for making such calculations does not exist' (*GT*, pp. 162–3).

According to Keynes, orthodox economists have neglected this 'embarrassing fact' by supposing that simple extrapolation of past events was a suitable guide for the future, that *natura non facit saltum*, as Alfred Marshall wrote on the title page of his *Principles* (Marshall, 1890). Thus, Keynes accuses 'the classical economic theory of being itself one of these pretty, polite techniques which tries to deal with the present by abstracting from the fact that we know very little about the future' (*GT*, p. 115).

11.2.2 Post-Keynesians, historical time and crucial decision making

However strongly they voiced their concern for the importance of uncertainty, both Knight and Keynes seem to have failed to convince economists that the vast majority of the theorems in modern economics dealing with uncertainty in fact analyse what both authors defined as risk. To highlight the difference between the traditional analysis of uncertainty by methods that are undifferentiated from those applied to the analysis of risk, many Post Keynesian economists have adopted the terms 'true' or 'fundamental' uncertainty to identify this original, but now often overlooked, definition of uncertainty originally formulated by Knight and Keynes. In doing so they hope to distinguish their extensions of the Knight–Keynes analysis from the traditional neoclassical approach in which agents are either presumed to know the future results of their actions, so that they are simply choosing the optimal set of future results, or are viewed as exploring possible decisions to discover those that are deemed to be suboptimal. The idea is simply to distinguish between two diametrically opposed traditions in analysing the impact of the future on the present.

Many Post Keynesians have attempted to elaborate the explanations of uncertainty given by Knight and Keynes in order to better distinguish the concept from the traditional analysis of risk.

They have thus attempted to develop Keynes's alternative analysis in ways that do not rely on the existence and/or the knowledge of the probability distributions of future events. In addition to emphasizing that they are interested in 'fundamental' uncertainty', they have sought to characterize the existence of such conditions in the conceptions of 'historical time' and crucial 'decision making'. Thus, 'Post-Keynesian theory ... is concerned primarily with the depiction of an economic system expanding over *time* in the context of *history*' (Eichner and Kregel, 1975, p. 1294; emphasis in the original) so that time is 'a real-world device which prevents everything from happening at once' (Davidson, 1981, p. 158).

Since the basic economic decisions concerning production and investment are processes that take time and are essentially irreversible, they are said to take place in 'historical' or 'calendar' time. As a result, actions cannot be reversed; decisions that lead to actions that cannot be reversed or repeated to produce more desirable outcomes are called 'crucial' decisions.

In the neoclassical approach, on the other hand, either time is considered as a logical and thus reversible process or agents are simply discovering an already known future; their actions cannot determine the future. As a result, when these issues are treated from the neoclassical perspective, it is in terms of probabilistic risk since true uncertainty as defined by Knight is not considered.[2]

Shackle was the first to note that historical time implied what he called 'crucial' decisions. An agent faces a crucial decision when he 'cannot exclude from his mind the possibility that the very act of performing the experiment may destroy forever the circumstances in which it is performed' (Shackle, 1955, p. 6). '[C]rucialness is the real and important source of uniqueness in any occasion of choosing' (Shackle, 1955, p. 63). Thus, as Davidson has pointed out, 'when agents make crucial decisions they necessarily destroy any stochastic processes that may have existed at the point of time of the decision' (Davidson, 1982–83, p. 192). In other words, crucial decisions describe situations in which the act of taking a decision destroys the existing distribution functions.

The identification of cruciality as an important element in economic decisions under uncertainty produces a clear line of demarcation between Post Keynesian authors and modern neoclassical theory. The latter assumes that there is sufficient information available in the present concerning the probability functions of future events, so that whatever decision is actually taken it is not considered crucial. As Shackle emphasizes, the existence of the distribution functions implies that the future 'is already existent and merely waiting to appear. If this is so, if the world is determinist, then it seems idle to speak of choice. Choice ... is originative; it is the start of a new train of influences' (Shackle, 1972, pp. 122–3).[3]

Among Post Keynesians Davidson has argued that these two characteristic features of uncertainty in the 'real world'—historical time and crucial decisions—imply that the stochastic process that generates real world events is 'non-ergodic'. He has used this observation as the basis for a modern reinterpretation of Keynes's distinction between probable and uncertain events. However, such a reinterpretation of the real world in terms of stochastic processes that are more usually associated with the frequency-based theory of probability appears to contradict Keynes's statement that it is impossible to calculate probabilities for some events.[4] Indeed, Davidson himself has pointed out that, in conditions of true uncertainty, 'objective probability structures do not even fleetingly exist, and a distribution function of probabilities cannot be defined' (Davidson, 1991, p. 132). Further, in order to apply the traditional frequency approach it is desirable to be able to repeat experiments in identical conditions so that the moments of the random functions can be calculated on the basis of a large number of realizations. This would be difficult, if not impossible, in the environment to which Keynes referred. All this seems to exclude any application of the mathematical theory of stochastic processes, which requires the existence, at least conceptually, of a universe of realizations.

However, a less extreme interpretation of Keynes's position is possible. For example, if probabilities are assumed to exist for all events, but agents do not possess sufficient information to construct satisfactory probability estimates for some future events they may conclude that the objective distribution functions are, to use Keynes's terms, 'subject to sudden changes' (Keynes, 1973e [1937], p. 119) over time, such that the economic environment cannot be assumed to be in a state of statistical control. Alternatively, agents may recognize that exogenous changes may produce radical reconsideration of the subjective distribution functions that they have formed. Either of these results would preclude the convergence of the psychological functions to the objective functions (even stochastically). And this would be true even if these latter functions are homogeneous over short periods of calendar time.

Such an interpretation would allow Keynes's analysis of uncertainty to be recast in terms of non-ergodic stochastic processes. Indeed, such an interpretation would explicitly integrate the possibility that the probability structures (both the objective and the psychological functions), even if they exist at every point in time, would be subject to sudden and violent fluctuations. It thus follows that the expectations produced on the basis of the calculation of probabilities may be completely independent of the actual future events.

Neither is the reformulation of Keynes's analysis in terms of non-ergodic stochastic processes incompatible with the rejection of the traditional theory of choice under uncertainty based on either objective or subjective probability distributions. The reformulation allows Post Keynesian criticism of objective probability analysis to be expressed in the fact that the traditional approach is valid only in an ergodic world. The criticism of subjective probability analysis appears less straightforward if probability is interpreted either in terms of 'degrees of conviction' (Savage, 1954, p. 30) or in terms of 'relative frequencies' (von Neumann and Morgenstern, 1953) because the hypotheses required are less strict. In particular, the model proposed by Savage does not even rely on a theory of stochastic processes.

This environment of potential ignorance about future results allows a more general theory of decision making on the basis of expected utility analysis. In the theory of expected utility, according to Sugden,

> a prospect is defined as a list of consequences with an associated list of probabilities, one for each consequence, such that these probabilities sum to unity. Consequences are to be understood to be mutually exclusive possibilities: thus a prospect comprises an exhaustive list of the possible consequences of a particular course of action ... An individual's preferences are defined over the set of all conceivable prospects.
>
> (Sugden, 1987, p. 2)

However, a close examination of this characterization of the theory of expected utility clearly shows that it is incompatible with Keynes's conception of uncertainty and with the reformulation in terms of non-ergodic processes.

Savage (1954, p. 10) defines an event as 'having every state of the world as an element' and insists on an order axiom implying that 'in deciding on an act, account must be taken of all possible states of the world, and the consequence implicit in each act for each possible state of the world' (Savage, 1954. p. 13). Further Savage notes that his approach 'makes no formal references to time' (Savage, 1954, p. 13). Thus, the decision maker seeking to maximize his utility is presumed to have a preference ordering that is both non-temporal and complete over the set of all possible realizations. It is clear that in a situation of real uncertainty these two conditions are rarely satisfied. In these conditions, it is understandable that Savage himself recognizes that his approach cannot be considered as a general theory because it does not cover 'true' uncertainty. The theory of expected utility appears to be more a code of coherent conduct for the individual than a system for the formation of expectations of future events. In other terms, it no longer deals with forecasting the behaviour of the majority of economic agents or of businessmen, but provides a specification of the behaviour that economic agents should adopt in order to be rational as defined by its initial axioms.

In this approach the antithesis of analytical structures (certainty/ uncertainty, logical time/historical time, ergodic/non-ergodic process) is superimposed on a divergence of objectives. In fact, the axiomatic construction has as its explicit objective the derivation of the optimal state or behaviour from its postulates, while Keynesian theory adopts, as we have emphasized, the opposite path, looking above all to characterize the decision making environment and economic decision making on empirical observations taken from the real world.

This Post Keynesian presentation of the characteristic features of the real world in terms of historical time and crucial decisions thus leads to the reinterpretation of Keynesian uncertainty as a non-ergodic stochastic processes which is clearly incompatible with the decision-making environment assumed in other, alternative approaches within the neoclassical tradition based on probabilistic risk, in terms of either objective or subjective probability. This result has even broader theoretical interest. The identification of the conditions of non-ergodicity and the rejection of the traditional probability-based analysis not only highlights the deficiencies of the way uncertainty is defined and analysed in neoclassical theory, it also calls into question the traditional analysis of economic rationality in a truly uncertain environment.

11.3 Instrumental rationality, cognitive rationality, and the structure of long-period expectations

11.3.1 New Classical Economics and Keynes's stochastic processes

The 'rational expectations hypothesis' (REH) appeared around the beginning of the 1970s as a new approach to rationality and uncertainty. It formed part of the analysis of equilibrium business cycles by the New Classical Economists. This hypothesis was supposed to satisfy the need for a theory of rational choice under conditions of uncertainty as the concept is defined in neoclassical theory. The central idea of this approach is that if individuals are presumed to be rational, then they should also be rational in their search for information and in their formation of expectations. Efficient expectations will thus be formed on the basis of the set of available information. A second hypothesis is taken from 'Walrasian' and 'classical' theory: the assumption of 'market clearing' (Lucas and Sargent, 1981, p. 304). A third assumption characterizes the nature of the movement of economic systems as stationary, stochastic processes (see conversation with Robert Lucas, in Klamer, 1984, p. 44). This latter assumption produces the regularity of the economic process that is at the basis of a succession of cycles.

The analytical structure defined by these assumptions inevitably produces an extremely simplified representation of the economic process. It is a abstraction in which 'Nature' undertakes 'independent drawings from a fixed cumulative probability distribution function' (Lucas and Sargent, 1981, p. xii), and each agent has the possibility of maximizing income on the basis of the mathematical forecast generated by given distribution functions that correspond to the conditional probabilities associated with the stochastic process that is supposed to describe the movement of the economy. The result of this maximization procedure is that 'on average' agents make optimal forecasts given the current and future states of the world (Lucas and Sargent, 1981, p. xiv). Following the approach indicated by Muth (1961), the problem of the formation of expectations becomes the identification of subjective probabilities with the observed frequency of the forecast events.

This new approach can also be evaluated from the point of view of the reformulation of Keynes's position in terms of stochastic processes given above. For example, as Davidson has argued, the most important characteristic of the stochastic processes assumed by the New Classical Economists is not that they are stationary but that they are ergodic. Then,

> for the REH to provide a theory of expectations formation which provides forecasts which are efficient, unbiased, and without persistent errors, not only must the subjective and objective functions be equal at any given point of time, but these functions must be derived from an ergodic process. In other words, the average expectation of future outcomes determined at any point in time will not be persistently different than the time average of future outcomes only if the stochastic process is ergodic.
>
> (Davidson, 1982–83, p. 185)

However, as emphasized in the first section, the Keynesian definition of the 'real world' is of a non-ergodic process. As a consequence, the forecasts obtained from the existing distribution functions can diverge consistently from the time averages obtained as a result of measuring the frequency of the actual observations of the events which are being forecast. As a result, Post Keynesians consider the assumptions of rational expectations and stationary processes as incompatible with analysis of the 'real world'.

Despite these attempts to clarify the importance of uncertainty in the sense given the term by Keynes and Knight for empirical analysis, mainstream evaluation of the question remains that represented by Walliser (1985, p. 17), who writes that Keynes's ideas on uncertainty have 'remained at the preformal stage, they do not seem to have had any general "cultural" influence on economic thinking except as complications or useless subtleties'. Indeed, for most economists better-known Keynesian concepts such as 'animal spirits' are considered to be purely subjective and thus irrational and unscientific. As a result, in the contemporary literature Keynes's analysis is either criticized or credited as an approach to macroeconomics that is incompatible with the traditional concept of individual behaviour based on the assumption of economic rationality.[5] This situation is in part linked to the identification of Keynesian uncertainty with radical subjectivism, and the associated scientific and theoretical nihilism. This is clearly the interpretation of Keynes adopted by Lucas, who writes that 'in cases of uncertainty, economic reasoning will be of no value' (Lucas, 1981, p. 224). It must be admitted that some Post Keynesian authors have given support to such an interpretation. For example, Shackle has claimed to be a 'nihilist', and applied the same term to Keynes (see Shackle, 1984, p. 391).

Further, as we have already pointed out, the definition of uncertainty associated with Keynes and Knight implies that it is impossible to provide exhaustive rendering of all possible future events *ex ante*. Thus the representation of uncertainty by means of probability encounters difficulty, not so much because of the estimation of the probability of any given event but in the representation of the set of possible future events. The use of the assumption that the agent can specify a 'residual even' appears as a completely arbitrary solution to the problem. As Shackle has pointed out,

> if the list of hypotheses in answer to some question is acknowledged to be endless and incapable of completion ... the language of subjective probability may seem unsuitable. That language distributes a total, representing the certainty of inclusiveness, over a finite number of specified rival answers. Or if not, then instead it includes a Black Box, a residual hypothesis of unknown content.
>
> (Shackle, 1972, p. 23)

While this criticism makes it clear that this approach is incompatible with Keynesian uncertainty and non-ergodic processes, its force has been ignored because it appears to be based on radical subjectivism and theoretical nihilism.

11.3.2 Keynes' conception of instrumental rationality

However, if we proceed from the conception of rationality adopted by Keynes and developed by the Post Keynesian economists, it is quite easy to show that this is not the case. There are two reasons for this. The first is that any complete analysis of Keynes's theory cannot ignore the two different notions of rationality that he took the pains to distinguish: instrumental rationality, which characterizes the adaptation of available means to desired objectives, and cognitive rationality, which adjusts the uncertainty concerning the environment to the available information.

The conception of instrumental rationality that Keynes proposes is hardly original with respect to traditional theory. Indeed, even in the context of strong uncertainty, such as proposed in the 1937 article in the *Quarterly Journal of Economics*, agents are not assumed to act in a purely random or irrational fashion: 'the necessity for action and for decision compels us as practical men to do our best to overlook this awkward fact and to behave exactly as we should if we had behind us a good Benthamite calculation of a series of prospective advantages and disadvantages, each multiplied by its appropriate probability, waiting to be summed' (Keynes, 1973e [1937], p. 114). This leads to the interpretation that Keynes in *GT* had deliberately accepted the traditional approach of instrumental rationality in order to ease the acceptance of his ideas. As a result, there can be little dispute over the notion of instrumental rationality, and it should not be necessary to point out that Keynes's theory does not imply the assumption of instrumental *ir*rationality. On the other hand, Keynes stresses the originality of his approach to the idea of cognitive rationality and gives it an important role in *GT*.

The second reason for the mistaken interpretation of rational behaviour in the face of an uncertain environment is that the majority of economies have never taken the time and effort to follow Keynes's explicit references linking the concept of 'animal spirits' to his *TP*. It is in this context that the relation between the tools of probability and the analysis of uncertainty is of importance. A number of Post Keynesian authors have dealt with this question and we can rely on this work to supplement *TP* (see Kregel, 1987; Davidson, 1987).

The point of distinction is Keynes's very conception of probability. We have already noted that Keynes did not embrace the frequency theory of probability. Further, as well as being more subtle,[6] Keynes's approach to subjective probability was also critical:

> In the sense important to logic, probability is not subjective. It is not, that is to say, subject to human caprice. A proposition is not probable because we think it so. When once the facts are given which determine our knowledge, what is probable or improbable in these circumstances has been fixed objectively, and is independent of our opinion. The theory of probability is logical, therefore, because it is concerned with the degree of belief which is rational to entertain in given conditions, and not merely with the actual beliefs of particular individuals, which may or may not be rational.
>
> (*TP*, p. 4)

On the contrary, in opposition to the usual 'frequency' theory of probability, Keynes viewed probability as a logical relationship between propositions rather than between event states of the world. Keynes is concerned with 'logical probability' or the 'degree of confirmation' or the 'degree of rational belief' defined as follows: 'Let our premises consist of any set of propositions h, and our conclusion consist of any set of propositions a, then, if a knowledge of h justifies a rational belief in a of degree α, we say that there is a probability-relation of degree α between a and h' (*TP*, p. 4).[7] The problem that Keynes seeks to resolve is the manner in which individuals determine their 'rational beliefs' concerning a proposition when their knowledge of a proposition is not certain.

Keynes considers two ways in which rational belief about a proposition may be reached when knowledge is uncertain. The first is based on the formulation of a probability reached on the basis of uncertain information or of 'doubtful arguments' (*TP*, p. 3). In the second it is impossible to determine a rational belief, so that it is rational to allow 'animal spirits' to determine actions. It is precisely these two types of uncertainty that traditional theory excludes by assuming that individuals have full or certain knowledge of what Keynes calls a 'primary proposition' (the relation that one seeks to validate, written as $p = a|h$ in *TP* (p. 11).

Criticism of any use of the frequency theory of probability has tended to combine, and sometimes confuse, these two separate forms of uncertainty. For example, as noted above, Shackle considers the investment decision as a 'crucial' decision that cannot be repeated. Thus, the facts of experience (or the 'premises' in 'h' as defined in *TP*) cannot contain any repetitions of the event. As a result, there is no reason for the probabilities to sum to 1. It is in this context that Shackle's rejection of the applicability of statistical probabilities should be understood. It is undeniable that the majority of investment decisions refer to situations in which the degree of rational belief or the 'secondary propositions' (*TP*, p. 11), $p|h$ exhibit uncertainty in the first sense defined by Keynes, that is, when the probability associated with the secondary proposition is less than one ($p|h < 1$).

However, even in this case it is possible to calculate a probability by formulating a secondary proposition concerning the primary proposition that, say, an investment in a particular project will produce a particular return given the information contained in '*h*'. In situations of this first type of uncertainty, the approach suggested by Keynes does not imply that the behaviour adopted will be 'irrational'. In fact, every entrepreneur confronting the same situation (and with the same mental capacity) should have the same degree of rational belief and should act on this in exactly the same way. A difference in behaviour could arise only from subjective differences associated with each individual entrepreneur, including differences in their evaluation of the information in '*h*'.

This definition of 'rationality' clearly differs from that employed by Shackle. Although the situation examined above is characterized by an inability to calculate a statistical probability based on a frequency distribution, in contrast to Shackle, who considers such decisions as 'irrational', Keynes could classify it as a decision based on a degree of rational belief that is less than perfectly certain. It is not a question of subjective 'caprice' or of any kind of 'irrationality'. This highlights an importance consequence of the distinction between the analysis of risk and Knight–Keynes uncertainty in an analogous divergence between Keynes's notion of rationality and the traditional concept underlying rational expectations.

It should first be noted that rational expectations theory shares Keynes's opinion that the theory of probability should refer not to the occurrence of events but to the assertions of individuals concerning the occurrence of events. As Kregel points out, 'rational expectations might thus be described as a theory concerning the formulation of secondary propositions containing primary propositions that are statistical probabilities of events generated on the basis of an economic model and which have probability approaching certainty as the observations of the events occurring over time included in *h* become large' (Kregel, 1987, p. 524). In the case of the analysis of the theory of rational expectations, the certainty of rational belief is linked to the hypothesis that the distribution of the subjective probability of the variable under consideration in *h* of the secondary proposition *p|h* can be assimilated to the objective distribution that actually produces the current values of the variable. But, as pointed out above, this is possible only if the process that determines the events that are the object of expectations is ergodic. Kregel's analysis thus completes the Post Keynesian critique of the theory of rational expectations initiated by Davidson (see, in particular, Davidson, 1982–83). According to Kregel 'the term "rational", as used by traditional theory, can only refer to the limited conditions of certainty of rational belief in a world governed by ergodic stochastic processes; the possibility of decision or choice in uncertain conditions is thus excluded, or classified as "non rational"' (Kregel, 1987, p. 524). In opposition, Post Keynesian analysis develops a theory of the formation of expectations applicable to situations in which the degree of rational belief is less than certain.

It should not be overlooked, however, that Keynes identifies a second type of uncertainly, which precludes the determination of any kind of rational belief. This second form of uncertainty in fact covers two types of uncertainty, which it is necessary to keep analytically separate. The first case corresponds to the possibility of the non-comparability of the probabilities associated with the secondary propositions. The primary reason for this is that the facts of experience that are incorporated in '*h*' can be extremely heterogeneous or even non-existent. This provides the basis for Keynes's affirmation that 'our knowledge of the factors which will govern the yield of an investment some years hence is usually very slight and often negligible. If we speak frankly, we have to admit that our basis of knowledge for estimating the yield ten years hence [of an investment] amounts to little and sometimes to nothing' (*GT*, pp. 149–50). In other terms, it will often be the case that it will be impossible to place an ordinal measure on the probability in question. In these conditions, the principle of 'insufficient reason' or the principle of indifference (which states that, if there is no reason to prefer a possible solution to another, each should have equal probability) must be rejected (see Keynes, *TP*, p. 45).

It thus becomes necessary, following Hicks, to reformulate the axiom of the comparability of probabilities in the following manner: starting from a certain set of information, it is possible to say of two propositions, *A* and *B*, that *A* is more probable than *B*, or that *B* is more probable than *A*, or that they are equally probable, or that they are not comparable.[8] It should also be noted that, contrary to certain interpretations of Keynes's analysis (for example, Lawson, 1985) that limit uncertainty to only those cases where the determination of probability is impossible, the author of

TP considered the non-calculability and the non-comparability to be equivalent as expressions of uncertainty.

However, if the non-comparability of probability implies uncertainty, it will be impossible for agents to formulate rational beliefs. To deal with this question Keynes introduces another essential element in his theory of logical probability: the weight of the argument. It is this factor that comes to dominate the decision to act:

> It seems that there may be another aspect in which some kind of quantitative comparison between arguments is possible. This comparison turns upon a balance, not between the favourable and the unfavourable evidence, but between the absolute amounts of relevant knowledge and of relevant ignorance respectively ... As the relevant evidence at our disposal increases, the magnitude of the probability of the argument may either decrease or increase, according as the new knowledge strengthens the unfavourable or the unfavourable evidence; but something seems to have increased in either case, — we have a more substantial base upon which to rest our conclusion. I express this by saying that an accession of new evidence increases the weight of the argument.
>
> (*TP*, p. 77)

11.3.3 Uncertainty and long-period expectations

In Chapter 12 of *GT*, when Keynes evokes the role of confidence in the decision to undertake an investment, it is precisely the 'weight of the argument' that he has in mind (*GT*, pp. 148–49). Thus, when probabilities cannot be compared and it is impossible to formulate a rational belief, it is the weight of the argument which becomes the determining factor, that is, which allows the evaluation of investment alternatives that produces a final decision to act. The subjectivity that resides in the evaluation of different individuals may then become dominant, since it is individual experience that will determine the weight that will be assigned to new information. As Kregel points out (1987, p. 526), it is only at this point that the idea of 'animal sprits' enters into the decision-making framework of *GT*. Animal spirits will be the final determinant of the moment at which the weight of the argument attached to a proposition is sufficient to make it dominant over all other possible propositions. They thus represent, in Keynes's words, the 'spontaneous urge to action rather than inaction'.[9] It is important to note at this point that Keynes insists that this 'spontaneous urge to action' does not depend on 'waves of irrational psychology' (*GT*, p. 162), but rather that this type of decision is securely founded in 'rational spirits' (Kregel, 1987, p. 526), by 'our rational selves choosing between the alternatives as best we are able, calculating where we can, but often falling back for our motive or whim or sentiment or chance' (*GT*, p. 163).

The importance of uncertainty in long-period expectations thus depends on the 'weight' of the type that we have just considered. However, when this weight is very weak, or even non-existent, no calculation, or use, of the concepts of logical probability is possible. At this point, and only in these conditions, is it possible to say that the probability is 'non-measurable'. Far from being rare, Keynes considered this the most likely case whenever expectations were formed over the long period.[10] This point of view appears very clearly in *TP*, which contains successive warnings against what Keynes calls 'numerical expression' (*TP*, pp. 21–22). In particular, he points out that

> [i]t has been assumed hitherto as a matter of course that probability is, in the full and literal sense of the word, measurable. I shall have to limit, not extend, the popular doctrine ... The calculus of probability has received far more attention than its logic, and mathematicians, under no compulsion to deal with the whole of the subject, have naturally confined their attention to those special cases ... where algebraical representation is possible.
>
> (*TP*, pp. 21–22)

Keynes thus considered that the possibility of obtaining a '"numerical" (cardinal) measure of the degree of probability as only occasionally possible': 'A rule can be given for numerical measurement when the conclusion is one of a number of equiprobable, exclusive, and exhaustive alternatives, but not otherwise' (*TP*, p. 122).

Now, in the majority of situations concerning decisions with long-period consequences, this is far from realized. It then becomes very difficult to endogenize the process of expectations formation and, as Keynes notes, 'the state of long term expectation [...] cannot be inferred from the given factors' (Keynes, 1973b [1934], p. 480) so that these decisions must be considered as being taken outside the 'realm of the formally exact' (Keynes, 1973d (1936), p. 2). In such conditions, Keynes suggests that the optimal behaviour to be adopted by decision makers is to fall back on their common sense as reflected in 'the actual observation of markets and business psychology' (*GT*, p. 149) rather than on the calculus of probability. Thus, entrepreneurs will first consider their past experience, and may presume that 'the most recently realised results will continue, except in so far as there are definite reasons for expecting a change' (*GT*, p. 51.) This initial response comes to the same thing as adopting an extrapolative behaviour that gives the present and the recent past an equivalent role to that which they play in the short period.

In the second place, conscious of the lack of information and of the reliability of their individual judgements, entrepreneurs will 'fall back on the judgement of the rest of the world which is perhaps better informed' in such a way that behaviour permanently conforms to that of the majority or the average and '[t]he psychology of a society of individuals each of whom is endeavouring to copy the others leads to what we may strictly term a *conventional* judgement' (Keynes, 1973e [1937], p. 114). It is against this background that Keynes's remark that 'in practice we have tacitly agreed, as a rule, to fall back on what is, in truth, a convention' (*GT*, p. 152) should be interpreted.

Finally, entrepreneurs may admit that the 'existing state of opinion' as expressed by the evaluation of the market is the only one that should be considered the 'correct summing up of future prospects' for investment (Keynes, 1973e [1937], p. 114). But included in this market evaluation will be 'all sorts of considerations ... which are in no way relevant to the prospective yield' (*GT*, p. 152). In fact, in these conditions the calculations of agents count for less than their 'nerves and hysteria, and even digestions and reactions to the weather' (*GT*, p. 162).

It thus becomes easier to understand why long-run expectations, and thus the marginal efficiency of capital, can be considered as being subject to sudden, sometimes violent, changes, marked by waves of optimism and pessimism. From this perspective, the conventional methods of calculation are 'compatible with a considerable measure of continuity and stability in our affairs, so long as we can rely on the maintenance of the convention' (Keynes, *GT*, p. 152). Long-period expectations are as a result volatile, but not violently unstable. However, the appearance of new fears and new hopes 'will, without warning, take charge of human conduct. The forces of disillusion may suddenly impose a new conventional basis of evaluation' (Keynes, 1973e [1937], p. 115). Thus, even in the most extreme conditions of uncertainty, Keynes rejects purely random decision-making. That his approach to decision making in the long-period has been termed 'irrational' is due to the failure to recognize that the traditional definition of 'rationality' does not apply in such conditions and must be reformulated.

11.4   Concluding remarks

Keynes's analysis of agents' behaviour under uncertainty is highly original and fundamentally different from the conventional approach that fails to distinguish between risk and uncertainty. The analytical representation of the informational environment facing decision makers is a first point of difference. In contrast to the standard approach, which follows the method of classical physics in assuming that outcomes of human actions are independent of their dates, Keynesian theory leads to the conclusion that economics has to deal with actions in historical time when random functions are not in a state of statistical control. This conclusion exposes a divergence of objectives between the two approaches. The axiomatic construction of neoclassical theory seeks to derive optimal states and behaviours. The Keynesian approach takes the opposite tack and seeks to determine the informational environment for decision making on the basis of observations taken from the evolution of the 'real world'. The identification of the two characteristic features of this approach in historical time and crucial decisions makes it possible for Keynesian economists to identify the chronic inability of standard theory to deal with conditions of fundamental uncertainty that may be defined in a way that is radically different from the familiar notion of risk. It also makes it possible to take into account a more complex economic environment based on non-ergodic processes in which decisions once taken will evolve in an indeterminate way.

In a non-stationary (non-ergodic) environment it is possible to highlight a second point of difference from neoclassical approaches, and more particularly from the New Classical Economists.[11] This point is associated with the elaboration by Keynesian economists of a conception of 'rationality' that is fundamentally different from that characterized by the 'robot mentality' of the theory of rational expectations. This type of rationality, which is capable of creating 'expectational instability', has little to do with 'irrational psychological fluctuations'. It is not based on the idea that, once uncertainty is taken into account, it is no longer possible to make theoretical statements about initial conditions and results. Rather, it leads to the identification of certain specific rational responses to uncertainty that may be identified and formalized. If, in fact, the notion of uncertainty calls into question the traditional approach to rationality, it can nonetheless be expressed in the form of 'law-like' rules of behaviour. It is thus possible to submit it to scientific analysis and debate. This conclusion applies in particular to the notion of 'rational spirits' that is the foundation of the Keynesian analysis of behaviour under fundamental uncertainty. 'Rational spirits' cannot be interpreted as the result of the cognitive irrationality of agents, as they are rather based on the notion of logical probability developed by Keynes in his *TP*, as well as on the 'conventional individual rationality' discussed in *GT* and further investigated in the 1937 *Quarterly Journal of Economics* article.

Notes

This chapter is a revised version of a paper originally published as 'Alternative Analyses of Uncertainty and Rationality: Keynes and Modern Economics', in S. Marzetti Dall'Aste Brandolini and R. Scazzieri (eds), *La probabilità in Keynes: premesse e influenze*, Bologna: CLUEB (1999), pp. 115–37.

1. While there is general agreement that both economists recognized the importance of the distinction between risk and uncertainty, there is less agreement about whether they had similar conceptions of uncertainty. See Hoogduin (1987) and Schmidt (1996).
2. As emphasized by Davidson (1991), the review of the literature by Machina (Machina, 1987), which is intended to give an exhaustive survey of the perspectives of choice under uncertainty, is revealing of the position of traditional economics on this question. While Machina does mention models of subjective probability, he never mentions the existence of other analyses of uncertainty that might be added to the 'probabilistic tool box' of traditional theory.
3. Some Post Keynesian authors such as M. Lavoie (1985, pp. 499–500) consider cruciality rather than the uniqueness of a decision—as in Knight, for example—as the fact that alters the future economic environment. Crucial decisions are, in effect, very common (for example, investment). As noted by Davidson (1982–83, p. 192), the uniqueness of an event in a finite realization could simply mean that the event has a very low probability.
4. See the passage from Keynes's *Quarterly Journal of Economics* article (1973e [1937]) cited above.
5. This is emphasized by Richard Arena (1989).
6. See Keynes's judgement of Ramsey's works in Keynes (1972 [1933]), pp. 338–9.
7. Keynes writes the probability relation thus defined as $a|h = \alpha$.
8. J. R. Hicks (1979, p. 114). In contrast to the traditional formulation of this axiom which states that given a certain set of information, of two propositions, either one is more probable than the other, or they are equally probable.
9. *GT* (p. 173). It is necessary to point out that the notion of 'weight' poses a very delicate problem of the determination of the point in time at which a decision will be taken. Keynes in fact excludes the idea of a maximum weight that would correspond to the existing set of available information (to put the point in the language of rational expectations). Rather, Keynes argues that it is not possible to equate the cost of additional information with an increase in weight in such a way that traditional theory relates an

increase in information with an increase in certainty: '[t]here clearly comes a point when it is no longer worth while to spend trouble, before acting, in the acquisition of further information, and there is no evident principle by which to determine how far we ought to carry our maxim of strengthening the weight of our argument' (*TP*, p. 83.)

10. See Keynes' analysis in Chapter 12 of *GT*.
11. Since the mid-1990s Joseph Stiglitz has led a group of authors called New Keynesian Economists in developing an approach in which agents face two types of uncertainty. First is 'exogenous' uncertainty, defined as being independent of the actions of agents. This is similar to simple probabilistic risk in which it is possible to know both the set of possible states of the world and their probability distributions. This probabilistic risk is not considered to have a great impact on the behaviour of agents or markets. More important for this approach is the second type of uncertainty, which is considered to be capable of impeding the operation of supply and demand and market clearing. This uncertainty is based on asymmetries in information. The rejection of the assumption of the equal distribution of information across agents is often considered the basis of the contributions of the New Keynesian Economists and the source of their differences with the New Classical Economists (see Stiglitz, 1992, pp. 38–86). Information asymmetry creates uncertainty that can be considered as endogenous to the extent that results depend on the actions of the best-informed agents in the model. However, this uncertainty does not appear to be the equivalent of the true uncertainty defined above by Keynes and Knight. This can be seen by recognizing that, although information is asymmetrically distributed, it remains true that full information, in the sense of probability distributions over all possible future states, is available to at least some of the agents in the economy, and further it is known that the present and future behaviour of market is determined by this distribution. As a result the criticisms that have been made of the New Classical approach in conditions of uncertainty also apply to the New Keynesian Economists. This judgement is reinforced by the fact that the latter group appears to accept the rational expectations hypothesis.

References

Arena, R. (1989), 'Keynes après Lucas, quelques enseignements récents de la macroéconomie monétaire', *Economies et Sociétés*, series 'Economie monétaire', n. 7 (April–May), pp. 13–42.

Davidson, P. (1981), 'Post Keynesian Economics: Solving the Crisis in Economic Theory', in D. Bell and I. Kristol (eds), *The Crisis in Economic Theory*, New York: Basic Books, pp. 151–73.

────── (1982–83), 'Rational Expectations: A Fallacious Foundation for Studying Crucial Decision-Making Processes', *Journal of Post Keynesian Economics*, 5 (2), pp. 182–98.

────── (1987), 'Sensible Expectations and the Long-Run Non-Neutrality of Money', *Journal of Post Keynesian Economics*, 10 (1), pp. 146–53.

────── (1991), 'Is Probability Theory Relevant of Uncertainty? A Post Keynesian Perspective', *Journal of Economic Perspectives*, 5 (1), pp. 129–43.

Eichner, A. S. and Kregel, J. A. (1975), 'An Essay on Post-Keynesian Theory: A New Paradigm in Economics', *Journal of Economic Literature*, 13 (4), pp. 1293–314.

Hicks, J. R. (1979), *Causality in Economics*, Oxford: Basil Blackwell.

Hoogduin, L. (1987), 'On the Difference Between the Keynesian, Knightian and the "Classical" Analysis of Uncertainty and the Development of a More General Monetary Theory', *De Economist*, 135 (1), pp. 52–65.

Keynes, J. M. (1972 [1933]), *Essays in Biography*, Vol. X of *The Collected Writings of John Maynard Keynes*, London: Macmillan.

——— (1973a [1921]), *Treatise on Probability*, Vol. VIII of *The Collected Writings of John Maynard Keynes*, London: Macmillan.

——— (1973b [1934]), Draft of Chapter 9 of the *General Theory*, in *The General Theory and After, Part I: Preparation*, Vol. XIII of *The Collected Writings of John Maynard Keynes*, London: Macmillan, pp. 480–5.

——— (1973c [1936]), *The General Theory of Employment, Interest and Money*, Vol. VII, of *The Collected Writings of John Maynard Keynes*, London: Macmillan.

——— (1973d [1936]), Letter of J. M. Keynes to G.F. Shove, 21 April 1936, in Vol. XIV of *The Collected Writings of John Maynard Keynes*, London: Macmillan, p. 2.

——— (1973e [1937]), 'The General Theory of Employment', *Quarterly Journal of Economics*, in Vol. XIV of *The Collected Writings of John Maynard Keynes*, London: Macmillan, pp. 109–23.

Klamer, A. (ed.) (1984), *The New Classical Macroeconomics: Conversations with the New Classical Economists and their Opponents*, Brighton: Wheatsheaf.

Knight, F. H. (1921), *Risk, Uncertainty and Profit*, Boston and New York: Houghton Mifflin Company.

Kregel, J. A. (1987), 'Rational Spirits and the Post Keynesian Macrotheory of Microeconomics', *De Economist*, 135 (4), pp. 520–32.

Lavoie, M. (1985), 'La distinction entre l'incertitude keynésienne et le risque néoclassique', *Economie Appliquée*, 37 (2), pp. 493–518.

Lawson, T. (1985), 'Uncertainty and Economic Analysis', *The Economic Journal*, December, pp. 909–27.

Lucas, R. (1981), *Studies in Business Cycle Theory*, Oxford: Basil Blackwell.

——— and Sargent, T. (1981), 'After Keynesian Macroeconomics', in R. Lucas and T. Sargent (eds), *Rational Expectations and Econometric Practice*, Minneapolis: University of Minnesota Press; London: Allen and Unwin, pp. 295–319.

Machina, M. (1987), 'Choice Under Uncertainty: Problems Solved and Unsolved' *Journal of Economic Perspectives*, 1, 121–54.

Marshall, A. (1890), *Principles of Economics*, (1st edn), London: Macmillan.

Muth, J. F. (1961), 'Rational Expectations and the Theory of Price Movements', *Econometrica*, 29 (3), pp. 315–35.

Savage, L. J. (1954), *The Foundations of Statistics*, New York: Wiley; London: Chapman and Hall.

Schmidt, C. (ed.) (1996), *Uncertainty in Economic Thought*, Cheltenham, UK and Brookfield, US: Edward Elgar.

Shackle, G. L. S. (1955), *Uncertainty in Economics and Other Reflections*, Cambridge: Cambridge University Press.

—— (1972), *Epistemics and Economics: A Critique of Economic Doctrines*, Cambridge: Cambridge University Press.

Shackle, G. L. S. (1984), 'Comments on the paper by Randall Bausor and Malcom Rutherford', *Journal of Post Keynesian Economics*, Spring, pp. 388–93.

Stiglitz, J. (1992), 'Methodological Issues and the New Keynesian Economics', in A. Vercelli and N. Dimitri (eds), *Macroeconomics: A Survey of Research Strategies*, Oxford: Oxford University Press, pp. 38–86.

Sugden, R. (1987), 'New Developments in the Theory of Choice under Uncertainty', in J. Hey and P. Lambert (eds), *Surveys in the Economics of Uncertainty*, Oxford: Blackwell, pp. 1–24.

von Neumann, J. and Morgenstern, O. (1953), *Theory of Games and Economic Behavior* (3rd edn), Princeton: Princeton University Press.

Walliser, B. (1985), *Anticipations, équilibres et rationalité économique*, Paris: Calmann-Lévy.

12
Moral Good and Right Conduct: A General Theory of Welfare under Fundamental Uncertainty

Silva Marzetti Dall'Aste Brandolini

12.1 Introduction

The methodological foundation of economic science is the postulate of rationality, which is its conceptual core. Simon (1978, p. 369) considers economics as that science which celebrates human rationality in all the ways that it reveals itself.

Traditionally, the positive conception of economics is distinguished from the normative conception in order to stress that 'what is' is different from 'what ought to be'. Positive economics requires economists to reveal economic laws and uniformities only about analysed facts, and to be neutral about competing moral systems. From this point of view, economics is an exact science, and agents behave rationally if they choose means which permit them to reach their established aims subject to the scarcity constraint. Normative economics, in contrast, allows economists a wider sphere of investigation by requiring them to deal not only with the laws that govern the real world but also with what the real world should or should not be, which depends on society's moral goods or values. Thus, from this other point of view, economics is a moral science, a science of thinking that is conditioned by the moral values established by society.

However, it is not always easy to treat the normative aspect of economics separately from the positive aspect, because the choice of ends, or moral values, may also be connected to the problems of their pursuit. In many cases, in fact, the rational choice of ends also becomes important. Consider, for example, a model where governments pursue partisan objectives because they use the public debt in order to influence the choices made by their successors (Alesina and Tabellini, 1990). When there is no agreement between governments that alternate in power on the composition of public expenditure, this situation may generate socially suboptimal public debt. When, in contrast, they share moral values that represent the foundations of social welfare, the composition of public debt may correspond to the socially optimal outcome. Therefore, we cannot deny that rationality has two main aspects: the aspect of the choice of moral values, and the aspect of right conduct.

Two fundamental conceptions of moral value exist, which justify the existence of different models of welfare economics: the *ethics of motive* and the *ethics of end*. The ethics of motive makes reference to subjective values, while the ethics of end recognizes intrinsic objective values. If we take instead the point of view of right conduct, two conceptions of rationality are also distinguished: Bayesian reductionism and rational dualism. These are two different ways of considering uncertainty about economic phenomena. Bayesian reductionism assumes that agents are always able to establish numerical subjective probabilities, and admits only the maximization procedure. Rational dualism, in contrast, distinguishes situations simple enough to be fully understandable by the human mind, where decision-makers are capable of applying the procedure of welfare maximization (substantive rationality), from situations too complex to be fully understandable (as in the case of non-measurable uncertainty).

In this chapter the main characteristics of competing models of welfare economics are analysed, from the point of view of the moral values on which they are based and from the point of view of the right conduct they suggest, in order to find an answer to the following question: from the point of view of rationality under uncertainty, what are the essential characteristics of a general theory of welfare? In sections 12.2 and 12.3 the main economic welfare models based on the ethics of motive and instrumental rationality are analysed. Section 12.4 examines the ethics of end and considers in particular Moore's doctrine of the ideal in order to better understand his criticism of hedonism and of the Humean view, and his influence on John Maynard Keynes's moral and economic ideas. Section 12.5 considers criticisms of expected utility maximization and justifies procedural rationality. Section 6 outlines the fundamental characteristics of a general theory of welfare (GTW) under conditions of fundamental uncertainty. The concluding section argues that a GTW has to allow all the possible values which a society espouses as well as agents' behaviour under conditions of non-measurable uncertainty.

12.2   Welfare theories based on the ethics of motive

The ethics of motive aims to establish the motives – the causes – of human conduct. It is an ancient conception which dates back to

Aristippus and Epicurus. In some of its expressions, the motive of human conduct is desire or will to survive; in others, it is the search for pleasure. Lorenzo Valla, Baruch Spinoza, John Locke, Gottfried Leibniz, David Hume, Cesare Beccaria, Jeremy Bentham, Immanuel Kant and Bertrand Russell espouse this ethical doctrine. Good is intended in the subjective sense, and it is perfection because it is desired. Establishing which is the most rational of alternative goods is meaningless, unless they are intermediate ends for reaching a superior good. More specifically, a thing is useful when it is desired as a means or is a means to attain pleasure; while when a thing is liked or desired for itself, it is good in itself (subjective intrinsic value). In both cases, the reference is always to *subjective* desire or pleasure. By identifying with pleasure or preference the motive that leads human beings to act, moral good is an object of desire (a natural object), and ethics is simply a discipline of conduct, or the science that guides human choices to the end of pleasure or in order to satisfy preferences.

Hedonism (egoism and utilitarianism) and the neo-Humean view are ethics of motive (see ss. 12.2.1 and 12.2.2 below). They are the ethical foundations of different economic welfare models. For our purpose, we focus on: i) the theory of social utility, which is 'the accidental deposit of the historical association between English Economics and Utilitarianism' (Robbins, 1984, p.141); ii) the new welfare economics (NWE) and the theory of social choice (TSC) which are instead based on the neo-Humean view; and iii) rule utilitarianism (RU), which is the result of a combination of assumptions associated with utilitarianism and the neo-Humean view.

12.2.1 Traditional utilitarianism: Benthamism

For hedonism, pleasure is the only *summum bonum* – the fundamental *motive* of human conduct. Pleasure is an emotional index of a situation favourable to the conservation of human species. According to Bentham (1948 [1789], p. 125), pleasure (and pain) governs us, and are the foundation of human life and legislation; while things such as freedom, truth, justice and nature are only means to reach the greatest pleasure.

Hedonism, intended as 'egoism', claims that pleasure for one person is good for that person only; while intended as 'utilitarianism', it claims that the general pleasure is good for a community. In particular, utilitarianism in Bentham's version (1948 [1789], pp. 126–7) claims that

> the community is a fictitious *body* composed of the individual persons who are considered as constituting as it were its *members*.

The interest of the community then is, what? – the sum of the interests of the several members who compose it. ... A thing is said to promote the interest, or to be *for* the interest, of an individual, when it tends to add to the sum total of his pleasures: or, what comes to the same things, to diminish the sum total of his pains.

The atomism hypothesis (methodological individualism in human sciences) and an aggregative conception of interpersonal impartiality (agent neutrality) are at the basis of Benthamism. According to atomism, society is a collection of independent parts, and not an organic whole. It is a stable structure, governed by material laws, not by psychological laws; thus, agents act with the regularity of heavenly bodies. The hypothesis of interpersonal impartiality, meanwhile, means that it is not rational to prefer the happiness of one person to that of another, so that the moral importance is attributed to pleasure alone, and not to whoever has pleasure (Brink, 1993).

Since the sole rational object of conduct is the greatest pleasure of the greatest number, Benthamism claims that the value of the consequences of any action is exactly measurable, and morality aims to maximize utility,[1] intended as the exact balance between pleasure and pain with respect to the total number of individuals in a community. Interpersonal comparisons are admitted without any discussion, and each agent is assigned the same weight. Bentham evaluated everything in money terms, and in doing this he was inspired by Cesare Beccaria. According to Bentham (Venturi, 1965, p. 563), Beccaria was the first to introduce into the field of morals 'the precision, the clarity and the incontestability of mathematical calculus'. Beccaria (1965 [1764], p. 20) specifies that, in political arithmetic, mathematical exactitude has to be substituted by the calculus of probability. Therefore, when the tendency of any action is estimated, not only are pleasures and pains numerically measurable and arithmetically additive, but probabilities, too, are numerically measurable and comparable.

Since private interest and social good have to be in harmony, Bentham's fundamental problem is to justify the belief that individual hedonism when it is rationally enlightened is utilitarian hedonism. Stark (1941, pp. 68–73) maintains that this belief is grounded in the assumption of 'human equality'. In particular, as regards economic situations, Bentham follows the principle of the natural identity of interests, which means that 'the various egoisms harmonise of their own accord and automatically bring about the good of the [human] species',[2] through free exchange and the division of labour. In other terms, Bentham's society is seen as a collection of homogeneous agents who regularly behave in a social environment in which laissez-faire is admitted. Each equally egoistic agent is equally able and free to behave according to reason, that is, to compare pleasures and pains. This gives a scientific foundation to the belief that private interest and social good are in harmony. Therefore, as Keynes (1972b [1926], p. 275) claims, 'the political philosopher could retire in favour of the business man – for the latter could attain the philosopher's *summum bonum* by just pursuing his own private profit'. This view considers economics as a moral science, where the main task of policymakers is to promote social utility through punishments and rewards.

12.2.2 The neo-Humean view

In the Humean view no single *summum bonum* emerges. According to Hume (1910 [1748]), considering that a thing is good means that people prefer it. Feeling and reason are equally involved in morals: feeling, intended as preference, is the fundamental motive of conduct, while reason is an instrument in the service of our preferences.

The welfare theories based on the Humean moral view assume an *impartiality among the ends*: morality requires every one of us to be impartial as between the ends of different persons. Welfare is identified with preferences, but preferences are not specifically identified with pleasure or happiness. Simply, a good is useful if it is preferred, and a utility function is considered a very convenient way to describe decision makers' preferences.

12.2.2.1 Ordinal utility: new welfare economics and the theory of social choice

New welfare economics (NWE) (Kaldor, 1939; Hicks, 1939) does not admit interpersonal comparisons of utility, so preferences can only be ordered. The welfare function is intended as a function that produces an ordering of social preferences (Bergson, 1938). Thus, the problem of aggregating individual preferences arises. A logical-mathematical criterion is Pareto optimality (Pareto, 1964 [1896–7]), which has been more successful as an ethical principle than Benthamism because its moral content is less controversial. The first value judgement admitted is the individualistic foundation: each agent is considered the sole judge of his or her own welfare. Given two allocations A and B, allocation B is better than A if B is preferred to A. The second value judgement establishes that allocation B is optimal compared to A if and only if at least one agent prefers B to A and nobody else prefers A to B. According to Hicks

(1939, pp. 700–1), changes 'which benefit some people without damaging others ... represent an increase in economic welfare – or better, an increase in the efficiency of the system as a means of satisfying wants, that is to say, in the efficiency of the system *tout court'*. A non- Pareto-optimal situation becomes optimal if the distributional constraint that a *sacrifice* (measured in terms of utility) *requires* a *compensation* (SRC) is satisfied, at least potentially (Brink, 1993, pp. 252–8). Therefore, *uncompensated sacrifices are morally unacceptable*. Thus a distribution is morally acceptable only if it does not impose an uncompensated or a net loss of welfare on one or more persons in order to provide benefits to others.

The compensation principle can apply to people of the same generation, but when present and future generations are considered, such as in sustainable development situations, some difficulty arises. The Pareto-optimal interpretation of SRC not only raises the issue of compensating future generations, if actions of the present generation impose losses on future generations, but also raises the philosophical issue of compensating the losses of the present generation when its behaviour favours future generations. This issue is still open, since future generations may not exist: they are only 'possible' individuals. Therefore, when a policymaker (who represents the present generation) applies a take-care-of-tomorrow policy, such a policy satisfies the moral value of intergenerational justice but is incompatible with the Pareto criterion of efficiency, because in this case nobody can compensate the present generation (Parfit, 1982; Temkin, 1993).

The Pareto criterion is also admitted by the theory of social choice (TSC), according to which voting is a way of aggregating individual preferences. Nevertheless, a well-known result of this theory is the Arrow impossibility theorem (Arrow, 1951), which claims that, given a minimum number of desirable value judgements or conditions (unrestricted domain, non-dictatorship, Pareto efficiency, independence of irrelevant alternatives), there is no social welfare function which produces a transitive order of preferences and satisfies those conditions.

12.2.2.2 Cardinal preferences: Harsanyi's rule utilitarianism

Harsanyi's rule utilitarianism (RU) combines Benthamism with the Humean view of preferences. It allows interpersonal comparisons of utilities. According to Harsanyi (1976, p. 50), 'the ultimate logical basis for interpersonal utility comparisons lies in the postulate that the *preferences and utility functions of all human individuals are governed by the same basic psychological laws'*. Nevertheless, RU does not identify utility with pleasure, and claims that a moral value judgement is a judgement of preference. Since preferences are assumed to be cardinally measurable, utility is identified with *cardinal preferences*.

The ultimate moral value is the welfare of individual members of a society. Each agent expresses his or her own preferences not only in his or her personal or individual utility function (*actual* preferences), but also in his or her personal social welfare function (*moral* preferences). Individual preferences are defined in terms of personal and partial criteria, while moral preferences are identified as the hypothetical preferences that each agent 'would entertain if he forced himself to judge the world ... from an impersonal and impartial point of view' (Harsanyi, 1976, p. ix)[3]. In this way the social good is not an objective quantity, but is fully determined by subjective preferences. More specifically, Harsanyi makes reference to the choice of a moral code which has the social function 'to enjoin people to do certain things and not to do some other things'. Therefore, individual rights and special obligations may be established without requiring the SRC principle to be observed. For example, it can satisfy the demand of justice (Harsanyi, 1976, p. 74).

Harsanyi's idea of moral or ethical preferences is used by the ethical social choice theory, according to which ethical preferences are included in sustainable growth models as moral duties (Asheim, 1996; Asheim, Buchholtz and Tungodden, 2001; Marzetti, 2007). Nevertheless, as regards practical applicability, Harsanyi (1986, p. 60) himself maintains that 'rule utilitarianism ... is not a criterion always easy to apply in practice'. In the real world, value judgements concerning social welfare may not be of the moral preference kind: in practice an agent is unlikely to choose a particular action in complete ignorance of his or her personal position.

12.3 Instrumental rationality and ethics of motive

What kind of instrumental rationality is associated with economic welfare theories based on the ethics of motive? In general, when we judge that a thing is good by reference to its consequences, we recognize that it is instrumental to an end. Rationality here is an instrument that coordinates the means with the ends, because those ends cannot be achieved if the decision maker fails to value the actions or instruments for pursuing them. A dispute about means is not an ethical one, but has to be solved on a purely scientific basis (Russell, 1954, p. 101); it consists of deductions from a series of postulates.

As for economic welfare theories based on the ethics of motive considered here, an action is approved or disapproved according to whether it increases or decreases utility. Therefore, the sole rational criterion of choice is the *maximization of the expected utility* (MEU). Let us assume that the possible events e_i, $i = 1 \dots n$, are mutually exclusive and exhaustive alternatives: utility v_i is associated with each of them. Until an event has happened, it is uncertain what value the utility will take, and therefore it is assumed that the probability p_i of each event is known. The sum of the weighted utilities, $\sum_{i=1}^{n} v_i\, p_i$, is the expected value, which has to be maximized by rational agents.

12.3.1 Substantive rationality

Since the consequences have to be predicted, there is a close relation between decision and forecast. When it is assumed that there are no cognitive limitations, agents behave in conditions of full or substantive rationality. The best action, which maximizes expected utility, is conditioned by the complete knowledge of all its possible consequences, of the degrees of value ascribed to that action and also to all its consequences; in addition, all the possible alternative actions, their consequences and their values have to be known. It would seem that in order to know the best action at a given moment, an agent should know the entire future of the world. In other words, decision makers are assumed to know the utility function, to have complete knowledge of the available means, to be able to foresee the relevant future with accuracy and to have no computational limitations. In these conditions their problem is purely logical. They will choose the action that maximizes expected utility, and they behave as if the expected value is the certain value of utility. The problem of choice has been transformed into an equivalent certainty problem, because the calculus of probability is 'supposed to be capable of reducing uncertainty to the same calculable status as that of certainty itself' (Keynes, 1973c [1937], pp. 112–13).

Individual and strategic rationality are distinct. The rational expectations hypothesis (REH) well describes individual substantive rationality. It assumes that (a) agents maximize their utility functions subject to some constraints, and (b) the constraints are perceived by all the agents in a mutually consistent way (the mutual consistency of beliefs). In the sense of Muth (1961), this means that decision makers are able to represent their beliefs as probability distributions, and that their subjective probability distribution coincides with the objective probability (also called frequency probability) distribution. This definition of rationality is stricter than that admitted by Bayesian rationality, which does not require subjective probabilities to be equal to objective probabilities. In a static situation, the REH equilibrium is that of a perfect competition model where all the agents have the same information set because they know the structure of the model and the true value of parameters. In a dynamic situation, in contrast, it is assumed that agents behave in recurring situations, which they have experienced before. Therefore, they know the laws that govern the economic system, and their forecasts are correct estimates of its future trends.

When we move from individual rationality to strategic rationality, agents' interactions are modelled through game theory. Agents have to consider that the economic environment is composed of other agents, that they are part of other agents' environment, that other agents are aware of this, and so on. This means that they must also be able to foresee all the possible actions undertaken by others according to a probability distribution. Von Neumann and Morgenstern (1947, p. 19) assume that, in a condition of risk, each agent knows the objective probability distribution that governs the random process. They justify this choice by maintaining that

> probability has often been visualized as a subjective concept more or less in the nature of an estimation. Since we propose to use it in constructing an individual numerical estimation of utility, the above view of probability would not serve our purpose. The simplest procedure is, therefore, to insist upon the alternative perfectly well founded interpretation of probability as frequency in long runs. This gives directly the necessary numerical foothold.

12.3.2 Maximization of expected utility, and bounded rationality

Models of bounded rationality are justified by the awareness that the assumption that agents take decisions guided by subjective probabilities equal to objective probabilities is unrealistic in many cases. In particular, 'when implemented numerically or econometrically, rational expectations models impute much more knowledge to the agents within the model ... than is possessed by an econometrician, who faces estimation and inference problems that the agents in the model have somehow solved' (Sargent, 1993, p. 3). In addition, when strategic rationality requires economic agents to be perfectly informed, they must have rational faculties that are even more unrealistic than those admitted by individual rationality.[4] They must also foresee all the ideas that can be conceived by the other agents. Since it is quite difficult to admit that in the future what is now inconceivable will instead be conceivable, it is more realistic to assume that subjective probabilities are different from objective probabilities, and that the objective probability of each possible event is unknown to the rational agent.

Sargent (1993) proposes to build models of boundedly rational agents by relaxing only the second requirement of the REH given by the mutual consistency of perceptions. The decision procedure is the MEU, but the condition in which it is applied changes since the agent's behaviour is modelled inductively (Arthur, 1994). Fully rational agents are replaced with boundedly rational agents who recognize the difficulty of knowing the distribution of objective probabilities and maximize their expected utility function by understanding the economic environment in a Bayesian context, where subjective probabilities – which may differ from individual to individual – are estimates of the objective probabilities. Under conditions of incomplete information, a rational Bayesian decision maker ascribes a subjective probability to each of the possible strategies adopted by other agents. She or he must establish subjective probabilities according to the best available information. In this way she or he maximizes expected utility and has good reasons to believe that the other agents behave in the same way.

Harsanyi, too, admits Bayesian rationality postulates, and in his RU model states that a moral action is chosen in two steps. First, all agents choose the *moral rule* or code that maximizes the expected social utility out of the set of all possible moral rules; in this step the ultimate criterion of morality is the consequentialist criterion of social welfare maximization. Second, each agent chooses a personal act consistent with the socially optimal code, and it is admitted that a code may evaluate individual acts by a non-consequentialist criterion, 'if such a moral code is judged to yield higher social utility' (Harsanyi, 1986, p. 59).

If we admit that agents can learn about probabilities, adaptive or learning models in a dynamic context deal with the formation of expectations when imperfectly informed agents are confronted with situations of which they do not know the objective probabilities. According to Pesaran (1987, p. 19), adaptation is 'a plausible "rule of thumb" for updating or revising expectations in the light of past observed expectations errors'. Agents' actions generate new information, and they adapt and learn; they can also learn from the experience of other agents.[5] The basic idea is that, through a learning process, agents may correct subjective probabilities until they are equal to objective probabilities. In order to face the uncertainty that characterizes the economic situation considered, they try to behave like econometricians, whose task is to transform the sample information and the conceptual probability model associated with it 'into more specific knowledge about the unknown model components and parameters' (Mittelhammer, Judge and Miller, 2000, p. 6).

Learning rational agents must be able to solve models more mathematically and econometrically demanding than those based on substantive rationality. In order to present the logic of a learning process in a very simple way, consider two agents who interact: the policymaker and the private sector. The policymaker maximizes utility under the constraint given by the model of the economic system that represents the behaviour of the private sector. Three potentially different probabilities exist: the a priori subjective probability that the policymaker uses in order to compute its optimal policy; the a priori subjective probability that the private sector assigns to the model of the economic system; and the objective probability that governs the economic system. Assume that the private sector is well informed and therefore 'substantively rational' because its subjective probabilities distribution is equal to the objective probabilities distribution; while the policymaker behaves like an econometrician who is boundedly rational and attempts to learn about the objective probabilities distribution. In this situation, rationality is bounded by the lack of a commonly understood environment. The policymaker's learning process may concern: (a) given the structure of the model of the economic system, the true value of (some of) its parameters; or (b) the correct structure of the model. In particular, when the policymaker must learn about the true form of the model, we can imagine that, by using some regression technique for learning, at time t the policymaker myopically maximizes the social utility function under the constraint of the incorrectly estimated model, and behaves according to the myopic decision rule obtained from the model solution. The policymaker observes the true reaction of the private sector to its policy, and at time $t + 1$, aware of its false perception of the economic system's functioning, updates its model estimate and behaves according to the estimated new decision rule (Sargent, 1993). By gaining experience, if this updating process eliminates the foreseen errors, the policymaker reaches the REH equilibrium, and the learning process is fully rational. Nevertheless, when the decision maker increasingly makes forecasting errors, the learning process is not fully rational and the REH equilibrium is not attainable; it is therefore realistic to assume that subjective probabilities are different from objective probabilities (Ghosh and Masson, 1991, p. 466).

A final question remains to be answered: how do we have to behave when it is also difficult to establish subjective probabilities? Harsanyi's (1997, p. 111) answer is that in practical decisions, if we do not know the objective probabilities, if we do not even have sufficient information for establishing the subjective probabilities, and if we have no reason for preferring one alternative to another, then it is reasonable to act as if their probabilities are equal. This means resorting to the Bernoullian principle of indifference, the application of which is analysed by Kyburg (s. 2.2.3), Levi (ss. 3.4 and 3.7), Fano (s. 4.5), Costantini and Garibaldi (s. 8.7), and Kregel and Nasica (s. 11.3.2) in this volume.

12.4   Welfare theory and ethics of end: from Moore to Keynes

As examples of ethics of motive, utilitarianism and neo-Humean views recognize only subjective values. Nevertheless, the simplification of excluding objective values is questionable. If we make reference to the moral values involved in sustainability, for example, non-anthropocentric ethics claims that, through reason, an intrinsic objective value (the primary value) also has to be ascribed to the natural system, considered as a whole. The primary value is independent of individuals' preferences, because a functioning ecosystem is essential to human lives and 'its services cannot be traded for other goods ... the substitution of ecosystem services is beyond human capacity' (Weikard, 2002, p. 21). Therefore, according to this view, the pursuit of sustainable development today requires a moral evolution which is well described by Hans Jonas (1974, p. 10): 'It would mean to seek not only human good but also the good of things extra-human, that is, to extend the recognition of "ends in themselves" beyond the sphere of man.'

In general, according to the *ethics of end*, reason also has to establish whether an end is desirable in itself. This is an ancient conception, which Plato and Aristotle refer to.[6] The Stoics, St Thomas Aquinas, Antonio Rosmini, the Cambridge neo-Platonists, Georg Wilhelm Friedrich Hegel, Johann Gottlieb Fichte, Thomas Hill Green and Benedetto Croce are leading scholars within this tradition. According to this point of view, good is a perfect reality, which is deduced from the rational nature of human beings. Rationality is intended in the universal sense, because reason is able not only to coordinate means to the end but also to understand the ultimate ends of humanity. According to Russell (1954, p. 17), 'the actions of human beings do not all spring from direct impulse, but are capable of being controlled and directed by conscious purpose. ... It is because of this power of acting with a view to a desired end that ethics and moral rules are effective, since they suggest ... a distinction between good and bad purposes'.

Objective values are preferred because they are perfect. They are justified by the attempt to remove doubts, criticism and negation from specific values. We focus here on Moore's doctrine of the ideal, since it is on this that Keynes's conception of moral value and economic welfare is based. Unlike the Humean view, it recognizes objective intrinsic values; and unlike hedonism, it admits a plurality of moral values.

12.4.1 The nature of the good: the ideal as a state of mind

In Britain at the beginning of the twentieth century, Moore's conception of the good as ideal had an important influence on ethics and on the theory of moral value. Moore's ethical conception is an important criticism of ethical naturalism or psychologism, from which modern ethics has profited. Moore calls naturalistic both hedonism and neo-Humean ethics, since they identify a property of a thing with the thing itself. Moore describes, as an example, two different kinds of philosopher: the hedonist who claims that 'good is pleasure' and the philosopher who states that 'good is what is desired'. 'Each of these will argue eagerly to prove that the other is wrong' (Moore, 1959 [1903], pp. 10–11). Nevertheless, their position is merely a psychological one, since 'desire is something which occurs in our minds, and pleasure is something else which so occurs' (Moore, 1959 [1903], pp. 10–11). In his *Principia Ethica* Moore defines ethics as the theory of the good in general. Ethical reasoning concerns two fundamental points: (a) the nature of the good in general (what is good and what is bad), and (b) the nature of good conduct (what good conduct is). In this section we consider the first point, in section 12.5 the second.

As for the nature of the good, Moore believes that 'our knowledge cannot be confined to the things which we can touch and see and feel' (1959 [1903], p. 110). Indeed, when we say that a thing is good in itself, its goodness is an object of thought, a state of mind. To the question 'How can the good be defined?', his reply is that it cannot be defined and analysed since it is a 'quality which we assert to belong to a thing'. A 'definition states what are the parts which invariably compose a certain whole; and in this sense "good" has no definition because it is simple and has no parts' (1959 [1903], p. 9). Each agent is intuitively aware of what good is, because nothing can prove the proposition that claims that the goodness of a thing is true. In other terms, each deci-sion about what is good depends on a direct intuition in each specific case. Nevertheless, intuition – as an original and independent source of knowledge, or immediate knowledge of a truth – is not an alternative to reason, because 'nothing whatever can take the place of reasons for the truth of any proposition: intuition can only furnish a reason for hold-ing any proposition to be true' (1959 [1903], pp. 6–10, p. 144).

The identification of what is good is a complex issue, because we do not always approve of what we like, and there is no doubt that com-mon sense believes that many less pleasant states of mind, are better than many others that are more pleasant. By admitting that the ends of human conduct derive from the rational and metaphysical nature of human beings, Moore defines the ideal as what is good in itself to a high degree. Life, nature, virtue, knowledge, truth, personal affections, beauty and justice may be good as ends in themselves.

The ideal (supreme good) has the characteristics of a complex organic whole. A thing may be judged to be good in different degrees: it may have intrinsic value, it may be bad, and it may be indifferent. According to Moore,

> a thing belonging to any of these three classes may occur as part of a whole, which includes among its other parts other things belong-ing both to the same and to the other two classes; and these wholes, as such, may also have intrinsic value. The paradox, to which it is necessary to call attention, is that *the value of such a whole bears no regular proportion to the sum of the values of its parts.*
>
> (1959 [1903], p. 27; emphasis in original)

Therefore, it is a mistake of the doctrines based on methodological individualism to maintain that, if a certain number of things form a whole, the value of that whole is the sum of the value of things that compose it.

Nevertheless, even if Moore provides the principles of ethical rea-soning and some conclusions about what is good, his ethics is not a complete system. Though he highlights that there is a contradiction in terms in the transition from egoism to utilitarianism that cannot be solved by assuming that the same conduct produces both these things, he does not provide a solution to the problem that private good and public good may not coincide (Skidelsky, 1983). In addition, he does not specifically admit any logical nexus between economic welfare and ethical good. Therefore, since a welfare theory requires a solution to these two problems, we focus on Keynes's thinking about social welfare, which tries to reconcile private interest and social good, and to justify the belief that there is no logical nexus between material welfare and ethical goodness.

12.4.2   Keynes's moral philosophy and theory of rational decisions

As regards moral good, Keynes adheres to Moore's idealism, which admits that ends, too, can be rationally established. Keynes's philosophical beliefs are expressed in his early philosophical writings (1904–6) and other writings such as 'The End of Laissez-faire' (1972b [1926]), 'My Early Beliefs' (1972e [1938]), *The General Theory of Employment, Interest and Money* (1973b [1936]), 'Art and the State' (1982 [1936]), and 'The Economic Possibilities for our Grandchildren' (1972d [1930]); while his theory of rational decisions is stated in *A Treatise of Probability* (1973a [1921]), where, as regards the consequences of a rational act, he also admits procedures different from those of MEU.

12.4.2.1 *Keynes' view of moral value: the principle of organicism*

As regards Moore's chapter on 'The Ideal', Keynes writes: 'I know no equal to it in literature since Plato. And it is better than Plato because it is quite free from *fancy*. ... I see no reason to shift from the fundamental intuitions of *Principia Ethica*' (1972e [1938], p. 444). He considers economic science a moral science, and identifies moral goods with Moore's ideals, intended as organic wholes. In *A Treatise of Probability* (1973a [1921], p. 343) Keynes claims that there are different examples of organic goodness,[7] and in particular, 'we may suppose that the goodness of conscious persons is organic for each distinct and individual personality. Or we may suppose that, when [two] conscious units are in conscious relationship, then the whole which we must treat as organic includes both units.' In addition, 'the organic good of the whole is greater the more equally benefits are divided amongst individuals' (1973a [1921], pp. 353–4).

From the awareness that the structure of ethical action is organic, it follows that the structure of social and economic action also has an organic component. The importance of this conviction is also highlighted by Karl Popper (1957), who claims that a social group is something more than the simple sum total of its members, and is also something more than the simple sum total of the purely personal relations existing between the individual members at some given time.

12.4.2.2 The sacrifice of individual good for the pursuit of the social good

Having established what moral good is, and having justified its organic nature, Keynes (1906, pp. 4–12) feels the need to give a convincing reply to the following question: If the duty to behave well is in conflict with the fact of being happy, 'ought I to sacrifice myself, my own goodness on the altar of humanity?' From the point of view of logic, nothing can prevent individual good and social good from competing: the duty of an agent as an individual is to acquire good states of mind for herself or himself, while as a citizen the duty is to help society to reach a good situation even if to her or his own detriment. In the awareness that both personal good and universal good have claims that are difficult to reduce to common terms, Keynes acknowledges that a personal sacrifice may be moralized by pursuing a social good. In 'Am I a Liberal?' he states: 'I am ready to sacrifice my local patriotisms to an important general purpose.' The objective nature of the ideal justifies, according to the situation, the sacrifice of the private interest for the pursuit of the social good (Keynes, 1972a [1925], p. 295; CW XXI, p. 375). Keynes' view about the relation between private interest and social good, by admitting situations in which someone has to sacrifice himself in order that others may benefit for social purposes without any compensation, not only denies the utilitarian harmony between private good and social good and the fact that no kind of loss is intrinsically more important than another, but it also conflicts with the Paretian criterion which is valid only if, because of a change, nobody suffers a loss. This view is, instead, shared by Harsanyi (1976), who admits that an individual can sacrifice his personal good in order to respect the moral rule that yields higher social utility.

By distinguishing between private good and collective good, Keynes also distinguishes between private action and public action. The link between ethics (which aims to determine what individuals ought to do) and politics (intended as art and science of government) is given by society, which establishes universal moral values. The organization of material welfare in order to attain the results of a good life requires actions by institutions that promote the public good as they interpret it, always 'subject in the last resort to the sovereignty of the democracy expressed through Parliament' (1972b [1926], p. 289). Following Edmund Burke, Keynes (1904b, p. 81) believes that politics deals with the doctrine of means, and not of ends. Therefore, political ends are not intrinsically good, but only instrumentally good. Government is an instrument whose aim is to satisfy the real needs of society. According to Keynes (1904b, p. 81), Burke provides a logically coherent political philosophy for justifying the intervention of the policymaker as means to promote the maximum good of the society, and the belief that the policymaker must pursue 'right aims by right methods' (1972b [1926], p. 294). In short, Keynes combines Moore's conception of moral good with Burke's practical ethics: the first conception states that ultimate ideals exist in heaven, while the second states that those ideals can be satisfied on earth through reason (Fitzgibbons, 1988, p. 62).

12.4.2.3 Ethical goodness and economic welfare

The fact that a policymaker ought to promote the public good by pursuing right purposes through suitable methods raises the issue of the relation between economic welfare and ethical goodness intended as good states of mind. In Keynes's system of thought, there is no immediate and precise logical nexus between economic welfare and ethical good, because the movement from material welfare to supreme good is an *art* that someone may not possess. Therefore, economic welfare is only one requirement of ethical goodness; it is an *intermediate good*, which in turn is a means for pursuing the supreme good (Marzetti, 1999). In particular, in 'Economic Possibilities for our Grandchildren', Keynes claims

> that the economic problem is not – if we look into the future – *the permanent problem of the human race*. ... Man will be faced with his real, his permanent problem – how to use his freedom from pressing economic care, how to occupy the leisure. ... But it will be those peoples, who can keep alive, cultivate into a fuller perfection, the art of life itself and do not sell themselves for the means of life, who will be able to enjoy the abundance when it comes.
>
> (1972d [1930], pp. 326–8)

In a context where the economic agent may not attain the philosopher's *summum bonum* by maximizing her or his utility, because private good may compete with social good and the logical nexus between ethical good and economic welfare may not be immediate and precise, Keynes – aiming towards the maximum ethical good – focuses not on maximum economic welfare but on national income. More specifically, he considers *intermediate objectives* – such as a just distribution of income and wealth, full employment and monetary stability – whose achievement is seen as the solution to the main issues related to the economic organization of society. Thus, the task of ethical rationality is to establish in which way and to which degree the possibilities of economic welfare are used. Keynes (1973b [1936], p. 379) leaves to classical theory the task of describing the behaviour of single agents (see Izumi Hishiyama chapter 10, this volume), and assigns to his macroeconomic theory the task of justifying policymakers' actions. If policymakers have to guide the economic system in order to promote the social welfare, they have to know the laws that govern the behaviour of the economic system as a whole. These laws are not completely atomistic, but have an organic component. To our mind, Keynes's sacrifice of the economic welfare function is the *Keynesian simplification of welfare*; it is designed to avoid all the difficulties that can arise when a theory makes reference not only to the concept of utility or preference, but also to the duty of calculating exactly the consequences of a moral action (Marzetti, 2007).

12.5   Ethics of end and right conduct

Though Moore (1959 [1903]) criticizes utilitarianism about the nature of the good, he recommends right conduct very similar to that recommended by utilitarianism. Among alternative possible actions, it is necessary to determine the one that will generally produce the expected greatest *good* – identified with the ideal. This is the 'ideal utilitarianism'. The pursuit of the greatest good is favoured by the general observance of rules or actions of general utility,[8] such as respect for liberty and private property, industriousness, and temperance. When rules or actions are proved to be of general utility, an agent 'should *always* perform them; but in other cases ... he should rather judge of the probable results in his particular case, guided by a correct conception of what things are intrinsically good or bad' (1959 [1903], p. 181). According to Moore, judgements based on frequencies should be the only cases of probability that have logical relevance.

Nevertheless, Moore (1959 [1903], pp. 149–54) specifies that rational decision makers meet difficulties in choosing the best action. The problem is about practical ethics, intended as the investigation of the probable reasons of action or the pursuit of the moral good according to a reasonable or probable expectation of obtaining it, given the agent's knowledge. He claims that

> it is obvious that our causal knowledge alone is far too incomplete for us to assure ourselves of this result. Accordingly it follows that ... we can never be sure that any action will produce the greatest value possible. ... The utmost, then, that Practical Ethics can hope to discover is which, among a few alternatives possible under certain circumstances, will, on the whole, produce the best result. ... But it is plain that even this is a task of immense difficulty. ... The first

difficulty in the way of establishing a probability that one course of action will give a better total result than another, lies in the fact that we have to take account of the effects of both throughout an infinite future. ... It is quite certain that our causal knowledge is utterly insufficient to tell us what different effects will probably result from two different actions, except within a comparatively short space of time.

12.5.1 Keynes' criticism of ideal utilitarianism

Keynes did not espouse ideal utilitarianism, but he seems influenced by Moore's awareness that in practical application ethics meets some difficulties in prescribing duties which produce the greatest sum of good. Mathematical expectation, intended as the product of a judgement of goodness and a judgement of probability, is based on two assumptions that Keynes (1973a [1921], pp. 343–4) finds unjustified: 'first, that degrees of goodness are numerically measurable and arithmetically additive, and second, that degrees of probability are also numerically measurable.'

Organicism justifies this belief, since the position of each element of the economic system, is (in some sense) dependent on that of the others. In fact, 'the atomic hypothesis which has worked so splendidly in physics breaks down in psychics. We are faced ... with the problems of organic unity, of discreteness, of discontinuity – the whole is not equal to the sum of the parts, comparisons of quantity fail us, small changes produce large effects, the assumptions of a uniform and homogeneous continuum are not satisfied' (Keynes, 1972c [1926], p. 262).

As regards moral good, if organic relations are admitted, it has to be also admitted that quantities of goodness are not always subject to the laws of arithmetic. As regards the measurability of probability, Keynes in his 'The Principles of Probability' (1907: unpublished, ch. 4) distinguishes between risk (measurable uncertainty) and (non-measurable) uncertainty before Knight (1921), and in his *Treatise on Probability* (1973a [1921]) he expresses his theory of logical or inductive probability and his doctrine of rational intuition, which admits that probabilities may be non-measurable and non-comparable. The lack of a scientific basis for computing probabilities would depend on the existence of continuous social interaction that can determine significant changes in the economic structure from the quantitative and qualitative points of view. This would determine the fundamental or true uncertainty of economic phenomena. Fundamental uncertainty means here that there is no scientific basis for establishing any calculable probability whatever, thus we also speak of non-measurable uncertainty (Keynes, 1973c [1937], p. 114).

Therefore, mathematical expectations of alternative courses of actions are not always measurable and, 'even if a meaning can be given to the sum of a series of non-numerical "mathematical expectations", not every pair of such sums are numerically comparable in respect of more and less' (1973a [1921], p. 344). According to Keynes (1972b [1926], p. 284), the philosophical problems about the application of mathematics and statistics to human conduct are not satisfactorily solved by resorting to the maximisation of the expected value, which 'deals with the present without any consideration for the fact that agents know very little about the future; so it is very difficult to make predictions about future facts'. In particular, statistics are built by assuming that past cases are certain; while uncertainty, when it is true, cannot ever be purely statistical (see Roberto Scazzieri, chapter 5, this volume).

12.5.1.1 *Logical probability*

Keynes pays specific attention to the concept of probability, since we cannot understand the scientific method if we do not investigate the meaning of probability. In his *A Treatise on Probability* (1973a [1921]) he searches for rational objective principles to justify inductive judgements in the awareness that science needs a concept of probability that is not merely dependent on a valuation that may be different from subject to subject.

In this volume, Kyburg (Chapter 2), Levi (Chapter 3) and Fano (Chapter 4) deal extensively with logical probability. For our purposes we note only that it is a logical relation that represents a degree of rational belief established objectively in the sense that every agent in the same circumstances establishes the same probability. More specifically, probability is subjective in the sense that

> it is without significance to call a proposition probable unless we specify the knowledge to which we are relating it. ... But in the sense important to logic, probability is not subjective. ... A proposition is not probable because we think it so. When once the facts are given which determine our knowledge, what is probable or improbable in these circumstances has been fixed objectively, and is independent on our opinion. The theory of probability is logical, therefore, because it is concerned with the degree of belief which is *rational* to entertain in given conditions, and not merely with the actual beliefs of particular individuals, which may or may not be rational.
>
> (Keynes, 1973a [1921],p. 4)

The appeal is to reason as source of knowledge. In particular, 'where our experience is incomplete, we cannot hope to derive from it judgments of probability without the aid either of intuition or of some further *a priori* principle' (1973a [1921], p. 94). In this way, Keynes (1973a [1921], ch. 3) claims to deal with probability in its widest sense, and this means that probabilities may be numerically non-measurable and non-comparable.[9]

An economic example of this measurability question is given by Russell (1948, Part V, ch.1). Consider the probability that a given insurance policy is good business for an individual. The problem of this individual is different from that of the insurance company, which is not interested in the individual case, since it offers insurance to all the members of a certain class of individuals, and so needs to know only the statistical mean. An individual, in contrast, may have personal reasons to expect a more or less long life. His or her health and way of life are important, and some of the details of these may be so rare that statistics cannot give reliable help. In addition, a doctor may not be able to give a scientific judgement about personal health conditions. In this case, the probability that taking out insurance is a good business for the individual is very vague and absolutely impossible to measure numerically.

In this volume Costantini and Garibaldi (Chapter 8), by considering events and not propositions, argue that 'nowadays the theory of probability is very different from the classical theory criticized by Keynes' and give a stochastic representation of an economic system where agents behave as organicistic and not as atomistic agents. Since long-time expectations change as time goes by, probabilities change with evidence. Therefore, changes in agents' strategy are governed by probability conditions which determine 'the statistical behavior of the economic system expressed by a probability distribution, hence its average behavior too' (s. 8.7).

12.5.1.2 *Weight of argument and moral risk*

Even if goodness and probability were measurable, the mathematical expectations of two alternative actions cannot be considered as the true measures of preferences because this method does not consider the weight of argument and the moral risk.

The epistemological concept of *weight* measures the reliability of probability. For an extensive analysis of this concept we direct the reader to the contributions by Levi (Chapter 3) and Vercelli (Chapter 7) in this volume. We mention here only that the weight of argument is the amount of relevant information available upon which a probability is established: if one argument is based on a greater amount of relevant evidence, it has more weight than another. Therefore, Keynes

(1973a [1921], p. 347) doubts that 'a good whose probability can only be determined on a slight basis of evidence can be compared by means merely of the magnitude of this probability with another good whose likelihood is based on completer knowledge'.

As regards *moral risk*, in contrast, the mathematical expectation procedure does not answer the following question: is it certain that a larger good, that is extremely improbable, is precisely equivalent ethically to a smaller good that is proportionately more probable? Therefore, Keynes (1973a [1921], p. 347) doubts that the moral value of a speculative action and the moral value of a cautious action 'can be weighed against one another in a simple arithmetical way'.

12.5.1.3 Right conduct when knowledge is not enough

What, according to Keynes, is right conduct? Keynes develops a concept of rational economic decision different from the maximisation of expected value. In his *A Treatise on Probability* the stress is on intuitive judgement. The distinction between deliberate reasoning and intuition has engaged the interest of many authors in recent decades (such as D. Kahneman, A. Tversky, and D. McFadden.) and prompts us to stress the topicality of Keynes's thinking about right conduct. Intuition represents all the forms of prior knowledge that guide agents' inductive inferences. In particular, Kahneman (2002, p. 451), when exploring the psychology of intuitive choices and examining their bounded rationality, maintains that 'the label "intuitive" is applied to judgements that directly reflect impressions', where impressions can be defined as opinions, ideas about facts, not grounded on certain elements and on logical reasoning but suggested by subjective impulses. Intuitive judgement is more frequent than judgements produced by deliberate reasoning, since agents are in general observed making choices according to a limited number of heuristics 'which reduce the complex tasks of assessing probabilities and predicting values to simpler judgmental operations' (Kahneman, 2002, p. 465).

In Keynesian terms, if

the question of a right action is *under all circumstances* a determinate problem, it must be in virtue of an *intuitive judgement* directed to the situation as a whole, and not in virtue of an arithmetical deduction derived from a series of separate judgements directed to the individual alternatives each treated in isolation. We must accept the conclusion that, if one good is greater than another, but the probability of attaining the first less than that of attaining the second, the question of which it is our duty to pursue may be indeterminate, unless we suppose it to be within our power to make direct quantitative judgements of probability and goodness jointly.

(1973a [1921], p. 345; emphasis added)

In this way Keynes (1972e [1938], p. 446) emphasises 'the right to judge every individual case on its merits, and the wisdom, experience and self-control to do so successfully'.

In addition, since moral good may be non-measurable and knowledge for establishing a numerical probability may be not enough, we cannot rationalize our behaviour by resorting to the principle of indifference, or 'by arguing that to a man in a state of ignorance errors in either direction are equally probable, so that there remains a mean actuarial expectation based on equi-probabilities. For it can easily be shown that the assumption of arithmetically equal probabilities based on a state of ignorance leads to absurdities' (1973b [1936], p. 152).[10] As reason cannot be defeated if we do not know the numerical value of probability, Keynesian rationality is more comprehensive than Bayesian rationality, since it can be applied to uncertain situations where Bayes's solution cannot be determined – that is, when the existence of an a priori distribution cannot be postulated, or when, even if the existence of an a priori distribution can be assumed, it is unknown to the experimenter (Wald, 1950, p. 16).

This firm belief influenced *The General Theory of Employment, Interest and Money* (1973b [1936]), where Keynes deals with the complexities of economic relations considered as a whole, which may compel agents to behave in situations of fundamental uncertainty. More specifically, the Keynesian formation of expectations about economic decisions affecting the future is considered in the short term and in the long term. In the short term, expectations generally have a high weight, because changes are mainly slow and each short term seems similar to the previous one. Since the amount of available information is great, it is possible to arrive at a probable inductive generalization. In the long term, in contrast, the amount of evidence is generally small, and so the weight of evidence is low, because there is no stability and expectations cannot be generalized through induction. Since our knowledge about long-term consequences is very vague and really uncertain, a rational basis for establishing numerical probability does not exist, so that mathematical expectation cannot be computed; and so agents would discard 'the calculus, the mensuration and the duty to know *exactly* what one means and feels' (Keynes, 1972e [1938], p. 442).

12.5.2 Rational dualism

In the literature, as regards instrumental rationality, two different and conflicting criteria of rationality are distinguished: Bayesian reductionism and rational dualism (Mongin, 1984, p. 11). In section 12.3 we have argued that, according to Bayesian reductionism, agents, through the calculus of probability, are 'capable of reducing uncertainty to the same calculable status as that of certainty itself' (Keynes, 1973c [1937], pp. 112–13). In this section, we will show how rational dualism works.

Rational dualism distinguishes situations (a) simple enough to be fully understandable by human mind, so that decision makers have reliable information and computing capabilities for applying the procedure of welfare maximization (substantive rationality); and (b) complex enough to be not fully understandable, so that decision makers have to simplify these situations in some rational way in order to make a choice (bounded rationality) since they do not have adequate information or computing capabilities for applying the maximization procedure (Marzetti, 1998).

Keynes, before Simon and Tinbergen, argued that the assumption of a calculable future wrongly interprets the principles of behaviour adopted in practice by agents, since it underestimates the situations in which they know very little or nothing, and gives rise to doubt, precariousness and fear. Therefore, the Keynesian view about right conduct leads to bounded rationality. This is a 'wild' research field, where there are numerous possibilities for modelling agents' behaviour that lack information. The bounded rational agent described by Sargent is only one possible kind of bounded rational agent. Simon (1987) generally speaks of cognitive limitations to decision making (internal constraints). Cognitive limitations mean that decision makers are never sure that a certain action will produce the maximum value. They cannot know, given certain circumstances, some of the conditions under which a specific action will determine its consequences, some of the consequences of these conditions, some of the events that will be influenced by the action in the future, and also the value of the action and that of some of its consequences. In addition, they cannot have information about all the possible alternative actions, and cannot know whether any other circumstances will interfere. This means that, as regards the structure of the model, the social welfare function and the representation of the economic system may be only partially known, or unknown. Furthermore, the model could be so complex that computational difficulties could hinder econometricians' efforts.

When due to cognitive limitations the basis for computing a mathematical expectation does not exist, agents have recourse to numerous practical procedures (heuristics) in order to behave rationally. In this case a decision depends not only on objectives and external constraints, but also on the procedure itself, which is the result of a process of choice (procedural rationality). In particular, when we relax one or more of the assumptions of the (expected utility) theory,

> instead of assuming a fixed set of alternatives ... we may postulate a process for generating alternatives. Instead of assuming known probability distributions of outcomes, we may introduce estimating procedures for them, or we may look for strategies for dealing with uncertainty that do not assume knowledge of probabilities. Instead of assuming the maximisation of a utility function, we may postulate a satisfying strategy.[11]
>
> (Simon, 1987, p. 15)

12.5.2.1 An example: from a substantive procedure to a bounded procedure

In order to give an example of the passage from substantive rationality to a bounded procedure, we may consider the theory of economic policy (Tinbergen, 1952).[12]

1. Consider first a situation of substantive rationality, where a policymaker has all the information for maximizing social welfare. For the sake of simplicity, let us assume a static context, and assume that in some sense and to some extent the ethical value is numerically measurable and described by the welfare function $V(y)$, where $y \geq 0$ is a vector of target variables. Uncertainty is included in $V(y)$ by using subjective probabilities for weighting the utilities of the different states of nature. Assume that the structure of the economic system $h(y) = 0$ is known. Therefore, we write:

$$\max_{y} V(y) \tag{1}$$

$$\text{u.c. } h(y) = 0 \tag{2}$$

$$y \geq 0, \tag{3}$$

where u.c. means 'under the constraint'. According to this model, the policymaker will choose y in order to make $V(y)$ a maximum, given $h(y) = 0$.

2. Tinbergen (1952, pp. 1–5) also maintains that in practice it is a difficult matter to estimate a social welfare function, and claims that in general social welfare

> will not be considered consciously but intuitively by those responsible for the policy. In principle, it must not only depend on individual ophelimity functions… but on a certain measure of combining and hence the weighting of these individual 'interests' as well. In practice, the stage of fixing [the welfare function] and trying to maximise it will often be passed over and the targets chosen directly.

In other terms, model (1)–(3) cannot be applied.

Assume that rationality is limited by lack of data for estimating $V(y)$, while $h(y) = 0$ is known. In this case a procedure that can be applied is that of the fixed target, which consists in the choice of a satisfying value for a certain number of target variables. Assume that y is distinguished in a subset of target variables x and instruments u, therefore $h(x, u) = 0$, and that x^* is a desired or satisfying value fixed a priori, therefore $x = x^*$. In this case the maximization procedure is substituted with a satisfying procedure as follows:

$$h(y) = h(x, u) = 0 \tag{4}$$

$$x = x^*. \tag{5}$$

Given $x = x^*$, the policymaking procedure consists in finding the values of instruments u which solve the system $h(x^*, u) = 0$.

This procedure is used in many Keynesian models, and it works even in situations where probabilities are non-measurable. When probabilities are unknown, Keynes (1973c [1937], p. 114) argues that the practical man or woman, in order to meet a minimum rationality requirement may ignore the prospect of future changes about which he or she does not know anything, and assumes that 'the present is a much more serviceable guide to the future than a candid examination of past experience'.

3. The procedure of fixed targets leaves some questions unsolved. In particular, how must the policymaker behave when the model has more

than one solution, or has no solution? In these cases the approximate optimization procedure can be applied, which consists in the search for the best approximation of the desired fixed target x^*, and therefore requires the use of a welfare loss function $L(x - x^*, u)$. The model is as follows:

$$\min_{u} \ L(x - x^*, u) \tag{6}$$

$$\text{u.c. } h(x, u) = 0 \tag{7}$$

$$u \geq 0. \tag{8}$$

The policy-maker will choose u in order to make the value of $L(x - x^*, u)$ a minimum, where $x - x^*$ is the difference between the actual value x and the desired value x^* (Preston and Pagan, 1982).

12.5.3 Other procedures: conventional judgement

We have shown that in economics the concept of rationality is problematic. Bounded rationality goes beyond the classical concept of rationality. In very few cases do agents behave according to substantive rationality, since they mainly act in a world of subjective beliefs (Arthur, 1994), where the procedures presented in the previous section do not exhaust the content of the real world. Bounded rationality represents, in fact, a rich psychological world of behavioural ideas and models, which cannot be always demonstrably ordered according to their degree of rationality.

Economists and psychologists also speak of ecological rationality, which goes beyond bounded rationality, since it stresses that agents are adaptive to the social environment in which they act. Ecological reasons describe not only bounded behaviours according to nature and sources of uncertainty in order to produce a choice, but also human interactions that determine conventions, norms and rules (Smith, 2003). It is not our task to analyse this interesting research field. For our purposes, we observe only that in ill-defined situations common sense admits the resort to inductive reasoning, in the form not only of intuitive judgement but also of conventional judgement. Social and economic life is also regulated by conventions, which are patterns of behaviour that are 'customary, expected and self-enforcing' since they are shared and sustained by other people (Young, 1996, p. 105). In Keynesian terms, when agents are aware that their individual judgement is worthless, they 'fall back on the judgment of the rest of the world which is better well informed. That is, [they] endeavor to conform with the behavior of the majority or the average' (Keynes, 1973c [1937], p. 114). In this volume, Hishiyama (Chapter 10, s. 10.4) specifically deals with conventional judgement as a pattern of behaviour in an organized investment market such as the stock exchange.

12.6   Discussion: A general theory of welfare

All the welfare theories considered so far are based on some moral value (also represented by sets of axioms) that can be intended as subjective values (pleasure or preferences) or objective values (ideals). As Russell (1954, pp. 100–7) argues, a rational choice between competing moral systems cannot be made since 'a genuine difference exists as to ends', and it is not possible 'to advocate any argument in favour of the one against the other', because 'what a man will consider to constitute his happiness depends upon his passions, and these in turn depend upon his education and social circumstances as well as upon his congenital endowment'.[13]

This argument prompts us to think in terms of a general theory of welfare (GTW). From the point of view of moral values, it must admit all the possible values that a society can espouse in all possible situations. This means that not only subjective values have to be admitted but also objective values. In terms of the models in which GTW is expressed, we believe that it is a branch of logic. 'Logic' is intended here in a wider sense than mathematical logic, because it is concerned not only with deductive arguments but also with inductive reasoning. In other terms, as regards instrumental rationality, GTW must be based on *rational dualism*, which claims that when it is not possible to obtain the knowledge necessary for applying the MEU procedure, or more generally the maximisation of the expected value, other procedures must be admitted in order to make rational decisions. Therefore, in order to present some actual cases, we refer to policymakers' practical capacity to pursue sustainable social welfare. Today, in order to pursue this aim, environmental policy not only recognizes the intrinsic objective value of nature (Bellamy and Johnson, 2000) but, depending on the particular situation, it makes reference to either substantive rationality or bounded rationality (Steyaert et al., 2007).

12.6.1 Subjective values

As regards subjective values, an actual situation of cardinally measurable social welfare is represented by the application of cost–benefit analysis

(CBA) to a project for the conservation of a given natural resource. Under CBA, not only do the benefits and costs measured through market prices have to be considered, but non-market benefits and costs must be considered and evaluated in monetary terms, such as the free use of the resource and its non-use values (option value, bequest value and existence value)[14]. Non-market values can be estimated through a well-designed contingent valuation survey, whose aim is to establish the willingness to pay of the relevant population for the conservation of that resource (McFadden, 1999; Polomé, Marzetti and van der Veen, 2005). The sum of the aggregated marketable and non-marketable values is a cardinal measure of the social welfare from that resource and, subject to known constraints, model (1)–(3) can be applied.

In a situation of ordinally measurable preferences, in contrast, preferences can be measured through a five-point Likert-type response scale (Whishman and Hollenhorst, 1998). Scores range from 1 (strongly non-preferred) to 5 (strongly preferred). A composite measure of welfare can be created by averaging scores on a certain number of items that contribute to social welfare, such as level of crowding, environmental quality, social experience and facilities. Even in this case a social welfare function can be estimated and, subject to known constraints, the maximization procedure can be applied.

12.6.2 Objective values

Sustainability in a strong sense stresses the importance of managing natural resources, with their primary value (PV) or the value of ecosystems as a whole taken into account. As Bellamy and Johnson (2000, p. 267) point out, the new paradigm of integrated resource management[15] recognises Moore's concept of 'the whole being more than the sum of the parts' and the 'diversity in values relating to natural resources'. PV is independent of individuals' preferences, since it is a *summum bonum*, that is, an intrinsic objective value ascribed to nature. Therefore, it is non-measurable. We have seen that Keynes's macroeconomics was conceived in the knowledge that policymakers have to organize material welfare in order to promote the ethical good, which may also be intended as ideal. In order to see how a macroeconomic model works when objective non-measurable values are admitted, consider the following situation: (a) PV of natural resources is recognized; (b) present agents can perceive this organic value by intuition, and in spite of this they have to behave rightly in order to respect future generations' rights to natural resources; (c) probabilities are numerically unknown, since there is very little or no experience about the future impacts of economic activities on the natural environment. Under these conditions, model (1)–(3) cannot be applied, while models (4)–(5) and (6)–(8) seem to be appropriate.

Since PV is non-measurable, it cannot be represented through a welfare function, and so it is rational to consider environmental physical indicators as *intermediate targets* or fixed targets, the achievement of which favours the pursuit of PV conservation. Let us focus on pollution, the reduction of which improves environmental quality and the functioning (health) of the natural system considered as a whole. Let us also consider the following simple input–output model of Leontief (1980, pp. 86–87):

$$y_1 = ay_1 + by_2 + c_1, \tag{9}$$

$$y_2 = cy_1 + dy_2 + ey_3 + c_2, \tag{10}$$

$$z = fy_1 + gy_2 - y_3, \tag{11}$$

$$L = hy_1 + iy_2 + my_3, \tag{12}$$

where y_1 is the agricultural production, y_2 industrial production, y_3 pollution eliminated through the industrial process of recycling, z the total quantity of pollution after waste recycling, c_1 and c_2 consumption of agricultural and industrial goods respectively, L employment, and the other symbols are known coefficients. Equations (9) and (10) describe the output levels of agricultural and industrial sectors, respectively. The net total pollution is represented by equation (11), which shows that pollution is the result of the production of agricultural and industrial goods, and it is reduced through recycling. Finally, equation (12) shows that the industrial process of recycling increases employment.

Let us use this model according the logic of model (4)–(5). Let us consider as fixed intermediate targets (a) a given level of total pollution, the control of which is needed for pursuing the PV objective, and (b) a given level of employment as follows:

$$z = \acute{z} \text{ and } L = \acute{L}, \tag{13}$$

where $\acute{z}$ is a fixed level of net total pollution, established according to the available scientific knowledge, and $\acute{L}$ is the established level of employment, which have to be pursued by means of two instruments: c_2 and y_3. The solution of model (9)–(13) is very simple. It is given by those levels of c_2 and y_3 that satisfy $z = \acute{z}$ and $L = \acute{L}$.

Model (6)–(8) can also be applied in this case. The solution is given by the values of instruments that minimize the difference between the actual values and the desired values of intermediate targets.

12.7   Conclusion

Since the moral values of society have to be rationally pursued, our analysis of the different welfare theories has demonstrated that they cannot be classified according to a single moral criterion, and a single kind of instrumental rationality.

Benthamism, NWE, TSC and RU are based on an ethics of motive, which considers only subjective values represented with a utility function; while Keynes's macroeconomic theory is grounded in an ethics of end, which also admits the rational choice of moral values, which are assumed to be not always measurable.

As for right conduct, when subjective probability is assumed to be equal to objective probability, welfare theories based on utilitarianism and the neo-Humean view are cases of substantive rationality because they describe agents' behavior in a situation of complete information about consequences and probability. When these theories admit bounded rationality, subjective probabilities are assumed to be different from objective probabilities in learning maximization models; on the other hand, when there is insufficient information to establish subjective probabilities, the principle of indifference should be applied. Keynes's macroeconomics, in contrast, also admits other situations of bounded rationality by recognizing that agents may act under conditions of fundamental uncertainty. In this case, bounded rationality focuses on non-maximization procedures (such as those of intermediate objectives and conventional judgment), not only because moral goods may be non-measurable but also because of the awareness that, when a numerical probability cannot be identified, the principle of indifference leads to absurdities.

Since no rational choice can be made between competing moral systems, a GTW is needed. GTW admits all the possible values that a society espouses. As for instrumental rationality, since agents may have inadequate information and insufficient computing capability for applying the maximization procedure, it must be based on rational dualism. Maximization models are applied when situations are simple enough to be fully understood and first-best solutions are found; on the other hand, models of bounded or procedural rationality are appropriate for addressing more complex problems which are only partially understood, as is the case with most practical applications and under conditions of fundamental uncertainty.

Notes

I am grateful to Roberto Scazzieri for his valuable comments and suggestions about this essay. The usual caveats apply.

1. Bentham (1948 [1789], p. 127) claims that utility is that property in an object which 'tends to produce benefit, advantage, pleasure, good, or happiness (all this in the present case comes to the same thing) or ... to prevent the happening of mischief, pain, evil, or unhappiness to the party whose interest is considered.'

2. Stark (1941, pp. 68–9) points out that Bentham observes two other principles: the principle of the artificial identification of interests, which claims that personal interest and general interest are artificially identified by legislators; and the principle of the fusion of interests, which affirms that personal interest and the general interest are spontaneously identified 'within each individual conscience by means of the feeling of sympathy'. Nevertheless, this last principle plays a minor role in Bentham's thought.

3. This hypothesis of *impersonality* and *impartiality* is based on the following principle: 'Treat other people in the same way as you want to be treated yourself' (Harsanyi, 1958, pp. 311–13).

4. See Simon, 1955.

5. Day (1975, p. 19) claims that, in general, the canonical form for learning algorithms is a

> system of switches and rules in which the switching sets are determined by performance measures. Learning takes place whenever behaviour is modified in responses to changes in these measures. ... Elemental principles of learning [are]: (i) successful behaviour is repeated; (ii) unsuccessful behaviour is avoided; (iii) unsuccessful behaviour is followed by a search for alternative modes of behaviour; (iv) behaviour becomes more cautious in response to failure.

   Models which incorporate these four principles can converge to the 'traditional optimisation equilibrium'.

6. Plato believed that happiness could not be identified with pleasure, and that it was connected to virtue; while Aristotle stressed the contemplative characteristic of happiness. See also Birks (1874, p. 213).

7. As regards the application of the organic principle to moral goodness, it seems that in Keynes's thought evolves. In his unpublished early writing 'Miscellanea Ethica' (1905, pp. 21–3), Keynes claims not only that utility belongs to the class of organic units, and that this 'leads to difficulties in the pure economic theory', but also that 'in ethical calculation each individual's momentary state of mind is our sole unit. ... But beyond each individual the organic principle cannot reach.' Nevertheless, later in his *A Treatise of Probability* (1973a [1921]) and 'My Early Beliefs' (1972e [1938])

Keynes admits other forms of organicism. At the beginning of the twentieth century, in fact, philosophical thought was leaving the atomistic vision for the organic vision of things, and this unavoidably influenced the evolution of all social sciences (see Gruchy, 1947–48, pp. 237–8).

8. Moore's emphasis on moral rules seems to have inspired Harsanyi's rule-utilitarian model, where a moral code, to which personal actions have to conform, is established in order to obtain maximum social utility (s. 12.2.2.2).

9. In *A Treatise on Probability* (1973a [1921], Part I, ch. 3) Keynes justifies his belief that 'only in a strictly limited class of cases are degrees of probability numerically measurable'.

10. This is also specifically discussed by Keynes in his *Treatise an Probability* (1973a [1921], chs 4, 5). See also Russell (1948, Part V, ch. 5). The problem is also explained by Franklin (2001, p. 279): 'To take the simplest kind of example, if there are three kinds of balls in an urn, white, red and blue, what is the initial probability that a ball to be drawn will be white? Is it 1/3 (because it could as easily be either white, red or blue) or 1/2 (because it could as easily be white or non-white)?'

11. Simon specifies that the Scottish word 'satisficing' is a synonym of 'satisfying'.

12. The theory of economic policy by Tinbergen (1952; 1956) distinguishes models of the maximization of social welfare (also named flexible objective models) from models whose aim is to reach numerically given objectives (fixed objective models), which represent a case of satisfying procedure.

13. Harsanyi (1976, p. 81), for example, admits: 'To my mind, humanitarian considerations should never take a second place to any other considerations, including egalitarian ones'.

14. From the economic point of view, as regards the value of a natural resource (a beach or a nature park, for example), we make reference here to the concept of Total Economic Value (TEV) (Turner, 1999). TEV is the sum of the use value and non-use values (such as option value, bequest value and existence value). Use value is the monetary amount ascribed to resource use by whoever makes the valuation, and it is distinguished in direct use such as informal recreational activities (walking and sunbathing), and indirect use (storm protection and flood control). With regard to non-use values, option value is the value ascribed to the resource in order to guarantee people the option of using it in the future, bequest value represents the responsibility of the present generation for resource conservation for future generations, while existence value is justified by the concern about the resource no longer existing. Free direct use, indirect use and non-use values are not established by the market, but can be estimated through specific valuation methods which make reference to individual cardinal preferences.

15. Integrated resource management is a result of the failure of the traditional rational planning approach based on scientific and technical methods sectorally applied to the multiple uses of natural resources.

References

Alesina, A. and Tabellini, G. (1990), 'A Positive Theory of Fiscal Deficits and Government Debt', *The Review of Economic Studies*, 57 (3), pp. 403–14.

Arrow, K. J. (1951), *Social Choice and Individual Values*, New York: Wiley.

Arthur, W. B. (1994), 'Inductive Reasoning and Bounded Rationality (the El Farol Problem)', *American Economic Review (Paper and Proceedings)*, 84, pp. 406–11.

Asheim, G. B. (1996), 'Ethical Preferences in the Presence of Resource Constraints', *Nordic Journal of Political Economy*, 23 (1), pp. 55–67.

———, Buchholtz, W. and Tungodden, B. (2001), 'Justifying Sustainability', *Journal of Environmental Economics and Management*, 41, pp. 252–68.

Beccaria, C. (1965 [1764]), *Dei delitti e delle pene*, in Venturi, F. (ed.), *Dei Delitti e delle pene. Con una raccolta di lettere e documenti relativi alla nascita dell' opera e alla sua fortuna nell'Europa del Settecento*, Turin: Einaudi.

Bellamy, J. A. and Johnson, A. K. L. (2000), 'Integrated Resources Management: Moving from Rhetoric to Practice in Australian Agricultural', *Environmental Management*, 25(3), 265–80.

Bentham, J. (1948 [1789]), *An Introduction to the Principles on Moral and Legislation*, in *A Fragment on Government and an Introduction to the Principles on Moral and Legislation*, Oxford: Basil Blackwell.

Bergson, A. (1938), 'A Reformulation of Certain Aspects of Welfare Economics', *Quarterly Journal of Economics*, 52, pp. 310–34.

Birks, T. R. (1874), *Modern Utilitarianism*, London: Macmillan.

Brink, D. (1993), 'The Separateness of Persons, Distributive Norms, and Moral Theory', in R. G. Freyand and C. W. Morris (eds), *Value, Welfare and Morality*, Cambridge: Cambridge: University Press, pp. 252–89.

Day, R. H. (1975), 'Adaptive Processes and Economic Theory', in R. H. Day and T. Groves (eds), *Adaptive Economic Models*, New York: Academic Press, pp. 1–38.

Fitzgibbons, A. (1988), *Keynes's Vision*, Oxford: Clarendon Press.

Franklin, J. (2001), 'Resurrecting Logical Probability', *Erkenntnis*, 55, pp. 277–305.

Ghosh, A. R. and Masson, P. R. (1991), 'Model Uncertainty and the Gains from Coordination', *American Economic Review*, 81(3), pp. 465–79.

Gruchy, A. G. (1947–48), 'The Philosophical Basis of the New Keynesian Economics', *Ethics*, 58 (4), pp. 235–44.

Harsanyi, J. C. (1958), 'Ethics in Terms of Hypothetical Imperatives', *Mind*, 67 (267), pp. 289–316.

——— (1976), *Essays on Ethics, Social Behaviour, and Scientific Explanation*, Dordrecht: Reidel.

——— (1986), 'Utilitarian Morality in a World of Very Half-Hearted Altruists', in W. P. Heller, R. M. Starr and D. A. Starrett (eds), *Social Choice and Public Decision Making*, Cambridge: Cambridge University Press, pp. 57–73.

——— (1997), 'Decisione e razionalità', in A. M. Petroni and R. Viale (eds), *Individuale e collettivo. Decisione e razionalità*, Milan: Raffaello Cortina Editore, pp. 101–25.

Hicks, R. J. (1939), 'Foundations of Welfare Economics', *Economic Journal*, 49, pp. 696–712.

Hume, D. (1910 [1748]), *An Enquiry Concerning Human Understanding*, New York: P. F. Collier & Son.

Jonas, H. (1974), 'Technology and Responsibility: Reflections on the New Tasks of Ethics', in *Philosophical Essays: From Ancient Creed to Technological Man*, Chicago: University of Chicago Press.

Kahneman, D. (2002), 'Maps of Bounded Rationality: A Perspective on Intuitive Judgement and Choice', *Nobel Prize Lecture*, 8 December, in T. Frangsmyr (ed), *Les Prix Nobel. The Nobel Prizes 2002*, Stokholm, Nobel Foundation, pp. 449–89.

Kaldor, N. (1939),'Welfare Proposition in Economics', *Economic Journal*, 45, pp. 549–52.

Keynes, J. M. (1904), 'The Political Doctrine of Edmund Burke', *The J.M. Keynes Papers*, UA/20/3, King's College Library, Cambridge.

—— (1905), 'Miscellanea Ethica', *The J.M. Keynes Papers*, UA/21, King's College Library, Cambridge.

—— (1906), 'Egoism', *The J. M. Keynes Papers*, UA/26, King's College Library, Cambridge.

—— (1907), 'The Principles of Probability', *The J. M. Keynes Papers*, TP/A/1, Cambridge, King's College Library.

—— (1972a [1925]), 'Am I a Liberal?', in Vol. IX of *The Collected Writing of J. M. Keynes*, London: Macmillan, pp. 295–306.

—— (1972b [1926]). 'The End of Laissez-Faire', in Vol. IX of *The Collected Writing of J. M. Keynes*, London: Macmillan, pp. 272–94.

—— (1972c [1926], 'Francis Ysidro Edgeworth', in Vol. X of *The Collected Writing of J. M. Keynes*, London: Macmillan, pp. 251–66.

—— (1972d [1930], 'The Economic Possibilities for our Grandchildren', in Vol. IX of *The Collected Writing of J. M. Keynes*, London: Macmillan, pp. 321–32.

—— (1972e [1938]), 'My Early Beliefs', in Vol. X of *The Collected Writing of J. M. Keynes*, London: Macmillan, pp. 433–50.

—— (1973a [1921]), *Treatise on Probability*, Vol. VIII of *The Collected Writings of John Maynard Keynes*, London: Macmillan. Italian translation by A. Pasquinelli and S. Marzetti Dall'Aste Brandolini, *Trattato sulla probabilità*, Bologna (1994): CLUEB.

—— (1973b [1936]), *The General Theory of Employment, Interest and Money*, Vol. VII, *The Collected Writings of John Maynard Keynes*, London: Macmillan.

—— (1973c [1937]), 'The General Theory of Employment', in Vol. XIV of *The Collected Writing of J. M. Keynes*, London: Macmillan, pp. 109–23.

—— (1982 [1936]), 'Art and the State', in Vol. XXVIII of *The Collected Writing of J. M. Keynes*, London: Macmillan, pp. 342–5.

Knight, F. H. (1921), *Risk, Uncertainty and Profit*, London: Houghton Mifflin Company.

Leontief, W. (1980), *Teorie, modelli e politiche in economia*, Milan: Etas libri.

Marzetti Dall'Aste Brandolini, S. (1998), 'Il comportamento razionale del policymaker', *Economia Politica*, 15 (3), pp. 475–517.

—— (1999), 'Bene morale e condotta giusta: la politica economica di J. M. Keynes', in S. Marzetti Dall'Aste Brandolini and R. Scazzieri (eds), *La probabilità in Keynes: premesse e influenze*, Bologna: CLUEB,pp. 139–87.

—— (2007), 'Happiness and Sustainability: A Modern Paradox', in L. Bruni and P. L. Porta (eds), *Handbook in the Economics of Happiness*, Cheltenham, UK: Edward Elgar, pp. 512–31.

McFadden, D. (1999), 'Rationality to Economics', *Journal of Risk and Uncertainty*, 19(1–3), pp. 73–105.

Mittelhammer, R. C., Judge, G. G. and Miller, D. J. (2000), *Econometric Foundations*, Cambridge: Cambridge University Press.

Mongin, P. (1984), 'Modèle Rationnel ou Modèle Économique de la Rationalité?' *Revue économique*, 35 (1), pp. 9–63.

Moore, G. E. (1959 [1903]), *Principia Ethica*, Cambridge: Cambridge University Press.

Muth, J. (1961), 'Rational Expectations and the Theory of Price Movement', *Econometrica*, 29 (3), pp. 315–35.

Neumann, J. von and Morgenstern, O. (1947), *Theory of Games and Economic Behaviour*, Princeton:, Princeton University Press.

Pareto, V. (1964 [1896–7]), *Cours d'économie politique*, Geneva: Librairie Droz.

Parfit, D. (1982), 'Future Generations: Further Problems', *Philosophy and Public Affairs*, 2, pp. 113–72.

Pesaran, M. H. (1987), *The Limits to Rational Expectations*, Oxford: Basil Blackwell.

Polomé, P., Marzetti, S. and van der Veen, A. (2005), 'Economic and Social Demands for Coastal Protection', *Coastal Engineering*, 52, (10–11), pp. 819–40.

Popper, K. R. (1957), *The Poverty of Historicism*, London: Routledge & Kegan Paul.

Preston, A. J. and Pagan, A. R. (1982), *The Theory of Economic Policy*, Cambridge: Cambridge University Press.

Robbins, L. (1984), *An Essay on the Nature and Significance of Economic Science* (3rd edn), London: Macmillan.

Russell, B. (1948), *Human Knowledge: Its Scope and Limits*, London: Allen & Unwin.

—— (1954), *Human Society in Ethics and Politics*, London: Allen & Unwin.

Sargent, T. J. (1993), *Bounded Rationality in Macroeconomics*, Oxford: Clarendon Press.

Simon, H. A. (1955), 'A Behavioral Model of Rational choice', *The Quarterly Journal of Economics*, 69, pp. 99–118.

—— (1978), 'Rationality as Process and as Product of Thought', *The American Economic Review*, 68(2), pp. 1–16.

—— (1987), 'Bounded Rationality?', in J. Eatwell, M. Milgate and P. Newman (eds), *The New Palgrave: Utility and Probability*, London: Macmillan, pp. 15–18.

Skidelsky, R. (1983), *J. M. Keynes: Hopes Betrayed 1883–1920*, London: Macmillan.

Smith, V. L. (2003), 'Constructivist and Ecological Rationality in Economics', *American Economic Review*, 93(3), pp. 465–508.

Stark, W. (1941), 'Liberty and Equality or: Jeremy Bentham as an Economist: (I) Bentham's Doctrine', *Economic Journal*, 51, pp. 56–79.

Steyaert, P., Barzman, M., Billaud, J. P., Brives, H., Hubert, B., Olivier, G. and Roche, B. (2007), 'The Role of Knowledge and Research in Facilitating Social Learning among Stakeholders in Natural Resources Management in the French Atlantic Coastal Wetlands', *Environmental Science and Policy*, 10, pp. 537–50.

Temkin, L. (1993), 'Harmful Goods, Harmless Bads', in R. G. Frey and C. W. Morris (eds), *Value, Welfare and Morality*, Cambridge: Cambridge University Press, pp. 290–324.

Tinbergen, J. (1952), *On the Theory of Economic Policy*, Amsterdam: North-Holland.

—— (1956), *Economic Policy: Principles and Design*, Amsterdam: North-Holland.

Turner, R. K. (1999), 'The Place of Economic Values in Environmental Valuation', in I. J. Bateman and K. G. Willis (eds), *Valving Environmental Preferences*, Oxford, Oxford University Press, pp. 17–41.

Venturi, F. (ed.) (1965), *Cesare Beccaria. Dei Delitti e delle pene. Con una raccolta di lettere e documenti relativi alla nascita dell' opera e alla sua fortuna nell'Europa del Settecento*, Turin: Einaudi.

Wald, A. (1950), *Statistical Decision Functions*, New York: Wiley.

Weikard, H. P. (2002), 'Diversity Functions and the Value of Biodiversity', *Land Economics*, 78(1), pp. 20–7.

Whishman, S. A. and Hollenhorst, S. J. (1998), 'A Path Model of Whitewater Boating Satisfaction on the Cheast River of West Virginia', *Environmental Management*, 22 (1), pp. 109–17.

Young, P. H. (1996), 'The Economics of Conventions', *Journal of Economic Perspectives*, 10(2), pp. 105–22.

Name Index[1]

---

[1] The name index does not include the references to John Maynard Keynes as these are too numerous through the volume.

331

Subject Index

348   *Subject Index*

Uniformity,
  'atomic'   17, 233–5, 251, 266
  deterministic   248–50
  limited   76–7
Uniformity of nature principle
  249
Utilitarianism   296
  ideal   311–2
  traditional   296
Utility
  expected   295, 301–5, 318
  general (in G.E. Moore)   311

Value
  desired   319, 323
  intrinsic   306–7, 319
  moral   294–5, 299–300, 305–6,
    308–9, 315, 318, 321, 324
  objective   305–6, 322–3
  primary   305, 322
  satisfying   319
  subjective   296, 305, 319, 321–2,
    324
Variety,
  limited and independent   17,
    233, 235

Wealth,
  accumulation of   239
  just distribution of   310
Weight of argument   5–7, 12, 14–15,
    20, 39–57, 151–68, 201, 236, 265,
    286–7, 290–1, 314–5
  and the timing of decisions   290
  in Shackle   56
Weight of evidence   6, 40, 43, 45,
    152, 316
Welfare,
  as an intermediate good (in
    Keynes)   310
  economic   310–11, 317–9
  general theory of   294–326
  material   308–10, 322
  social   295, 299–300, 303, 311,
    317–9, 321–2, 326
  sustainable   321
Welfare loss function   320
Wholes,
  as aggregates (in Russell)   266
  as units (in Russell)   266
  organic   234, 237–8, 267, 308
  versus parts   20, 233–4, 238, 241–4,
    248, 250–6, 259, 264